Perspectives on
Musical
Aesthetics

Perspectives on Musical Aesthetics

Edited by
John Rahn

W. W. NORTON & COMPANY • NEW YORK • LONDON

Library of Congress Cataloging-in-Publication Data

Perspectives on musical aesthetics / edited by John Rahn.
     p. cm.
    Essays reprinted from issues of Perspectives of new music.
    1. Music—20th century—Philosophy and aesthetics.   I. Rahn, John.
II. Perspectives of new music.
ML3845.P25   1994
781.1'7—dc20   93-40287

ISBN 0-393-03614-6 (cloth)
    0-393-96508-2 (pb)

W. W. Norton & Company, Inc., 500 Fifth Avenue, New York, N.Y. 10110
W. W. Norton & Company Ltd., 10 Coptic Street, London WC1A 1PU

1 2 3 4 5 6 7 8 9 0

Perspectives on Musical Aesthetics

Edited by
John Rahn

W. W. NORTON & COMPANY • NEW YORK • LONDON

Library of Congress Cataloging-in-Publication Data

Perspectives on musical aesthetics / edited by John Rahn.
        p.   cm.
    Essays reprinted from issues of Perspectives of new music.
    1. Music—20th century—Philosophy and aesthetics.   I. Rahn, John.
II. Perspectives of new music.
ML3845.P25   1994
781.1'7—dc20   93-40287

ISBN 0-393-03614-6 (cloth)
    0-393-96508-2 (pb)

W. W. Norton & Company, Inc., 500 Fifth Avenue, New York, N.Y. 10110
W. W. Norton & Company Ltd., 10 Coptic Street, London WC1A 1PU

1 2 3 4 5 6 7 8 9 0

CONTENTS

Perspectives on Musical Aesthetics

INTRODUCTION:
THE AESTHETICS OF
PERSPECTIVES

What is aesthetics, and why worry about it? For people who produce art, aesthetics is an everyday working issue, one that comes up at every decision point: What shall I do next? When I am composing a piece of music, and have reached the natural end of a phrase or subsection, what shall I do next? When I am about to start on a new painting, what shall I do next? When I have composed one opera, and have a commission for another, what shall I do? Am I happy with the sounds of my previous work, the harmonies and the tunes and the way they work together—do they in fact work together? The rhythms and timbres and sound quality, the kinds of textures—do all these work well musically and dramatically with the libretto? Did the piece succeed formally; did it put everything together into the kind of whole I wanted, if I wanted a whole? What about the new libretto—does its nature demand changes in the way I compose, or is there an opportunity hidden in it for doing something excitingly new?

These are not merely technical decisions. There is a lot riding on them. An artist puts herself on the line with every new work, exposing herself to the world. The dimensions of the creative act are at once intimately personal—this is *me* out there—and intensely, inevitably involved with ideologies, religions, metaphysics, politics, matters that constitute a dangerous arena in which to present oneself naked.

Art is intimately personal even if the artist is unconcerned about self-expression, abjures expression, or believes with the Buddhists that a sense of self is a great hindrance on the path. We know about other people from their actions, verbal or otherwise. A work of art is an act which is a complex nexus of many subactions and interactions of great implication. It is like a large, formal garden full of rare plants, designed and developed and worked on over a period of decades by a single person, so that the garden distills the actions of a life into a living form. We read the person in the actions as represented by the form, and the form is so intricate that its representation of the person is both deep and relatively complete, more complete than any normal social inter-action could provide. Moreover, while it is not civilized to be judgment-al about a person as shallowly represented in normal social interactions, it is the privilege of everyone upon whom a work of art impinges to judge that work, sometimes by merely fleeing or embracing it, but often by praising or deprecating it to others in terms that one would never use about a person one knows. It takes guts to be an artist.

Actions take place in cultural and historical contexts, which at once supply a larger set of possibilities than would be available in the absence of such context and pretty much constrain choices to that set or a related set of possibilities, if only by abreaction. The artist's sensitivity to this environment determines the depth or subtlety of his response in art, the quality of the art as a contribution to the culture. An artist wants to further an artistic tradition, building on its past accomplish-ments and sensibilities, and to make the art trenchant, something that people will enjoy paying attention to in its contemporary context, something people actually have an appetite for and want, because of its insight as well as its elegance or novelty of form. Intellectual grasp allows a relation to the cultural environment that is not reflexive or programmed by that environment. It is at this point that reading essays such as those in this book actually can help, both those who produce art and those who actively receive it. Even when one disagrees with the positions taken in an essay, the kinds of thinking developed in it can set standards, open new possibilities, and provoke independent thinking of similar scope.

The chapters in this book are collected from a professional journal called *Perspectives of New Music*. This journal has an audience of composers, theorists, performers, and other musicians and intellectuals who are interested in contemporary art music of all kinds. Its contributions reflect the practical orientation sketched above: in addition to the pure pleasures of speculation, these essays serve the interests of the working musical artist. The issues that are alive in this context are not necessarily those of traditional academic or philosophical aesthetics. For example, there is very little here about Beauty or the Sublime, probably because these concepts are not strong factors in everyday aesthetic decision-making nowadays, at least among composers. Nor is there much here about non-Western music; there might fruitfully be more, but the focus would remain on how to advance artistic traditions within the Western culture that is ours by definition. The discourses that do find representation here include Continental ones such as the Frankfurt School (Theodor Adorno in the article by Rainer Rochlitz and elsewhere); contemporary French thought such as that of René Girard (in articles by Douglas Collins, Eric Gans, and John Rahn) and that of Michel Foucault (most explicitly in the article by Foucault and Boulez); John Cage's brand of Zen (in his own article); artificial intelligence (in Robert Duisberg's essay); James Joyce's modernism (in Arthur Nestrovski's article); Platonism (in the symposium of Arthur Berger and friends); the ideas of Tolstoy, Collingwood, and Dewey (in Fred Maus's "Recent Ideas") in their newly conceived contemporary avatars (Benjamin Boretz, Elaine Barkin, and James K. Randall); and a certain native Californian discourse on expanded consciousness and the environment (in the David Dunn contributions) and linguistic politics (in Kenneth Gaburo's "LA"). This particular set of interests is in no sense a manifesto—another collection from the journal might have another cast to it, as the journal changes, evolves, and simply takes advantage of whatever comes its way that seems most lively.

These essays are arranged here in six sections: Aesthetic Theory; Contemporary Music and the Public; On Being a Composer; Environment, Consciousness, and Magic; Music and Literature; The

Survival of Aesthetics. Each of these sections is preceded by a separate introduction, in which I attempt to provide some orientation to what follows. I hope you enjoy the book.

—John Rahn
Editor, *Perspectives of New Music*

AESTHETIC THEORY

As its title implies, "Aesthetic Theory" is the most theoretical part of the book. It is certainly the most difficult. A reader might prefer to postpone this section until some of the others have been assimilated. The six sections may be read in any order—naturally, but here is official permission to do that!—though reading the essays in "Aesthetic Theory" at some point will reflect additional depth and substance on the rest of the book. Because of their complexity, I will provide a rather extended introduction, hoping to clarify the framework of these discussions.

Douglas Collins's essay, "Ritual Sacrifice and the Political Economy of Music," originated as a review of Jacques Attali's book *Noise*, which was controversial and influential in France when it first appeared and which has since become visible in the United States in translation. Attali's neo-Marxist view of history and, by extension, his evolutionary view of a future age, is lent credentials by his activities as a prominent economist, first in Mitterand's French government, then in high posts in the European Economic Community. He is one of the men who runs Europe.

Realizing that Attali's book and his critique of it would be incomprehensible to most American readers, Collins supplies some invaluable background in recent French intellectual history. The major terms of debate here are framed by the works of Theodor Adorno and, more recently, of the popular and widely influential René Girard, both largely present but largely unacknowledged in *Noise*—Adorno the Frankfurt School neo-Marxist, Girard the very conservative French Catholic thinker. Although I will not summarize Collins's argument, I do want to point out his surprising and valuable conclusions, lest they be overlooked by a mind already numbed by novelty. Eschewing any simplistic art-versus-society model (as does Attali), Collins invokes Georges Bataille's ideas about "homogeneous and heterogeneous social elements": "The laboring homogeneous mass, which is tied to the world of practical reason and effort and of desire that is never overcome, must locate the principle of its organizing identity outside itself, thereby discovering that which is not itself, heterogeneous form—the mediation that makes possible an otherwise unavailable cohesion." Thus both elements, locked in an "intrinsically unresolvable struggle," are required to sustain an economy such as ours. Any evolutionary progress or political victory that effectively suppressed either would destroy the matrix supporting both.

Rainer Rochlitz's article "Language for One, Language for All: Adorno and Modernism" is a masterly exposition of the best in the tradition of thought that originates in Adorno, but Rochlitz has refined Adorno's thinking and has moved on. In place of the oppositional political aesthetics of Adorno, Rochlitz offers an aesthetics no longer anchored in ethics (or metaphysics). In a sort of echo of Collins's conclusions, Rochlitz says, "In a society which plays against the universality of egalitarian commerce the card of singularity and of the 'difference' of each one—including anarchist and ultraconservative impulses—aesthetics cannot of itself represent the normative basis of criticism." In fact, an ethically oppositional art ironically serves the interests it opposes: "Tolerance for the expression of singularities serves often as a safety valve for persistent injustices."

In a series of brilliant books, Eric Gans has expounded a coherent theory of society based on a reworking of a concept of "originary scene" whose most immediate source is René Girard. Gans's essay "Art and Entertainment" rather pessimistically concludes that art in the sense we used to know it is no longer possible: "The disappearance of the illusion of essential social difference is also that of the socially transcendent evaluation of the real differences that exist. Entertainment provides solace from the anxieties of the market on which those differences are bought and sold, the stock-exchange on which we are obliged, for well or ill, to spend our lives." This particular view eventually provoked a response in my own article, "What Is Valuable in Art, and Can Music Still Achieve It?," whose rather didactic tone survives from its original form as a talk read to an audience of younger composers. I will not restate the argument of my article here, but refer readers to a section from that article called "Music and the Sacred," which explains some of the background for the "originary" thought of René Girard and Eric Gans.

Eric Gans developed his ideas more specifically for music in his keynote address to the Society for Music Theory at its 1990 annual meeting, "The Beginning and End of Esthetic Form." In fact, the series of articles—Collins, Gans, Rahn, Gans—constitutes an ongoing conversation, one that is currently being continued in the pages of *Perspectives of New Music* with feminist reactions and alternatives to Gans and Girard, showing (I hope) that differences of opinion can be productive.

Ritual Sacrifice and the Political Economy of Music

Douglas Collins

The Prajapati, in the beginning, created men together with sacrifice, and said: "By this shall you multiply. Let this be the Cow of Plenty and yield unto you the milk of your desire."

Bhagavad Gita, III, 10

The sacrifices and music, the rites and the laws have a single aim; it is through them that the hearts of the people are united, and it is from them that the method of good government arises.

Ssu-ma Ch'ien

A MERICAN ACADEMICS HAVE often been suspicious and even envious (sometimes justifiably so) of the stereotypical French intellectual—a brilliantly facile, awesomely prolific, highly politicized, media-hip, publicly unembarrassed discipline-hopper, who is contemptuous of the modesties of academic divisions of labor, whose name and face have national visibility, and who is at least offered the illusion of being taken seriously by those with real political power. Jacques Attali is one of the most remarkable present-day embodiments of this mythic figure. He is the author of more than a dozen books that include technical works on economics, a biographical study, a novel (*1492*), a best-selling volume of memoirs, an essay on health delivery systems, and, at issue here, a book on the function of music as mirror and prophecy in the modern world. Formerly a professor of economics at the École Polytechnique and currently chief executive officer of the European Economic Community's new central bank, this polymath has functioned at the Elysée Palace as Special Counsellor to President Mitterand.

One of Attali's recent works has been the cause of considerable scandal, as it was revealed that this very public figure had been involved in some large-scale, unacknowledged, verbatim borrowing. The plagiarisms moved a journalist in *Les Nouvelles littéraires* to suggest that henceforth all published books should be tagged as belonging to either of two categories: the word *livre* would be reserved for volumes that contain material ascertained to be original, while the neologism *lavre* would designate texts that pretend to no such distinction. This newer term would apply selectively to Attali's *Noise: The Political Economy of Music*[1] because of a dependency on Theodor W. Adorno (noted by Susan McClary in her afterword) and a more profound, but just barely admitted, debt to the anthropologist and social-literary critic René Girard.

The "political economy of music" is grounded on the notion that the aesthetic phenomenon has its origins in ritual murder. This idea can be located in a number of passages in Adorno's works, but most dramatically in the essays he wrote together with Horkheimer that appear in *Dialectic of Enlightenment*.[2] "Odysseus or Myth and Enlightenment" offers the best introduction to their view of the fate of sacrifice in modern culture: "The history of civilization is the history of the introversion of sacrifice. In other words: the history of renunciation."[3] Adorno further discusses the idea of music as the residue of ritual murder in his various critiques of Stravinsky, as well as in the powerful, sinister essay "The Natural History of the Theater," where the component elements of theater and public music events are strikingly assimilated to aspects of violent, archaic ritual. Of the applause for a musician's performance, for example, he writes: "This act forcibly returns us to the ancient sacrificial

rites that have been long forgotten. It is possible that once our ances-
tors struck their hands together rhythmically as the priests slaughtered
the animals who were offered in sacrifice."[4] And, scarily, "The radio decisively concludes the demystifications of the character of applause.
Transmitted over the airwaves, the clapping sound unmistakably resembles the crackling of the flames that surround the altar prepared to
receive the body of the sacrificial victim."[5] Adorno condemns the Stravinsky of *Le Sacre* because he seems to exalt the murderous mob; on the
other hand Adorno praises Schönberg for his identification with the
broken victim.

Though in general quite sovereignly indifferent to American intellectual life, the French "intellocrates" (to use their own self-dismissive
term) have lately been amused to discover that the thinkers they have
outgrown—as if they were childhood maladies—have come to know a
posthumous success on the other side of the Atlantic. In a recent editorial in *L'Express* Alain Besançon writes: "In America, after a bit of a delay, the prominent thinkers of the School of 1968 [so contemptuously
designated are our translated favorites—Foucault, Deleuze, and Derri-
da] have come to know a success we refuse them in Paris."[6] Contrary to
the evidence of what has been translated into English, René Girard has
become one of the most influential of French intellectuals. An enormous number of publications in the most varied fields either resist or
embrace Girard's compelling views of desire and human culture, as well
as his renewed discussion of the cultural centrality of ritual sacrifice, an
idea introduced in the 1930s by the members of "Le Collège de sociologie," in particular Georges Bataille and Roger Caillois. If Attali's
book appears at all novel to us, it is because *Noise* is one of the few of
the many such texts to have been translated.

Briefly and crudely, here is Girard's argument as exfoliated in his
three major books (*Mensonge romantique et vérité romanesque*, 1961; *La
Violence et le sacré*, 1972; *Des choses cachées depuis la fondation du monde*,
1978).[7] After our basic physical requirements have been met, and
sometimes even before, desire becomes mimetic—it reproduces the
preexistent desires that it discovers in an impressive other. Our desires
are never our own, but are always part of a triangle. On this point Girard is a good student of the Russian-French philosopher Alexandre
Kojève, who writes: "Desire directed toward a natural object is human
to the extent that it is 'mediated' by the desire of another directed toward that same object: it is human to desire what others desire, because
they desire it."[8] Girard shows, for example, that Don Quixote embraces
an archaic fantasy of chivalric values not because of the intrinsic virtues
of this world view but rather because he is reproducing an attachment

of an admired figure, the medieval author Amadis of Gaul, in whose works he had found this atmosphere described. By means of associating with these manners, Quixote imagines that he can himself possess the superior power of the envied model. Amadis exemplifies what Girard calls "the external mediator," an envied other who is not present in our own experience, except perhaps through a text—Amadis had lived some centuries before Quixote. Much more significant levels of not merely textual trouble begin when we are faced with an "internal mediator" whose brilliant, and immediately present, example leads to our reproduction of his or her desires. This reproduction results in a mimetic rivalry, the universal character of which constantly threatens the stability of society. Mimesis is common to animals as well, but animal societies function according to saving natural systems of subordination that are not found in man.

The apocalypse of mimetic rivalry is the "sacrificial crisis." During this perilous moment for the community, all of the categories and individual distinctions that have made civilized life possible are blurred as each person repeats the violent strategies of his or her own esteemed or despised models. In mythology this moment is often described as a period of natural disaster, of degree- and difference-leveling plagues, floods, famines, and fires. According to Girard, the difficulty is resolved by the mechanism of "the emissary victim." Just as the group verges on extinction from the murderous rage of each against the other, a scapegoat is unanimously designated who is accused, quite falsely, of being responsible for the dysfunctionalizing violence. The choice of the victim, Girard argues, must be thoroughly arbitrary; otherwise the violence would not be brought to an end. After the victim is expelled or devoured, the attitude toward this unfortunate figure is radically altered—the person whom the mob had viewed as the most abominable of creatures comes to be viewed as the most sacred of humans, because his or her expulsion has been responsible for the return of the community to a unified and productive condition. Among Girard's many examples is the shift of the public attitude toward Oedipus that occurs from *Oedipus the King* to *Oedipus at Colonus*. This mechanism would be the basis of human society and its symbolic forms: language, technology, institutions, and culture. For the renewed human community, the rite consists in the regularized revival of the crisis in an attenuated mode, in order to reap the dividends of the initial success. The rescued group recreates the disorder, again leading to the sacrifice of a victim, whom it presents simultaneously as responsible for the disorder and finally as the source of safety. Power is always the sacred, Girard argues, and not the brute force that a certain reductive sociology imagines it to be—it is the victim in so far as it remains embodied in a person still living in the community.

Girard holds that it is in the Judeo-Christian texts (but certainly not in what he terms *historical* Christianity) that we encounter the only truly radical critique of sacrifice that man has ever known. By siding with the victim against the falsely accusing mob, Jesus and the prophets reveal a thorough understanding of mimetic desire and the sacrificial mechanisms that were thought to be the only way to prevent a monotonous collapse into suicidal strife. Jesus is unlike all other sacrificial victims of myth in that he demystifies the persecution device. Unlike the Oedipus of Sophocles, he refuses to accept responsibility for the disorder for which he is declared accountable. The mimetic drive is the culprit, Jesus demonstrates—he teaches that what is to be condemned is man's morbid fascination with man as idol and the turning away from the one, imageless God.

In modern society the mechanisms for victimizing can no longer function overtly, and disturbances in human relations are no longer resolved in a ritual manner. In destroying the effectiveness of sacrificial mechanisms of defense against violence, Christian revelation gradually deprives humanity of all escape routes. History constrains us to renounce violence and to refrain from all retaliation. It destroys the positivity of violence, its capacity in the paroxyms of crisis to be transformed into a stable and pacified order. Ironically, because Christian revelation demystifies and attenuates the power of ritualized sacrificial mechanisms, the Judeo-Christian texts have in fact contributed to an increase in the level of violence in our more recent history. As we are without our pacifying collective rituals, we thrash about desperately and anarchically in search of new forms of relief from the consequences of mimetic rage. In this situation the renunciation of violence becomes our only chance of survival: it ceases to be the utopian desire of the dreamer and takes on a fearful reality. It is our uncontrollable destiny and responsibility, Girard argues in *Des choses cachées*, to confront the impossibility of apocalyptic violence: either to experience it, or to fully imagine and then renounce it by embracing the only solution, namely, the nonviolence of Jesus as described in the New Testament. Establishing a nonviolent society does not so much imply that one act and do something, but that one give oneself up to the necessary and implacable movement of a history rich in meaning and hope, until the decisive and inevitable day of the absolute alternative between total destruction and universal reconciliation in the Kingdom of God.

Attali's *Noise* must be read as a revealingly selective purchase of Girard's points of view—an acceptance of his founding theory of desire and violence and the anthropology that is declared logically to follow. However, Attali resists Girard's "conservative" theological conclusions and instead advocates an aesthetic, "liberal" solution to the central problem of the race: the creation of a non-violent society. I would argue that it is no accident that this particular book has appeared in translation, while the many others will be ignored. France is a reluctantly modern, Catholic country.

"I will show," Attali writes in his introduction, "that the musician is an integral part of the sacrifice process, a channeler of violence, and that the primal identity *magic-music-sacrifice-rite* expresses the musician's position in the majority of civilizations: simultaneously *excluded* (relegated to a place near the bottom of the social hierarchy) and *superhuman* (the genius, the adored and deified star). Simultaneously a separator and an integrator" (p. 12). Clearly recognizable here are the victim position and function that Girard described. To control the victim is to control the tools of unification. Music is the quintessential mass activity, which, like the crowd, is simultaneously a threat and a necessary source of legitimacy. "All music, any organization of sounds is then a tool for the creation or consolidation of a community, of a totality" (p. 6). And: "[The theorists of totalitarianism] have all explained, indistinctly, that it is necessary to ban subversive noise because it betokens demands for cultural autonomy, support for differences or marginality: a concern for maintaining tonalism, the primacy of melody, a distrust of new languages, codes, or instruments, a refusal of the abnormal—these characteristics are common to all regimes of that nature" (p. 7).

Attali offers a caricature history of music that is divided into four phases, each described according to a characteristic relation of music to power and to the position of the victim. In his chronicle, noise is a weapon, and music is the formation, domestication, and ritualization of that weapon, functioning as a simulacrum of ritual murder. The first of the four networks, or forms of musical distribution, is termed "sacrificial ritual." Gregorian chant, which is offered as an example, typifies this period's form of music: it exists prior to exchange, it is thoroughly a captive of power, it produces an amnesic response to the possibility of violent change, and it permits no significant or disruptive differences.

A new network of music, labeled "representation," is said to emerge in the eighteenth century. At this moment, when ritualized belonging to the community becomes mere "representation," and when capitalism develops in opposition to the more stable feudal world, music becomes a commodity; it comes to have an exchange value, as performers are now specialized functionaries who are paid by the spectators. Music is unmoored in this phase—regulatory codes, prohibitions, and sacrificial rituals lose the organizing, disciplining force they possessed in the earlier era.

The third phase, called "repetition," appears at the end of the nineteenth century with the invention of recording techniques. "This technology, conceived as a way of storing representation, created in fifty years' time, with the phonograph record, a new organizational network for the economy of music. In this network, each spectator has a solitary relation with a material object; the consumption of music is individualized, a simulacrum of ritual sacrifice, a blind spectacle. The network is no longer a form of sociality, an opportunity for spectators to meet and communicate, but rather a tool making the individualized stockpiling of music possible on a huge scale" (p. 32). Attali views this moment as a most darkly feckless phenomenon. "When music swings over to the network of repetition, when use-time joins exchange-time in the great stockpiling of human activity, excluding man and his body, music ceases to be a catharsis; it no longer constructs differences. *It is trapped in identity and will dissolve into noise*" (p. 45). Evident here are the clearest echoes of Girard's "sacrificial crisis." This dissolution is the telos of the cultural entropy process, the frozen, repetitive society that Lévi-Strauss predicted for the difference-insulting, "hot cultured" West when it reaches the end of what Ricoeur terms "the hermeneutic of recovery," when it finally absorbs all that is alien and ceases to confront that which is other than itself: "Today, music heralds—regardless of what the property mode of capital will be—the establishment of a society of repetition in which nothing will happen anymore" (p. 5).

The final utopian phase, in which we do not yet live, but which certain artists predict through their work, is termed the period of "composition." In this moment, made possible by the semiological anomie that characterized the preceding phase, music "would be performed for the musician's own enjoyment, as self-communication, with no other goal than his own pleasure, as something fundamentally outside all communication, as self-transcendence, a solitary, egotistical, noncommercial act. In this network, what is heard by others would be a by-product of what the composer or interpreter wrote or performed for the sake of hearing it" (p. 32). In a society organized by ritualized sacrifice, and this is the case to varying degrees in each of the three preceding phases, according to Attali, self-pleasure is repressed and music has social value only when it functions to unify the social order.

Attali's most original point is that music does not simply mirror a given economic configuration, but has the power to predict future developments within the economy and the general evolution of the social organization. Music prophecies and heralds future modes of production—its styles and economic organization are ahead of the rest of society because it explores, much more rapidly than material reality can, the full range of possibilities in a given code. The composer is in a strange situation, belonging to a category of worker who has succeeded in preserving ownership of labor while avoiding the position of wage earner. The composer, like the entrepreneur, is what Attali terms a "molder," an individual whose income is independent of the quantity of work performed, who produces a mold from which an industry is built, making audible now the world that will emerge in the future.

In a manner that I do not find satisfactorily clear, however, Attali depicts the age of "composition" as emerging naturally from the universalization and decadence of the previous network. Attali reasons, as did the Benjamin of "The Work of Art in the Age of Mechanical Reproduction," that the simulacrum of power will always contribute to the deritualization and hence the deligitimation of authority: "The first recording of speech was a representation of the king's legitimacy. But the android of the king, repeating his legitimacy, could not remain a representation of power for long" (p. 86). An irreversible liberating process is made possible by this humiliated—because repeated—replica of grandeur. "Accessibility replaces the festival" (p. 109). After the process of identical repetition has permeated the field of production, and as the deritualizing thrust concludes its trajectory, the disappearance of stabilizing differences will unbridle violence and shatter all codes. Attali here sounds much like "philosopher of desire" Gilles Deleuze, co-author of the briefly influential *Anti-Oedipus*: "Violence, then, threatens more than ever to sweep across a meaningless, repetitive society. Outlined on the horizon is the real crisis, that of the proliferation accompanied by the absolute dissolution of the place of sacrifice, of the arena of political action, and of subversion. But at the same time, the loss of meaning becomes the absence of imposed meaning, in other words, meaning rediscovered in the act itself—composition: in which there is no longer any usage, any relation to others, except in the collective production and exchange of transcendence. But composition necessitates the destruction of all codes" (p. 45). Composition can then emerge, born from this semiological holocaust that Attali finds most dramatically evident in the repetitive economy of rock music, which represents the alienation, commodification, and banalization of the liberationist content of jazz.

I would quarrel with the argument here developed for two reasons. First, I believe that the "composition" phase of development may be neither as subversive nor as anti-capitalist as Attali appears to suggest. The universalization and democratization of unmediated relation with objects that he valorizes as utopian and emergent in the "composition" phase is arguably the most publicly esteemed value of the culture with which it is declared to cleanly break. In support of this point, consider together the positions of Georges Bataille and Jean-Pierre Dupuy, another economist who has been influenced by Girard's hypothesis.

In his great essay "The Psychological Structure of Fascism," Bataille describes the relation between what he terms homogeneous and heterogeneous social elements.[9] The laboring homogeneous mass, which is tied to the world of practical reason and effort and of desire that is never overcome, must locate the principle of its organizing identity outside itself, thereby discovering that which is not itself, heterogeneous form—the mediation that makes possible an otherwise unavailable cohesion. He describes the heterogeneous as a mode of being that at least appears to be self-coincident and to exist for itself alone. The exigency toward closure that characterizes the homogeneous elements of society drives it to identify with the figure of identity to self that suggests the transcendence of mere survival, the transcendence of the logic of the primacy of utility. It is through sacrifice that the homogeneous elements realize this fantasy; it is through the exigency of loss—ostentatiously gratuitous expenditure—that the identification with heterogeneous elements is achieved.

The sublime died with the triumph of the bourgeoisie, argued Georges Sorel. He was exaggerating, to be sure, but he had a point that cannot be ignored. The energies generated by the sublime will continue to be required, reasoned Jules Monnerot, a student of Sorel and colleague of Bataille: "The sublime is an element which western societies cannot afford to do without."[10] In a vital society, then, heterogeneous elements must be permitted to circulate freely, producing the migrating desires and rivalrous relations that fuel its vitality. But, if we accept Bataille's logic, undiminished and unalloyed heterogeneous form can only pass out of existence as it produces around itself the homogeneous/ heterogeneous mass that is undynamic because the character of its libidinal economy is monolithic and uneffervescent. As Dupuy acutely notes: "The economy presents itself as the negation of the crowd: the economy poses itself against the crowd; it is the return of the crowd that it seeks at any price to prevent."[11] The first three of Attali's phases, because they involve the production, at various levels of attenuation, of cohesive group formation, are incompatible with the requirements of the market economy.

How are the precious, energizing, but always beleaguered heterogeneous elements to be preserved without producing the feared crowd or unacceptably stabilizing the desires of the collectivity? By atomizing the

imagery of self-identity, which is precisely what occurs within the
"composition" moment, any dynamism-stultifying unanimity is blocked:
"Beyond the rupture of the economic conditions of music, composition
is revealed as the demand for a truly different system of organization, a
network within which a different kind of music and different social relations can arise. A music produced by each individual for himself, for
pleasure outside of meaning, usage and exchange" (p. 137). I do not
understand how this position can be described coherently as other than
reflective of the mode Attali declares it to transcend.

Attali scorns the idea of "the organizing conductor" as the image of
the legitimate and rational organizer of a regressive, undemocratic field
of production—he is thus the physical representation of power in the
economic order, as leader of men, simultaneously entrepreneur and
State. It would seem more reasonable to suggest that the conductor-
orchestra relation is rather nostalgic for a stable libidinal economy that
involves the unanimous focus, a hegemonic patterning of desires that on
the contrary must be free to migrate if there is to be anything that resembles the affective anomie that characterizes an advanced consumer
society. The conductor-orchestra relation thus mirrors a devolved, feudal network, and is not at all expressive of the values of an advanced entrepreneurial bourgeoisie.

Sociologist Cornelius Castoriadis has written that the major conflict
in the most advanced societies is not the largely resolved one between
the haves and have-nots, but rather the intrinsically unresolvable struggle between normalizing, reifying, homogenizing pressures in culture
and countervailing forces that seek to subvert these rigidifying tendencies. Adorno describes the same pair as "the antinomies of bourgeois
society." The modern argument between these two positions is never
resolvable in the context of a modern society because this society, in
order to exist in the sense that we recognize it, requires their endless
interplay to remain at once dynamic and disciplined, productive and innovative. Attali's last two phases, which he sees as occurring *sequentially,*
must coexist *spatially* in a kind of antagonistic complicity. Much of the
infectious, evolutionist drama of his story, therefore, would appear to
be historically incoherent.

NOTES

1. Jacques Attali, *Noise: The Political Economy of Music,* trans. Brian Massumi, foreword by Frederic Jameson, afterword by Susan McClary (Minneapolis: University of Minnesota Press, 1985).

2. Max Horkheimer and Theodor W. Adorno, *Dialectic of Enlightenment,* trans. John Cumming (New York: The Seabury Press, 1972).

3. Ibid., 55.

4. Theodor W. Adorno, *Quasi una fantasia,* trans. Jean-Louis Leleu (Paris: Gallimard, 1982), 75.

5. Ibid., 76.

6. 10 January 1986, 18.

7. The first two volumes have been translated as *Deceit, Desire and the Novel* (Baltimore: Johns Hopkins University Press, 1977). Girard's masterpiece, *Des choses cachées depuis la fondation du monde,* remains sadly without an English version. Other untranslated books of Girard include *Le Bouc émissaire* (Paris: Grasset, 1982) and *La Route antique des hommes pervers* (Paris: Grasset, 1985).

   In France there is widespread popular appreciation of Girard. His last three books have made sustained appearances on the best-seller lists, and he has appeared often on radio and television.

8. *Introduction to the Reading of Hegel: Lectures on the Phenomenology of Spirit,* trans. James H. Nichols., Jr. (Ithaca: Cornell University Press, 1980), 6.

9. Now available in English, in Georges Bataille, *Visions of Excess: Selected Writings, 1927–1939,* translated and very well introduced by Allan Stoekl (Minneapolis: University of Minnesota Press, 1985), 137–60. In the same volume see also the hair-raising essay "Sacrificial Mutilation and the Severed Ear of Vincent Van Gogh," 61–72. The University of Minnesota Press will also soon publish a translation of Denis Hollier's valuable anthology *Le Collège de sociologie* (Paris: Gallimard, 1979).

10. *La Poésie moderne et le sacré* (Paris: Gallimard, 1945), 45.

11. *La Panique* (Paris: Les Empêcheurs de penser en rond, 1991), 54.

[Editor's note: Since the original publication of this article in 1985, the following titles have been translated: René Girard's *Des choses cachées depuis la fondation du monde*, as *Things Hidden Since the Foundation of the World*, trans. Michael Metteer (Book 1) and Stephen Bann (Books 2 and 3) (Stanford: Stanford University Press, 1987); and Denis Hollier's *Le Collège de sociologie*, as *The College of Sociology (1937–39)*, trans. Betty Wing (Minneapolis: University of Minnesota Press, 1988).]

Language for One,
Language for All:
Adorno and Modernism

Rainer Rochlitz

M ODERNITY CAN BE assigned a minimalist as well as a maximalist definition. In the first case, one would go back to the birth of modern
subjectivity, to the Renaissance, the Reformation, the French Revolution,
and modernity would be understood as the perpetual re-questioning of the
normative criteria on which a posttraditional society is founded, as a
chronic tension between the demands of profitability, of efficaciousness, of
maintenance, and the demands of validity, of the autonomous logics in the
sciences, of norms, and of arts.[1] From this perspective, the historical catastrophes of the nineteenth century do not justify the verdict which
denounces modern reason as such. In the second case, modernity can be

This article was originally published in French as "Langage pour un, langage pour
tous," *Critique*, nos. 488 and 489 (January/February 1988):95–113.

seen as the absolute radicality of the political and artistic avant-gardes and
of their continuous bid for change, especially since the middle of the nineteenth century, a radicality which opposes to the apocalyptic negativity of
modern societies a demand for rational reconciliation without compromise.
In this latter case, after the successive defeats of the radical movements,
there appears a deceived and bitter, cynical or desperate "postmodernity,"
and a sceptical realism which ends up denouncing as utopian the perspectives of minimalist modernity.[2]

Adorno's thought is situated midway between these two definitions,
and leans strongly toward the second. What separates Adorno from postmodernity is his paradoxical effort to save normativity and the emancipat-
ing potential of reason, whose totalitarian drift he nevertheless denounces.
As for his successors, the principle of all essential change is resolutely confined to a force which is exterior to reason, and notably to the imagination
without which it would be sterile and repressive.

Historically, Adorno's thought stems from a triple failure: the failure of
Western humanism at Auschwitz, a catastrophe which the culture of Bach
and Beethoven, of Goethe and Hölderlin, of Kant and Hegel, did not
know how to prevent; the failure, in Stalinism, of the political movement
which had claimed "to realize philosophy";[3] the failure, finally, of Western
culture in a cultural industry dominated by the American model. In all
three cases, Adorno (and Horkheimer, with whom he wrote *La Dialectique
de la raison,* completed in 1944) sees the triumph of instrumental or practical reason in the modern subject, a subject which ends up by abolishing
itself as subject.

However—and it is this which links Adorno to the first definition of
modernity—philosophy "keeps itself alive" by virtue of its practical failures.
It strives to save that which instrumental reason can only miss or destroy:
the nonidentical, the individual, and the particular.[4] What permits thinking, in opposition to the spontaneous tendency of thought—"to think
means to identify"[5]—is the very failure of an identification which misses its
object; by a sort of return of the repressed, that which is nonidentical forces
thought into a "dialectic," that is to say, into a critical reflection on itself,
and into a mimetic relation with its object, much like the processes which
are expressed in art. Instead of identifying its object, dialectical thought
identifies itself with it, while at the same time retaining its identity as critical
thought.

As Habermas has shown, this conclusion is inevitable within the framework of a philosophy of the subject, such as Adorno's philosophy remains.
It can apprehend only by objectification—and thus by "reification"—that
which arises from an essentially intersubjective "identity" of persons and of
relations of reciprocity on which, in a final analysis, the social fabric relies.

That is why it attempts to offer a remedy by a mimetic approach and a conceptuality founded on "affinity." The recent theory which grounds society, language, and personal identity on the activity of communication, anterior to any reifying objectification, can avoid this stumbling block and more accurately assign a place to the pathologies of modernity. It escapes the aporias of maximalism and its postmodern consequences, because it is not compelled to attribute to the catastrophes of the twentieth century a meaning tied to the totalitarian essence of the modern subject.

I

Among the theories of modern art, the aspiration of the Adornian project is unique; it is comparable only to the three or four great syntheses of German philosophy, to the aesthetics of Kant and Schelling, of Hegel and the young Lukács, and to the collection of essays by Walter Benjamin which served as a model for the musical and literary studies of Adorno himself. Of all these theories, that of Adorno is the only one which was able to take into account, not only romanticism and postromanticism, but also the avant-gardes, their decline, and their influence up to the threshold of postmodernism.

In spite of the pessimistic tone which he consciously adopts, Adorno still speaks of an artistic modernity of the future. For him in 1969, not only is this adventure, menaced by cultural industry, yet to be concluded, but he places in it his hope for the survival of the critical spirit, since, according to him, dialectical thought itself relies on a conceptual equivalent of the mimetic attitude. Right up to its negation by a radically demystified art, aesthetic appearance is for him the basis of hope. It is this and this alone which maintains the perspective of a reconciled world, a view which philosophic thought is incapable of preserving without the aid of art.[6] Demystified and reconciled myth, rational mimesis, art, and especially the disenchanted art of the avant-garde constitute the normative base of Adornian philosophy; this is the base which authorizes its critique of society.

The ultimate and incomplete synthesis of all Adorno's essays, his *Aesthetic Theory*, attempts to reconstruct all of artistic modernity as a function of the same historical situation. All modern works should be understood as responses to one and the same problem, that of myth, of disenchantment which is the process of an Enlightenment ongoing for thousands of years, and finally of reconciliation. It is a reflection on art seen from the interior, from the point of view of creation and of the work, with all the complexity and all the reflexive character that this implies for a modern artist. This is why the *Aesthetic Theory*—with its concentric structure

and its aphoristic writing—draws close to being a work of art in itself, playing with the concepts to render them more permeable to their objects, and
denying itself the transparency of a linear reading. No aesthetic connects art
and modernity as closely; art is only realized by liberating itself from all heteronomy; it is the art of the avant-garde which reveals the essence of all art,
but also its aporias.

Adorno's thought is paradoxical. Dedicated entirely to modernity, at the
same time it gnaws away at its very foundations. In spite of the disastrous
balance sheet which he draws up, Adorno nevertheless refuses to abandon
the project of modernity. It is this which constitutes his intermediate position between the two definitions of modernity. There is no *other* root of
reason for him; if the dialectical concept tends to be mimetic, the mimesis
of modern art is rational and—contrary to Nietzsche and Heidegger—does
not thrust its roots into a past which is anterior to Reason. It is this which
saves Adorno from irrationalism, without however permitting him to differentiate art and philosophy as much as he would like to do.

One can say—in reflecting on Albrecht Wellmer's analysis[7]—that the paradox of Adornian thought is due to his fusion of two types of criticism, that
of a rational philosophy of history and that of a critique of reason in the
name of its other. The appeal to reason's other becomes inevitable once
Adorno and Horkheimer begin to interpret the rationality of the historical
process according to the Hegelian and Marxist dialectic of progress as well
as to the Weberian analysis of bureaucratic rationality.[8] Instrumental reason, which governs the development of the Mind (or of the productive
forces), thus escapes all rational control, to the extent that *all* reason is
instrumental, is the objectification of a reality by a subject. From this perspective, the critique of reason can only be carried forth in the name of reason's other, in the name of the nonidentical (nature, urges, poetry, the
oppressed). Adorno's originality with regard to Nietzsche lies in the fact that
for him the nonidentical is not irrational, but rather a deformed element of
integral reason. The dynamic which connects the two sides of reason, the
"dialectic of reason," is fundamentally a dialectic of mimesis: domination
mimes the violence of natural forces in order to master them by work and
by conceptual thought—it is a mimesis of death in the name of the conser-
vation of self—whereas aesthetic affinity mimes that which is dominated.

As with Heidegger, the development of the modern subject coincides
with the progress of reification, of the objectifying and dominating relation
to nature, both external and internal; but analogously, the development of
the subject is accompanied for Adorno by an internal differentiation whose
effects are beneficial. Dominating reason gives rise to the birth of mimetic
reason in the arts and in dialectical thought. To the extent that it is contrasted with magic, art is a rationalized mimesis, an appearance conscious of

its unreality. Alone, it cannot reconcile a reality which has been oppressed and destroyed by instrumental reason; it can only testify to a possible reconciliation, evoked by aesthetic appearance, while representing nonreconciled reality.[9] Modern works—those of Schönberg, of Kafka, or of Beckett—thus call forth reconciliation and at the same time deny it by their use of dissonance; to present dissonance as resolved in creating a harmonious work of art would deprive art of its critical force.

According to Adorno, humanity will escape its self-destruction by instrumental reason only to the extent that the two sides of mimesis reach a reconciliation. Now, the imbalance of modernity results from the fact that avant-garde art is already a synthesis of mimesis and of rationality—of the most advanced techniques and principles of organization—whereas positivist philosophy, sciences, technology, economic administration, and management have eliminated every mimetic element. As a successful synthesis of the human endeavor, art thus once again becomes the model for philosophy.[10]

If modern art is obscure and refuses itself to immediate comprehension, this is because its apparent irrationality is the inverse of instrumental reason. In exploring the repressed domain of the nonidentical which it is in the business of saving, this art incarnates a form of reason which would no longer be instrumental. It is thus that in speaking of artistic modernity Adorno does not cease to consider current problems in philosophy.

The dialectic of mimesis appears especially in connection with concepts of innovation and experimentation; it culminates in that which Adorno calls the "subjective point," a sort of point of no return for artistic radicality.

Designed on the model of a commodity which must affirm its competitive uniqueness, the novelty of the modern work is at the same time a mortal parody of itself, to the point of the self-destruction of art. Contrary to appearances, a new work shows reality as it is, increasingly damaged under its polished surface, disfigured by the universal reign of merchandise, a final avatar of classical domination. The novelty of avant-garde art is its incessant transcendence of negativity. At the same time, the work nonetheless remains an artistic appearance, and in this manner a promise of happiness, thanks to a form, in itself new, which projects a distanced light on the reality which it reveals. This entanglement of disillusion and of utopian promise constitutes the dialectic of artistic modernity according to Adorno; it associates the content of truth with a quasi-messianic function of appearance in general.

If the new is "irresistible,"[11] that is because each work which is truly new forces itself as a conquest upon other artists, analogous to a scientific discovery, henceforth not to be dismissed. It is this which connects the development of art both to the history of truth and to the development of productive forces, including the knowledge of artistic techniques. A work of art is intimately linked to a commodity in a capitalist society and can only affirm its autonomy by pulling itself away from the circulation of exchange by dint of its uselessness, in the manner of a "ready-made" by Duchamp.[12] The truth of an avant-garde work consists in revealing all the violence, all the inhumanity, all the reification which crystallizes in a commodity produced by modern society.[13] It remains to be known if art can be associated this closely to truth and to a philosophy of history univocally reduced to a course toward the catastrophe, whose Benjaminian image seems to have profoundly impressed Adorno.[14]

Dominating reason being irrational—the destruction of nature and of humankind—apparent irrationality in modern art is according to Adorno a form of rational reaction which denounces false instrumental logic. More precisely—and in this Adorno undoubtedly intends to take into account the Kantian systematic—art opposes to instrumental rationality the very finality of reason. In its continual reaction to the development of productive forces, art follows their logic by anticipating the diversion of technical potentials to human ends.[15] It is to this intimate relation with the movement of history that aesthetic novelty owes its "irresistible" character.

By establishing such a close relation between art and historic reality, Adorno denies himself the concept of a logic proper to the artistic creation itself, founded on the emancipation and the differentiation of subjectivity, in the sense of a minimalist theory of modernity. This, moreover, is why he relativizes the autonomy of art from the very start of his *Aesthetic Theory*.[16] The seductive force of the Adornian aesthetic is tied to the fact that a great number of modern artists were themselves involved with a logic of transcendence, devolving from the motion of the historic process toward the worst, even if they did not adhere to the dialectic of reason and of its mimetic inverse. The debate on the "end of the avant-gardes," ongoing since the 1970s, has revealed a break with this logic of transcendence. In this context, the renunciation of the maximalist model could open out into two opposing perspectives: a pure and simple inversion of radical logic, or the elaboration of another logic, compatible with the minimalist model. Discussions on postmodernism fall within the first hypothesis; rather than a pursuit of radicalization, there is a provocative acceptance of all that which former reasoning had banished from modernism: a taste for the eccentric, for kitsch, for luxuriant excess rather than ascetic rigor; rather than a critical conscience going against the stream, a complacent adherence to what is in vogue. This inversion remains attached in a negative sense to avant-gardist dogmatism: "one must be absolutely postmodern." In the second hypothesis, it is a question of reconstructing a logic of artistic modernity which is not simply the obverse of economic and social history, but which reacts in its own way, according to its own proper logic. The first path follows, in spite of itself, the logic of maximalism through a new global turning point and a new sectarianism which this time is eclectic; the second separates out the elements of a subjective singularization of language, even as in the apocalyptic logic of the avant-gardes.

If the dialectic of modernism tries to establish a relation between art and historic truth, the analysis of experimentation is concerned with the status of the subject in modernity; it defines the procedure which a subject impaired by identifying reason must follow—to bring about that which is modern. Originally, the concept of experimentation "simply meant that a self-conscious will set out to explore unknown and illicit ways of doing things;"[17] at a later time—a time that was current for Adorno—this concept designated "the fact that the artistic subject uses methods the results of which it cannot foresee."[18] By abandoning itself to heteronomy—in aleatory music, in action painting, and in automatic writing—the subject exposes itself to regression while trying to remain master of itself at the point of contact with that which is the most alien to it.[19] Artistic modernity is thus a test for the sovereignty of the aesthetic subject before the insignificant and the nonaesthetic; but for Adorno, the irrational element which thus imposes itself upon the subject has the characteristics of truth repressed by reason.

The theory of the "subjective point" relates to the same problematic of the subject: "If modern art as a whole can be understood as a continual intervention of the subject, which is no longer at all disposed to let the traditional game of forms of works of art play in a nonreflective way, then to the continual interventions of the self, there corresponds a tendency to give up in powerlessness."[20] For when everything is a construction of the subject, "there remains only abstract unity, freed from the antithetical moment by which alone it became united."[21] Art is at the same stroke "rejected at the point of pure subjectivity,"[22] by the cry of expressionism, by cubist construction, by the gesture of Dada, by the intervention of Duchamp. After having reached this extreme point, the artist—as Picasso and Schönberg themselves illustrate—can only come back to a more traditional order. In this, Adorno sees signs of the end of an art which renounces itself rather than compromise; truth content risks destroying aesthetic appearance. Beckett alone succeeds at this *tour de force*: "The space assigned to works of art, between discursive barbarism and poetic prettification, is hardly more vast than the point of indifference in which Beckett has set up shop."[23]

This restrictive concept of subjectivity as an integrative force—which, once having lost the aid of tradition, could only choose between sterile domination and abandonment of self—is due to the limits of the philosophy of the subject, the domain within which Adorno's thought remains.[24] According to this philosophy, the subject is essentially an objectifying

activity, even when it examines itself; it would thus not be able to constitute any meaning, since meaning is always intersubjective. According to
Adorno, the growing weight of the absurd in modern art is due to the
increasing force of a subject which dismantles all valid meaning. One might
thus believe that Adorno expresses a regret vis-à-vis the objectivity of meaning in traditional societies, but this is not at all so. In truth, the stakes of art
are for him foreign to the signification; art is a kind of "nonsignifying language,"[25] as he characterizes both natural beauty and a modern art
which—as does music—moves away from all narration. The progressive
intellectualization of art contributes to this just as does its primitivism, the
taste for fauvism. But in spite of this refusal of signification, Adorno
attributes a very precise message to the language of art: it is the "language
of suffering"; it evokes the negativity of reality and exorcises it through
form. All "authentic" works convey this same message, which converges
with the ultimate goal of philosophy.

II

Recent attempts to liberate aesthetics from this metaphysical heritage
which—for Adorno, but also for Heidegger—makes of art the preserver of a
precise truth, generally have the flaw of remaining negatively dependent on
these concepts. Thinking to return to Kant or to Nietzsche, they substitute
something for truth, be it the play of subjective faculties, authenticity, or a
relativization of the concept of truth.

Albrecht Wellmer and Martin Seel,[26] who endeavor to reinterpret
Adorno in light of the thought of Habermas, are drawn to aesthetics as a
means of completing a theory of the forms of rationality. Their analysis con-
centrates on the contribution of art and of aesthetic reception to the collective process of communication. Thus, Wellmer opens aesthetics to art, an
aesthetics which is posterior to the *Aesthetic Theory*, by attributing to modern subjectivity the same power of regeneration and integration that
Adorno had reserved for the open forms of art. This allows him to reformulate the Adornian aesthetic utopia as a salvation for the socially excluded
and repressed, not only in an aesthetic testimony of truth, but in a communication constantly enlarged through the action of art.

As for Martin Seel, he renounces such a utopia to conceive a social game
of rationalities in which art serves as invitation to make experiences—experiments—for their own sake. The work of art presents a "way of seeing"
which cannot be objectivized (p. 272) but which, if it succeeds, can be
actualized and made the object of a discourse showing others the mode of
perception which leads to such a comprehension.

In the history of aesthetics, Martin Seel distinguishes two great, erroneous tendencies: the "privative," which considers a work of art as inexpressible, radically foreign to a discursive apprehension of the real (Seel cites Nietzsche, Valéry, Bataille, Bubner); and the "superlative," which sees in the aesthetic phenomenon the manifestation of a truth superior to that which discursive reason can attain; the first tendency is purist, the second fundamentalist (pp. 46–47). Now, Seel's endeavor consists in defining a more rational relation with art, that of attention to a content of experience presented in the form of a nonpropositional articulation. The criterion for the aesthetic value is not truth but rather aesthetic "success" (pp. 126ff.). Those works or artistic manifestations are successful which express the contents of lived attitudes to which they alone give us access; of which they reveal to us a new sense; and which appear to us as adequate and essential for a "just" life in the present time (pp. 210–11). Aesthetic rationality appears initially in an argumentative form highlighting that which shows itself to be expression in the artistic phenomenon (p. 214). Such an emphasis is both interpretation (commentary) and actualization (confrontation, immediate emotion), and becomes criticism by combining these two aspects. Criticism specifies the mode of perception which reveals the signification of the aesthetic phenomenon (p. 296); the artists themselves do not communicate any signification but make something which is significant in itself (p. 291).

For Seel, art does not aim for anything other than to acquaint us with the experiences that are possible on the horizon of the historic present—and first to draw our distancing attention to the experience which is ours; it does not convey any other utopia (p. 330). That of a widening message, integrating what up until then was inexpressible, is not specifically aesthetic, but rather political. Those who make the experience aesthetic live the fragile presence of liberty, not its ever-vanishing future (p. 332). Seel thus rejects all aesthetics of "preappearance" or of the anticipation of a real utopia, where he sees nothing but illusion.

His book is an important attempt to articulate a domain which is difficult to grasp, that of an expression which is neither idiosyncratic nor conceptual. He represents the most recent example of a paradoxical effort characteristic of German thought since Kant: to make sense of art through philosophy, while at the same time making art a privileged object of reflection, and keeping guard against its philosophic overevaluation. Reason has need of an art which clarifies, but art is not the totality of reason (p. 326).

Wellmer and Seel react against the privilege Adorno assigns to the creative process and to the work of art. As does H.R. Jauss (and Paul Ricoeur, who develops in *Time and Narrative* a theory of mimesis as refiguration of reality through the configuration of the artwork itself), they endeavor to reintroduce the receptive subject that the *Aesthetic Theory* had dismissed. This option actually recommends itself when one perceives the limits of the

philosophy of the subject, which lead Adorno to admit of no social impact
on the part of modern works, and to conceive only the evocation of a utopian reconciliation with nature, one which balks at all practical realization.

It remains that aesthetics—unlike ethics—is concerned with historically
dated and completed objects which have the particularity of being able to
influence well beyond the time of their creation.[27] If aesthetic judgment
renders "present" an experience crystallized in the work, one must admit
that the work itself is not devoid of that rationality that criticism realizes; "a
moment of reason is affirmed in the autonomy of the radically differentiated domain of avant-garde art."[28] Before analyzing the activity which consists in appropriating and making available the experience contained in the
work, it is thus necessary to examine the rationality inherent in the aesthetic object, without which there is neither aesthetic nor critical experience. Without it, the work of art remains reason's irrational other and gains
access to rationality only in critical discourse.

Traditional art—narrative, coherent, significant by itself—often seems to
be rational in that it is composed of elements arising from a cognitive or
moral rationality; on the other hand, modern art distinguishes itself precisely—and Adorno stresses this—by its apparent irrationality. It is this
which led Nietzsche to see in the work of Wagner a resurgence of "pre-
socratic" Dionysianism, radically foreign to the modern *logos*. The problem
thus consists in identifying, precisely in this modern art which is reduced to
that which is unique to it, the element which constitutes aesthetic validity—that in the name of which a work is considered a success—and which
allows it to be judged. This brings us back to associating the rationality of
the work of art with its validity as a work.

Aesthetics always comes up against the difficulty of reconciling the virtually universal validity of the successful work, the equivocal or polysemous
character of this universality, and the singular character of the experience to
which it gives form (often even of the material in which it is realized). Kant
thus speaks of a universality without the intervention of a concept, Adorno
of a nonsignificant eloquence. In both cases, one of the terms has a particular connotation: for Kant, the nonconceptual aspect expresses both a deficiency which turns art into the "symbol of morality," and a path which
leads to a moral life; for Adorno, eloquence is paradoxically univocal: it tells
of the suffering that knowledge cannot express, and thus the difference
between works becomes secondary in relation to the "nonrepresentable"
which is the content of truth.

Art—especially modern art—is thus a language, but a language charged
with intense energy and which denies communication.[29] Aesthetic eloquence establishes itself in two ways: by a break with the established sig-
nifications of ordinary language and by the creation of a singularized and
intensified language, a language "for one." The elaboration of this language

"for one" transforms it into a language "for all," made virtually universal by dint of its intelligibility, which necessitates a deciphering.[30] Aesthetic comprehension—and criticism—is thus an art of translation which causes the apparent singularity of the work (and of the experience which constitutes it) to attain a virtually universal signification, but which is for its own part a function of a particular actualization. The unity of aesthetic "validity" does not in any way reduce the diversity of the "nonsignificant eloquence" particular to each work, nor the plurality of interpretations of which each can become the object, precisely to the extent that it is successful.

For Adorno, the particular nature of modern art was a function of reality—of absolute suffering under the reign of totalitarian identity—about which artworks unfurled their eloquence. According to the concept which has just been sketched, modern art is essentially a function of an internal necessity of decentralized subjectivity; a language "for one" charged with individual energy, which becomes "language for all" when the work is successful, is a proposal of meaning[31] in the form of contingent figures and ordered materials.

The intensified proposals of meaning do not form a continuous tradition, according to the concept of hermeneutics; nor do they reveal a hidden essence along the line of the truth of being, but rather, a fragile construction whose internal coherence is always a little strained. That which saves the meaning— that rare commodity of postmetaphysical modernity—from contingency and total arbitrariness, is the fact that its elaboration is subterraneanly a collective work, constantly nourished by the social exchange of experiences, which is the foundation of artistic configurations; no singularity deprived of all supra-individual signification can crystallize into a work.

Proposals of meaning reflect an interpretation and an arrangement of sensitive perception for which the accuracy of tone and the original character of the experience (and of the language found to express it) count more than the conformity to facts and to norms. Art is not in the order of the everyday, even though it seeks its epiphanies in the most ordinary life; it can take the liberty—and this is in fact what one expects from it—of ignoring the intersubjective demands which constitute daily life in society. Only in this way does the stylization of the proposal of meaning become possible. For the receiving subjects, impressed by this ordering of meaning acquired at the price of a certain number of abstractions, the proposal will be confronted with suitable experiences, but also with quotidian demands, and its pertinence will be tested against the true and the just.

From here onwards, one can attempt to explain—without premature reference to historical reality—certain characteristics of modern art, notably the status of negativity and its avatars. According to our hypothesis, the proposal for a coherence of meaning based upon an absolutely singular experience brings into play the demand for a radical expression of self which—from Baudelaire to Beckett—comes up against rigid and intolerant social structures. It is this which gives to aesthetic singularity the appearance of the destructive, satanic, revolted negative. It breaks with the everyday and the constraints of rational subjectivity to bring to life an instant of absolute presence. The sudden shock of ecstasy or of sacred horror snatches it away from all habit and from all familiarity and plunges it into a lucid rapture. Extreme singularity wounds hopes for inviolable personal integrity, whose pathological deformations it denounces while at the same time becoming attached to them in as much as they are images of singularity. So long as the singularity of the subject is not established, it appears demoniac, and art is inhabited by a spirit of revolt; once it is recognized—and it is this which seems today to be the case—art loses its role of representing the "accursed part." Initially subversive, artists tend to become public characters, proposing each of their singularities as a model across the schemas of their experience. Contrary to that which maximalist modernity dreads, it is not the absolute singularity whose existence is menaced, that will be mutilated, leveled, or abolished by social normalization. What risks generalization is a singularity that is without universal bearing, a pluralism of "differences," empty and flatulent.[32] At the extreme, current culture tends to multiply voiceless narcissisms one upon another, and to confuse the fugitive attention that they arouse with aesthetic or intellectual expression. Hence also, during a certain time, the cult of madness, of perversions and of abnormalities of all sorts, which themselves have no aesthetic value, but only documentary interest. The demand for aesthetic validity which characterizes an intensified proposal of meaning calls for a symmetry between the "voice" emanating from the work and that of the receiving subject; so long as it is a "proposal of meaning," the work is not a psychoanalytical "case" which one studies, and this symmetry is the basis of aesthetic rationality.

In accordance with its subversive side, aesthetic singularity thus questions the forms of social normativity which uselessly limit the expression of self. Inversely, coherence of meaning, placed under the demand for originality, is ceaselessly confronted with the resistance of the nonmeaningful and the untenable. From Manet and Baudelaire to Beckett and Bacon, the sovereignty of art affirms itself in the face of the negative and the insignificant. The work is a "proposal" of meaning at the risk of failure: of a meaning which can remain private or of limited interest. In the course of this process, the means employed to affirm the sovereignty of the artist are continually reduced to the "essential": to the expression of an invincible singularity, inexpressible in existing artistic languages. Basic geometric shapes, primitive strokes, pure or elementary colors, bidimensionality, distanced daily objects, raw materials, displayed in the context of a show, can play this role, and arouse the shock of the inartistic annexed by the sovereignty of the artistic sphere.

"Proposal of meaning" signifies finally that the language "for one"—the singularity of the work which seeks to be recognized as singular universal[33]—must be presented to an audience, in order to put to the test its virtually universal intelligibility, its effect of aesthetic coherence as a singularized language, and its power to make the singularity of its experience resonate in the historical experience of the receiving subjects. It is thus necessary that the work overcome at least the three stumbling blocks of absolute singularity: being nonintelligible or stripped of interest; the obstacle of aesthetic incoherence, or that of a break in tone incompletely mastered; and of inadequacy to historical expectations of originality, or of the nontopicality of the dissonance to which it responds.

Contrary to dramaturgical activity in daily life, which aims at influencing others to attain a precise goal, the presentation of works before an anonymous audience—a sort of generalized Other—establishes a contract between the work and its viewers.[34] Nothing, in fact, obliges them to subject themselves to the discipline of the work, but once they have freely abandoned themselves to it, they will experience—or not—the internal necessity, and will recognize it by their aesthetic emotion and their critical judgment. It is this logic which makes of art (and of the aesthetic experience) a sphere of a demand for validity analogous to those which define science and ethics, but of a weaker demand, incapable of assuring the cohesion of society; it is a demand without an immediate "illocutory force," without necessary consequence for daily life. That which could have welded together the audience of certain works in the past—recited epics, tragedies presented before the entire city on special occasions—was due to values other than aesthetic. The modern novel and painting, or recorded music, address themselves to an isolated individual; and the collective experience of the concert, of the theater, and of the cinema, even if it can mobilize shared values, does not create any real tie capable of uniting individuals outside of the aesthetic space.

The demand for truth always comes back to a necessity inherent in the arguments, and only in the second place to facts and events (which cannot of themselves assert their truth). The demand for moral justice is already inherent in the norms themselves, whose legitimacy is presupposed in every modern society, and only secondly in the arguments which justify them.[35] As for the aesthetic demand, it is expressed by each singular, historically situated work which offers itself to the public, and only secondly by the criticism which justifies it, which recommends it or contests its value. But unlike truth and justice, no subject is obliged to accept the proposal of aesthetic meaning. If truth and justice are fallible, their demand is peremptory once one is obliged to admit its pertinence; the universality of a

work of art, and more recently, of certain films evoking solidarity, remains
on the contrary precarious and tied to the possibility of actualizing singular
experience. That is why there exists a mortal rivalry among the works for
the conquest of a universality of meaning; in this rivalry, the contingency of
the subject's situation—which gives the subject access to a privileged experience—escapes the will of the artist. It is the "natural" part of the "genius";
only the capacity to exploit it, to confer upon it the form of a language "for
all," is within the province of the artist.

   The cognitive and moral dimensions of language tend to parenthesize
the particular meaning of the historic situation; the existence or the nonex-
istence of the facts and events, the normative adequation or inadequation of
maxims of action and of institutions do not imply in themselves any relation of these demands either to the plans of the subjects or to the ultimate
goals that they are pursuing. Intensified proposals of meaning schematize
in pregnant materials the historical interpretations of the desires and the situations of the world; they thus reduce the metaphysical projects of the past
to horizons of meaning that subjectivity assigns to itself in the aesthetic
space.[36] In modern society, this meaning must prove itself in the process of
artistic reception, where it interacts with other demands for validity and
with rival proposals. Postmodern "aestheto-centrism," inspired by the
Nietzschean theory of the "artist philosopher," can thus be understood as
a refusal of this reduction of metaphysics to a hypothetical status, to simple
proposals of meaning; it is through loyalty to the lost absolute that everything is reduced to a game of appearances.

*   *   *

What makes Adorno correct in his analysis of radical modernity is that,
until recently, most artists themselves admitted the logic of the worst and
of apocalyptic anticipation. From Baudelaire to Beckett, including Kafka
and Schönberg, modernity constantly repeated an apocalyptic blackmail
which aimed to force the course of history. It is this implicit theology which
collapses along with maximalist modernity. But just as the moral catastrophes of the twentieth century prohibit, in ethics, a simple "return to" a
classical doctrine, and necessitate instead a redefinition of moral theory,
neither can aesthetics go back in time. To reformulate the conditions of recognition of an action or a work does not mean to dissolve all criteria in
"contextuality."

   Writers like Thomas Bernhard illustrate the passage from the apocalyptic
vision (e.g., *Corrections*) to a proposal of meaning of the minimalist type (*Le
neveu de Wittgenstein*). One may regret the passing of the fascinating beauty
of the apocalyptic works, animated as they are by a certainty which transcends singularity, for even the nonmeaningful in them is more powerful

than the risk of triviality that lies in wait for the atheological creator; but the decline of this type of creation has seemed inevitable since the banalization of singular difference. At the same time, the proposal of meaning that was apocalyptic blackmail—"going beyond real negativity by the despair of the imagination," according to Adorno's formula—becomes an option among others, somewhat historically dated, and one would seek in these works that which connects with the stylization of a singularity. In this sense, postmodern "sensibility" is a proposal of meaning that is legitimate in itself.

Such an aesthetics—and it is still this which distinguishes it from that of Adorno—is not the principal support of a critical theory of society; it is complementary to an ethics inscribed in the ordinary language of modern societies. This ethics constitutes the normative expectations of reciprocity which allow for evaluation of the legitimacy of the social order and of equity in interpersonal relations. In a society which plays against the universality of egalitarian commerce the card of singularity and of the "difference" of each one—including anarchist and ultraconservative impulses—aesthetics cannot of itself represent the normative base of criticism. Tolerance for the expression of singularities serves often as a safety valve for persistent injustices. As for works of post-avant-gardist modernity which content themselves with seeking a "secular illumination" in the frame of a world which is neither the worst nor the best, their critical force will be all the greater as their normative reference is no longer an inverse image of redemption, but rather a meaning which is conceivable here below, here and now.

—translated by Roberta Brown

NOTES

1. Cf. Jürgen Habermas, "La Modernité: un projet inachevé," translated by G. Raulet, *Critique*, no. 413 (October 1981): 950–69.

2. Jean-François Lyotard, *La Condition postmoderne* (Paris: Éditions de Minuit, 1979) and A. Wellmer, *Zur Dialektik von Moderne und Postmoderne* (Frankfurt: Suhrkamp Verlag, 1985) converge in this way up to a certain point in their criticism of Habermas. [Jean-François Lyotard, *The Postmodern Condition: A Report on Knowledge*, translated by Geoff Bennington and Brian Massumi, foreword by Frederic Jameson (Manchester: Manchester University Press; Minneapolis: University of Minnesota Press, 1984).]

3. Theodor W. Adorno, *Dialectique négative* (Paris: Éditions Payot, 1978), 11. [Originally published in German as *Negative Dialektik* (Frankfurt: Suhrkamp Verlag, 1966). English edition, *Negative Dialectics*, translated by E.B. Ashton (London: Routledge & Kegan Paul; New York: Seabury Press, 1973).]

4. *Dialectique négative*, 15.

5. *Dialectique négative*, 12.

6. The *Aesthetic Theory* defines the content of the verities in works of art as "the act of freeing oneself from myth and bringing about a reconciliation with it" [trans. C. Lenhardt (London: Routledge & Kegan Paul, 1983), 266]. This definition is borrowed from Walter Benjamin's essay on Goethe. The schema is invariably applied in all the concrete interpretations of Adorno, whether it is a matter of Goethe or Balzac, of Schönberg, of Kafka, or of Beckett. [This and subsequent references to the English translation of *Aesthetic Theory* are for the convenience of the reader. In most cases, we have translated directly from the French translation by Marc Jimenez (Paris: Éditions Klincksieck, 1974), as cited in the original form of the article.]

7. Albrecht Wellmer, "Wahrheit, Schein, Versöhnung. Adornos ästhetische Rettung der Modernität," in *Zur Dialektik*, 9–47 (cf. note 2).

8. Cf. Jürgen Habermas, *Théorie de l'agir communicationnel*, translated by Jean-Marc Ferry and Jean-Louis Schlegel (Paris: Éditions Arthème Fayard, 1987), vol. 1, 371ff. [Originally published in German as *Theorie des kommunikativen Handelns*, 2 vols. (Frankfurt: Suhrkamp Verlag, 1981–85). English translation, *The Theory of Communicative Action*,

2 vols., translated by Thomas McCarthy (London: Heinemann; Boston: Beacon Press, 1984–87).]

9. This is what Wellmer calls the "dialectic of aesthetic appearance," *Zur Dialektik*, 15ff. Cf. Horkheimer and Adorno, *La dialectique de la raison*, trans. E. Kaufholz (Paris: Éditions Gallimard, 1974), 35–36. [Originally published in German as *Philosophische Fragmente* (New York: Institute of Social Research, 1944). English edition, *Dialectic of Enlightenment*, translated by John Cumming (London: Allen Lane; New York: Seabury Press, 1972).]

10. *Dialectique de la raison*, 36: "In so far as an expression of totality, art claims the dignity of the absolute. It is this which has at times prompted philosophy to concede the primacy over knowledge to art. According to Schelling, art begins at the point where knowledge fails; art is 'the model of science and is already found where science has yet to penetrate.' According to his theory, the separation of the image and the sign is 'completely abolished each time that there is an artistic representation.' The bourgeois world was only rarely inclined to show such trust in art."

11. *Aesthetic Theory*, 31.

12. In connection with the young Marx, it was often observed that his criticism of alienated work was based upon a creativist model close to the human ideal of the Renaissance and of German idealism. If this model disappears in *Das Kapital*, *Aesthetic Theory* goes back to a normative basis founded on the model of artistic creation.

13. This is why Adorno's aesthetics remain in a sense an aesthetics of "reflection" (cf. Wellmer, *Zur Dialektik*, 29).

14. With the exception of Peter Bürger, the German critics of Adorno question the predominance of the concept of truth in his aesthetics. They propose either a theory of aesthetic pleasure, indifferent to truth (Karl Heinz Bohrer, Rüdiger Bubner), or a relativization of the concept of truth (authenticity with Franz Koppe; "potential for truth" with Albrecht Wellmer).

15. Art is truly modern, according to Adorno, "when it has the capacity to absorb the results of industrialization under capitalist relations of production, while following its own experiential mode and at the same time giving expression to the crisis of experience." *Aesthetic Theory*, 50.

16. "To be sure, autonomy remains irrevocable....Today, however, autonomous art begins to manifest an aspect of blindness....It is not

certain that after its total emancipation, art would not have undermined and lost those presuppositions which made it possible." *Aesthetic Theory*, 1–2.

17. *Aesthetic Theory*, 35.

18. *Aesthetic Theory*, 35.

19. *Aesthetic Theory*, 36.

20. *Aesthetic Theory*, 43.

21. *Aesthetic Theory*, 43.

22. *Aesthetic Theory*, 44.

23. *Aesthetic Theory*, 47.

24. It is this which Jürgen Habermas (*Théorie de l'agir communicationnel*, and Albrecht Wellmer (*Zur Dialektik*) demonstrate.

25. "The total subjective elaboration of art, in so far as it is a nonconceptual language, is, at the stage of rationality, the only figure in which something is reflected which resembles the language of Creation.... Art tries to imitate an expression that would not contain human intention." *Aesthetic Theory*, 115.

26. Wellmer, *Zur Dialektik*; Martin Seel, *Die Kunst der Entzweiung: Zum Begriff der ästhetischen Rationalität* (Frankfurt: Suhrkamp Verlag, 1985).

27. Cf. György Lukács, *Philosophie de l'art (1912–1914): premiers écrits sur l'esthétique*, translated by Rainer Rochlitz and Alain Pernet (Paris: Éditions Klincksieck, 1981), 159ff. [Originally published in German as *Heidelberger Philosophie der Kunst (1912–1914)*, edited by György Márkus and Frank Benseler (Darmstadt: Luchterhand, 1975).]

28. Jürgen Habermas, *Der philosophische Diskurs der Moderne* (Frankfurt: Suhrkamp Verlag, 1985), 117. [English edition as *The Philosophical Discourse of Modernity: Twelve Lectures*, translated by Frederick Lawrence (Cambridge: Polity, in association with Basil Blackwell; Cambridge, Mass.: MIT Press, 1987).]

29. Wellmer (*Zur Dialektik*, 62ff.) emphasizes the equal importance of signifying and energetic aspects in the aesthetic object.

30. It is this process which is dealt with by the phenomenology of the creative process developed by Lukács in his *Philosophie de l'art*, 41ff.

31. "The power to create meaning, presently confined for the most part to aesthetic domains, remains contingent as does any truly innovative

force." Habermas, *Der philosophische Diskurs der Moderne*, 373. According to Lukács's *Philosophie de l'art*, a work of art is the utopia of a world which can satisfy our expectations of integral self-realization. Such a definition excludes negative works from art, whereas the "proposition of meaning" accepts the affirmation of an experience of nonmeaning.

32. Michel Foucault had observed this phenomenon of a deceptive individuation in contemporary society, attributing it unilaterally to a result of power; cf. *Surveiller et punir* (Paris: Éditions Gallimard, 1975) [English edition as *Discipline and Punish: The Birth of the Prison*, translated by Alan Sheridan (London: Allen Lane; New York: Pantheon Books, 1978)] and *Volonté de savoir* (Paris: Éditions Gallimard, 1976) [English translation as *The History of Sexuality*, vol. 1, *An Introduction*, translated by Robert Hurley (London: Allen Lane; New York: Pantheon Books, 1978).]

33. Cf. Jean-Paul Sartre, *L'Idiot de la famille: Gustave Flaubert de 1821 à 1857*, 3 vols., Bibliothèque de philosophie (Paris: Éditions Gallimard, 1971–83), vol. 1, 7. [English translation as *The Family Idiot: Gustave Flaubert, 1821–1857*, translated by Carol Cosman (Chicago: University of Chicago Press, 1981–).]

34. Cf. *Aesthetic Theory*, 108: "The viewer unknowingly and unintentionally signs a contract with the art work, as it were, pledging to subordinate himself to the work on condition that it speak to him."

35. Cf. Jürgen Habermas, *Morale et communication*, translated by Chr. Bouchindhomme (Paris: Édition du Cerf, 1986), 80ff. [Originally in German as *Moralbewußtsein und kommunikatives Handeln* (Frankfurt: Suhrkamp Verlag, 1983).]

36. Cf. Lukács, *Philosophie de l'art*, 213–26.

Art and Entertainment

Eric Gans

THE FAMILIAR OPPOSITION between "high" and "popular" culture, born in the romantic era, is inherently always in the process of dissolving. The justification of the market can never quite satisfy the producers of popular art; but, at the other end of the spectrum, the differential claims of high art are belied by their very need for articulation. It is in this ever-problematic distinction that the founding opposition between the sacred and the profane maintains its experiential relevance for modern culture.

The dichotomy "art" versus "entertainment" redefines this opposition in terms closer to a contemporary intuition that refuses the simplistic division of society into a self-conscious elite and a presumably unself-conscious mass. It reflects the fact that the opposition between high and low art no longer distinguishes so much two audiences as two attitudes. The traditional dichotomy has the residual value of differentiating between those who are "cultured" and those who are not. But the most explicitly "cultured" persons—particularly academics—tend with increasing frequency to emerge from lower middle-class strata where they have not merely been exposed to popular culture but formed a part of its normal audience, whereas those who more actively seek power and wealth are no longer, at least in the United States, required or even expected to make any great use of whatever cultural knowledge they may have acquired in the course of their studies. Hence not only do the same individuals tend to engage in both "highbrow" and "lowbrow" cultural activities, but the insistent preference for the former over the latter tends to appear more as a compensation for a lack of social status than a sign of membership in the "leisure class." On returning from the ballet, one turns on the television set as a relief from a cultural askesis that few really enjoy. Our respect for the enduring significance of art in contrast to the ephemeral products of "consumer culture" is not in question; but it is certainly possible to suspect that the contemporary judgment of what constitutes "art" makes boredom a more central criterion than esthetic pleasure in any reasonable sense of the term.

The term "entertainment" is often interpreted as implying the assimilation of esthetic objects to objects of consumption, but the analogy is insubstantial. Even television series are saved on tape and in some cases rerun year after year. Trashy literature may appear in paperback, but there are trashy paperback editions of the world's greatest literature. In terms of individual esthetic experience, popular music enthusiasts listen to more repetitions of their already repetitive favorites than classical music-lovers; and many treasure old pop records not only as collector's items but as "classics" in their field. The pejorative notion of the "consumption" of inferior art-works finds no real basis in the practice of the actual consumers of popular art. It would be all too easy if we could distinguish between a great novel and a merely amusing one by examining the residue of a reading to see whether or not the novel had been "consumed." This is not to say that the intuition that associates entertainment with consumption is altogether without merit; but its anthropological basis is more fundamental than can be provided by the one-line condemnation of the "consumer society."

It has long been our contention that the appropriate method for dealing with any significant cultural distinction such as art versus entertainment is to trace its component elements back to a hypothetical originary scene.[1] The effect of this procedure is necessarily to abolish the dichotomous symmetry of the distinction, not by "dialectically" transcending the binary opposition forward in a ternary structure, but by revealing the asymmetrical origin of its components that ultimately derives from the infinitely signifying opposition between center and periphery that is the heart of our originary hypothesis. Semantic dichotomies, implying as they do that both components emerged coevally, by a kind of synchronic mitosis, are an artifact of the passionless scene of rational analysis, where the center/periphery opposition becomes the unproblematic one between observing subject and observed object, thereby reducing the "cultural" to the merely "natural." The synchronic oppositions that emerge in the originary scene reflect on the contrary the maximal dissymmetry between the powerless multitude at the periphery and the sacred uniqueness at the center.

The potential symmetry of these poles is revealed in historical time through the dissipation of their tension, which is to say by the desacralization of the scene. This desacralization is a great cultural achievement, but we honor it poorly when we seek to impose it on a reality whose lack of symmetry was precisely what required the scene to come into being in the first place. Binary oppositions are a feature of the very animal pecking orders that the original protohumans found wanting; animal societies resolve conflicts that limit themselves to such oppositions. A potential leader challenges the old one for supremacy. When battle is joined, the opponents occupy symmetrical positions; the result of the conflict is to restore peace by reestablishing a hierarchical order. But animal mechanisms must fail when rivalry becomes generalized to the entire group; at this point each individual may be said to oppose the remainder of the group as a whole. The resolution can only take place when the group recognizes the object of its generalized rivalry as the universal, absolutely asymmetrical element of the fundamental opposition.

The moment of "art" in the originary scene is the moment of desiring contemplation of the central object, a contemplation we are fully justified in calling "esthetic." This contemplation is evidently not a form of consumption. Yet there is in it a movement toward consumption. The time of contemplation is a time of hesitation between the aborted gesture of appropriation, converted to the designation of the object, and the renewed successful effort in which each acts in function of the already constituted community. The intervening contemplation is not "timeless" and homogeneous. On the contrary, it generates the ensuing scene of consumption without the intervention of extraneous elements, and should thus be understood as effecting a transition between the two moments in which the object is a center of appetitive interest. This transition between two appetitive states consists of a movement away from such interest followed by a return toward it. These movements are by no means symmetrical; indeed, the relative stasis of contemplation is dependent on the dissymmetry between the abrupt turning-away from appropriation and the slow turning toward it. Contemplation is a single activity, not a couple of disparate moments. The imaginary movement of desire toward its object is not checked by an opposing force; its relocation on the imaginary scene of representation is all the "opposition" it requires.

The transitional nature of contemplation makes it clear nonetheless that the participants' attitudes toward the object at the end of the interval of contemplation must have been quite different from those held at the outset. The sacralizing fear to appropriate gradually dissipates, with a concomitant difference in the quality of the imagination. From compensatory, imaginary possession becomes anticipatory; the transcendental joy of the impossible possession of the sacred gives way to the more concrete pleasure of the anticipated renewal of appropriative action. What divides these two tendencies of the imaginary may be expressed in terms of an internal equilibrium. When the object appears as sacred and inaccessible, the pleasures of the imaginary are so to speak paid in full by the accompanying sacrifice of appetitive satisfaction. When, in contrast, appropriation becomes once more conceivable, the sacrality that makes the desiring imagination more than a mere anticipatory function of appropriative activity (like the cat anticipating the movement of the mouse) contributes to an imaginary satisfaction for which no sacrifice is necessary. At this point the participant may be said to have his cake and eat it too. These two moments of the contemplative desiring imagination will serve as our hypothetical originary source of the distinction between high and low art, or between art and entertainment.

The contemplators of the isolated central object of desire are individuals separated by this desire from each other as well as from the sacral center. But as soon as contemplation becomes anticipatory, the separation of the uniquely desiring individual comes to an end. It is not the communal nature of the feast, but the anonymity of what we have called the "consumers' satisfaction" in it that is primordial. Uniqueness is lost once one not only agrees but looks forward to mere participation as a substitute for unrealizable unique possession. Entertainment is a mass phenomenon because it exalts the joys of the anonymous periphery over the solitary dreams of the center. Its inauthenticity derives from the fact that only the center can guarantee the scene on which these joys must be enacted. The recipient of imaginary entertainment appears to be getting something for nothing—the proof of this being that he is willing to pay for the privilege. But the increased pleasure of anticipation is merely the counterpart of the preceding culturally (and not biologically) determined deferral of satisfaction. Entertainment is a dividend in natural currency from humanity's investment in the cultural. In the originary scene as reproduced in ritual the consumption of the central object is not suppressed but merely deferred. Entertainment insists on the promise implicit in this deferral, whereas art emphasizes the irreversibility of the sacrifice it requires.

But today it is less the contrast between these two categories, as described over the years with vast complacency by the critics of "consumer society," than their complicity which interests and troubles us. So long as a clear distinction could be felt to obtain, the sacral element in culture could be said to have survived intact, albeit already menaced by forms the denigration of which became increasingly urgent in proportion to their threat. Mallarmé, the high-culture hero of the post-modern age, expresses the intensity of this threat with great lucidity, albeit not yet with resignation. The post-romantic era was marked, indeed, defined by heroic attempts to preserve the difference of a self-conscious cultural elite from submergence in the "mass." Scheler's attempt to make use of the Nietzschean category of "ressentiment" for this purpose illustrates the problematicity of this position; in the guise of exposing the resentment of the mass as the sign of their non-election to the status of "authentic" man, here assimilated to the true Christian, Scheler only manages to demonstrate the ferocity of his own resentment against institutions that fail to distinguish him from the mass of the resentful. All modern attempts to create an ethic that will distinguish between the authentic and the inauthentic are doomed to failure, because they are *cultural* defenses rather than testable theories, and indeed are ideologies in very nearly the Marxian sense of defending the interests of a class—the intelligentsia—by giving an illusory picture of the structure of social production. That this structure is primarily an ethical rather than an economic one is an affirmation I shall not attempt to prove here.

In contrast with Europe, at least the Europe that existed before the Second World War, fragments of which still survive in the old cultural capitals, the United States has never felt altogether comfortable with the aristocratic notion of a "high culture." Thus while professors of literature, in the great tradition of Henry James, still nourish themselves *outre-atlantique*, their sociological colleagues have for many years implicitly defended American popular culture by presenting it as at the very least the culture of a social group, and therefore equally worthy of our "value-free" esteem. The thrust of this defense has been taken up and radicalized by social-science-minded humanities faculty who surely have much to point to in decrying the snobbery of those who would maintain at all costs the distinction between culture and "kitsch" or "schlock." Yet defenses of popular culture, let alone pseudo-profound analyses that demonstrate its long underestimated potential for providing critics with material for articles, are of interest only to the extent that they permit us to observe the interminable agony of cultural difference at first hand. The analysis transforms the entertaining into its opposite, and thereby "saves" its cultural significance. But the real interest of human science is to build theories of the whole, not to defend or attack isolated dichotomies, which because of their dependency on the whole spring ever anew from their ashes. The most cogent demonstration of the profundity of a work of popular art cannot abolish the high/popular distinction, but only titillate us with intimations of its forthcoming demise.

How do we go about judging a society—our own—that can no longer clearly distinguish between the experience of desire as infinite loss and the anticipated pleasure of its satisfaction, but which can nevertheless recognize the difference in the cultural productions of earlier eras? Evidently the relation of desire to its object in modern market society is no longer what it was in the past. What has changed is not the structure of desire itself, but the way our society expects us to implement it. Utopias of desire are suspect, and we should not rush to condemn the "materialism" or "utilitarianism" that this suspicion betrays. What is suspect is not the sacrality that is behind desire, but our ability to figure this sacrality. Rather than an age of materialism, we may just as well call ours an age of mysticism. The figure of impossible desire is a dream of production in a time when consumption is the only relation available between the worshiper and his divinity. The figure is available, but not the reality—this is the very essence of representation by which means man came into being. We have changed our attitude toward the figure because we can no longer distinguish a priori between the representation of our desire and the reality of its object. This development stems from no peculiar perversity, but from the realities of our experience. Our society's need, not for goods but for distinction, has given birth to a productive agency that makes our desires, as soon as they can be given form, already all but realized. Yet not only is technology no independent "motor of history," but insistence on it is heuristically as well as ontologically unfortunate. The domination of modern society by information-processing, which is to say by the exchange and transformation of representations, reflects the imperatives of the interpersonal relations that dictate not so much the content of these representations as their indefinite multiplicity.

Let us recall the line of a popular song of some years ago, "dream the impossible dream." Modern high literature may seek to realize such a dream, but an imperative of this sort would never be found there. The imperative implies precisely the possibility of realization that is anathema to our mysticism. To dream the impossible dream is to make it no longer impossible, but accessible to the heroic figure who will, we are certain, eventually realize it. The rhetoric of "impossible" desire is here turned to practical use; rather than a (tragic) outcome firm enough for comedy to mock, the impossible, by becoming a mere figure, is already unworthy of its task of incarnating desire. The dream we are asked to dream is the very stuff of which markets are made; the "impossible" is what is only just rare enough to acquire a market value.

Our spontaneous reaction to this rhetoric is to call it "romantic," thereby assimilating it, presumably as a degenerate form, to the first great cultural movement of modernity. The romantics, indeed, believed in the figural utopia of desire; they saw no difficulty in painting a picture of it and declaring it inaccessible at the same time. They were thus the last great artists for whom the opposition between art and entertainment was irrelevant. The intuitive assimilation of the popular to the romantic is thus anything but unjustified. On the contrary, we intuitively give significance to the popular by tracing it back to its most recent culturally significant ancestor.

The romantics thought one could paint a picture of desire because such pictures had been repressed within traditional society in its neoclassical "early modern" configuration. *Imitatio christi* had merely been replaced by *imitatio graecorum*; the romantics imagined themselves the first to reveal the hitherto secret images of individual desire. Although these images are not in fact particularly revolutionary—the true revolution in artistic form being a product rather of the post-romantic rejection of romantic subjectivism—their importance was not in form but in content. Romanticism posed for the first time the characteristically modern problem of the originality of individual desire, which is to say, as the more lucid romantics recognized, the problem of its essential non-originality. Post-romantic disillusionment followed hard upon romantic illusion, which was far from shared by all the romantics themselves. But for the first time there was a specifically *cultural* illusion to share; and thus, for the first time, the familiar opposition between the authentic and the inauthentic took form—indeed, became identified with "form" in the well-rounded, classical and post-classical sense of the term. Romantic "art" could already be opposed to romantic "entertainment" to the extent that it revealed or dissembled the fundamental unoriginality of the *form* of desire.

"Revealed or dissembled" implies an opposition that is far from innocent: the equivalent, in fact, of that between the authentic and the inauthentic that has dominated our consciousness since the romantic era. It was the romantic vision of originary desire that first declared itself authentic in opposition to the tired figures of tradition. Yet a mere generation later artists would wince at the naivety of this opposition while valorizing its opposite term. The stake in this dichotomy is the infinite distance between damnation and salvation, but its basis is the esthetic intuition that was the nineteenth century's most potent—and most volatile—source of anthropological truth. This translation of the ultimate question of fidelity to the originary scene—to the essence of humanity—from the ethical to the esthetic is fraught with danger, as the twentieth century would so clearly reveal. In approaching it from the standpoint of art versus entertainment, a dichotomy that remains ironically within the domain of its original formulation, we seek not to deny the danger but to extenuate it; our justification for this procedure is the fact that this formulation is indeed originary.

The error of romanticism is not its claim to have returned to the originary scene abandoned by the neoclassical tradition; all movements and theories that pretend to originality, including our own, make this same claim. The error lies in the utopian conception of this scene as the locus of individual fulfillment. It is this secret link between the individual and the collective that explains the romantics' mysterious combination of egocentricity and worship of "organic" collectivities; these collectivities are conceived as the ideal habitat for the ego. The romantic's desire is for him a guarantee of the authentically originary character of its content—the naivety of attributing figural "content" to desire is his, not ours. The concept of authenticity is necessary here because for the first time in cultural history the desiring imagination is given priority over the constituted forms of the community. No battle is engaged over worldly supremacy; on the contrary, a status of worldly defeat is claimed as a sign of election. Romanticism thus constitutes a radical break with a ritual order stigmatized as degenerate, most visibly in its art-forms.

The radicality of the romantic position is compromised by its overconfident reliance on the figures of desire, but this is no mere mistake. Romanticism is a tragedy, not a farce; it had no way of knowing that the appeal to the originary would produce structures—in politics as well as art—distinguishable only by their sentimental portentousness from the old. The romantic, as the first bourgeois opposing the bourgeois universe, conceives of it as unpleasant, unentertaining because cut off from the originary wellsprings still available to the private individual. The cultural/mediate appears to refuse all satisfaction to the immediacy of nature. The artist's complicity with his "inauthentic" surroundings has not yet reached the stage where he will suspect his own desire as the involuntary product of such mediations.

This assimilation of the originary to the utopian is the source of the energy of romanticism as well as of its naivety. Its anthropological watchword, simply put, is "ritual as pleasure." Ritual itself divides the moments of production and consumption that the romantics assimilate; but ritual is its own theory incarnate, not an attempt, however misguided, to understand one's cultural other. Romantic misunderstanding of ritual is the first great step beyond the sacred, and any anthropology, however scientific, consists only in relatively less egregious such misunderstandings.

The romantics had presented themselves as authentic artists in opposition to the academic sterility of their recent predecessors; the post-romantics, with what appears to us the greater justification, relocated this opposition between them and the romantics. Because the romantics' criterion for esthetic authenticity was not formal prowess but the intuition of desire guaranteed by the figure, their dichotomy could be conceived as encompassing the ethical in all its manifestations, most notably the political. The post-romantic reaction, at its most radical, subordinated the ethical to the esthetic, making the "discovery procedure" into the truth itself. It is precisely here that the art/entertainment dichotomy emerges. For the romantics, the inauthentic had been synonymous with the boring, as witness Stendhal's *boutade* that the romantic is what pleases us whereas the classical is what pleased our grandparents. In the romantic utopia my desire interests you a priori— "Insensé qui crois que je ne suis pas toi!" We have only to follow our "nature." Desire takes us to our origin because that is what we all desire. That this premise fails to imply the romantic conclusion reflects no mere error in logic, but a preliminary optimism about modernity, however "tragically" expressed. To conceive, on the other hand, art as essentially unamusing is the sign of a peculiarly modern pessimism with which we are far more comfortable.

The post-romantic reaction was obsessed by its intuition of an internal distinction within secular culture between "true" art and entertainment, between the beautiful (but this word would no longer be felt appropriate) and the merely attractive. The artists of this generation have been said to have made a religion of art. No doubt; but as in Marx's making a "religion" of politics, their accomplishment is belittled by the implication that they merely projected onto one domain the categories of another. To make a religion of art is not merely to grasp the after all rather facile analogy between the two cultural forms, but to seize in the esthetic the essential moment of the sacred, precisely in its capacity to figure desire as unfulfillable. The location of the division between the sacred and the profane within the esthetic rather than on either side of it reflects an anthropological intuition of a refinement absent in previous ages.

At this point, art is not merely the source of something more than pleasure; it suspects pleasure as something worldly and utilitarian. The romantic utopia of desire falls under suspicion as uncritically open to the facile satisfactions of the bourgeois market-system. Desire can no longer be trusted; the romantic separation between the individual and "the others" is no longer confidently located in an objective worldly space. Henceforth the struggle between the higher and lower forms of desire, familiar to the religious sphere, is fought on the battleground of the individual imagination. The war-cries that accompany the artists' charge may strike us today as shrill, and their mission as chimerical as that of their less doubting precursors, but it is only with such means that one can sustain the intuition of a new discovery procedure for anthropological truth.

To think art as separate from the satisfaction of desire is to eternalize the originary moment of contemplation, to cut it off from the appetitive satisfaction that ritual had always preserved, in however attenuated a form. The worldly, communal moment that allows a society to be created is seen as the devil's work; as though Adam's primary sin had been not pride but gluttony, the artist's role is to create new non-alimentary fruits with the same spiritual content. To "entertain" is after all to nourish (as the French verb *entretenir* makes clear); the self-sufficient contemplative moment must free us from the illusion that something more concrete will follow. What is contemplated in the originary scene is an object of a universally felt appetite. Its sacrality springs from this universality; its exclusion from our world proceeds from the intensity of our worldly attachment to it. The post-romantics understood the impossibility of reproducing this form in a market society. But what they could not well appreciate was the critical role of the market in establishing the esthetic moment—the moment of pure desire— as the dominant one. The infinite value to which they aspired was that of the infinite deferral of use; in contradistinction to the communal art-market, they set up an "absolute" market of their own. Their exaltation of the contemplative was and remains dependent on a dialectic with the appetitive that is the essence of "capitalist accumulation." No vulgar parallel need be drawn between the respective asceticisms of banker and poet; our notion of the market-system can easily accommodate the specificity of both if we bear in mind that markets are not merely, or even primarily, loci for the exchange of goods. The primary market is and has always been the market for human praxis. The Marxists have well noted the "workmanlike" qualities of post-romantic artistic production, whether to denounce the complicity of its practitioners with the system they purported to oppose or to exalt their inversion of its aims—the latter being surely the more subtle interpretation. But the centralization of production, far from revealing the mortality of the market-system, only demonstrates its invulnerability to the socialist ideal that would replace it. All production requires a market; it is for this reason that in *The End of Culture* we called the originary desire for the center "producer's desire."

In short, the post-romantic utopia was that of an art divorced from any considerations of entertainment. That this utopia was neither truly realizable nor merely chimerical is well demonstrated by the quality and, one is tempted to add, by the entertainment-value of the work it inspired. For the very absolute nature of this divorce made it a guarantee rather of intention than of fact; under the protection of his contempt for bringing pleasure to the masses the artist was able to reinforce his intuition of the ultimate truth of the contemplated central object. The angelism of this attitude, so visible in Mallarmé, is more apparent than real, because what was in effect being grasped was not an elitary mystery but the very basis of the collectivity. Mallarmé's anthropological intuition, a subject I have dealt with elsewhere,[2] was nourished by his insistence on the indefinite and non-anticipatory deferral of satisfaction, which became for him a discovery-principle. The significance of the *crise de Tournon* in his personal and creative history can be described most succinctly as the moment at which he discovered, if not this principle itself, the fact of its existence. The early works like "Les Fenêtres" that breathe resentful contempt of the "mass man" *à l'âme dure* give way to a mode wherein the unsubstantiality of the image becomes the guarantee of something more than the displeasure of the reader ("le plaisir aristocratique de déplaire")—the guarantee of the conjunction between the imaginary scene and its originary sacral counterpart. The absence of nourishment is no mere snobbish exaltation of the sign over its referent, but a reflection of the posteriority of the cultural to its appetitive origin; the food is absent not because man should really be able to do without it (as Mallarmé had implied in "Les Fenêtres" by speaking with contempt of the mass man's need to "nourrir ses petits") but because culture arises as a reflection on what has already been consumed. But the subtlety of this distinction, although it guaranteed the greatness of Mallarmé's poetry, was easily lost on his followers; not only could its intuitive basis never be thematized—the case for all esthetic movements however "lucid"—but more significantly, it depended on a sense of individual difference that was in effect an extreme, one would like to say, an ultimate concentration of the romantic paradox of a movement composed of unique individuals. Mallarmé's experience of death and rebirth that made of him an impersonal "voice" was inimitable in its very impersonality, since it left its imitator no space for personal differences; Proust's and Joyce's enterprises were equally so. And the socio-ethical concomitant to this increasing lack of space, to this raising of the stakes to their ultimate human limits—so that one would have somehow to give more than his life to write a poem after Mallarmé, a novel after Proust or Joyce—is the growth, not of "imperialism," nor even of mass production ("Taylorism"), but of the techniques of consumer-oriented merchandising, in a word, of entertainment in the

economic as well as the artistic sphere. The artist-as-hero had come to the end of
his rope because the heroic rhetoric of the romantics had been made available on
the assembly-line. Mallarmé belonged to the last generation in which one could
claim to be invulnerable to the blandishments of the advertising techniques he
contemplated for his "Livre." For once the artist allowed himself a second of
human desire, his imagination would be forever corrupted by the foreclosure of
this desire by the products designed to satisfy it.

   This extreme position was not the last line of defense for the high culture; it
was in fact the first, from which it has been retreating ever since. But it was the
last point from which primary anthropological intuitions could be obtained.
The twists and compromises of modern esthetics, from futurism to the *nouveau
roman*, have substituted ever-more-strident a priori doctrines of the esthetic for
the free exploration of its imaginary domain. The results are not so much lacking
in interest as they are derivative of the doctrines themselves; and in writers like
Artaud and already Mallarmé's chief disciple Paul Valéry, the interest of the doctrine is in inverse proportion to its productivity. Meanwhile, a whole entertainment industry had taken over the functions that had formerly devolved upon
the quasi-sacral artist whose role had become the object of such theorizing. The
ultimate outcome of this process would appear to be the fusion of art with entertainment as before, but from the opposite direction; the sacral artist who enter-
tains by revealing man to himself gives way to the sacral entertainer whose art
sacrifices the self to its distraction.
   It would nevertheless be an unfortunate mistake to assume that this transition is or could ever be complete. No doubt the most curious feature of the
contemporary esthetic scene is the persistence of the high culture, subsidized
with taxpayers' and granting agencies' funds. Few eras have been more favorable
to the "fine" artist; art, or in any case its purveyors, benefit from civic and corporate pride as well as from a favorable climate for investment in "collectables."
The growth of an educated upper-middle class provides the social basis for a
flourishing of the arts surely comparable on an economic scale to any in history;
even poets, notorious worst-sellers, can eke out a living by traveling from college
to college as "writers in residence." The suspicion that the emperors of modern
art are scantily clad, that their undoubted creativity is derivative and its source
the search for distinction rather than for human truth, has little or no impact on
the social interactions that sustain the arts today; one is not really expected to
enjoy them, scarcely even to "appreciate" them, but to congratulate oneself on
the askesis one has obtained from the boredom they inevitably inspire. The
high-cultural artist is no longer scarcely anyone's idol, but he commands the
respect due the successful. The idolized popular entertainer, on the other hand,
is viewed with envious detachment by the educated; one accepts to be enter-
tained, but one refuses to worship at the altars of the media. High-artistic askesis
acts as an antidote to absorption in mass pleasures; as high art tends ever more to

empty formality, its very abstraction from content guarantees its persistence as a reminder of the formerly lofty aims of esthetic *Bildung*.

Yet the inauthenticity, or to put it another way, the anesthetic nature of these high-cultural esthetic experiences gives a clear indication that mass "popular" culture not merely threatens the dominance of high culture in the esthetic realm, as it did in Mallarmé's time, but has already overturned it. It is not the mere numerical appeal of mass culture that is decisive, although its financial success parallels the democratization of disposable income that is the market society's bottom line in cultural as in other matters. The threat to the educated elite, or rather the victory realized over it, is clear from nearly every conversation one has outside the strictly professional sphere concerning cultural matters. I have taught for many years in French departments and have had precious few conversations about recent French literary works—particularly since the already long-gone heyday of the *nouveau roman*. On the other hand, I am quite well aware of my colleagues' recent trips to the cinema, and often hear of popular novels they have read. Not only are these esthetic activities more pleasurable in themselves than the high-cultural variety, they are more pleasurable to discuss. This last point, apparently so nearly tautological, is really the key; unlike the more secret forms of forbidden pleasure that one forebears to discuss in public, those procured by the mass culture participate fully in the social dialectic. Their full-fledged inclusion in the professional discourse of professors of literature is hampered only by the nagging suspicion that we have really no particular qualifications to speak of them, that our much-vaunted techniques of textual analysis are not inapplicable but largely—and increasingly—irrelevant to the understanding of how these works produce their effect. The move from new-critical to deconstructive rhetorical analysis clearly reflects the quasi-conscious search for a technique that, by avoiding the esthetic experience altogether, constitutes its textual objects as canonical a priori.

The question posed by entertainment to the modern age is whether the chief thrust of the never-ending process of decentralization in market society is the production of difference or of similarity. The oxymoric syntheses "similarity in difference" and "difference in similarity" only say the same thing on the centerless scene of metaphysics. To the inhabitant of the modern world, the difference between these similar formulations is the whole difference, the fear of their collapse into similarity the only fear. If, as I have claimed, the originary foundation of human society is difference as absolute otherness, then the fundamental problem of the self will always be the preservation of the specificity of its participation in this otherness and not the mere fact of participation as such. For once this specificity is lost, what remains to guarantee that of the originary, sacred difference—of difference *tout court*?

The high/low cultural distinction that has been the theme of this essay is not founded on the sociological opposition between mass and elite, but on that between individuality and participation. The great lesson of modernity in advanced societies is that the class differences that animated hierarchical society since its inception, and which Marx rightly found unjustifiable, were not anthropologically fundamental, but rather stood as social guarantees for a far more intractable structural opposition within the originary scene itself and within the imaginary scene that preserves its structures. The art/entertainment dichotomy helps teach us this lesson because, precisely, it undercuts sociological oppositions and forces us to face the ontological dichotomy within ourselves.

It is necessary but not sufficient to trace this dichotomy back to the originary scene. The heuristic value of our hypothetical derivation, like that of all such derivations, is to afford a perspective on the future, which alone can be of real interest. Anthropology can never be a fully predictive science, but it can and must become a *projective* one, one which continually refines its ontology of the human on the basis of the revelations afforded by the projective temporality of our present experience. The future of the art/entertainment dichotomy is significant precisely because it cannot be in any sense determined; because its future determination depends on an ongoing process of freedom through self-understanding.

The contrast between the sacralized art of the past and the profane works of entertainment that dominate esthetic experience in the present does not imply any pessimistic conclusions concerning the individual in the modern age. The esthetic means for the promotion of unique individuality may be no longer available, but we cannot therefore justifiably conclude that modern popular entertainment reduces us to the level of the undifferentiated mass. It merely leaves us with our social differences without making a case either for their significance or for their insignificance.

What this implies is that entertainment in the modern age is not the equivalent, either for well or for ill, of the popular art of the past. The choice between high and low, individuation and massification is no longer available in art, and the result is not a mere reduction of the esthetic to its lowest common denominator, but a perceptible moving-away of art from both its original aims. The "alimentary" nature of entertainment no longer implies a necessary complicity with the anonymous violence of the periphery. Instead, there is an exploration of the surface of experience which, by offering easy solutions to insoluble problems, permits us to defer the necessity of finding such solutions. We can no longer take seriously the ritual techniques of significant closure, but we can appreciate the illusion of closure in a world where it is no longer a realistic possibility. Thus we grow ever less self-conscious of our search for entertainment, which accepts the inevitable relativity of the modern experience while feigning to transcend it.

So long as one could say, "art for the few, entertainment for the masses," the anthropological truths that art revealed were confounded with those of mere sociology. Now we can understand that individuation is an aim that cannot be limited to a social class or its weltanschauung. But as soon as this becomes apparent, the very possibility of self-substantive individuality as a rational aim becomes problematic. What art could achieve concretely must now be conceptualized in abstracto. The disappearance of the illusion of essential social difference is also that of the socially transcendent evaluation of the real differences that exist. Entertainment provides solace from the anxieties of the market on which these differences are bought and sold, the stock-exchange on which we are obliged, for well or for ill, to spend our lives.

NOTES

1. This hypothetical scene is presented at length in Eric Gans, *The End of Culture* (Berkeley: University of California Press, 1985), Chapter 2. Very briefly, the scene consists of a group of proto-humans surrounding an object of extreme appetitive value. The strength of the appetitive attraction of the object is opposed by the fear of each that he will be subject to the violence of the others if he attempts to procure it for himself. This stasis expresses itself in the abortion of the appropriative gesture of possession and its conversion into a sign of designation; in our theory this is the first linguistic act and by the same token the origin of the human as such.

   The center/periphery distinction defines the unique and therefore "sacred" center in opposition to the anonymous mass at the periphery. This "massification" as a precondition of the collective projection of significance onto a central desire-object contrasts with animal forms of collective behavior, which create hierarchies based on series of binary "pecking-order" conflicts. In such hierarchies, conflict is averted because it never expresses itself in the form of a desire so strong that it abolishes all pre-existing differences. Thus the difference between man and the animals can be expressed as that between creatures for whom the primary problem of existence comes from without (survival in nature), and for whom internal conflict is a secondary problem, and a higher form for which the principal problem is the cohesion of the group itself against primarily internal sources of conflict, to be resolved by "cultural" means.

2. "La femme en X: Mallarmé anthropologue," *Romanic Review* 72, no. 3 (May 1981), 285–303.

What Is Valuable in Art,
and
Can Music Still Achieve It?

John Rahn

THESE IMPORTANT QUESTIONS resist any definitive or absolute answer, intrinsically.[1] Imagine someone giving the absolute answer to these questions. Inescapably, such an answer would circumscribe the personal artistic space of the answerer, presenting the shape of that space as its essential quality. This is why pronouncements on such subjects are usually interesting when they emanate from people whose artistic space is of general interest, from a Babbitt or Xenakis or Boulez, a Carter or a Stockhausen, a Glass or Cage. Rather than answering the questions, this essay will explore some of the possible shapes discerned dimly out there, as it were puzzles in a looking-glass, or like shadows on the wall of the cave through the smoke of the central fire.

The stance of this essay is that of the composer of music in Western culture. Creators in other cultures may, we hope (because diversity is valuable), have not only other answers, but other questions. Scholars have traditional directions from which to approach questions of value in art, but the roads they have chosen to travel are not ours. Often scholars ask, Valuable for what?, responding with some functionally oriented answer. The eminent ethnomusicologist Bruno Nettl, writing in a recent book called *The Western Impact on World Music*, concludes that in the polyvalent musical culture of today, where many different musical cultures may coexist in a given time and place, a music is valuable as an "emblem of ethnicity"— valuable for its social function of promoting cultural identity and cohesion. The space so revealed is not in an aesthetic dimension, but an anthropological one. ("Interpretive" ethnomusicological approaches derived from Clifford Geertz's kind of anthropology escape the toils of functionalism, which is rather *vieux jeu* in anthropological circles, without renouncing the tendency to flee from the aesthetic core of the musical to its cultural causes and effects. However, I had better not cast such stones too vigorously, lest they invade the anthropological house of glass that will be built later in this essay.)

Functionalism also underlies less sophisticated views on these questions. The married couple who value Our Song because of its personal associations with a period in their history illustrate the phenomenon of *induced aesthetic value*: they have learned to love the song, beyond their initial aesthetic reaction to it, as the great personal-historic value they use the song to contain spills over into the aesthetic domain. The immigrant, or exile, living in a foreign land, may use the native or folk music of his homeland to focus and contain his nostalgia, his *Heimweh*, to keep his feelings about his native country alive while sequestering them from his day-to-day activities. The powerful and deep emotions evoked may well spill over into the aesthetic domain, investing the music with a beauty of a kind not pertinent to it in the old country.

As a farewell to functionalism, consider the values prevalent in the music industry. There, a piece of musical property is valued to the extent that it can make money for the owners of the property. The induced aesthetic value referred to above is unlikely to manifest under these conditions, though one might imagine tears coming to the eyes of a recording-company executive lounging by the pool late one night, hit unexpectedly by the sounds of the song that built the pool, unexpectedly grateful for it all.

What music is valuable *for* is not what is valuable *in* music. Musicians— those who create or recreate the music—judge music in some mysterious musical fashion independent of the uses that music may be put to. It is possible to say, "This is a great protest song, but a poor piece of music." Much of the foofooraw in the current visual art scene has to do with the wavering boundary between use (say, as an investment) and aesthetic value: the intensity of the collision is proof of the distinction.

CRAFTSMANSHIP

One of the things musicians (again, within the tradition of Western music) value in music is craftsmanship, technique. Those who create or recreate each passing quaver, who as listeners note each precise placement of the smallest musical entities making up the musical piece, know (like the toad beneath the harrow) where every separate toothpoint goes. If the creator of the music stumbles, misplaces his points, at any level of musical structure from the tiniest detail to the most global levels, such listeners perceive the fault, and (perhaps) mourn the loss of something potentially more perfect. The concern is not only a negative one. There is a positive joy in perceiving a flawlessly intricate musical structure, one which leads the mind to startling discoveries as it is unfolded, offering depths upon depths into which we peer, within which we play, but which are never exhausted, never leave us low and dry.

This is not the flash of a Richard Strauss, not the meretricious craftsmanship of the mere technician, unconnected to the wellsprings of his human existence; it is, rather, the kind of craftsmanship that apes the divine, or from which the notion of divine creation is extrapolated. It is the grand tradition of a highly evolved art music, and whatever the virtues of traditions of less polished, less evolved music, they do not offer this sublime experience. Cultures which do offer such a tradition, such as our Western art-music culture or those of India or Japan, are incontrovertibly superior in this respect to those that do not.

Composers who number themselves among the champions of the positive value of musical craftsmanship include Igor Stravinsky, Arnold Schönberg, Milton Babbitt, Elliott Carter, Pierre Boulez—the list is long. Krzysztof Penderecki was recently asked in a public forum whether he thought some contemporary composers might have lost touch with their audience, might have gone too fast for the general taste. His reply: "Never too fast." The problem arises for composers who do not wish necessarily to repeat the technical solutions and achievements of the past, whose musical minds are bent on exploration rather than colonization. Colonization is defensible, even noble, if the territory is unoccupied. For creators of original art, there is no knowledge base built into the audience. Music which moreover requires the ability to hear where every separate toothpoint goes has difficulty with audiences anaesthetized by inability to perceive the elements from which the piece is constructed. They have ears, but do not hear. There are even composers who lean back in the overstuffed armchair, in the embrace of dead musical tradition, as it were musical couch potatoes, themselves unmoving amid familiar *immeubles*, living on inherited wealth.

There is no general solution to this problem, though it is exacerbated by a cultural environment which legitimizes mass taste and commercial values above all else. The point I wish to make is that the positive joy of musical craftsmanship is one ingredient of that which is valuable in music, one curve in the shape of aesthetic space. As with any musical tradition in any culture, music exhibiting this value is independent of uncomprehending audiences, and dependent for its legitimacy only on members of the musical tradition, that is, those who are actually capable of perceiving the music.

EXPRESSION

Musicians will often characterize part of the value of a musical piece as having to do with expression. Of course a protest song is construable as expressive of political ferment, a folk song as expressive of ethnic values, but these are only functionalist descriptions in expressive clothing. Program music is explicitly expressive, in a way that still refers to the extramusical, but which integrates the extramusical with the purely musical—its musical essence might be intimately involved with telling a story, for example. However, of music that falls outside the above categories, one may ask, What then does it express? And in general, What does it mean for music to express something?

Expression is often parsed as reference. Thus, music that expresses an emotion does so by referring to that emotion. This seems preferable to parsing expression as evocation, since music that expresses sadness should still do so if sadness is not in fact evoked in a particular listener on a particular occasion, even though the listener recognizes that the music expresses sadness. It remains a problem, however, that the notion of reference itself is either trivial or opaque.

Let us suppose that a piece of music does express sadness, referring to it and perhaps evoking it. Wherein lies the value? Things are sad enough already, one might say. It is possible to refer the value of expression to a kind of Aristotelean catharsis, and a distancing of emotion that allows us to get a perspective on it. The intricacies of musical development within a piece work through a kind of analogy to the structure of world-situations, of ourself experiencing not only the world but our emotional and intellectual concomitants to the world as part of that world. (There is no need for any Husserlian epoché abolishing distinctions of existence: we can pay attention to everything as qualified in original experience.) In this view, the value of expression in music would partly lie in its providing a kind of jungle-gym on which to exercise our capacity for dealing with reality, increasing our survivability and teaching us wisdom. The pleasure we gain from this aspect of the musical experience would derive from the same sources as the pleasure of learning, of satisfying curiosity, of increasing our abilities.

This kind of expression is, as is the positive joy of craftsmanship mentioned above, a dimension along which traditional judgments of art music graph in a monotonic if not linear fashion: the greater the degree of expressive wisdom (or craftsmanship), the higher the musical value. It would be tempting to say that music might gain value from the contribution of the dimension of craftsmanship, but gain relatively little from the dimension of expression; or vice versa; or it might succeed or fail in both dimensions at once. The dimensions of craftsmanship and expression are in fact not orthogonal. Without craftsmanship, the musical structure must lack the complex coherence necessary faithfully and imaginatively to express the world; and if there is high craftsmanship, there must be a structure of world-like complexity and coherence, whose expression is immanent in its existence.(Indeed, this gives some handle on how to begin to describe the distinction between music that is art, and music that is not.)

SELF-EXPRESSION

Many who have approached the questions from another perspective, that of the producer of music rather than its receptors, have asserted that the value of the music lies in its ability to function as a medium in which the producer can express himself. It is the activity of expression that is valuable, not the resulting object, which might be regarded as a sort of fumet on the trail of the artist. The role of an audience, any audience, is radically devalued, as are artistic products designed for an audience. Technique of any kind is suspect, since it is aimed at an audience, and can be construed as a form of discipline from outside of the individual. The roots of such an attitude go back to Romanticism, in which cultural forms were seen as an artificial barrier to the apprehension of reality, a reality that was approachable directly by the individual who broke free of the conventions and gave voice to his unfettered, and largely emotional, experiences. Dewey and Tolstoy merely democratized Romanticism, purging it of its notion of the inherent aristocracy of the individual, the noble savage: now we are equally noble, equally savage all together. Who then can be the audience? The very notion of audience stinks of invidious distinction. Authenticity is all. As Eric Gans puts it in his brilliant and controversial essay "Art and Entertainment,"

> The romantic, as the first bourgeois opposing the bourgeois universe, conceives of it as unpleasant, unentertaining because cut off from the originary wellsprings still available to the private individual. The cultural/mediate appears to refuse all satisfaction to the immediacy of nature. The artist's complicity with his "inauthentic" surroundings

has not yet reached the stage where he will suspect his own desire as the involuntary product of such mediations.[2]

There's the rub. For one who does "suspect his own desire as the involuntary product of [cultural] mediations," the spring of authenticity is no longer of Castilian purity—hence the advance of the "post-romantics," such as Mallarmé, away from the personal toward an episteme of impersonality, inimitable in its majesty: the significant world is no longer self alone, and the self is no longer the only road to knowledge. When Milton Babbitt says, "I have met my Hypothetical Other, and he is I," he distinguishes himself from those who do not write for an audience: his audience is out there, and he reaches out there for his music.[3] The protocol and discipline of writing for an Other remain.

Yet, to express the world is to express *Dasein*, Being-in-the-world. In this sense, all expression is both existential and personal. It transcends trivial particularity neither through the Romantic's naive belief in self, nor through the post-Romantic's (perhaps only relatively less naive) belief in his access to an experience independent of self, but through the necessary conditions of existence for an individual as individual.[4]

MUSIC AND THE SACRED

Technique and expression admitted, music retains a mystery at its heart that is connected with its intimate, if not indeed genetic and originary, involvement with religion. It is necessary to avoid clichés about religion in this regard, and to take rather the broadest possible anthropological and cultural approach to it. Such an approach would not trivialize religion, neither as "the religious experience," fodder for some positivist science, nor as the obscure if colorful doings of benighted indigenes. Nor would it be paralyzed from the outset by the awe and observance of dogma due some particular religion by one of its adherents.

There is a strand of humanistic anthropology in Europe, which offers an interesting balance between the Scylla of secular trivialization and the Charybdis of esoteric circumscription. Motivated by the hermeneutics of the life of Christ, its theories have transcended their origins so as to apply to the most general idea of the religious. One of the attractions of this approach is its explanation of language and culture in general, as well as religion, within its terms of reference. Another is its methodology, which is neither that of the natural nor the empirical social sciences, but instead employs a hypothetical "originary scene."[5]

The hypothetical originary scene has several versions. A crowd of proto-humans surrounds an object desired by each of them. The potential violence of this periphery is defused, this time, by the beginnings of human culture: either by an act of communal designation or reference, putting off violence and the appetitive and allowing a moment of contemplation that constitutes the central object as sacred, partly by virtue of that very deferment of conflict and constitution of community; or by the selection of an "emissary victim" on whom the violence of the whole group is concentrated, also serving to constitute a community and defer conflict. In the latter version, "The group of murderers surrounding the body experience a sudden release of tension, their violence spent, and they contemplate the body as the source of this miraculous transformation of violence into peace. The body of the victim thus becomes for [René] Girard the object of 'the first noninstinctive attention,' which turns it into a *sacred* object, the first signifier and the source of all signification."[6] (The relevance to Christianity is obvious.)

The primal infinite, because indefinitely deferred, desire for the central object becomes the basis not only for all language and religion but also for culture in general, and high culture in particular. It is high culture in its aesthetic aspects that re-evokes the originary scene by presenting an infinitely desirable and utterly unattainable object to a crowd of people who redeem their violent tendencies by renouncing the appetitive or acquisitive, and affirming the contemplative, with respect to that object. Thus high art serves the function of reaffirming the foundation of culture in general. The essence of that foundation is representational.

Mass consumer culture presents a problem for high art (in these terms), because the circuit is shorted: objects are represented as desirable, pseudo-infinitely desirable, only to provoke their acquisition and consumption. There is no contemplation of an unattainable, which affirms the community; no sacralization. What Lola wants, Lola gets. Art in particular stimulates a desire in which the appetitive reigns unchecked. The consumer possesses the painting, possesses the music, via an ordinary commercial transaction. In such a context, the kind of music that has proven commercially successful is predictable: loud, shallow, and sentimental, with maximum appeal to the kind of group identification in which possession of the music becomes indeed an emblem of ethnicity. In the words of one teenager, talking about a rock band, "As soon as I heard the group, I wanted to be like the kind of people that listened to them"—a pathetic remnant of the sacralizing impulse.[7]

None of this analysis is predicated on class distinctions of any kind. Acceptance of the outdated cliché that art music is upper-class music has led to vilification that can only be adequately explained by resort to something like the hypothesis of the emissary victim. It is in fact false by any definition of class except a circular one, that the upper class is the class of people that like art music.

Has art music irretrievably lost its grip on the sacred, on the wellsprings of culture, or have changed cultural conditions made such art irrelevant? The operas of Philip Glass illustrate what may be a rebirth of a sacral connection. Each of his operas has been a ritual of ostention, pointing at various quasi-sacred facets of contemporary culture: Science (*Einstein on the Beach*), Religion (*Akhnaten*), Politics (*Satyagraha*).... The hieratic staging, the absent plots, the mesmerizing ritualistic music, the device of the lone mythic (but human) figure seated silently above and behind the rest of the stage action, the opposition of crowd and individual in a way that is positively not romantic, the absolute avoidance of conventional expressivity in the music and its reliance on very large-scale rhythmic structures of almost frightening asceticism, all point to an aesthetic that makes a radical reconnection with the sacred. It is arguably a specifically Indian conception of the sacred that suffuses Glass's music with its particular flavor, as witnessed by this description of the Tantric conception of time:

> On the vast time-scale imagined by Indian thinkers, variation and individuality seem to mean nothing. Each apparently unique pattern of events is felt to be the result of overlapping cycles of different rhythm, conceived, perhaps, somewhat too spatially, always reproducing eventually a resonance they must have produced before.[8]

The resemblance of Glass's pitch world to conventional tonality may obscure for some musicians the radicality of these operas, in their break with conventional expressivity, and their reconnection to an eerily impersonal mythic world at the roots of our culture. The amazing thing is that the operas have been a popular success—that the power of the successful reconnection has outweighed the strangeness of their musical idiom on the one hand, and what some might perceive as their relative poverty in the dimension of musical craftsmanship on the other hand—though surely, to succeed holistically as they do is proof itself of craftsmanship at some levels.

The idiom is almost beside the point. So long as the music does break with outdated expressive forms and idioms, that do nothing but deepen the ruts of musical futility, any kind of music will do that dares to evoke the powerful roots of our culture. People need real art—art whose craftsmanship expresses the world and reconnects to the Sacred, in the general sense outlined above. Yet there is more required of art, as I will explore below.

ART AS COMMUNICATIVE ACTION

If the foundations of culture are representational, it may be time for the asymmetry of the originary scene (the violent crowd on the periphery

versus the victim in the center) to begin to lose its influence as a primary
determinant of cultural forms. Hierarchy gives way to networks, to interactions within a framework of discourse, or of Habermas's "communicative
action." The originary scene itself could be reinterpreted as the very model
of communicative action, broadly construed. By the action in the originary
scene, action which is essentially communicative, culture becomes possible
and is actually created.

One aspect of communicative action is discourse, which may be characterized as a web of purposive semantic interactions under the discipline
of the goal of truth, a truth which is built up by and evolves within
the web itself.

The identity of such a web, and therefore of its kind of truth, is assured
across time and participants by the same kind of process by which the
identity of anything is constituted. As some thing, for instance a physical
object, changes aspect over time and space (as when we walk around it), we
constitute it as one thing rather than several things, just in the case that we
have some coherent theory which links, not any one of its manifestations to
any other (which would make the linkage an equivalence relation), but at
least each pair of manifestations which neighbor one another in some
ordering—for example, any two time-successive perceptual "snapshots."
The relation of linkage is then (in the language of axiomatic set theory)
formally reflexive, symmetric, and nontransitive—not an equivalence but a
relation of "similarity." Relying on a similarity relation for identity of
things in a transforming world nicely captures the common-sense para-
doxes of thinghood. (Wittgenstein's notion of family resemblance might be
appropriate here.) As with physical objects, so with things like discourses.

Is music a discourse? Certainly it is ontologically akin to a discourse, and
the kind of constitution of identity described above is recognizable, both in
identity of a piece from performance to performance, and also in identity of
smaller or larger musical traditions. But discourse needs a truth as its focus.
Perhaps music has a kind of truth of its own, though attempts to transplant
logical or linguistic truth to music inevitably founder. (Is the countertheme
false? How can one negate that chord?) The relation of music to truth is in
fact less literal, and considerably more complex, as I have suggested above in
my remarks on expression. For support and amplification, one can refer to
Heidegger, Ricoeur, and Adorno.[9]

Habermas's "communicative action" is discourse with added dimensions. Here is how Habermas has described four models of action, the
teleological, the normative, the dramaturgical, and the communicative.

> [The teleological concept of language]—developed from the limit case
> of indirect communication aimed at *getting* someone to form a belief,
> intention, or the like—is, for instance, basic to intentionalist semantics.

The normative model of action presupposes language as a medium that transmits cultural values and carries a consensus that is merely reproduced with each additional act of understanding. This culturalist concept of language is widespread in cultural anthropology and content-oriented linguistics. The dramaturgical model of action presupposes language as a medium of self-presentation; the cognitive significance of the propositional components and the interpersonal significance of the illocutionary components are thereby played down in favor of the expressive functions [N.B. self-expressive—JR] of speech acts. Language is assimilated to stylistic and other aesthetic forms of expression. Only the communicative model of action presupposes language as a medium of uncurtailed communication whereby speakers and hearer, out of context of their preinterpreted lifeworld, refer simultaneously to things in the objective, social, and subjective worlds in order to negotiate common definitions of the situation.[10]

Each of these kinds of action models an aspect of music. We can easily recognize in music the normative and dramaturgical models of action. The advantage of modelling music as something like Habermas's "communicative action" is that doing so brings clearly forward the interdependence of the "objective, social, and subjective" in music, even if we do not follow Habermas in all the details of his theory of communicative action, or in its neotranscendentalist bias. The very idea that music is an action is pregnant. To conceive of our musical activities as actions in the worlds of the world, and as communication in the sense of communion, at once stimulates us to open our eyes on those worlds, and to cherish the cultural community as the subsistent source of our enterprise, even as we value that necessarily individual spontaneity which makes any act possible. Such spontaneity crystallizes the act of art in the work of art. The work of art thus affirms, and exhibits, the value of spontaneity itself to and within the community of culture.

THE NECESSITY OF ORIGINALITY

Iannis Xenakis has referred to "the profound necessity for music to be perpetually original—philosophically, technically, aesthetically."[11] If we accept the dialectic inherent in the concept of art as a "communicative act," a concept of art as that in which the community recognizes the existential value of individual, personalized spontaneity, which crystallizes the act of art in the work of art—then it is clear that in losing originality art loses itself. That which we point to as the essence of the relation between the individual and the others, the center and the periphery, the represented and those representing, the sacred and the congregation, the essential and the existential—this essence collapses and voids itself, infertile, unless it cherishes both halves of its dilemma. Art celebrates spontaneity in community. To the degree that some act of art, and its resulting work, merely follows the rules, ploughs another furrow, devolving with mechanical consequence from some set of givens, it is inauthentic as act and as art, and useless to its culture.

NOTES

1. A shorter version of this paper was delivered at the Annual Meeting of the Society for Electro-Acoustic Music in the United States, Olympia, Washington, 22 October 1988.

2. Eric Gans, "Art and Entertainment," *Perspectives of New Music* 24, no. 1 (Fall–Winter 1985): 24–37. Quote from p. 31. (See p. 47, this volume.)

3. Milton Babbitt, "On Having Been and Still Being an American Composer," *Perspectives of New Music* 27, no. 1 (Winter 1989): 106–12. (See pp. 145–51, this volume.)

4. The preceding paragraph is indebted to, and responds to, Eric Gans's very kind private response to a draft of this paper.

5. "But the progress of our theory of representation requires that it become increasingly rigorous precisely in the sense of situating the origin of all determining elements of the evolution of human representation within our originary scene. It is this necessity that differentiates what we have called elsewhere 'human science' or 'radical anthropology' from the natural as well as the empirical social sciences. Because we seek not merely to observe the regularities of human conduct as though from without but to reconstruct the significant moments of its evolution, we cannot accept any institutionally given form as an inexplicable *donné*. . . . The cultural significance of hypothetical construction is precisely that it constitutes an attempt to understand the fundamental human constructions 'non-culturally,' that is, without the benefit of *fictions*." Eric Gans, *The End of Culture* (Berkeley and Los Angeles: University of California Press, 1985), 16.

6. Gans, *End of Culture*, 13. See also René Girard, *Violence and the Sacred* (Baltimore: Johns Hopkins University Press, 1977).

7. Elsa Bowman, "The Relationship of Music and Popular Culture in Schooling," *Perspectives of New Music* 27, no. 1 (Winter 1988): 118–23.

8. Philip Rawson, *The Art of Tantra* (Greenwich, CT: New York Graphic Society, 1973), 141.

9. See in particular Heidegger's *Being and Time,* Ricoeur's *Time and Narrative* (which includes an interpretation of Heidegger in its Chapter 3), and for Adorno and Habermas, the article "Language for One, Language for All: Adorno and Modernism" by Rainer Rochlitz, in *Perspectives of New Music* 27, no. 2: 18–36. (See pp. 21–39, this volume.)

10. Jürgen Habermas, *The Theory of Communicative Action,* 2 vols., trans. Thomas McCarthy (Boston: Beacon Press, 1984–87), 1:95.

11. Iannis Xenakis, "Concerning Time," *Perspectives of New Music* 27, no. 1 (Winter 1989): 92.

The Beginning and End
of Esthetic Form

Eric Gans

DESPITE THE GENERALITY of the term "esthetic," it is virtually impossible to talk about esthetics without referring to a specific art.[1] And of the major arts, music is no doubt the one students of esthetics refer to least. Even for those who have more than a music-appreciation background, it is difficult to integrate within esthetic discourse an art that in principle makes no reference to worldly experience.

And yet any discussion of esthetic form should take music as its model; for music alone of the arts is all form. In my own case, I plead a very limited technical knowledge of musical form. But I shall attempt to discuss esthetic form in such a way that the musical can serve as its general model, forcing the discussion away from its natural affinity for the more obviously representational arts.

I shall proceed on the basis that the overall structure of cultural experience, including esthetic experience—which I shall shortly characterize more specifically—is that of a crisis that is brought to a conclusion. But because this conclusion is not really definitive, because the end of one crisis is the beginning of another, I shall speak not of "crisis-resolution" but of "crisis-deferral." The difference between a "classical" and a "modern" cultural consciousness is that the former still thinks of the conclusion of a crisis as its resolution; we moderns have learned better.

Because the crisis-deferral model is a temporal one, it comes more readily to literary (and musical) scholars than, say, to art historians. It goes against the grain of classical esthetic theory, which takes its conception of the "beautiful" from the plastic arts. But even the formalist theory of narrative, which follows the classical crisis-resolution model, mistakenly banalizes the notion of crisis.

Isn't a crisis just a perturbation in the homeostasis of everyday life? Isn't all experience a series of crises and deferrals? But this common-sense explanation explains nothing. Even if all worldly projects had the structure of crisis and deferral, that would not tell us why we should be interested in more of same in esthetic form. But in fact a project, even a life-and-death project, is not a *crisis*. For crisis is not an individual but a *collective* concept. As an exemplary illustration, we may turn to everyone's favorite literary work. At the beginning of the *Oedipus Rex*, Oedipus conceives a project: to find the murderer of Laius. But that is not the crisis. The crisis precedes and inspires Oedipus's project: it is the plague afflicting Thebes.

The function of the cultural—ritual or esthetic—enactment of collective crises can best be explained from a generative standpoint. Before there were imaginary crises, there were real ones. Although the cultural repetition of an *individual* experience of crisis would be inexplicable without resort to dubious psychoanalytic mediations, the reenactment of a *collective* crisis is more obviously functional. Culture reproduces in controlled fashion the real crises that threaten the violent breakdown of a social order. The Theban plague is a good example of such a crisis; plagues spread by contagion, and so does human violence. Reenactment reinforces the community's mastery of the factors that led to crisis; the culturally imposed imitation or *mimesis* of ritual and art preempts the runaway imitation that can turn the human community into an uncontrollable mob. By helping to prevent, or, more precisely, to defer real violence, the make-believe of esthetic culture clearly contributes to the viability of the society that practices it.

But even if we assume that the repetition of a pattern of crisis and deferral can help head off real crises, we must still explain the specific relevance of the *esthetic* enactment of crises. This requires us to define the esthetic *form* in which this enactment takes place.

Esthetic repetition, or mimesis, is not simply the reproduction of a real event. The first thing everyone knows about the esthetic domain, as opposed, most crucially, to the related sphere of religion, is that it is not only wholly representational, but unreal; we are able to imagine it to be real without *believing* it to be so. We operate Coleridge's "willing suspension of disbelief." This operation becomes less mysterious if we reflect on the obvious parallel between art and language. Words too are not real in the worldly sense, and yet we understand them by constructing imaginary models that correspond to their meaning, whether we believe in their truth or not. It is the strength of this parallel that makes it appropriate to consider all art, even so nonobjective an art as music, as a form of representation. Yet the esthetic domain occupies a specific place within that of representation in the general sense. The esthetic experience is that of *form*. The signs of language and other sign-systems are "transparent" to their meanings. In everyday communication, we do not *contemplate* words, we consider what they are trying to tell us and take the appropriate action. But we contemplate art and take as a result of this contemplation no worldly action at all, since art does not refer to the world.

What then is the "form" we contemplate? Here the visual arts give the clearest examples: the form of a painting is what keeps it in its frame, what separates it from the desire it arouses. Of course, whatever the quality of the painting, it will remain in its frame, but the adequacy of the content to the form is measured by the extent to which the painting gives *itself* a frame through its organization as a pictorial composition. It is the painting's internal form, what we might call the "form-of-its-content," that justifies its external form as a picture in a frame. "Form" is not a merely formal matter. If we take the example of the portrait in Balzac's *The Unknown Masterpiece*, what we call the "form" of the painting is what confines within esthetic experience the desire inspired by the representation in the portrait. The failure of Balzac's artist to confine his desire is a failure of form; when he falls in love with the woman in the portrait, in his desire to possess her he turns his painting into a formless chaos.

But we can go further than this; the desire a painting—any painting—inspires is generated not in the first place by its subject but *by the form itself*, by the internal coherence that forces the spectator to *want* it to remain in its frame at the very instant in which he desires to possess it outside the frame. It is this oscillatory movement between the form-as-object-of-desire and the form-in-itself that defines esthetic experience. The spectator oscillates between imaginary belonging to the world of the artwork and awareness of the formal barrier to this belonging, a barrier on which the spectator's desiring imagination depends. The beauty of the portrait preserves its object from desire within the context of desire itself, because it is the inviolate form we desire and possession would destroy it.

With the transfer of desire from the subject to the form itself we may now leave the visual terrain of the portrait for the domain of "pure form," where music awaits us.

For once we are no longer concerned with the mimetic content of the sign, it is no longer necessary that this content be identifiable. Much of twentieth-century painting exemplifies this condition; for the plastic arts, the twentieth century is the historical moment when representation loses contact with its representamen to become truly opaque. But the independence of sign from content that in the plastic arts required the revolution of modernism had been accomplished in music by the end of the seventeenth century. Because the fundamental relationships of music—rhythm and pitch—are objects of experience in themselves rather than means for depicting such objects, music is of all the arts the first to liberate itself from the narrow conception of artistic mimesis as depiction. The words of the song, the movements of the dance are not essential to music; their musical "accompaniment" can stand on its own as an art-form. The rise of "program music" in the nineteenth century only confirms the formal autonomy of music. Program music is not music subordinated to and thus remindful of some other worldly or cultural activity. On the contrary, it makes use of the representational possibilities—both descriptive/synchronic and narrative/diachronic—inherent in music itself to construct an imaginary world.

We have seen that the attribution of esthetic form to an object introduces a formal closure that resists the desire directed at the object, thereby deferring the crisis its presence had provoked. But this attribution of form is not the gift of a *deus ex machina*; it is generated by the crisis itself. In a situation of collective crisis, the circular configuration of actors designating a central object suffices of itself to produce "form." The focusing of many desires on a single object renders that object both more desirable and less accessible. No one dares approach the object, fearful of the wrath of the others. The object is surrounded as it were by a protective shield composed of the desires of the encircling collectivity. The formal closure attributed to the object is in the first place the product of the desires that surround it.

But these desires are not manifestations of individual subjectivities. They are *expressed*, communicated among the members of the group, through the *sign* by which they designate the central object of their desire. The sign communicates the significance of the object and simultaneously the renouncement by each of its possession. The sign is *an aborted gesture of appropriation* that points to the object without seeking to abolish its separation. Each, for his[2] own safety, must communicate to the others that he does not intend to disturb the equilibrium by asserting personal designs on this object, that his interest is "purely formal."

In order to designate its referent, the sign must itself be formally closed, detachable from and ultimately independent of the referent. It is indeed *this* formal closure, that of the *sign*, that is primary. The sign lends its closure to the object, or more precisely, it transforms the experienced closure (*Gestalt*) of an object of perception, which had been processed automatically by the perception-system in the prehuman state, into a *formal* closure capable of provoking an esthetic experience. The object is given its "beauty" by the collective desire through the mediation of the sign.

That it is the form of the sign rather than the form of its referent which is the primary source of esthetic experience explains why "natural beauty" is a derivative of artistic beauty rather than the other way around. This is not to deny that certain natural sounds or sights are more agreeable than others, just as certain tastes or odors are more agreeable than others. Formal closure, even in the most refined of the arts, cannot be indifferent to these realities, but they are the raw material of esthetic pleasure, not its cause. Appetite is prior to culture, but *desire* is not; desire depends on the sign, and the esthetic in turn depends on desire.

The elements of music have never been referential in the sense that words are signs of their referents and the relations among them. To say that music "represents" emotions or mental states is not very perspicuous. Yet, at the level of synchronic analysis, the sounds of music form a system analogous to Saussure's model of language. True, for Saussure the differential system of sound-signs ("signifiers") occupies only one side of a piece of paper, with a differential system of ideas (or "signifieds") on the other. But the heart of Saussure's definition of the sign is not signification but location within a differential system, where the values of the elements are determined wholly by their difference from one another.

The analysis of language as a purely differential system is a matter of controversy. But in music we seem to have an object to which this analysis should apply unproblematically. Music, like language, constructs temporal sequences of elements presented in a well-defined order, subject to often complex rules of composition or "syntax," but without any "semantics" to speak of. The differential nature of the musical system is most obvious with respect to pitch; at least for those without perfect pitch, a piece of music sounds the same when transposed. Yet the analysis of music as a synchronic differential system cannot tell us either how music originated or why it continues to exist. It denies or "forgets" the human historicity of music, just as Saussure's analysis forgets the human historicity of language. The ahistorical mode of such models is a dissimulation of their origin in the temporal event of crisis.

Structure is in the first place ethical; it serves to defer conflict. And the first ethical structure is the structure of signification itself. But signification in its most fundamental sense does not follow the pattern of Saussure's sheet of paper. It is not differential but differentiating. Signification is primordially *the designation of what is significant*. In terms of the circular figure of crisis, the significance of the central object is guaranteed by the uniqueness of its position. The significant is indifferently the cause and differentially the outcome of the crisis. The operation of signification begins with indifference and creates difference. But the indifference it begins with is not systematic, "always-already" differentiated. There is no set of interrelated differences from which the significant element is selected. Before a single center is chosen, there is no structure at all.

Although there is perception of difference in the prehuman state, it is impossible to speak of the *significance* of prehuman difference. Significance and signification are inseparable from human language, which could only have arisen if animal representations of difference had proved inadequate. The crisis that brought about the origin of language must have disabled any prehuman (and therefore presignifying) systems of differences, such as the one-on-one "pecking order" that regulates conflict among many higher animals. The fundamental structure of signification is defined by the many-one periphery-center relationship of the circle of actors designating a central object. Any structure of significant differences must emerge from this single difference between the significant and the nonsignificant.

The Saussurian system of differences is not the source but the consequence of signification. The designation of a significant center (in mathematical terms, the "origin") determines for every point in space a "value" corresponding to its distance from this center. The absolute difference created by this designation between the meaningful and the meaningless begins to be relativized. Some objects are near the center, others become analogous centers; analogy and association, metaphor and metonymy suffice for the creation of the entire lexicon. Once a single difference is established, it becomes, like a single crystal in a solution, the seed for the differentiation of the whole.

The application of the same reasoning to the origin of music implies that the only meaningful way to conceive of the originary musical work is as the musical component of the originary sign. This proposition, if nothing else, should make us think about what the essence of music is. But instead of a Platonic idea, the sort of essence that can be derived from a hypothesis of origin is rather a potential for independent categorial existence. Why after all do we need categories like "music" or "painting"? Are such things determined a priori? Or is it not rather that "music" designates an ensemble of activities with enough in common to give rise to a common or *institutional* name? The "essence" we seek is not the pure form of which all real works of music are imperfect copies, but an originary opening to this institutional complex.

Our analysis must avoid the error of those, for example, who "explain" tragedy as a derivative of ritual, forgetting that the derivation itself, which is also a deviation, is precisely what must be explained. After the birth of tragedy, after all, ritual continues to exist: why did it thus split in two? A more promising line of inquiry seeks an explanation for the successful survival of the derived form; it asks, "what new niche does tragedy fill? or music?" But this empiricist interrogation after the model of biological evolution is not adequate as anthropology. Music (or tragedy) does not fill a new niche by "mutation" from a previous form. Because cultural adaptation is *intentional*, it requires an entirely different model. The material of human culture is best understood as *potentially present from the beginning*. This point is methodological; but in the anthropological domain, there can be no real distinction between methodology and ontology. How we understand man cannot be distinguished from what we conceive him to be.

Why are the phenomena of human culture best understood from the standpoint of their originary potential rather than from that of their "empirical" emergence within history? Because, unlike genetic material with its indefinite plasticity, the material of human culture is intentionally self-fashioning. Our understanding of what it is at a given moment is dependent on our historical awareness of what it is capable of becoming. At the root of this difference between the understanding of nature and the understanding of humanity, or between the natural and the human sciences, is the ultimate reference of any explanation of cultural activity to a universal human community made up of the author and all other human beings as the potential audience. I only understand an element of human culture, including those of the past, when I understand under what circumstances I might participate in it. This means that my understanding is dependent on the premise that I, and all other human beings, have the potential to participate in it. But it is only possible for this potential to be present in all human beings if it is an originary constituent of humanity.

Let us take as an example of cultural evolution the emergence in the baroque period of a focus on "pure" instrumental music, in which the instruments were no longer mere substitutes for human voices. It is not useful to speak of the composition of full-scale works for instruments alone as a mutation of medieval and Renaissance musical practices. On the contrary, not only do we understand these practices better because we know that they contained within them the possibility of liberating the musical from its subordination to activities that reenact crisis more directly (ritual, dance, song), but it is only as a result of this liberation that we can speak of something like "medieval music" at all. Only once voices singing sacred texts can be assimilated to instruments can we decide that the essence of what they are doing is "making music." The development of "pure music" opens a perspective on earlier music that was unavailable at the time but that in retrospect is more adequate to its object than the medieval perspective. And just as we cannot understand medieval music today unless we can see within it the germ of later musical culture, including the possibility of "pure music," we cannot understand the origin of humanity unless we can find within it the possibility of all the cultural phenomena, including music, that we consider to be essentially human.

To hypothesize that the originary sign has a musical "component" or "moment" does not imply that music occupies a predetermined niche in the production of this sign. It is only to suppose that there is, inherent in the act of signifying, a musical element that has the potential of becoming an independent form of cultural activity. What then is music that it can be thought of as a component of the originary sign?

The usefulness of signs is a function of their *economy*. Because the sages of the academy of Lagado in *Gulliver's Travels* have decided to abolish verbal language, they are obliged to lug about heavy sacks full of things to use in the place of words. Swift's satire points up the absurdity of using signs that are no more economical to produce than the things they represent. Following this reasoning to its ultimate—Platonic, or metaphysical—conclusion, the "ideal" sign would be infinitely economical, that is, it would have no material cost at all. But of course signs for human communication (and even those manipulated by computers) cannot be "ideal" in this sense, since they must be perceptible to the receiver of the message. In particular, they must have intensity and duration.

Let us assume to simplify matters that the originary sign is sonorous, as the universal use of verbal language suggests. Then we may reason concerning the sound of the sign in the same way as in the matter of its reference. That is, once one sound is significant, then other things connected with it through association or analogy can become significant as well. Just as difference *within* the significant is not primary but a mere corollary of the difference between the significant and the nonsignificant, so difference *within* sound, of the sort music thematizes (difference in pitch, duration, timbre . . .) is secondary to the difference between the significant sound and other, nonsignificant sounds, or noises.

So far, this reasoning sounds like an explanation of the expansion of the domain of the *signifier* in parallel with that of the *signified*. Just as things become significant on the model of the original significant object, so may sounds or other physical manifestations become differentiated along these lines. But now the point is different. The sound-as-sign is a "signifier," but its very materiality, its distance from the Platonic ideal, makes it, by analogy with its referent, an "object" of significance in itself. The name of God is itself a terrible thing. It is only as a consequence of its materiality that the sign can have form; but inherent in form is "formal" independence from its referent. Hence relationships may be recognized between the significant sound and other sounds metaphorically or metonymically associated with it, independently of the significance-relationship with its referent or "signified"; in the terms of Saussure's image, such relationships remain on the same side of the paper. The formal closure of the unique sign can be extended to other sounds, to combinations of sounds: this is the originary possibility of music.

The existence of music is dependent on the potential internal complexity of the unique signifier. The sign, however economical, is an act. As a sign, its internal structure is unimportant. But the sign-as-act inherits from its hypothetical provenance in the aborted gesture of appropriation an internal temporality, a beginning, middle, and end, that the sign-as-sign lacks. The sign-as-sign is one, although it will eventually be combined with other signs. But the existence of music depends upon the fact that the sign-as-act is necessarily temporally divisible and extensible. The materiality of the sign is the materiality of human action, and has from the outset the rhythm and tone of human action.

The mathematical aspect of music depends on the ear's sensitivity to arithmetical relations of sound frequencies. But this is not an independent piece of data. Natural *rhythms* are "mathematical" by their very nature, and differences in frequency are nothing but condensed rhythms. To raise a note an octave is to make it twice as "fast."

Although music depends on the materiality of the sign, we are justified in calling it the art of "pure form" because the materiality with which it operates is the minimal materiality of the signing activity itself. A plastic art like painting involves intentional painting-gestures that cannot be derived directly from the signing activity of originary language. Not only did such an art originally emerge as an aspect of ritual—this was certainly true of the art of music as well—but its constitutive acts could not have arisen outside of it.

Painting is usually termed a "mimetic" art, in the sense that it imitates an external object, something not itself. But the mimetic element is present in all art. Its origin is in the imitative nature of the first sign; each participant passes from the "animal" imitation of the others' appropriative gesture—the mimesis of potential conflict—to the human imitation of the others' sign, which can be indefinitely repeated with the same meaning. Because music, unlike painting, is a direct consequence of the unavoidable materiality of the signing activity itself, its mimesis remains limited to this primary level and has no need for the secondary imitation of the form of its object. Music's nonobjectivity stems directly from the nonmimetic nature of language, the "arbitrariness of the signifier" by which words designate their referent without resembling it. The sign, contemplated in its own materiality, independently of its referent, does not resemble or "imitate" its referent.

We might ask whether there is not something perverse in the fact that it is the unavoidable *inefficiency* of the maximally economic sign that is the source of music. But this inefficiency reflects the necessary limitation of the sign in a different sense: as a means for the deferral of violence. Emission/reception of the sign substitutes for the satisfaction of appetitive interests; but this substitution cannot be indefinite, because, *pace* the metaphysicians, we cannot conceive of the use of signs separately from the materiality of their users.

Thus we may say that the sign is destined to fail in its ideality, because if this ideality were indeed realizable, the sign would not be needed and would never have been invented in the first place. But the "failure" of the sign is at the same time the occasion for its supplementation through music. The sign-as-sign is instantaneous, transparent to its object. The time taken to emit or receive it is minimal, and therefore functionally insignificant. If we gloss over this fundamental quality of the sign, we cannot understand the origin of language which is the origin of the human. But once the sign comes into being, the materiality of the sign-as-act becomes on a secondary level analogous with that of its referent. The sign is no longer a gesture that can be prolonged into an appropriative act; but it is an act of designation that can be experienced as *analogous to* an appropriative act. Within the newly created domain of signification, the act of producing the sign provides a temporal and material distraction from the loss of the object. For the desiring imagination by means of which each participant in the originary event "possesses" the object he must renounce, the materiality of the sign is a supplementary guarantee of the figures it constructs on his internalized "scene of representation." And whatever material qualities the sign may have include those of rhythm and (presumably) sonority, that is, the fundamental components of music.

The *cultural* function of the sign, its function as the originary model of all cultural activity, derives from the concentration on internal relations within the medium rather than on their "transparent" referential signification. The value of esthetic form in resolving a crisis is that the form's inviolability both arouses desire and keeps this desire at a distance, thereby maintaining the desirer in the oscillatory relation characteristic of esthetic experience. In music, which builds its forms from the minimal signing material, the interplay of formal elements is self-sufficient. Formal closure is the sole "desire-object," and the paradoxical tensions of desire are aroused by the potential endangerment of this closure through the introduction of apparently discordant elements that require assimilation into the form.

Signification is a means of deferring crisis, of avoiding conflict. The "musicality" of the sign, the independence of its formal closure from its signifying function, with the consequent potential for the independent, supplementary elaboration of this formal element—the clearest example of which is perhaps the early medieval *melisma*—encourages the members of the community to participate more actively and cooperatively in its production and contemplation. The ethical connotation of the musical term "harmony" is not accidental.

I would emphasize that the consciousness of the relations of which music is composed is not a mere abstract capacity of human perception. It is not sufficient that man perceive musical relations; he must have the potential to *experience them as significant* with sufficient force to make their formal closure, independently of reference to other activities (including the other arts), an adequate motivation for the oscillatory experience we call the esthetic effect. It is not enough to be able to hear music; one must be capable of perceiving it as beautiful. This is not a self-evident, "analytic" consequence of having ears that can detect differences in pitch, or of possessing an internal clock for rhythm. It requires that these physical capacities become culturally significant, that their utilization become exploitable as a means for the deferral of violence.

But if human musicality cannot simply be deduced from the originary hypothesis, neither is it merely posited. It must be integrated, as I have attempted to do here very briefly, into a model of the scene of human origin. This is a model that tends toward the deductive while remaining fundamentally narrative. By adding "musicality" to it we do more than merely increase its content. We understand the capacity to appreciate the play of pure form as a necessary consequence of man's fundamental capacity for linguistic representation; but this necessity cannot be said to be inherent in the concept of language, or in the concept of the human. This extension of the concept is the originary model for Kant's "synthetic a priori."

We conclude that if man can speak, he must be musical. But we cannot deduce this abstractly, because there is no abstract Idea of speech or music to refer to. There is only human speech, and human music. To study either speech or music, or both, is to engage in anthropology.

* * *

This having been said about the beginning of esthetic form, I shall turn in conclusion to a few reflections about its end. If the "end" of pure form is to attach the audience's desire to its closure, provoking thereby a temporary renouncement, or deferral, of the attempt to possess desire's potentially conflictive worldly object, what happens when form itself reaches its "end," when the very principles of formal closure are challenged?

My knowledge of atonal music is largely confined to what I have learned from John Rahn's admirably lucid introduction to the subject.[3] I am struck by how much the atonal theory he describes has taken over from traditional tonal music, most notably the chromatic scale. Why not, after all, divide the scale into seven, or twenty-three intervals? Why not get rid of it altogether? (I understand that such ideas have indeed been put into practice.) But even the limited deviation of atonality constitutes a revolutionary step. For instead of constructing musical theory as a consolidation of untheorized practice, modern theory becomes a precondition of practice. Since "practice," in the sense of what sounds good, is always the final arbiter, this means that theory has become the basis for *experimental* creation, in music as in the other arts.

Atonal theory has prudently retained the basic formal relations of tonal music, including pitch class and of course rhythm. Nevertheless, it asks that we train ourselves to listen to music differently, to acquire an "atonal filter" to go along with, if not to replace, the "tonal filter" we have absorbed with our mother's milk, or perhaps while riding in elevators. But if tonal music is played in elevators, this is not a sign of its decadence, but of its "naturalness." That is, "natural" in the sense of "natural language," not in the sense of the pseudo-Rousseauian opposition between "nature" and "culture." Like languages, musical traditions vary, and although not all of them are tonal, they are all "natural" in a way that atonal music is not. What modernist art in general has had to persuade us of is that experimental, theory-driven art can be esthetically effective, that its innovations will gradually wend their way into the general esthetic consciousness.

Yet it is a curious fact that modernism has not received the same degree of acceptance in music as in the plastic arts. Contemporary music is still "avant-garde" in a way no longer true of painting or sculpture.

From the standpoint of the average educated person, music is the least contemporary of the arts. It is the only one the large majority of whose devotees prefer the creations of past centuries to those of the present, not just in principle but in practice. The "education" required to hear the structures of an atonal work has reached only a fraction of the university-educated population, and virtually none of the rest. And whereas the various branches of commercial plastic art and design have been strongly influenced by modernist concepts and techniques, this is far less the case for popular and "commercial" music.

This suggests the following paradigm, which for reasons that will become clear in a moment, I shall call "maximalist": Modern music will always remain in advance of its hearers; as soon as they become accustomed to its structures, it will move on to still more audacious ones. Hence new music will always require a special education, will never come to appear "natural." For the vast majority, the appreciation of contemporary music will remain paralyzed by a sense of alienation and inadequacy, and few will reach the point, not indeed of understanding its new principles of formal organization, but simply of *hearing* them. In the art of pure form, the extension of "natural" form will remain an essentially problematic operation.

But it is hard to believe in the viability of this model. Even music must come to terms with the postmodern renouncement of the exaggerated ambitions of modernism. Hence it befits the postmodern era that the most characteristic contemporary music is *minimalist*. This is a form of atonal music that circumvents the need for an "educated" listener by incorporating the learning process into the composition itself: learning by repetition. Rather than seek new sonorities, it ceaselessly recombines nearly identical ones. In a Mozart symphony, we feel a harmony between the form itself and our appreciation of it, as though we understood the esthetic experience in the very act of experiencing it. In minimalist music, we are forever on both sides of this understanding: this form of music is trivially easy to understand in its broad lines, yet far too complex to grasp in all the variety of its variants. It both overwhelms and underwhelms us.

In the Mozartian model, when the crisis is resolved and the piece comes to an end, we feel as though harmony will reign forever. Minimalist music, on the other hand, incarnates the recognition that crises are never resolved, only deferred. The piece stops when it reaches the conclusion of a series of combinations that no ordinary musical mind is capable of experiencing as closed. The paradoxical oscillation that defines esthetic experience takes place here not in the synthetic framework of the working out of a chord progression, but at every instant of hearing. At every moment there is repetitious form and unrepeatable complexity. Dramatic "identification," as with a tragic hero or a tragic theme, is impossible. We only identify in fragments; our safeguard against conflict is a preoccupying agitation.[4]

According to this model, postmodern art promotes neither the destruction nor the stasis of form, but its proliferation. Like a fractal, the formal line is raised to a higher dimension. At the dawn of esthetic culture, form was conceived as an "Apollonian" repose that contained or deferred the audience's "Dionysian" agitation. The oscillatory nature of esthetic experience was a human reaction to what seemed in itself to be absolute. Today we no longer believe in absolutes. At the "end" of esthetic form, the form itself mirrors in its oscillatory fragmentation the human experience of the formal. We have passed from an esthetic of transcendence to an esthetic of immanence.

Minimalism's quasi-ritual repetition, in which nothing is ever exactly repeated, sums up the combinatorial dilemma of postmodern culture: the infinite variety of imaginable forms must be mapped upon the limited scope of human experience. This operation (of which I think Bruckner was a great anticipator) brings the listener strangely close to religious awe. Ritual has always had its combinatorial element, as illustrated by the Buddhist monks working forever to solve the "tower of Hanoi" or to recite the billion permutations of a prayer. But now the work itself, cut off from even the living memory of religion, invents its own ceremony.

At a moment when belief is no longer credible, the only remaining source of form is our *esthetic* experience. The art that makes us realize this most sharply is music, the art of pure form, and this realization is, at least implicitly, collective. The obsessive, omnipresent form of a minimalist work imposes on us the awareness that esthetic form provides our only protection from the disorder of undeferred crisis. It is our collective sense that only *this* form stands between us and chaos that was formerly known as the sacred.

NOTES

1. This essay was originally a lecture delivered at the 1990 Annual Meeting of the Society for Music Theory. I have made minor revisions and added some new material. Fuller accounts of the anthropological theory presented here may be found in my books, *The Origin of Language* (Berkeley: University of California Press, 1981), *The End of Culture: Toward a Generative Anthropology* (Berkeley: University of California Press, 1985), and *Science and Faith: The Anthropology of Revelation* (Savage, MD: Rowman & Littlefield, 1990).

2. I have assumed that the members of the originary human community-in-crisis, the inventors/discoverers of the sign, were male, since the male sex, among primates as well as humans, has always had a near-monopoly on violence. In the works mentioned in footnote 1, this "originary event" is described as taking place on the occasion of a hunting party.

3. *Basic Atonal Theory* (New York: Schirmer Books, 1980).

4. This dominant sensation is associated with forms of modern popular culture as well, e.g., music videos *à la* MTV. But the visual agitation of these videos is by no means minimalist; it operates through the accumulation of sensation rather than the continual controlled passage over the same terrain. Furthermore, the *musical* element of rock is never experienced as fragmentary. It is "Mozartian" music, but written for an audience with a short attention span. It must be such in order to hold together the sometimes disparate imagery of the video, which would otherwise overcome the esthetic subordination—dictated by the economics of the popular arts—which the very name "music video" implies.

CONTEMPORARY MUSIC
AND THE PUBLIC

The chronically troubled relation in the twentieth century between
contemporary art music and the public is one with which every
composer has to come to terms. There is an enthusiastic mass audience
for music, but its appetites are assiduously catered to, controlled, and
created by a music industry that leaves little room for music that
deviates from one of the few formulae, or for music that is artistically or
technically difficult. Yet there are many of us who love music, who
know a lot about music, and who try to compose music we like, "good"
music in some sense, that is nevertheless seldom commercially viable in
today's market. We cannot, or will not, compose music we dislike just
because it would be a commercial success, because for us the point is
not primarily to produce a marketable product but to serve Music.

   Apart from economic concerns, recording technology has effected a
de facto change of venue for listening (I eschew the word "consumption" here), from the concert hall (or arena) to the living room.
To many, the spectacle of a hall filled with rows and rows of sitting
people looking at a stage seems archaic. In fact, the basic structure of
musical production/performance/consumption has been put into
question.

In his book *Noise,* Attali responds to these issues by advancing an evolutionary theory whereby changes in musical forms and methods of musical production herald significant changes in economic structure (see Collins, "Ritual Sacrifice," in section one). Pierre Boulez and Michel Foucault's "Contemporary Music and the Public" consists of a lively conversation about these problems, from the perspectives of a distinguished composer and a philosopher of society whose thought has been seminal in Europe and the United States. Their view is basically a conservative one, working within social and artistic structures that are essentially unchanged. J. K. Randall, Fred Maus, and Benjamin Boretz in their essays adumbrate a situation in which the relations of music and society have been changed radically. Randall and Boretz, long-time collaborators, have been the focus of a subculture of free-improvisation music-making since around 1974. Both remain concerned with audience/performer/composer relations, as these two essays testify; they are in fact already working outside conventional social structures for music, in a way reminiscent of the final, "composition" stage of Attali's evolution. Fred Maus, in "Recent Ideas and Activities," provides expert commentary on the philosophical connections (e.g., to the thought of John Dewey) inherent in the position of the Boretz/Randall culture.

Contemporary Music
and the Public

Michel Foucault and Pierre Boulez

M ICHEL FOUCAULT. It is often said that contemporary music has drifted off track; that it has had a strange fate; that it has attained a degree of complexity which makes it inaccessible; that its techniques have set it on paths which are leading it further and further away. But on the contrary, what is striking to me is the multiplicity of links and relations between music and all the other elements of culture. There are several ways in which this is apparent. On the one hand, music has been much more sensitive to technological changes, much more closely bound to them than most of the other arts (with the exception perhaps of cinema). On the other hand, the evolution of these musics after Debussy or Stravinsky presents remarkable correlations with the evolution of painting. What is more, the theoretical problems which music has posed for itself, the way in which it has reflected on its language, its structures, and its material, depend on a question which has, I believe, spanned the entire twentieth century: the question of "form" which was that of Cézanne or the cubists, which was that of Schönberg, which was also that of the Russian formalists or the School of Prague.

I do not believe we should ask: with music at such a distance, how can we recapture it or repatriate it? But rather: this music which is so close, so consubstantial with all our culture, how does it happen that we feel it, as it were, projected afar and placed at an almost insurmountable distance?

PIERRE BOULEZ. Is the contemporary music "circuit" so different from the various "circuits" employed by symphonic music, chamber music, opera, Baroque music, all circuits so partitioned, so specialized that it's possible to ask if there really is a general culture? Acquaintance through recordings should, in principle, bring down those walls whose economic necessity is understandable, but one notices, on the contrary, that recordings reinforce specialization of the public as well as the performers. In the very organization of concerts or other productions, the forces which different types of music rely on more or less exclude a common organization, even a polyvalence. Classical or romantic repertory implies a standardized format tending to include exceptions to this rule only if the economy of the whole is not disturbed by them. Baroque music necessarily implies not only a limited group, but instruments in keeping with the music played, musicians who have acquired a specialized knowledge of interpretation, based on studies of texts and theoretical works of the past. Contemporary music implies an approach involving new instrumental techniques, new notations, an aptitude for adapting to new performance situations. One could continue this enumeration and thus show the difficulties to be surmounted in passing from one domain to another: difficulties of organization, of placing oneself in a different context, not to mention the difficulties of adapting places for such or such a kind of performance. Thus, there exists a tendency to form a larger or smaller society corresponding to each category of music, to establish a dangerously closed circuit among this society, its music, and its performers. Contemporary music does not escape this development; even if its attendance figures are proportionately weak, it does not escape the faults of musical society in general: it has its places, its rendezvous, its stars, its snobberies, its rivalries, its exclusivities; just like the other society, it has its market values, its quotes, its statistics. The different circles of music, if they are not Dante's, nonetheless reveal a prison system in which most feel at ease but whose constraints, on the contrary, painfully chafe others.

MICHEL FOUCAULT. One must take into consideration the fact that for a very long time music has been tied to social rites and unified by them: religious music, chamber music; in the nineteenth century, the link between music and theatrical production in opera (not to mention the political or cultural meanings which the latter had in Germany or in Italy) was also an integrative factor.

I believe that one cannot talk of the "cultural isolation" of contemporary music without soon correcting what one says of it by thinking about other circuits of music.

With rock, for example, one has a completely inverse phenomenon. Not only is rock music (much more than jazz used to be) an integral part of the life of many people, but it is a cultural initiator: to like rock, to like a certain kind of rock rather than another, is also a way of life, a manner of reacting; it is a whole set of tastes and attitudes.

Rock offers the possibility of a relation which is intense, strong, alive, "dramatic" (in that rock presents itself as a spectacle, that listening to it is an event and that it produces itself on stage), with a music that is itself impoverished, but through which the listener affirms himself; and with the other music, one has a frail, faraway, hothouse, problematical relation with an erudite music from which the cultivated public feels excluded.

One cannot speak of a single relation of contemporary culture to music in general, but of a tolerance, more or less benevolent, with respect to a plurality of musics. Each is granted the "right" to existence, and this right is perceived as an equality of worth. Each is worth as much as the group which practices it or recognizes it.

PIERRE BOULEZ. Will talking about musics in the plural and flaunting an eclectic ecumenicism solve the problem? It seems, on the contrary, that this will merely conjure it away—as do certain devotees of an advanced liberal society. All those musics are good, all those musics are nice. Ah! Pluralism! There's nothing like it for curing incomprehension. Love, each one of you in your corner, and each will love the others. Be liberal, be generous toward the tastes of others, and they will be generous to yours. Everything is good, nothing is bad; there aren't any values, but everyone is happy. This discourse, as liberating as it may wish to be, reinforces, on the contrary, the ghettos, comforts one's clear conscience for being in a ghetto, especially if from time to time one tours the ghettos of others. The economy is there to remind us, in case we get lost in this bland utopia: there are musics which bring in money and exist for commercial profit; there are musics that cost something, whose very concept has nothing to do with profit. No liberalism will erase this distinction.

MICHEL FOUCAULT. I have the impression that many of the elements that are supposed to provide access to music actually impoverish our relationship with it. There is a quantitative mechanism working here. A certain rarity of relation to music could preserve an ability to choose what one hears, and thus a flexibility in listening. But the more frequent this relation is (radio, records, cassettes), the more familiarities it creates; habits crystallize; the most frequent becomes the most acceptable, and soon the only thing perceivable. It produces a "tracing," as the neurologists say.

Clearly, the laws of the marketplace will readily apply to this simple mechanism. What is put at the disposition of the public is what the public hears. And what the public finds itself actually listening to, because it's offered up, reinforces a certain taste, underlines the limits of a well-defined listening capacity, defines more and more exclusively a schema for listening. Music had better satisfy this expectation, etc. So commercial productions, critics, concerts, everything that increases the contact of the public with music, risks making perception of the new more difficult.

Of course the process is not unequivocal. Certainly increasing familiarity with music also enlarges the listening capacity and gives access to possible differentiations, but this phenomenon risks being only marginal; it must in any case remain secondary to the main impact of experience, if there is no real effort to derail familiarities.

It goes without saying that I am not in favor of a rarefaction of the relation to music, but it must be understood that the everydayness of this relation, with all the economic stakes that are riding on it, can have this paradoxical effect of rigidifying tradition. It is not a matter of making access to music more rare, but of making its frequent appearances less devoted to habits and familiarities.

PIERRE BOULEZ. We ought to note that not only is there a focus on the past, but even on the past in the past, as far as the performer is concerned. And this is of course how one attains ecstasy while listening to the interpretation of a certain classical work by a performer who disappeared decades ago; but ecstasy will reach orgasmic heights when one can refer to a performance of 20 July 1947 or of 30 December 1938. One sees a pseudo-culture of documentation taking shape, based on the exquisite hour and fugitive moment, which reminds us at once of the fragility and of the durability of the performer become immortal, rivalling now the immortality of the masterpiece. All the mysteries of the Shroud of Turin, all the powers of modern magic, what more could you want as an alibi for reproduction as opposed to real production? Modernity itself is this technical superiority we possess over former eras in being able to recreate the event. Ah! If we only had the first performance of the Ninth, even—especially—with all its flaws, or if only we could make Mozart's own delicious difference between the Prague and Vienna versions of *Don Giovanni* . . . . This historicizing carapace suffocates those who put it on, compresses them in an asphyxiating rigidity; the mephitic air they breathe constantly enfeebles their organism in relation to contemporary adventure. I imagine Fidelio glad to rest in his dungeon, or again I think of Plato's cave: a civilization of shadow and of shades.

MICHEL FOUCAULT. Certainly listening to music becomes more difficult as its composition frees itself from any kind of schemas, signals, perceivable cues for a repetitive structure.

In classical music, there is a certain transparency from the composition to the hearing. And even if many compositional features in Bach or Beethoven aren't recognizable by most listeners, there are always other features, important ones, which are accessible to them. But contemporary music, by trying to make each of its elements a unique event, makes any grasp or recognition by the listener difficult.

PIERRE BOULEZ. Is there really only lack of attention, indifference on the part of the listener toward contemporary music? Might not the complaints so often articulated be due to laziness, to inertia, to the pleasant sensation of remaining in known territory? Berg wrote, already half a century ago, a text entitled "Why is Schönberg's music hard to understand?" The difficulties he described then are nearly the same as those we hear of now. Would they always have been the same? Probably, all novelty bruises the sensibilities of those unaccustomed to it. But it is believable that nowadays the communication of a work to a public presents some very specific difficulties. In classical and romantic music, which constitutes the principal resource of the familiar repertory, there are schemas which one obeys, which one can follow independently of the work itself, or rather which the work must necessarily exhibit. The movements of a symphony are defined in their form and in their character, even in their rhythmic life; they are distinct from one another, most of the time actually separated by a pause, sometimes tied by a transition that can be spotted. The vocabulary itself is based on "classified" chords, well-named: you don't have to analyze them to know what they are and what function they have. They have the efficacy and security of signals; they recur from one piece to another, always assuming the same appearance and the same functions. Progressively, these reassuring elements have disappeared from "serious" music. Evolution has gone in the direction of an ever more radical renewal, as much in the form of works as in their language. Musical works have tended to become unique events, which do have antecedents, but are not reducible to any guiding schema admitted, a priori, by all; this creates, certainly, a handicap for immediate comprehension. The listener is asked to familiarize himself with the course of the work and for this to listen to it a certain number of times. When the course of the work is familiar, comprehension of the work, perception of what it wants to express, can find a propitious terrain to bloom in. There are fewer and fewer chances for the first encounter to ignite perception and comprehension. There can be a spontaneous connection with it, through the force of the message, the quality of the writing, the beauty of the sound, the readability of the cues, but deep understanding can only come from repeated hearings, from remaking the course of the work, this repetition taking the place of an accepted schema such as was practiced previously.

The schemas—of vocabulary, of form— which had been evacuated from what is called serious music (sometimes called learned music) have taken refuge in certain popular forms, in the objects of musical consumption. There, one still creates according to the genres, the accepted typologies. Conservatism is not necessarily found where it is expected: it is undeniable that a certain conservatism of form and language is at the base of all the commercial productions adopted with great enthusiasm by generations who want to be anything but conservative. It is a paradox of our times that played or sung protest transmits itself by means of an eminently subornable vocabulary, which does not fail to make itself known: commercial success evacuates protest.

MICHEL FOUCAULT. And on this point there is perhaps a divergent evolution of music and painting in the twentieth century. Painting, since Cézanne, has tended to make itself transparent to the very act of painting: the act is made visible, insistent, definitively present in the picture, whether it be by the use of elementary signs, or by traces of its own dynamic. Contemporary music on the contrary offers to its hearing only the outer surface of its composition.

Hence there is something difficult and imperious in listening to this music. Hence the fact that each hearing presents itself as an event which the listener attends, and which he must accept. There are no cues which permit him to expect it and recognize it. He listens to it happen. This is a very difficult mode of attention, one which is in contradiction to the familiarities woven by repeated hearing of classical music.

The cultural insularity of music today is not simply the consequence of deficient pedagogy or propagation. It would be too facile to groan over the conservatories or complain about the record companies. Things are more serious. Contemporary music owes this unique situation to its very composition. In this sense, it is willed. It is not a music that tries to be familiar; it is fashioned to preserve its cutting edge. One may repeat it, but it does not repeat itself. In this sense, one cannot come back to it as to an object. It always pops up on frontiers.

PIERRE BOULEZ. Since it wants to be in such a perpetual situation of discovery—new domains of sensibility, experimentation with new material—is contemporary music condemned to remain a Kamchatka (Baudelaire, Sainte-Beuve, remember?) reserved for the intrepid curiosity of infrequent explorers? It is remarkable that the most reticent listeners should be those who have acquired their musical culture exclusively in the stores of the past, indeed of a particular past; and the most open—only because they are the most ignorant?—are the listeners with a sustained interest in other means of expression, especially the plastic arts. The "foreigners" the most receptive? A dangerous connection which would tend to prove that current music would detach itself from the "true" musical culture in order to belong to a domain both vaster and more vague, where amateurism would preponderate, in critical judgment as in creation. Don't call that "music"—then we are willing to leave you your plaything; that is in the jurisdiction of a different appreciation, having nothing to do with the appreciation we reserve for true music, the music of the masters. When this argument has been made, even in its arrogant naiveté, it approaches an irrefutable truth. Judgment and taste are prisoners of categories, of pre-established schemas which are referred to at all costs. Not, as they would have us believe, that the distinction is between an aristocracy of sentiments, a nobility of expression, and a chancy craft based on experimentation: thought versus tools. It is, rather, a matter of a listening that could not be modulated or adapted to different ways of inventing music. I certainly am not going to preach in favor of an ecumenicism of musics, which seems to me nothing but a supermarket aesthetic, a demagogy that dare not speak its name and decks itself with good intentions the better to camouflage the wretchedness of its compromise. Moreover, I do not reject the demands of quality in the sound as well as in the composition: aggression and provocation, *bricolage* and bluff are but insignificant and harmless palliatives. I am fully aware—thanks to many experiences, which could not have been more direct—that beyond a certain complexity perception finds itself disoriented in a hopelessly entangled chaos, that it gets bored and hangs up. This amounts to saying that I can keep my critical reactions and that my adherence is not automatically derived from the fact of "contemporaneity" itself. Certain modulations of hearing are already occurring, rather badly as a matter of fact, beyond particular historical limits. One doesn't listen to Baroque music—especially lesser works— as one listens to Wagner or Strauss; one doesn't listen to the polyphony of the Ars Nova as one listens to Debussy or Ravel. But in this latter case, how many listeners are ready to vary their "mode of being," musically speaking? And yet in order for musical culture, all musical culture, to be assimilable, there need only be this adaptation to criteria, and to conventions, which invention complies with according to the historical moment it occupies. This expansive respiration of the ages is at the opposite extreme from the asthmatic wheezings the fanatics make us hear from spectral reflections of the past in a tarnished mirror. A culture forges, sustains, and transmits itself in an adventure with a double face: sometimes brutality, struggle, turmoil; sometimes meditation, nonviolence, silence. Whatever form the adventure may take—the most surprising is not always the noisiest, but the noisiest is not irremediably the most superficial—it is useless to ignore it, and still more useless to sequestrate it. One might go so far as to say there are probably uncomfortable periods when the coincidence of invention and convention is more difficult, when some aspect of invention seems absolutely to go beyond what we can tolerate or "reasonably" absorb; and that there are other periods when things relapse to a more immediately accessible order. The relations among all these phenomena—individual and collective—are so complex that applying rigorous parallelisms or groupings to them is impossible. One would rather be tempted to say: gentlemen, place your bets, and for the rest, trust in the *air du temps*. But, please, play! Play! Otherwise, what infinite secretions of boredom!

—translated by John Rahn

From *CNAC magazine* no. 15 (May–June 1983), 10–12, by kind permission of the Centre national d'art et de culture Georges Pompidou.

Are You Serious?

TO SOME PEOPLE I
HAVEN'T MET YET:

KENNETH MAUE
FRANETTA McMILLIAN
CATHERINE SCHIEVE
JOHN D. VANDER WEG

AND TO ALL THE
USUAL SUSPECTS

J. K. Randall

Marseilles   **1.**   *Spring 1972*

We watch some old men play boules in the ww2 bombcrater across the alley from the rub-out *The French Connection* starts with. Petanques up north, bocce in Italy. A small ball gets tossed out there, then each player tosses his two big heavy balls at it 'til they're all out there. Closest to it at the end wins. The balls knock each other and the target ball around so the picture doesn't just thicken, it cancels itself. A ball arcs along a sideslope past the target ball, hits a rock, and zigzags back in front of it relocating some other balls. Or knocks one into the target ball which rolls over next to another which was out of it. Crafty—lucky—can't tell; —more like exploratory. And good and bad don't last long enough for any habits to form: they're transient secondary attributes like direct vs. banked or pitched vs. rolled or topspin vs. backspin. I like the preliminaries to a toss: hefting, siting, limbering, posturing; and the deliveries: elbowed, wristed, palmed, fingered, twisted, hooked, pushed, heaved. Deciding which ball is closest at the end can take a while in Italy or New York but in France it's just a nod during the pickup, then the next game goes back the other way. Players and spectators come and go. Newcomers shake hands.

Were these players topnotch?

Was this game topnotch?

Dunno.

Wrong question.

It's not like Steve Mizerak running 150-and-out or the bottom of the 9th in the 7th WS game or boules on level ground.

But I'm riveted:

Qualities, energies are engaged which I'd rather cultivate than siphon off.

10 days later we saw *The French Connection* in Basle.

Hopewell NJ   **2.**   *late Nov 1984*

She fishes a multipaged twotone beige paperthing out of her wastebasket and shoves it toward me. "Here. You might be interested in this."

SUNRISE
CENTER FOR THE HEALING ARTS, INC.
46 Bayard St., Suite 323, New Brunswick NJ

Fall Expansion . . . . . .
Full Expression . . . . . .

Major Event: Spiritual Expression through Music and Dance: A Weekend Festival

—The Genteels
—Middle Eastern Belly Dancers
—Meryl Olson-Stern
—Afro-American Dance Ensemble
—Laraaji
—Group Motion of Philadephia
—Laura Shapiro
—Karl Fury
—Sunrise Percussion Group

Sat/Sun Dec. 8/9 1984, from 1PM on.
3rd World Center, Princeton University

We kick it around. I'm looking for some current events to bounce off of. She's looking for some fellow therapists to talk to. On into the paperthing, therapies profuse: { . . . . . . Massage Therapy (Shiatsu, Swedish, Intuitive) . . . . . . Feldenkreis: Awareness through Movement . . . . . . Massage Therapy, Polarity, Breath Awareness . . . . . . Channeled Readings . . . . . . Mind/Body Therapy (Removing Emotional Blocking) . . . . . . Integrative Bodytalk . . . . . . Psychic Healing, Readings, Consultations (An African Herbalist and Traditional Healer) . . . . . . }

We decide A. we ought to know better and B. let's go.

3rd World Center   **3.**   *Sat 1PM*

a survivor of cancer whose life was turned around by a John Denver song—the lyrics, the message of it—Kay speaks movingly about her work with children dying of cancer in a Buffalo hospital; she playacts her own and the institution's foibles, the agonies and incomprehensions of the children, and their successes with her in giving musical vent to their feelings (:in silent haste one reviews one's own triumphs and comes up anxious)

{ . . . . to entertain and stimulate children and adults aged 7 to 107.

The Genteels: Kay Johnston-Gentile
Ron Gentile, Ph.D.}

then she sings; and all at once she's the apple of a loving mama's eye on best behavior in her brand new dress at her birthday party, and the loving, gently didactic pretty young mama herself; in her straight-on stance(—faraway misty-eyed; palmpressed prayerful; fingerwagging cautionary—), accompanied at the piano by her husband Ron (on his own an unabashed, if uplifted, Tom Lehrer), she conveys to us and reinforces what at lifedepth, over liferange we all of course comfortably agree to and confidently hope for.

Standardized is no accident: with confections of thought and sound which were tested widely some time ago and found pleasing (—modest; upbeat; humorous even, though always in good taste—) (agonies of cancer blindeyed), she reminds us that we Already Know; that it'll all come up AOK.

Deep Wholespirit Message Massage.

It Soothes.

But what particular standardizations matters not at all, and that's among the messages. With the same unflagging friendliness that now evokes the smalltown parlor or church social, or the family channel, Kay and Ron will join us later on in essaying meditational conventions of Baghdad and Cairo.

yet some Unthinkables nag:

: to challenge us or stretch us would count as aggressive, manipulative;

: individual, as divisive—as separating herself from us, or her and us from others;

: debatable, as contentious;

: and any of the above as impolite, out of bounds, a gaffe, a faux pas, a fart in church.

Co-opted into a handholding circle to sing the We Shall Overcome strand of the Genteels' culminating fantasia, my gorge rises a little. (my friend and her husband are already sitting this one out in another room with their lunchbucket)

<table>
<tr><td>*3rd World Center*</td><td align="center">**4.**</td><td align="right">*Sat 4PM*</td></tr>
</table>

Speaking of spirituality, Sondra commends lightness of touch, some buffoon-ery even.

{Sondra Watson, M.A.; dancer, painter, counselor, mother, clown; student of New Thought, Yoga, Rebirthing, Spiritual Healing, Sufiwork; studies with Sufi Master Adnan Sarhan.}

She is quoting someone to the effect that the paths to illumination sometimes seem so strewn with potholes and boobytraps that you wonder if God Himself could make it.

(In memory twinges a complaint that our INTER/PLAY sessions bring out in us the long faces of high transport bordering on depression or nagging pain rather than any skinglow of joy never mind just a friendly smile once in a while.)

Rhea-Linda, dance therapist and proprietor of Give-a-Gram {Belly Grams, Gorilla Grams, Show Gal Grams, Hula Grams, Create-A-Gram} demurs: she knows that everything Sondra says comes from God but even so she couldn't go so far as to question the fullness of His power.

{Sufi. The word means purity. The process is concentration, meditation, exercises, breathing, whirling, dancing, singing—the feeling of rapture that comes from them. These combine to awaken the forces within the body that lead to higher consciousness . . . . Sufi techniques bring better contact between the inner self and the outer cosmic power. – Sufi Master Adnan Sarhan in *EAR magazine*, Nov/Dec 1984}

As Sondra mugs her way through a dressup & peeldown skit (–a woman waits, paces, smokes; gets 2nd thoughts and sexy; bellydances–), I don't see myself tangling with her.

Now Djuna introduces herself and we adjourn to a smaller, warmly-carpeted room where she sits down on the floor at the front crosslegged facing us. A cassette-tape of elusive ethnicity quietly fills the room.

{Every sound has a certain power, on the mind, on the psyche, on the emotions, on the feelings, on the senses . . . . . . When I drum, I go into deep concentration, a very meditative state. Everything falls away. There is no sense of environment or identity, only the sound. I feel a oneness with the drum and a unity with existence within myself. I hear an eternal sound that cannot be heard by the ear, and no sound on earth can compare to it. It is an overwhelming power . . . . . . It gives healing to all the people who hear it . . . . . . They go into a deep meditative state, which is actually a state of receptivity bringing on healing and contentment . . . . . . There's a power and mercy that comes. – Adnan Sarhan, *ibid.*}

Following Djuna's instructions we distribute ourselves through the room, leaving space to move, and sit down on the floor crosslegged facing her. Nervous about my recuperating back, I keep to my chair along the side: Djuna notices, and includes this possibility among her instructions.

{Djuna Wojton, student of ballet and modern dance, is certified to teach yoga; she began studying Oriental dance in Egypt in 1978, and has appeared on the TV show 20/20.}

She will lead us in some Middle Eastern movements known to induce a relaxed, meditative mindset: we'll become aware of our bodies, of our breathing. She'll keep it simple so we can copy her easily. (My friend and her husband are back in action and will go the distance this time, he in longjohns.)

Lines of attention bind each of us singly to Djuna.

" . . . . . inhale . . . . . . ; . . . . . exhale . . . . . .

(The sound intermingles with the sounds of the cassette-tape, which will be fast-forward wound or changed several times in the course of the hour.)

" . . . . . now this arm . . . . . .

(Djuna's right and the facing roomful of lefts undulate snakily.)

" . . . . . then this arm . . . . . .

Balkily approximating Djuna's actions in my chair or standing up, I'm aware of the fifteen or so others filling the room like flowers in a flowerbed, all basking in the same sun and bending to the same breeze.

" . . . . . inhale as we lean this way . . . . . .

Right in front of me I've become aware of Moses (—a very black Ghanian with a loose, solid, eminently grounded, body; an ordained Christian minister who has returned to traditional African healing rituals and is engaged in a Native American vision quest; co-director of Sunrise, and member of its Percussion Group—) managing to be unproblematically himself in remote emulation of Djuna's elegant, floating, eminently skypointed, movements.

" . . . . . exhale as we lean this way . . . . . .

Resisting the indignity of someone else's breathing rhythm, I vamp rather than copy; as does a member of the Sunrise staff lounging on a bench with his congadrum up front over behind Djuna.

" . . . . . now contact a partner . . . . . .

(Sondra has replaced Djuna as leader!)

" . . . . . now join hands with your partner . . . . . .

(Not by chance, I grab Sondra.)

" . . . . . now make a sound like this . . . . . .

(Perhaps pursuant to an earlier colloquy about Gorilla Grams, Rhea-Linda is raking my longjohned friend pretty good with rapidfire wholebody bumping movements.)

" . . . . . now make a face like this . . . . . .

(I shove, drag, and obstreperate, giving Sondra no problem at all, nor damming the flow of her instructions any.)

As I twist my way out the door, Setarah replaces Sondra as leader (—the tape and the conga are frantic by now—) and gets everyone into that pelvic jiggle that bellydancers do.

{Setarah: specialty teacher at Jack LaLanne/European Health Spas and the East West Center for Creative Dance, Drama, and Music; for many years a student of Serena of New York, Ahmad Hussein of Egypt, and Sufi Master of the Mevlevi Order of Whirling Dervishes Adnan Sarhan of Baghdad.}

The next day I'll welcome chances to chew the fat with Sondra and Djuna. Sondra is glad, as I am, to clear any air that needs clearing, and expresses complete sympathy with my unscripted responses. Djuna explains that Sufi exercises are intended merely to induce a mindset from which . . . . . .

Yet I retain a reservation: salvation is less common than saviors; and our quests lead rarely to the former, but inevitably to the latter, whose potencies somehow become our whole vehicle, not just the training-wheels.

I'll chew on Moses's ear the next day also, in the same vein: I'm getting allergic to carrying out instructions and I'm agog at the coupling of 1. find your true self & unblock your creativity & get in touch with the cosmos with 2. do exactly what I'm doing & saying as I transmit to you by rote what I got by rote from somebody who got it from God by rote. (I'm giving Moses no problem: he understands, accepts, appreciates, —in fact, enjoys—my popping off; and smiles, comfortably. That evening he will teach us an African healing song (, by rote).)

But for now it's back to the big room where we wait around for Djuna to emerge from a dressingroom in heavy cosmetics and glittering well-below-the-navel skirt to bellydance her solo. About six or eight of us remain in a semicircle of chairs, and Djuna dances very close to us in the space we outline. My reactions surprise me: I am not, it turns out, put much in mind of old Errol Flynn or Hope/Crosby movies; nor struck all that much by spirituality's fated scavenging on what Cotton Mather would surely have pegged as its enemy and opposites—in this case harem pussypushing, in the Genteels' case the ersatz erotica of yesteryear's subclassical music entertainments; nor concerned with any articulately complex anchoring of the heights of spirit in the depths of flesh (; or in the heights of flesh either); or with the confusions—hers, mine, yours—that have eased us into this awkward do-it-for-an-audience ritual. What I catch myself noticing as she twirls and jiggles right up close among us is that she does reach you, with of all things her face: no dancerly opaque slab, that; she really lays her eyes right on you, and her smile; and I pick up plenty of open clear light, nothing of the come-on.

Davey Williams　　　　**5.**　　　　

. . . . . . have access to an instrument, voice, body, or any other sound-maker which you are intuitively "at home" with. Forget all notion of your "favorite" music; even of what you think music is at all . . . . . . If you are alone, listen only to silence inside . . . . . . If you are playing with others listen more closely to them than to yourself.

Always begin with silence. Let things happen . . . . . . Do not get outside the sound in anyway . . . . . . Do not make value judgments of the sound as it occurs. Once it begins, be committed to it. Expect the impossible to happen . . . . . .

Pauline Oliveros   *EAR, Nov/Dec 1984*

Sitting by the river on a clear warm morning . . . . . . I focus my attention on a
particular rock, listening intently to the way the water keeps smacking against
the rock and bubbling all around it . . . . . . I expand to take in all I can possibly
hear: water, birds, insects, humming, whistling and bubbling . . . . . . I listen
to the manifesting stillness in me as I become attuned to the whole sphere of
sound . . . . . . I begin playing mentally with the river, imagining counterpoints
and harmonies, melodies and rhythms, opposing sounds . . . . . . Relaxing
again I open more fully, my mental space stretched by imagination and play.
A feeling of well-being rises in me as my ears follow the streaming river. I
realize that any sound can be a cue for the energy one needs . . . . . . In this way
listening is healing.

La Rochelle   *Oct 1984*

. . . . . . the arcaded, swinging city opens out—pitches you out—
onto the inlets . . . . . . & a carpet of fishingboats (—two sailors mend a net; a
leashed mutt watches—); cafés all around . . . . . . & out towards the twin tow-
ers & what's left of the ramparts: you go on out thru the gap & bam it's
behind you, a whole sound—dead . . . . . . it's the harbor now (—a schoolclass
practices sailing—) . . . . . . & beaches & parks; a vacant sidewalk runs along
the edge . . . . . . I keep walking . . . . . . (I can't get so far I can't walk farther) . . . . . . even the harbor falls off behind me; more & more it's the Atlantic
out there: me & it (, we've had this date from the beginning) . . . . . . no
dogshit even . . . . . . bracing grey intimate mean necessary . . . . . . (: "Love
Song—the sound of a locomotive far out at sea . . . . . ." . . . . . . (Davey
Williams) . . . . . .)

3rd World Center   **6.**   *Sun 9 Dec*

It's the announced startingtime and there's nobody here but me and Laraaji.
Also three members of the Sunrise staff. My friend and her husband won't be
here; weren't here last night either, for Meryl or the Slideshow. Chickened
out. Meryl wasn't all that bad: nice rendition of Summertime which she introduced as "a bluestune." (The Slideshow wasn't what I needed though. Split
after about five minutes.) Her act was showy.—Campfire showy, sort of:

babies & all. Except God writes her songs. Hits you in segregated compartments where you can wallow in it and know it's Not for Real just Entertain-.
ment. In her spikes and highcrotched skintights she's putting some gloss on
her massage therapy biz. You can reach her at . . . . . . The Slideshow was something else again. Meryl massages you some other time, the Slideshow does it
right now. Like Kay. Only nonverbal. Actually it was an onfilm with music-
track slideshow. It's played both houses of Congress! Played here because the
Afro-American Dancers didn't show, and the guy that produced this film (or
rather "through" whom it was produced; I'm still getting used to this "channel" thing) rushed a copy over to us on short notice. Went all over the world
for visuals: wildflowers, mountainscapes, blue skies, no famine in Ethiopia
though, no athlete's foot. Nice arpeggios. —Alright I get it: the world's about
choked itself already on all its shit, so let's inject what's needed: some love,
some beauty, some assuagement. A Nonfrantic Alternative, right? OK fine. So
why does it hit me like treacle and make me puke. I think I'm getting a handle
on it, and it relates to Kay too. These images of love and beauty are what?
They're the sanitized prettypatty prefab our shit's managed to cohabit with
for quite some time now thank you, that's what. Shoved at you at lifedepth,
over liferange, it puts the wrong bite on you. Just about tells you to look the
other way, don't work it thru. Almost says: since what's wrong makes you
feel so bad let's grease your feelings. Almost tells lies about what's out there,
or in there. I'll have to try this one out on Moses. Doesn't clean out any new
space in you for love and beauty. Just rings your chimes. If those're your
chimes. Certainly doesn't drag your shit out there where you can't dodge the
stink like the Frantic Alternative. Just plugs your nostril. Soothes. Except if
you're not right there where the grease is, it's a weird number gets run on
you. (That's Djuna over there jawing with Laraaji.) —some Group Motion
people already. Guess they'll play and we'll move. Later on when they do—
and we don't—Manfred'll holler out from his keyboard. "Come on dance!"
(This I can handle. Laying for it in fact.) But after that I'll balk some more.
At doing prefab in Laura Shapiro's scenario. (Liked watching it though.) I'll
go a little ways with Moses that night on his African song. Not with David
Winston at first though but he's got a hook in me he doesn't know about:
to coddle my back I've been sitting home on a heatingpad grooving on the
Folkways stack of American Indian records thinking if I were onto the phys-
icalities the music's a part of, it'd really click in. Proved true. I fell in at the rear
of the passing Alligator Shufflestomp line snaking around the room, David
whoopsinging in the lead and doing that Indian thing on his Taos drum that
always grabs me cuzzits a speed of pulsation not a "beat". (Manfred's pushing
the Group Motion stuff rearstage so Laraaji can unroll his rug upfront and go
first.) Once Group Motion's on, I'll dance. A "beautiful dancer" is what
they'll call me afterwards, I shit you not . . . . . . Sondra! . . . . . . I go for the
idea. (A few enclaves of hugging and deep bodywork have resumed from

yesterday.) Aside from the back, I'm fiftyfive and fat. My movements will be gnarled, minimal, untrained, all tangled up in two plastic chairs. (Laraaji turns out to be a slowmotionfreak too. He'll dance with us. And Djuna and Sondra and Moses.) Beautiful: not like "you were really expert and rate recognition." (Laraaji's shoes are sitting alongside his rug now.) More like "you were right there and we picked you up loud and clear." Rack one up a long ways from skill and the admirable. (And his instruments are spread around on it.) And get their credentials: the cameraperson was a woman; Laraaji is a coffee-with-cream black in a plain floorlength white tunic and white beanie; Mahan Rishi wears a Sikh turban; and Manfred ought to know. (We've sort of settled down by now, in remote chairs around, while Laraaji gets into his sound.) The Sunrise MC says I guess we're ready, I'll give you an intro. Laraaji says no no don't, I'll start up from right here, I'm there already. Crosslegged on his rug, facing us with closed eyes; nonsmiling; back straight, more hung from the shoulders than resting on the floor; our chairs drawn up now into a small arc just in front of him; his instruments around him thus:

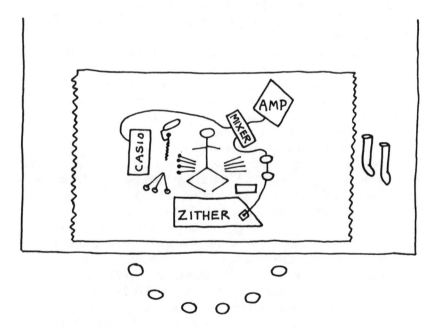

it's his whole presence that reaches us. (Smiling would count as deliberately ingratiating; or as privately reflective. Open eyes, as windows of a distinct personal emanation under his own direction; as a selective singling-out of this or that, of you or me.) Tuned to a wavelength along which anything and everything can pass nondestructively to the channel, he looks centered and

calm, not ecstatic; not closed off, or exclusive, or elsewhere; something like:
warm, permeable, in place. (Not like that agate-eyed Kalifornia Kool where
inner energy doesn't quite reach the skin and homicide lurks rampant and
unexplored a millimeter beneath the mask.) He's more listening than inventing or performing: lots of time spent raining sticks (, mallets later) on his
reverberated, amplified zither, in rapid singlestroke right-left alternation moving to and fro across the strings. No sweat. But also no "skill," let alone
"imagination": any of us could "do" this. It's as if he's listening to sound-
actuating energy pass thru him and out his instruments as sound; like us, he's
a receiving-, not a sending-, center for the quiet sound he fills the room with.
I'll get a different fix on Karl Fury's sologig that evening. Hunchedover, fret-
focused; tentative hardened into memorized; self-absorbed in his digital operations, sound leaking out like a proofreading of the operations; Karl,
introvertedly, is "presenting" (—himself; his tunes—) just as surely as Meryl.
(". . . . . thank you, thank you . . . . . ."). A qualm though: one recalls
Kierkegaard's Knight of Faith who works whitecollar, eats burgers with fries,
catches the sitcoms, finishes off a sixpack and turns in early. Well, at least
Laraaji looks the part. (Among us in the small arc, the chaired version of
Laraaji's rugposture—eyes closed, nonsmiling face forward, back straight—has
become endemic.) Mahan Rishi too: that evening, the workforce, which he's
almost limply transmissive of, will surge thru him; and on out the suspended
gong: as din—ferocious; joyful. (In a brief improvisation just before, Karl's
nonstop selfreactive guitar had passed thru Mahan Rishi and emerged gently
adumbrated with bells.) Minutes along now, but still facing us with closed
eyes, Laraaji sings recurrent instruction-texts: "now have your highest
vision" . . . . . (the voice is natural, direct, forceful, outreaching; and
unprocessed; the curtain of zither sound, dense and transparent) . . . . . "now
your warmest loving" . . . . . { . . . . . offers his channeled music inspired by
inner vision. Known not only in New York City where he performs regularly,
Laraaji travels throughout the United States lending joy to conferences,
retreats, conventions, and gatherings.} Shaking some bells with one hand,
Laraaji is rewiring and donning a headmike with the other. No tour-de-force:
just keeps sound live enough for us to stay in it. No big deal. (This guy gives
the Sologig a good name.) He's pivoted sideways to us now facing his Casio
so we see his headmike in profile and he's doing a radio interview with a
dietfreak. Latest News from the Trenches of Uplift. Seems this guy's guru's
got him on a 21-day birdseed ration or something. A real breath of fresh air.
Some fleshly foibles bygod. Laura will raise the issue later: how do we feel
about watching her solodance version of women's 19th-cent. factory work as
"spiritual expression"? Felt fine. I wised off about overpopulated instant nir-
vanas of dreamy eye, waterfalls, and D-flat major triads. (Went over like a fart
in church.) I liked that about the Group Motion session: roughedged; con-
torted. Individualizing; isolating even; in a supportive, multitracked way:
OK if you're like this and you're like that here's what I'm like. We've had

INTER/PLAY sessions like that. Also a kind where each of us feels the others as an extension: personalized illusions of bloated singletracked, where what anyone else does, whatever it is, must now be for me as if I had done it. (You are Responsible for the World: be thou allabsorbed and allabsorbing.) —& then there's the tape of it. Another trip all its own. I'm in no hurry to "evaluate" it; just to get with it. Let it evaluate me: where'd I get so much smarter than it so fast? It'll prod you, stretch you, get you off it. Recommended. Also the Sunrise Percussion Group's soundfest that evening. (We need 'em all, my friend, and then some. —Just ease off with the orders and the Slideshow.) Multitracked; supportive; welcoming (:noticing me hung for an ax, Mahan Rishi comes across the room with claves): in the chorus of joy in which no voice is lost or even stops, Exude; Overflow. Let Health Glow. Smile. —Sure, but what about the music? —& what about INTER/PLAY tapes as music? — not the sound or the symptoms of this or that activity or mindset, but as music; on the map of other music that's—you know—music? (Sure. I know. I'm afraid there may be no such thing, my friend. That music of ours that's "just music" is quite possibly, in your ear, the sound of our nasty social and psychological habits. I say "nasty" because I think music we love engages and supports lots more in us than just our soundpattern detectors, and I interpret your insistence that it's "just music" as a refusal to look into what-all that might be, i.e., as a cover-up, and I don't think it's your virtues you're trying to cover up from yourself. Also I've personally cultivated plenty of the nasties I've got in mind (:even invented a few), and it takes one to know one, my friend.) The sideways-to-us half of Laraaji's sologig is more complex; intriguing. After the soundfest I'll cheat on some hugging to lay a short rap on him about it. In fact nothing jagged or repellent or demonic had come down the channel (—why not?—); but playful did. On the Casio especially: and no "Attitude" showing. No cop-out like "hey don't get me wrong, we know we're not Serious about this" which turns playful silly. And his deadpan transmission of a pair of jerks like the interviewer and the dietfreak didn't just give me some realworld grounding. A lot crunchier than that. Defused any chance I might have grabbed to get the jollies looking down my nose at jerks. What Krishnamurti pushes as "choiceless awareness." A helluva projection.

Fontainebleau   7.   *Oct 1984*

At once vast and sparse. Not a flower in sight; nor a star in the greenguide. A "garden": the "Parterre." To one side, the flat palace. (3 stars.) Elsewhere, massed beyond our ken: trees; clouds. Here it's manmade grounds: bull-dozed flattened straightedged layered. Spent the end of the afternoon here yesterday. Couldn't wait to get back this morning. Got it to myself. Dirtplots and dirt borders. Grassplots. Stone borders and steps and patios and benches. Geometrically stonepooled water. A few, a very few, shrubs; all shaved conical. The layout, symmetricized. Grandly. Mercilessly. The named curve. The named shape. A knockout. Nothing over your head, my friend. Or even up to your armpits. One is master here. Domesticates infinity, even. At a deep sublevel out from the foot of the defunct falls, facing away. Straight lines of divine length, going away. A canal, treelined: on either side, the long thin colonnade. The alternative promenade. In far country. The path not taken. Within bounds, what there is. Not dense with dense subpockets like Versailles. Nor a dusty drag like the Tuileries. Same guy though. Le Nôtre. Should be a household word. Physical embodiment, as the very space we occupy, of thought; art. And rawly so. Undisguised, the theft from us; the violation; the intent to overawe. No rollicking fancy. Or sensuous intimacy. Or mindblowing revelation. Hardcore. No shit. Truths: a system of: uncovered. Powers: empowered: imposed. Correctitude to the nth. To be grasped in selected, static acts of vision. One's Will has been Worked. Under shifting cloudcover, the lone walker meanders; traces queer paths.

Commentary #0 "creativity"

The texts put it this way:

"creativity could use some redeeming orientations; some mirrors to see itself in; some noninvidious images"

text #1 "work"

"it's yourself you're working on"

Commentary #1

Advocates amplify thus:

"use whatever turns you on (Greek manuscripts, rocks, electronic sound) to stretch yourself, purge yourself, redirect yourself, hypothesize yourself, ..."

and less pleasantly:

"you're trying to make yourself available (—get that: it's a long ways up, but it's the top—) not praiseworthy"

text #2 "play"

"let'er rip"

Commentary #2A

We cite three abbreviations of this text:

1. "celebrate"
2. "wail"
3. "fly"

Commentary #2B

Some have asked:

" . . . . . . or is play maybe just the hardest kind of work and work is maybe just the funnest kind of play

To which advocates reply:

"Dunno.

What's vital is some outright counterpurpose.

"Work" says Get off your Ass.

"Play" says Get off your Back.

text #3 "communicate"

"at the depth, at the warmth, of workplay: interact"

Commentary #3

We're here to make a space we never knew of before, into which we can flow and return changed, not foreseeably by some plan, but by opening ourselves to acknowledge ourselves and each other, with whatever outcome; to hang in there; to regard and include; to give each thing (, anything) a fair shake, its full ride; to heed and nourish the newly becoming space which each of us sustains, inhabits, inherits.

The world contains no "them" to change: just "us."—lots of us. And in changing us, who can be sure?

text #4 "output"

"what you're roping us into is a tryout of a Way to Be, a Way to Go: please arouse in me a sense of my wherewithal to be that way or go that way my way"

Commentary #4A

This text was once considered earnest but friendly. Then five corollaries were circulated:

1. "you're not trying to grease me right where I wallow"

2. "you're not trying to dazzle us with your superlative and inimitable gifts"

3. "you're not confirming for those who Can't their special dependence on those who Can"

4. "you're not launching the Next Wave in some deracinated preserve known as an "art" or a "field""

5. "you're not packaging nostrums to do it for us so we won't have to bother"

Commentary #4B

We're not talking what's printed on the giftcard my friend we're talking what the gift is, says, does:

No. 1 (: Not Bad): "do your thing with this" also "try this out and get back to me"

No. 10 (:Not Good): "here's where it's at, fans" also "dig this and watch my smoke" also "smell me and drop dead"

text #5 "utility, quality"

"masterwork art, definitive formulation, validated method are among the crotchety gluttons at the feast of brotherhood; not its hosts"

Commentary #5A

The attempt to heal familiar fissures between the two titular concepts is the least of this text's provocations. Consider its canonical amplification:

"in the nittygritty of your creative processes, implicitly or explicitly, in the very germination of any immediate or eventual "outputs": what kinds of person are you being or becoming? what kinds of present or future interaction are you fostering?""

Commentary #5B

Outrage lingers over "the threat to treat their sacred cows as bunfiller."

Others cool it; hang tight with their pet cows and vedgies.

Commentary #5C

Texts tend towards a ripe inwardness. It's corollaries and amplifications that smart off. So we propose a swap: read In The Nittygritty Of as the text #5 entitled "utility, quality"; then read Crotchety Gluttons as a corollary.

text #6 "knowledge, craft"

"not a repository; not a technique: but "sensitivity training""

Commentary #6

"what you're developing is your clarity—your ability to get the most out of the least;

and your openness—your capacity to take in and to give"

text #7 "success"

"May you always arrive at ground zero afresh."

Commentary #7A

Advocates are entranced by what "afresh" says about "ground zero" in fusing "again" (meaning it's the same) with "fresh" (meaning it looks different so it's different) with "refreshed" (meaning not just you feel good but also it's what you've been up to that got you there so no wonder it looks different).

Commentary #7B

"The navelgazing solipsism encouraged by many of the preceding texts reaches its incorrigible nadir in this one. Exactly what's wrong, we ask frankly, with the urge to achieve, to stand out from the crowd, to make people sit up and take notice? Are these among the energies we're supposed to "siphon off " (:talk about invidious!) rather than "cultivate"? As if they were any more antisocial than navelgazing! Or as a "canonical amplification" puts it, "sniffing your armpits." Alright then: what about just giving pleasure? Or making a contribution?"

These and the next comments we pass along.

text #8 "reputation"

"May those whom you feel involved with be as free from adulation as from condescension."

Commentary #8

"And speaking of blindeyed, are all standards of excellence, all distinctions of merit, to be invalidated?"

text #9 "remuneration"

"the real world sucks"

Commentary #9A

A fruit of experience, this text was created by composer David Madole in seeking re-entry to Academe.

Commentary #9B

The following three corollaries are apocryphal imitations of the original:

1. "composing sucks"

2. "performing sucks"

3. "professoring sucks"

Commentary #9C "Go Ahead"

push the product; life is no weekend retreat

text #10

Recent Ideas and Activities of James K. Randall and Benjamin Boretz: A New Social Role for Music

Fred Everett Maus

1

DURING THE 1960s James K. Randall and Benjamin Boretz were closely associated with Milton Babbitt at Princeton University. The best known and most widely available evidence of Babbitt's influence on Randall and Boretz is Boretz's dissertation essay "Meta-Variations," submitted to Princeton in 1970 and published in *Perspectives of New Music*.[1] It can serve as an illustration of the relation among Babbitt, Randall, and Boretz in this period. The dissertation was supervised by Babbitt and Randall; more precisely, it was written in close consultation with Randall, and is involved throughout with Babbitt's ideas on theory and composition. The provocative claims of Babbitt's early writings—the depiction of twelve-tone structure as fundamentally different from tonality but equally rich, the defense of Schenker's theory of tonality and suggestions about possible reconstruction, the invocation of analytic philosophy as a basis for the methodology of music-theoretical thought, and more generally the belief that composers and other musical thinkers can draw on the best intellectual tools of their time in working toward a clear, explicit understanding of what they are doing—these positions develop, in Boretz's essay, into an elaborately articulated account of pitch structure, distinguishing between order-determinate and content-determinate systems, drawing on work of the philosopher Nelson Goodman to construct an explicit theory of structural relations, and eventuating in remarkable analyses and a discussion of Boretz's own composition *Group Variations*.

"Meta-Variations" is, among other things, an account of the thought that was involved in Boretz's work as a composer. Like Babbitt, the Boretz of "Meta-Variations" emphasizes the liberating effect of explicit theoretical thought for a composer: the claim is that music theory, rather than being a source of inhibiting constraints, can serve as a tool for extrapolating from known musical properties and structures to unforeseen possibilities.

More recently, especially since the mid-seventies, the ideas and activities of Randall and Boretz have changed considerably. The change has been gradual, an evolution rather than a sharp break, but the extent of the change can be dramatized by contrasting their recent orientation with the model formerly provided by Babbitt's work. To put it briefly and simply, in place of Babbitt's insistence on intricately calculated compositions and explicit, literal descriptions of music, Randall and Boretz have explored various improvisational activities, and they have communicated about music in poetry and narrative.

Some musicians still think of Randall and Boretz primarily in relation to Babbitt; others, aware of the divergence of Randall's and Boretz's recent work from Babbitt's concerns, remain uncertain of the nature and motivation of the change. Recent developments in their work have become known largely through publications in *Perspectives of New Music* and to some extent through the distribution of Randall's tapes of improvisations under the title "Inter/Play." But the publicly available material can seem fragmentary and enigmatic. The complexity of Randall's and Boretz's thought and writing, and the misleading resemblances between their work and that of better-publicized innovators, John Cage especially, have created some confusion about Randall's and Boretz's purposes. In this paper I hope to make their ideas more approachable, paving the way for the comprehension that must precede any serious evaluation.

2

I believe it is helpful to regard Randall and Boretz in light of an important radical tradition in general aesthetics, vigorously presented in writings of the late nineteenth and early twentieth centuries. The works that I will discuss have not directly influenced Randall and Boretz, but they are closer in substance to their recent thought than any material I have seen that deals specifically with music. The relatively comprehensive and widely known writings of these aestheticians can provide a helpful introduction to the musical material.

Tolstoy's *What is Art?*, Collingwood's *The Principles of Art*, and Dewey's *Art as Experience* are centrally concerned to offer theories of the *importance* of art, clarifying the nature of artistic value. They agree in attacking traditional theories that explain the value of art in terms of beauty; arguing in somewhat different ways, they all agree that the notion of beauty, supposedly an intrinsically valuable property of successful art, does not clarify the aims and value of art.[2] To clarify the nature of art, these writers focus on art's function in the lives of artists and audiences, describing the role of art in satisfying important personal and social goals. The importance of art, they argue, lies in its ability to articulate and communicate inner states, or more briefly in its expressive nature.[3]

The suggestion that art should be understood primarily in relation to personal and social contexts, as a medium for articulating and communicating experience, may seem familiar or even banal. But Tolstoy, Collingwood, and Dewey draw radical consequences from this starting point. First, these writers concentrate on *activities* rather than *objects*, stressing that art exists in processes of creation and apprehension rather than as a realm of beautiful objects awaiting contemplation. Tolstoy defines art as follows:

> Art is a human activity, consisting in this, that one man consciously, by means of certain external signs, hands on to others feelings that he has lived through, and that other people are infected by those feelings, and also experience them. (p. 50)

Art is an activity of communication, and individual works of art are to be understood in light of their role in this activity. According to Collingwood,

> By creating for ourselves an imaginary experience of activity, we express our emotions; and this is what we call art. (p. 151)

Art is defined in terms of the activity of expression, though Collingwood, unlike Tolstoy, emphasizes that the artist creates by clarifying an initially obscure emotion, so that the artist learns in the process of creation. Collingwood stresses the importance of aesthetic experience to the extent of denying that physical objects such as paintings are works of art: rather,

> a work of art proper is a total activity which the person enjoying it apprehends, or is conscious of, by the use of his imagination. (p. 151)

Dewey's title, *Art as Experience*, already signals his focus on activities rather than objects. Dewey emphasizes the distinction between an art product such as a statue and "the *work* of art":

> The first is physical and potential; the latter is active and experienced. It is what the product does, its working. (p. 162)

Dewey gives a more central place than Collingwood to the externality and physicality of art objects, but he insists that art can be understood only by studying the *interaction* between art object and audience in experience.

> When artistic objects are separated from both conditions of origin and operation in experience, a wall is built around them that renders almost opaque their general significance, with which esthetic theory deals. (p. 3)

> [A]n esthetic experience, the work of art in its actuality, is *perception*. (p. 162)

For all three writers, aesthetics, in order to show the value of art, must direct its attention to the activities in which art figures, rather than isolating the products of art from these activities.

Second, these writers dispute conventional boundaries between art and other activities, finding art in many ordinary contexts where it is not usually recognized. Tolstoy asserts that

> All human life is filled with works of art of every kind—from cradle-song, jest, mimicry, the ornamentation of houses, dress and utensils, up to church services, buildings, monuments, and triumphal processions. It is all artistic activity. (p. 51)

As an example of art, Tolstoy refers to a boy who has been frightened by a wolf: if the boy relives his feelings while recounting the event, and creates those feelings in his audience, then the storytelling is art (pp. 48–49). According to Dewey, the essential task for aesthetics is "recovering the continuity of esthetic experience with normal processes of living," (p. 10) and his book is full of examples and arguments to establish such continuity. To illustrate expression, he describes an irritated man who orders and objectifies his emotion by straightening his room:

> if his original emotion of impatient irritation has been ordered and tranquillized by what he has done, the orderly room reflects back to him the change that has taken place in himself. He feels not that he

has accomplished a needed chore but has done something emotionally fulfilling. His emotion as thus "objectified" is esthetic. (p. 78)

Collingwood's theory is the most extreme: having identified art with expression, Collingwood concludes that "Every utterance and every gesture that each one of us makes is a work of art." (p. 285)

Third, these aestheticians tend to blur the distinction between artists and non-artists. Obviously the conventional distinction is not respected in the passages I just cited, where a broadened concept of art brings with it a broadened range of artistic creators. But even in describing situations where an artist or performer presents his work to an audience, all three writers stress the similarity between the activity of artist and audience. For Tolstoy and Collingwood, understanding expression means finding in oneself the state of mind that is being expressed, matching it to the external art object somewhat as the artist has done (Tolstoy, 153; Collingwood, 117–19, 250). Dewey quotes Tolstoy's remarks with approval, and develops an elaborate account of the similarities between artistic creation and the temporally developing experience of an audience (pp. 52–54). Collingwood also emphasizes the collaboration that is common in art, including the audience's role in shaping and confirming a performer's self-awareness and, consequently, in determining many details of the continuation of the performance. He laments that writing separates the writer from his audience, preventing such interaction and collaboration (pp. 315–24).

Fourth, a focus on experience and communication motivates a pervasive distrust of professionalism, artistic institutions, and artistic schooling. Tolstoy is particularly vehement on this issue, writing, for instance, that art schools

destroy the capacity to produce real art ... [and] generate enormous quantities of that counterfeit art which perverts the taste of the masses and overflows our world. (p. 126)

Dewey writes of the confusions created by museums, in which objects are isolated from the contexts that would have given them meaning (pp. 7–9), and Collingwood writes angrily of the "cliques of artists and writers," which

consist for the most part of a racket selling amusement to people who at all costs must be prevented from thinking themselves vulgar, and a conspiracy to call it not amusement but art. (p. 90)

For all three writers, artistic institutions are important sources of misunderstanding about art, weakening the connection between art and vivid personal experience and substituting connections between art and dexterity, art and information, or art and social standing.

3

The ideas I have summarized are remote from the working assumptions of most musicians and musical scholars. Consider, for instance, the normal practice of musical analysis or composition instruction, with its exclusive focus on internal relations within the individual piece. Music theory generalizes about musical properties across different pieces, but seldom addresses questions of value. Technical discussion of music is almost always the study of musical objects, abstracted from any personal or social settings in which their importance might become intelligible. Mainstream musical studies are still preoccupied with the canon of Western art music. Performers, scholars, and audiences tend to agree in centering their activities on a small range of major compositions, displaying relatively little curiosity about a wide range of musical behavior. Performance institutions and much else in musical life reinforce a sharp distinction between productive, highly-trained musicians and their audiences. These generalizations apply to the work of Randall and Boretz during the 1960s as well as to many less imaginative instances.

In such a milieu, it is easy to sense the radical potential of the ideas of Tolstoy, Collingwood, Dewey, and related writers. The recent work of Randall and Boretz involves a reinvention of the general position I have been outlining. That is, Randall and Boretz, in seeking to understand the nature of musical value, have come to regard music primarily as self-articulation and communication, and their elaborations of this view have recovered many of the claims previously argued in aesthetics.

The most striking, or at any rate the most literal, evidence of this is a talk by Boretz, "If I am a musical thinker...," published in *Perspectives of New Music* and separately as a book.[4] Boretz stresses that "the authentic perception that I need of my real needs, of my real interest in the activities I pursue" will not be available unless thought and music are seen as "the palpable emanations of intense human identity-seeking expressive activity." He writes that musical awareness and conception deal properly with occasions and activities, not pieces or works, and he identifies listening as "the primal expressive act, moving us "exactly insofar as it expresses *us,* the listeners." He warns of the consequences of "the reification of competence and skill":

Status replaces identity, erudition replaces experience, technique replaces awareness. Discipline replaces engagement. Knowing replaces searching. Self-congratulation replaces self-fulfillment—and in the end it must be that cynicism replaces yearning. (p. 507)

These paraphrases are suffcient to show the closeness of Boretz's thought to that of the earlier aestheticians. It would be rewarding, on another occasion, to consider Boretz's talk at length, following such parallels in greater detail and exploring the novel features of Boretz's position and of his presentation.[5]

James K. Randall's "Are You Serious?" is mostly an autobiographical recounting of his experiences at a "weekend festival" of "spiritual expression through music and dance," involving a range of New Age teachers, healers, and so on.[6] The title suggests the complex tone of Randall's account: the question can be read as an incredulous retort, a put-down of the ambitions of modern spiritual teachers, but equally as a hopeful or wistful query, seriously intended in the hope that these unfamiliar activities may contain something valuable. The question is certainly addressed, in a challenging way, to the reader of *Perspectives:* are *you* as serious, in your own musical activities, as these New Age teachers are trying to be?

For present purposes, what matters is the background of assumptions that could lead Randall to take an interest in quasi-religious music and dance, and to present his experiences to the readership of *Perspectives.* The autobiographical form is likely to strike some readers as impertinent, involving a change of subject from music to some mingling of self-obtrusion and amateur sociology. Randall indicates his reply when he anticipates a question about the quality of the New Age music, or indeed of his own improvisations:

—Sure, but what about the music?—& what about INTER/PLAY tapes as music?—not the sound or the symptoms of this or that activity or mindset, but as music; on the map of other music that's—you know—music? (Sure. I know. I'm afraid there may be no such thing.... I think music we love engages and supports much more in us than just our soundpattern detectors, and I interpret your insistence that it's "just music" as a refusal to look into what-all that might be, i.e., as a cover-up ...) (p. 83)

Randall refuses to isolate music from the personal and social contexts in which it functions, and he intimates that the desire to isolate it may be motivated by self-protection or self-deception. Turning his attention from patterning of sound to social contexts, he finds the New Age emphasis on the function of music initially promising, at least enough so to inform himself about it.

Generally the New Age performances turn out to be disappointing. A musician might react to Randall's disappointment with some complacency, finding it predictable. But Randall's qualms have obvious implications for classical music practices as well:

> I'm getting allergic to carrying out instructions and I'm agog at the coupling of l. find your true self & unblock your creativity & get in touch with the cosmos with 2. do exactly what I'm doing and saying as I transmit to you by rote what I got by rote from someone who got it from God by rote. (p. 78)

Randall points out a confused mingling of an ideology of self-exploration with firmly authoritarian practices; clearly in doing so he hopes to lead conventional classical musicians to speculate on the seriousness and clarity of their own self-understanding, and in particular on the relation between self-discovery and acceptance of authority in their musical activities.

The varied literary forms in which Randall and Boretz have recently written of music reflect quite directly an attentiveness to the expressive aspects of their writing. More strikingly, Randall and Boretz have embodied their beliefs in a practice of improvisation in which several people play, with no predetermined schedule of events, making a tape that they will later hear and discuss. Musical works disappear, replaced entirely by musical activity. The notion of musical communication and collaboration becomes straightforward and predominant, with continuous interaction among the participants. The later listening and discussion, made possible by relatively recent technology, makes the activity of self-scrutiny essential and inevitable. Distinctions among composers, performers, and audience no longer find application. These improvisations evade the distinction between serious, professionalized music-making and everyday social interaction. The radical innovations of Randall and Boretz correspond precisely to the radical implications of theories of expression in aesthetics.

At the least, the parallels I have cited indicate a wide area of shared attitudes between some well-known works in aesthetics and some recent musical developments. More specifically, the interest of the aesthetics texts is enhanced by their relation to current musical experimentation, and a link to celebrated works in aesthetics makes it possible to ponder the musical material more deeply by turning to fuller presentations of related ideas.

If there is a polemical edge to this paper, it lies in my desire to argue against casual, unreflective dismissal of an interesting and important range of current musical activities. The ideas that motivate Randall's and Boretz's recent work are not so very different from ideas of Tolstoy, Collingwood, and Dewey; the musical developments cannot be easier to dismiss than the positions taken in those classic books.

NOTES

1. Parts 1–6. *Perspectives of New Music* 8, no. 1 (Fall-Winter 1969): 1–74; 8, no. 2 (Spring-Summer 1970): 49–111; 9, no. 1 (Fall-Winter 1970): 23–42; 9, no. 2/10, no. 1 (1971): 232–70; 11, no. 1 (Fall-Winter 1972): 146–223; 11, no. 2 (Spring-Summer 1973): 156–203.

2. Leo Tolstoy, *What is Art?*, trans. Aylmer Maude (New York: Funk & Wagnalls Company, 1904), 38–45; R. G. Collingwood, *The Principles of Art* (London: Oxford University Press, 1938), 37–41; John Dewey, *Art as Experience* (New York: Perigee, 1980), 129–30. Further page references for these books appear in the text of the paper.

3. This summary captures the central focus of Tolstoy's and Collingwood's theories. Dewey's splendid book is more comprehensive and complex; expression plays a crucial role in his account, along with other aspects of art.

4. *Perspectives of New Music* 20, nos. 1 and 2 (Fall-Winter 1981/Spring-Summer 1982): 464–517; Barrytown: Station Hill Press, 1985. Neither is paginated.

5. For instance, his emphasis on expression as self-articulation is particularly close to Collingwood's position. In writing of the expression of *identity*, Boretz improves upon the earlier writers' focus on feeling and emotion. A full account should also address the visual impact of the published versions: the text appears in large type, with relatively few words to a page, along with inkblots and sketches. Boretz arrived at this format in order to achieve some of the control of pacing and tone that he would have in an oral performance. But as he has pointed out, the format also creates somewhat the effect of a children's book. I find that this contributes to the impact of the text: it is easy to feel that one is encountering ideas that have been familiar for many years, but recently ignored or forgotten.

6. *Perspectives of New Music* 23, no. 2 (Spring-Summer 1985): 72–88. (See pp. 90–106, this volume.)

Interface
Part I:
Commentary:
The Barrytown Orchestra
on Hunger Day
November 15, 1984*

Benjamin Boretz

WE COME INTO this public space. Your space, somehow, though not less, supposedly, ours. We come in, having spent most of the just elapsed afternoon here, setting the space up, and strenuously—in the edgy refraction of too much previous experience—thinking how to engage you, this time perhaps, in the spirit and sense of what we engage ourselves in. Wanting to offer you something which feels to us like ourselves, and to you like a possibility of your-selves. Lusting to stimulate you to awareness of what might be possible for per-sons to do rather than exhibit to you us, that we can do it. Speculating, ear-nestly, that we, coming into this public space in our own name and on our own account, might be in particular the intelligent instruments of such a transaction; because we have ourselves convinced that only in a world admitting of such

*(for "Text #10" of J. K. Randall's "Are You Serious?")

transactions are we likely to attain some acceptable identity, can we imagine that we, as ourselves, might be acceptable persons, might survive, acceptably. What we have set up is a faintly amoebic curvature of chairs and low tables, implicitly, rather than explicitly, enclosed; articulated mildly, with tinges of formality, occlusion, elevation, from the normal corridors and enclaves of this place, instead of dissolving indistinguishably into that normalcy: this is to be an offering, an occasion; we have solicited and have been tendered an invitation, quite formally, to contribute to this communal fast day, with a two-hour soundmaking alternative to dinner, from five to seven. What our preparatory exertions have to do with famine in Africa, to us seems obvious.

At five the setup, though architecturally complete, is still shy a few electronic links, creating, because you have begun to accumulate in what the clock tells us must be meaningful agglomeration, twinges of anxiety, oppressive prehensions, a sudden familiar alienating spasm of obligation to you, rushes of conflict between the pressure and explicit rejection of that obligation, resisted not out of indifference to you, not seeking alienated distance from you, but from a poignant need to remain true to the thing within ourselves we want to touch here, out of a sharp dread of alienation from our own recognizable selves, from the sound we ourselves make, from the activity of ourselves making it. When adaptors arrive, and don't fit, decisions have to be made to proceed without (some) amplification. At five-fifteen no sound has yet been heard from the eight of us around our amoeba. But your sound, self-contained, has been rising steadily over us, a paralyzingly neutral noise, simultaneously stonewalling and demanding, blank and loud, abusive.

We, silent, are challenged to respond with corresponding aggression, just where we most want to stay within, not ourselves, but the space we had been planning to join with you. (You, of course, have been free to sit, move around, walk through, enter and leave, the space, your own familiar space still, usurped by us only fractionally, and even that fraction structured to minimize your, and our, sense of invasion.) As we struggle for composure within our growing timidity, fear, feeling out here the absurdity of our paradoxical condescension in offering ourselves as ourselves, in our own name and on our own account, as fellow-citizens, to a space in which we feel, and are felt to be, ill-fitting aliens, as we struggle in our vanity to offer a model of unalienated communal expression, an unintimidating, accepting, environment of expressive activity, within a space in which everincreasingly we feel ourselves unacceptable, our sound begins to rise, in a suddenly muted crevice of yours. Our score is: think of melody, and make sound within the sound you hear. We pursue our score, over and under each other's and your sound, for perhaps half an hour.

Until one of us, arriving late, experiences us from your perspective. Perceives us, balefully, making public fools of ourselves, playing this pathetic pinched restrained introvert sound. Perceives us, painfully, being selfindulgent cultfreaks, subjecting you, innocent dropins, deserving auditors, to an excruciating exhibition of weird autism, eliciting your attention just to show how contemptuously we can hold out on you, murmuring mumbly and indecipherably into our own miserable chops with dismal disregard for your edification. And then she jumps into our midst with bongos blazing to retrieve us from disgrace, wake us from numb sloth, redeem whatever fragment of respectability might still be redeemable.

With some edge, we, humorous, cagey, resist, subsiding, rather than rising, to the challenge. With some sharper energy, we keep on trying to hold hard-won accumulations of coherence, purpose, sensibility. With some effort, we adjust and accommodate, finally, congenially, and for the next forty or so minutes our sound goes through a coil of complex, vivifying transformations. We end, ignorant of your attitudes and opinions, feeling relief: we have survived. And when we hear the tape, we love it, especially the sensuous responsive interplay between your sound and ours; and the magical transformation from sensitive roomfeel to intense interactive expression, pivoting around the zapping catalytic bongo entry. Our bongo drummer, herself, now within the tapesound with us inside our sheltered listening space, in your absence, is embarrassed by what suddenly to her (but not at all to us) is heard as gross overreaction to mistaken perception. (But in your presence it had been different, and for you, immune from conciliating dialogue or relistening in congenial surroundings, the reality experienced, some unspeakable untoward social event, persists unmodulated:)

selfindulgent?

(the sound on the tape.)   :   how?

hostile?

(the shape of the space.)   :   how?

pathetic?

(the awareness of the interaction.)   :   how?

frivolous?

(the sensibility within the circle.)   :   how?

In our own name: being present, in this public space, making sound *as ourselves* being present, *as ourselves* making sound, we violate a first principle of public edification: there are these wooden molds, into which a person may insert oneself, therein to fulfill responsibly—even with distinction, even with distinct individuality—a known social function, with known social valuation, with a known set of appropriate actions, resulting in a known range of appropriate

sounds; such insertion carries with it the secure expectation that one will perform these actions correctly, and with appropriate results (one has, after all,
been taught; and others are in a position to judge). This is to serve the public
interest: to honor and respect the dignity and standing of the equally well-
inserted onlookers, who just as satisfyingly well know how to satisfy the functions appropriate to their wooden molds in the space gratifyingly provided for
them to do so by one's appropriate actions. To give oneself thus responsibly to
such a securely validated public function is the very antithesis of selfindulgence.
And to enter a certain particular wooden mold, that, say, of the good and
faithful servant of high musical culture (imported from Vienna by way of New
York), to be, namely, a Serious Musician, is the very antithesis of frivolity. From
within such a wooden mold, one will do it right. One has been taught. One can
be trusted. One is Serious.*

On our own account: being present, in this public space, *with ourselves, with
one another*, making sound, in this public space, *for ourselves, for one another*, we
violate a first principle of public entertainment. You are bereaved of your
detachable role of the courted, they whose favor and approval are ardently sup-
plicated; you are deprived of the fulfilling satisfaction attaching to the dispensa-
tion of terminal, ultimate judgment. To the extent that these people do this
with each other, for themselves, they deprive you of the passive gratification of
their being there wholly with you, of their doing this exclusively for you. (We
face *into* our circle; respond to one another; we do not appear to be beseeching
your approval, only leaving room for you to invent—outside of any known context—your own mode of reception or response. Hostile—in its selfenclosure,
this. And pathetic—in its fortressed insularity.)

When you are my students, and I invite you to engage, you ask, "What
should I do?", thus declining to engage even my invitation to engage, and putting me in my place—as teacher—so as to restore yourself to your place of
safety—as student. This is *my* trip, right? So don't expect *you* to get involved.

When you are in this public space we enter, to make sound, and we invite
you to engage, you turn us into Performers (or Composers, or Improvisors, or
Avantgardistes) for yourselves to be an Audience of, to be able safely from that
safe place to celebrate or repudiate us, and our sound, with no danger of
unforeseeable engagement:

*[*Serious*: As in: Get serious, boy—find yourself
a steady job, save yourself up some money, raise yourself
a family.]

So what do *we* want of *you?*

And in what name, on whose account, in what form, do we presume to seek to be acceptable, to feel ourselves acceptable, as conveyors of a communal soundsense, as we enter this public space?

And in what way, for what reason, do we seek that you acknowledge us, and that we perceive ourselves, as having been, in our soundmaking in this public space, legitimate interlocutors in the communal dialogue about the needs and forms of everyone's interaction?

And how is just surviving, enough?

(The Barrytown Orchestra, playing in Kline Commons lounge at Bard College on a fast day for the benefit of Ethiopian famine victims, November 15, 1984, consisted of (counterclockwise from corridorside) Ann McLellan, Frank Carter, Mike Woodward, Bruce Huber, Penny Hyde, Chuck Stein, Ben Boretz, Dan Sedia, Kathy Osgood.)

Interface
Part II:
Thoughts in Reply
to Boulez/Foucault:
"Contemporary Music
and the Public"

Benjamin Boretz

*(". . . a pseudo-culture of documentation [is] taking shape . . .
the performer become immortal, rivalling now the immortality
of the masterpiece . . . an alibi for reproduction as opposed to real
production . . .")* *

Perspectives of New Music 24, no. 1 (Fall–Winter 1985): 9 (p. 86, this volume)

"We've all been there, haven't I?"

IMMORTALITY: EVEN SNEERED AT, it won't go away. (How can it? wasn't there to begin with.) Hang out the 'masterpiece' shingle and— composerperson, performerperson, professorperson, or whoever you are— you've just opted wholehog for 'reproduction,' for reincarnating by some token music-making exertions the old Beethoven (either as Himself or as rolled over) ghost-balloon. Nothing less than an archetypal prefixture at Square 1: hardly 'real production' (though maybe Missouri and Paris offer radically differing perspectives), and as for Creative Expression, that's only for simps anyway. Doesn't matter if your masterpiece ritual is reverent or iconoclastic or heretical, either: same lofty ur-Meta-pedestal you're hoist-ing onto, same Importance you're figuring to rate, since it's already there and those that credentialized it eternally (being dead) have no further need (and if you don't happen to make it all the way to Pope you can always start one of your own). Otherwise, down at street level, Performance and Composition's no big issue—just a natural way to make a fairly simple dis-tinction between the 'action' and the 'reflection' facets of some stretch or other of music-making. And if you are into the 'masterpiece' action, don't blame the paying unwashed (mythical-beastly ill-natured ontological trivia that they are) if they prefer the heavy sermons at the plastic church down the street, which they happen to *like* (and which, non-coincidentally, are felt to like *them*), over those which (on both accounts) feel nasty.

There is an issue about listeners; it may be historical: it may be that mas-terpiece composition no longer yields its struggle to its auditors, it may be that it no longer projects a sense of urgent, earnest striving, of strenuous process in progress. Maybe it became opaque to people because it was stonewalling them with images of *mastery*, rather than dangling the old-masterpiece humbugs of fellow-suffering, sensory titillation, or even dema-gogic hassling or some other kind of histrionic availability; what else other than stonewalling is that notorious acoustical modern-music 'complexity,' anyway?: well short of the Grosse Fuge, expressive inscrutability stands in adequately for comprehensional 'difficulty.' The Stings of Command hav-ing lost their authority, only S/M cultfreaks and fellow inflictors would go for them voluntarily (and, remember, the people *do* have *their* music).

Prying apart the social alienation without giving up the global Me lust drives aspirants two different ways: one way is to see that the baggage of Lofty is a white elephant impeding the briskness of commerce, not to men-tion that it's mostly a hypocritical scam anyhow, and so to shed it clean and enter the lists with knockout exploits of pure techno-Classic chops, fabri-cating tasty consumer Pop for symphony orchestra, chamber group, or something mod. Where Serious looks like just an elitist inhibition of Going For It, it's entropic already: in such a case, frankness does pay. The other way is to do an extreme retreat into the thwarted Public-Serious esteem hangup itself (James Joyce on his couch of composition deciding to "retire from public life"), going for either Technique, detached, polished, and virtuous, or Discipline, like legitimate research in the field of Musical Composition. As the popular artist seeks love, the true professional seeks respect, and requires recognition only from other true professionals (but how come it's *recognition* that's always *the* issue of choice?). Blowaway playing chops, scintillating composition craft, intimidating discourse virtuosity: great axes for a species of aggressive self-assertion which has alienation itself already built into the bedrock of status-justification (Liszt: "Das versteht Ihr Alle nicht"). Strenuous withdrawal: the ultimate pure (entropic) Public-social maneuver.

There may be an insight here. Social climbing before the multitude may be avoidable without anyone's having to give up music as an expressive language. Seeing how the culture fractures Public from serious and social, space opens up for other ways of slicing musical needs and uses, like personal navigation and interpersonal negotiation, serious aplenty and social for sure, just not implicitly public, and real weak on Number-One status claimability. If music-making rituals are getting stripped of their global dignities and noble obligations then it maybe becomes more imaginable to liberate them into shapes that configure naturally to perceived needs to explore, identify, integrate, aiming at realizing authentic domestic purposes—which could even be avowed non-fraudulently—such as: to help put ourselves together, as people; with people.

In *Meta-Variations,* struggling to create a perspective from which to grasp the origins of music-epistemic confusions while enclosed within their grip, I argued, with what might have seemed obscurely motivated vehemence, for the cognitive distinction between the referents of 'music' as an epistemic probe, and 'music,' invoked as an honorific epithet, and implicitly signified alarm over the threat to cognitive-aesthetic survival lurking in the elision of that distinction. I see it now, sharper for having been gnashed by Foucault and Boulez, as the distinction between 'work' as a way of life, and as an advance obituary celebration, aspiring to coerce enforcement of an inert symbolic historical position. In music, as in everything, the disappearing moment of experience is the firmest reality; but the fictions of permanence, invented for the benefit of discourse and contemplation, are so much more firmly graspable by the conscious minds whose invention they are, that they, rather than the vanished traces of elusive experience, are the referents on which the firmest conceptions—intuitions, even—of reality are built. And thus do sanity—that is, the fact of sanity—and rationality—that is, the sensation of sanity—come into mortal conflict, threatening to dissolve the sensible integrity of existence. Music is what people can do to work at harmonizing that contradiction: to save significance while still sustaining identity as a continuous mental structure.

What I as a musician, as a music-experiencing and music-expressing person, choose, as a musical thinker, to disdain, and to engage, bears critically on the capacity of my music-making to be mobilized in the cause of my survival. It cannot, survivably, be squandered in making myself, or my music, an object of admiration or esteem or—especially, if we are talking about Foucault and Boulez—of authority.

Benjamin Boretz
October/November 1986; February 1987

Interface
Part III:
Relevance. Liberation.

Benjamin Boretz

for the Society for Music Theory, November 6, 1987

RELEVANCE. LIBERATION. Slogans which at one time politicized our universal concerns with social responsibility and personal significance. At that time it was conspicuous how self-consciously music was engaged in pushing at the frontiers of those issues. There was revolutionary rock. There was free jazz. There was Zen, there was indeterminacy. There was the Movement; there was meditation; there was the media. Pulling away, with equal zeal, from those same frontiers, there was the radical Ivy cult of the dictatorship of the scientific intellectual, socially nonresponsible and personally detached. For me, personally, in counter-reaction to the blatantly ideologized character of every one of these cultures, and in need,

amidst all the pressuring and confusing noise of their sonic and verbal emanations, of a private ideological articulation of my own, there was *Meta-
Variations*.

Relevance is addressed in the first sentence of *Meta-Variations*: it says
that I needed to find a way of thinking *about* music that would be adequate
to that thinking *in* music which, for me then, identified the substance of
value in the interpersonal space of a musical transaction. And it was the idea
of music as thought, too, on which *Meta-Variations* grounded its program
for my liberation: proposing the imaginative liberation of my musical ideas
by the depth and acuity of my receptual reconstruction of what music there
already was; promoting the liberation of my musical experience by the comprehensive self-determination of the contexts, contents, and structures
which I could make palpable to myself in my interactions with musical phenomena; and envisaging the liberation of my world-sense by the extension
of its boundaries, and the deepening of its insights by discovering and composing the fantastic non-physical worlds of sensations and dimensions and
untranslatable events which could be experienced, in music form, as wholly
real and totally sharable, just like the domestic normal worlds we all share as
real without special definition or conscious imaginative effort.

Meta-Variations was, in sum, an extended meditation on these points,
putting my world together from its musical center, in terms of my personal
experience, insight, and intuition. And it served me, too, as a program for
an imaginable music culture—an anarchic pluralist culture of independent
thinker-imaginers, experiencing with transcendent depth their own music-
thought experiences, but equally accessible to one another for communication, empathy, mutual inspiration. The possibility of such a culture was
given to me by the distinctions I was making between the determinacy of
the Chosen and the determinism of the Given; between cognitive intersub-
jectivity and universal necessity; between the firmness of a musical identity
by its determinate feel within music language alone, and the dependency of
that identity upon paraphrasability or extracontextual specification; by the
distinctions between definition and proof, between assertion and demonstration, and—perhaps most poignantly—between understanding and judgment. The section of *Meta-Variations* entitled "Music Theory, Aesthetics,
and Ear Training" was a modest glimpse in this direction; there were
broader sightings elsewhere.

But in the subsequent history of *Meta-Variations*, after its composition,
some of its broader visions began to unravel; contradictions began to
appear that were implicit in the very breadth and scope of its attempt to
both universalize and relativize a highly particular world-view. For when it
emerged into the actual world of other persons, into the real-time world of
its real-world time, when, in fact, it materialized in *Perspectives* as a public,

published, document, *Meta-Variations* projected not really as a personal confession interpersonally shared, but rather as a public manifesto publicly enforcing a specific musical viewpoint, a particular intellectual style, a culture-centric world-view. Paradoxically indeed, this documentation of one person's operation of the politics of individual liberation, both manifesting and advocating a maximum independence and self-determination of experiencing and imagining in both the personal and the interpersonal space, now in actual political space came down as an instrument of coercion and prescription. And thus it was exposed that the conceptions of relevance—social responsibility—and of liberation—personal fulfillment—embedded in *Meta-Variations* were in structural conflict with one another. And that they would be inevitably in conflict in any texts or practices grounded, like *Meta-Variations*, in a conception of music as a domain of autonomous sound-thought objects and phenomena. For the implications—and retroactively, even the intentions—of such texts and practices appear radically different when they are viewed as modes of transcendent self-development within private space, and when they are brought into public space looking like hard, formed, created objects built to invade and survive in the real world. And this conflict between ideology and function, this functional hypocrisy of one's sincerest intentions, infects all the contemporary manifestations of public music and music-intellectual culture. Is, perhaps, built in to the very conception of 'public' which has become our culture's principal communal mode. And certainly marks every one of the self-consciously idealistic contemporary music practices which I mentioned at the beginning of these reflections, despite the enormous ideological-conceptual gulfs apparent among them.

All of those contemporary music cultures, in fact, and *Meta-Variations* culture along with them, are modelled on *masterpiece* culture—which freely translates into *celebrity* culture in some versions—and which entails as an indispensible image the autonomous identity of either the masterful work of art or the masterful artist. It is a model whose relation to the history and culture of its surroundings is either mythologically one-dimensional and provincial, like that of Scripture, or blank, like that of theoretical science. In masterpiece culture, musical behavior is strictly the symbolic behavior of abstract Ideas, idealized Figures, and schematized structures of quantified sonic particles. Music History, the official record of musical phenomena within masterpiece culture, is merely the recorded chronology and taxonomy of these idealized behaviors. It is only when music is seen as something that is done by and among *people*, as a form of *people's* behavior among other forms of behavior, that real-time, people-size circumstances of history, culture, and experience become indispensibly relevant, both as input to and as output from, our conceptions and practices of music.

If musical thought is to be relevant, if it is to be liberating, if those two conceptions are to be consonant rather than contradictory, a conception of the materials, character, and activity of music broader in scope than that of *Meta-Variations* needs to be pursued. In saying this, I regard myself as the direct beneficiary, rather than the recuperating victim, of the conceptions, constructions, and gropings which carried me through to the 'All-Musical' scope of *Meta-Variations*; for the very exhaustiveness of this scope of conception and construction was crucial to exposing and specifying its intrinsic limits. From within the mind of *Meta-Variations*, a virtually unlimited universe of musics is imaginable; but all these musics are ultimately constrained by what turns out to be a single possible, bounded conception of music, among many possible others. The materials of music under this conception are understood as a vocabulary of sound qualities inferable from sonic particulars. And the contents of music are understood as the expressive experiential output of the cumulative networks of relational time-objects formed among these qualities.

If, on the other hand, music is received as behavior, then our musical and our metamusical behavior both are significant content in the global interpersonal space in which we act upon one another, creating and exhibiting and cultivating messages of social form and interpersonal experience. How we choose to understand music is not passive; it is positive social action. And how we scope the range of what we can count as the materials of some music, how we can learn to embed the sonic data of a musical occurrence within its ontological context as an implicative occasion within a particular cultural vocabulary, traditional or newly being created, will determine our capacity to reactivate our own musical culture, to reconnect our musical thinking and behaving with what is alive in us as questing people, wanting to understand, experience, and cultivate the actual world of our actual lives with our living music.

I end with three soundstretches, each of which is the sound of a significative musical behavior, whose salient qualities as music, the senses in which it is music, are not adequately accessible from the strategies made available by *Meta-Variations*, nor any other current practice of musical thought based on the construal of autonomously structured, autonomously ontologized, sonic formations, however copiously, and even trivially, they may suffice to account for its ostensible data:

[Soundstretch 1: J.D. Short: Train, bring my baby back
   (from Folkways FTS 31028: *Delta Blues*)]

[Soundstretch 2: Procession of the colour-bearers/Song of the Alfereces
   (from EMI-ODEON 064-18218: *Musical Atlas: Chile*)

[Soundstrech 3: from B. Boretz's *forM. (a music)* (a tape convergence of
   texts and occasions)]

Interface Part IV: On Thinking about Various Issues Induced by the Problem of Discovering That One Is Not a 'Composer', and That the Space Which One Inhabits Musically Is Not 'America'

Benjamin Boretz

I

A TIRADE (FROM MY DIARY)

1.

. . . Do I have to tell you about the spiritual cannibalism of the culture, our culture, which has been bombarding us with ultrasensory overstimulation aiming to reprocess us into fulltime consumption machines, stealing above all from us our time (not an inch of time without an imprint of message), and even our very *sense* of time (to be measured in lengths of no more than one message unit each) under the guise of entertainment, and even of 'art', commoditizing the eternal, hyping the primal? Our time is the *sine qua non* of our identity. We need to take extreme measures to reclaim it for ourselves and each other. (3/88: about *("... my chart shines high where the blue milk's upset ... "*))

2.

Postmodernism in music is premised on the idea that people have to compose, perform, listen to, and review music no matter how useless, pointless, rootless, disengaged, culturally archaic those practices have become. Business, after all, is business. And what is called minimalist music, in postmodernist talk, strenuously and overtly celebrates the pervading poverty of our cultural spirit, and the mechanical functionality which has increasingly become what passes for our relations to one another. On the grounds that we need our music for vital matters of survival and salvation, and that we can't afford to squander it on marginal ego-iconography that doesn't even have the immediate culture-wide expressive bite of popular entertainment, I am—politically—opposed to the stances and practices of postmodernist and minimalist music. And in favor, insofar as I can imagine needing a high-cultural music medium at all, of stances and practices currently striped, historistically, as 'modernist': frontiers are still there; they need to be confronted and extended; they *are* that which people need to confront and extend; symbolically at least, but tangibly, also, in the sense of science, every people in every age has its own assemblage of obsessions and terrors—alienations. These need to be spoken for to and with by activities among one's own kind, activities which strain to articulate the inarticulate inchoate lucidly, which name the unnameable, bear the unbearable, make survivable the affirmative recognition of the terrifying, take the journey for us, within, to the places we desperately need to go to and equally need to avoid the pain and fear of going to, experience with us for us everything we are too vulnerable to experience alone, too alone to survive not experiencing. In our age, for our people, the requisite forms of these practices are in principle always unknown, their perpetual reconstruction the endless task of those whose compulsion—whose obligation to us to which we obligate them—it is to travel to the unknown, to seek and discover and unravel there the endlessly evaporating texts which enable and constitute, both, our life-giving, ineluctable struggle against the inevitable deficit. If we need public-functional musicworkers, it is these public functions for which their services are required. The person, the monument, which is larger than life, we no longer believe or trust or endorse. Nostalgia will not do our business. The cold metaphors of lockstep windup tin militias may chill our heart but I doubt they scourge our consciousness. Something authentically new is still always going to be needed. As it always has. (4/88).

II

RECOGNIZE THAT THERE ARE MISUNDERSTANDINGS WHICH ARISE FROM FUNDAMENTAL AND UNRESOLVABLE CONFLICTS REGARDING WHAT IT IS, WHAT IT'S ABOUT, AND WHY PEOPLE CARE ABOUT IT

1. WHY I NEED TO ELIMINATE 'SKILL' AND 'TECHNIQUE' FROM MY EXPRESSIVE AND EDUCATIVE PRACTICES:

To do something you have to be able to do it. That is not 'technique'. 'Technique' is not a fact. 'Technique' is a way of looking at things which creates facts of a certain specific type. Facts created from the 'technique' perspective have a peculiar way of putting together a doing; they construct it as the manifestation of an abstract, meta-experiential, content, discursively attributable to the doing and the doer, detaching the doing from its experiential nature and functional purpose as a fused unitary doing-in-particular. 'Technique' and 'skill' serve not as aids in the effectiveness or substance of doings or of the experiencing, observing, or interfacing with doings, but only in the symbolic commerce of competitive status-acquisition and status-conferral. The power to get and give points, not to be effective or affected. Significance institutionalized, sanitized, domesticated as metric. The regimentable quantity, the disinvolved observation, in trade for the self-determined quality, the uncontrollably involving 'is-ness' of 'an experience'. 'Technique' and 'skill' are technique and skill directed toward the result of calling attention (essentially, *discursive* attention) to themselves, that their presence is (satisfyingly and satisfactorily, or not) manifest, that the candidate passes the test, proves himself and his work worthy of respect and attention in designable ways, from a detached perspective. To perceive 'technique' and 'skill' this way is in no way to endorse carelessness or mindlessness or random-intentional drift; on the contrary, it constitutes a demand for critical rigor in the definition of what business you're in and requires that you maintain your focus on the purpose and significance of your enterprise of expression. Sloppiness in the conduct of musical doing, and especially music-educational doing, comes from separating out technique and skill from the purposes for which they are employed, not from keeping them fused and inexplicit.

2. WHAT EXPRESSES YOU, PERSONALLY, IS *NOT* 'SELF-EXPRESSION':

To speak of your identity is to speak essentially of your ontology. It's fundamental: your sense of being sane requires that your intuited ontology be sustained: it's threats to that bedrock sanity-giving sense of what is and happens that gives rise to such strenuous defenses as moralities, standards, judgements, ideologies, righteousness.

So 'expresses you' does not mean expresses any image of your person self-reflexively, but rather means resonates, corroborates, confirms, substantiates your intuitions of what there is and what happens: the ontology that constitutes your identity.

What is 'non-personal' expressing then? Borrowing identities, for one, in the service of some ulterior strategy of public self-creation. Objectifying, for another, your own identity—the image of your person or the contents of your ontology—to enforce it as obligatory upon, or to make it enticing to, the hypothetical or actual Other.

So what's a non-bullshit sense of 'authenticity'?: means being (out of an acutely felt need to serve an acutely demanding self-interest) strenuously *for real*; that is, true to the deepest available layer of your perceptions and intuitions—your own best possible access to your own observation language. The familiar traditional (pre-Postmodernist) cultural ethos includes a myth of 'personalness' as a critical role-condition of 'artisticness': your obligation as an artist is not that you have ideas which are *good* (or true, or deep, or original), but that you have ideas which are convictually *yours*.

So it's a *direction of effort*, never a result. An aspiration, never a claim; a way of thinking and striving which manifestly gives rise to ideas, observations, awarenesses that have not come other ways, which contrast signally and blatantly with those that have come other ways.

Two ways something identifies *you*:

1. you identify *with* it as a 'rightness' in harmony with your intuited ontology;
2. you identify *against* it, locating yourself in some specific alienation with respect to it; not just 'otherness' but some specific content of otherness; not just 'alienation' but in some specifiably locatable geography of elsewhere.

3. WHAT I UNDERSTAND TO BE THE ESSENTIAL DISTINGUISHING CHARACTERISTICS OF ENTERTAINMENT ART AND HIGH ART:

Entertainment surrogates our time; relieves us of it for a spell; lives through it for us while it's on loan; does what it takes to keep it for just so long as that feels nonconsequential, not threatening our ultimate reappropriation; returns it refreshed but otherwise intact, unsullied by any lingering tarnish or blemish of content; cleansed but not altered, corroborated but not invaded, renewed but not re-formed.

High art surrogates our time exactly so also; but aspires to not only surrogate our time but also to transform it permanently and substantively: purports to return it to us comprehensively reconstructed: such that not just immediately during or following, but always thereafter, and even with cumulative effect, our time (= the world) will not be the same. Its intentions toward us are serious (as is our use for it) and sinister: someone is invading our psychic space with the intention of appropriating our identity and remaking it at their will; or it is we ourselves who appropriate ourselves to it so as to have it do this to us: 'take us over', make us more thereby, give us by surrogation the authority of its own visionary grasp, of its own devouring subjugation of us ourselves.

4. WHY INTERFACE IS A PROBLEM:

Our survivals depend on one another's. Trouble begins the moment you try to persuade me (and thereby yourself) that *your* struggle is *my* struggle too; or even—especially even—when you try to persuade us both that *mine* is *yours* too. And yet, of course they are. And yet, that's never what we're addressing when we're operating the institutionalized ideology that they are: The spiral of incoherence is perpetual: Self-assertion is the problem; self-assertion is the only means we have available by way of which to attempt a solution. The problem is, obviously, insoluble; also, inescapable.

Is there a way of acting that converges the personal and the 'political' needs? That expands awareness to the size of the issues, reduces the sizes of the issues to the sizes of persons, works to harmonize rather than to conquer the immovable contradictories which not only trouble but define our existential identity?

Interface
Part V:*
The Inner Studio
(Strategies for
Retrieving Reality
in Music Experience
and Practice)

Benjamin Boretz

[*There is an amphitheatrical indoor space. Black mostly, with black-upholstered chairs on blackpainted risers, the chairs rimmed with silvershiny chrome framework. Two midsize video monitors, left and right, a chair center with musicstand and microphone, at the flatfloored bottom of the amphitheatrical slope. Large numbers of persons who have entered the amphitheater from both sides fill the left and right thirds of the seatspace—along the video sightlines—leaving the center swath facing the speaker near dead vacant. A video—an interactive documentation of the Barrytown Orchestra in a sound-making session at home—runs silent on the monitors behind the speaker, for as long as he speaks.*]

*A talk for the music department seminar, University of California at San Diego, 26 April 1990.

FOR ME PERSONALLY, this is no gig. I accepted John Silber's invitation to talk here now because there are some things I needed to try to articulate—and they have a lot to do with the issue of a person communicating their personal thoughts or expressing their personal musical ideas in an environment of people they don't know. I imagined and materialized an occasion recently that dealt with this problem in one way—it was a multi-textual environment including videotext, slidetext, oral-verbal vocal text, and realtime ensemble musictext, called "The Purposes and Politics of Engaging Strangers." In a way, this, for me, needed to be that sort of occasion also—but instead, I've gotten interested in the idea of trying to articulate for a group of people I mostly don't know some thoughts I've never articulated and really don't know how to articulate, or even whether I can. But one of the points I need to make, if I'm going to come before you in this highly symbolicized configuration, is that I'm not a lecture jock with a prefabricated routine or even a preconceived message. There are some things I want to think about that only make sense to think about in a situation like this. I wrote them down to read to you. That's why I'm here. I hope you have a good reason for being here too.

If I want to understand how to do music, I need to understand why I do music. Or, better, what I'm doing when I'm doing music. What I'm doing, that is, for myself—whether it be the indulgence, or expression, of some peculiarly personal, or interpersonal, energy; or the purposeful, or even conscious, cultivation of my own development, or the pursuit of my own mental health; or, the conditioning in some form or sense of my surrounding environment—however locally or globally I conceptualize it—toward some condition in which I anticipate I will feel more at home, more normal, more safe, more sane, or something like that, within it. I have to try to know, accurately and without self-deception, where I'm coming from doing music (or anything, for that matter) so that the direction in which my activities are evolving in relation to music making, music thinking, music talking, music learning, make satisfactory sense in themselves, and, maybe even more poignantly, make satisfactory sense in relation to one another. And from my point of view—and all through, I'm going to be speaking of myself in a concrete sense, not as an abstraction standing for you and me both as well as everyone else, recast into my image—I need urgently to know what I'm doing when I'm doing what I'm doing, most especially when it involves my primary and deepest-lying personal and interpersonal actions—music—because I need to take responsibility for myself and for my actions, in relation to myself and to my surrounding world of other creatures. I need to be responsible for myself because I am the only one who *can* be, because without that responsibility being taken by me for me I am psychically in freefall in an empty universe. And that wouldn't be good news for any hope I have of sustaining sanity, of, that is, keeping my focus on the effort to survive, personally.

Why do I think I need to articulate this stuff, why do I need to think about and try to understand what I'm doing when I'm doing what I'm doing? It's an important question, right here and right now, because it involves the issue of me being right here right now talking to you in your room: what am I doing here, and what's in it for you? Unless I'm so narcissistic that I think that everything and anything about me has got to be inordinately fascinating to you—or, unless I'm too crazy to be aware of your place in this transaction or your presence in this your own space—I've got to put together for you and me both how what I talk about handles the distinction of me from all of you, from each of you, and even more especially, of each of you from each other of you. This kind of issue doesn't usually come up in one-on-one conversation—but you know what it's like when someone comes on to you alone like they're talking to a crowd, to a solid mass of collective onehood, whose main characteristic appears to be its reproduction in the huge of the individual personality of the speaker. No moral issue, here—it's just that that effect would utterly defeat my pur- poses, and if I'm going to risk using the intrinsically absurd situation of me, personally, putting out thoughts to you, collectively, I'd better try to get it right, or at least to keep it straight. And I can't manage to do that, and still worry about being eloquent, or entertaining, at the same time.

So what it is is that I need to think and talk explicitly and consciously about what I'm doing when I'm doing what I'm doing because things going along in unreflective space start to not feel right. Because it feels like just doing what comes up, going for what seems plausible to go for, doesn't work out right—feels like a problem down there where there wasn't sup- posed to be one. That's the only reason I suppose that I think, because something's not working right in a holistic unselfconscious way; there's a problem that needs to surface, become exteriorized consciously, identified, understood, responded to. So anything I think about is my problem, right? So what's your interest in it? Well, first of all, despite all the personal, cultural, generational differences between me and any of you, I imagine there are significant things we have in common—maybe these aren't they, in any given case, but my hope is to uncover unknown connections, to mutually identify with kindred spirits who care about the things I care about, so we can think and work and do music for each other's benefit, give each other the support of mutual permission and mutual validation.

OK; here's how I understand what I'm doing, these days, when I'm doing music: my most intense personal need for musical expression I *don't* experience as a need for *self* expression, or even for something felt as 'expression' as such. What I do experience is an acute need for rationality—for sanity. For, that is, the verification of the validity of the reality which is intuitive to me. The personally impersonal, the only objectivity available to an individual consciousness. My identity doesn't rest on the constant reflection and re-reflection back to me of images of myself. That way lies non-sanity, really, not just the closure of vanity. My personal expressive identity is the identity of *the world I perceive as real*. From that emerges the complex web of world-building entities and phenomena which ramifies and stretches and expands torrentially and limitlessly—and includes, crucially, *you* and *your* independent reality, as components of *my* reality. Empathy—the most crucial characteristic of expression in a social context—comes only from a critical operation of sanity from a secure ontological base. It's the only way any kind of altruism, commonality, sharing, loving, and—at the other extreme—arguing, disaffecting, hating, make any sense. To begin with, and to end with, such interpersonal transactions are never really you doing something for or against me, or me doing something for or against you, but always you doing something for or against yourself, me doing something for or against myself. Somewhere in the middle, though, there are other transactions that mediate the ontological issues at the extremes. These transactions reflect the tensions and problems that engender structures and concepts, like: moralities, judgments, codes, forms—things that enable people to perceive and respond to hostile *alien* realities such as threaten to overwhelm and annihilate their own reality—to respond with social-symbolic acts like rejection, condemnation, dismissal, or even submission, rather than by sheer defensive overt violence, by, that is, physical murder. That's how I see music-socializing transactions too. I see every music-doing act by a socialized person as an act heavily implicated in social energies, processes, and intentions: me doing something for or against me; you doing something for or against you. At the very least, I need to articulate my thoughts out loud among you, to put my music sound out there where others are, to disseminate my articulations of word ideas and music ideas, so that there will be some resonance of *my* reality, or my ontology, for me to hear coming back at me from within the world I inhabit, too, not just the resonances of everyone else's, or some generalized resonance of everyone's.

But I inhabit that world with you together. And my output, if it has genuine ontological energy, is probably implicitly aggressive—in principle, just because it's mine, not yours—in relation to you. So we have a problem; a mutual problem if mutual survival is what we both want. And we'd better come up with some social structures within which we can try to build a solution. I don't think that the intensely competitive, skill-oriented structures for doing and learning music which have mostly been institutionalized in our culture are going to help us deal with the problem of mutually wasting each other, because the problem arises precisely in a competitive form: each of us seems to need all the psychic world-space there is; and, therefore, we need to devour and subsume everyone else's space within our own. That's what our conventional structures mostly promote in fact; and I don't know about you, but *that* is the principal killer of personal and social-expressive value and sanity for me, in my world, as I experience it. And if what you want to be doing when you're doing music is anything like what I want it to be, you're also going to need to evolve some different kinds of music-doing structures, and even to invent some different kinds of music.

One reason for that necessity is in a sense historical: I don't believe that, at this point in our culture-time, the practice of high-art music is anymore believable or even available as an alternative way of expressive life, as a way of actively resisting participation in, and reinforcement of, the collectivizing and commoditizing structures of mainstream culture. What it seems to be these days is just flat a tool of mainstream capitalist culture providing leisure-time entertainment for the conspicuously acquisitive. It used to seem—I mean when I was your age—that there were actually gaps in the institutional structures, legitimate possibilities of countercultural resistance, built into the principles of the institutional structures them-selves. And it seemed that, explicitly, it was in particular high art, along with serious intellectual activity, which bore within their natures both the implication and the responsibility of such resistance—even if in practice that implication seemed not always to be realized or the responsibility fulfilled. It seemed back then that what you called 'art' was precisely something whose very identity implied resistance to personal repression and rejection of social oppression—that it was its very superposition of the ever-threatening, ever-present backdrop of oppression and repression that made it be, in fact, 'art'. That it was that quality of defiant persistance in the face of the overpowering institutional counterforce that gave high-art music its sharpest expressive significance, its edge and depth and intensity—not some admirable exhibition of athletic skills, or of some elusive genetic 'talent', or the ability to construct and control monster complexities of structure or texture.

But retroflectively, I can now see that even back then our high-art music was ultimately compromised in its ostensibly individualistic, counter-cultural message by the fact that it always internalized, in its very sonic and aesthetic and *physical* structure, the principle—and the intention—of hegemony: expressive value equals moral virtue equals personal superiority equals the right to dominance, at least symbolically. That ultimately counter-countercultural message was carried equally by high-art and frankly commoditized music, by traditionally crafted music, esoteric intel-lectual modernist music, outrageously irreverent funky avant-garde music. And when in the sixties the valorous individualist stance of high art was unmasked as an elitist scam—as, that is, a snobwise road to gross hegemony—that not only cleared the ground for the legitimation of every-one's music, it also destroyed the psychic foundation—false, as it proved—

which the image of high-art composition had provided, for an expressive musical practice based on an intense quest for the particular and the authentic, as not only indispensible personal values, but as possible social values as well.

If we could separate the counter-elitist insights of sixties culture from its hegemonic legacy which took the form of the universalization of commerce and of commercial values, that could give us some real benefits in the task of putting together new structures for the mobilization of musical practice to articulate and confront the predicaments of our contemporary lives. We could, for example, greatly profit from the structure of the rock band as a medium, detaching it if possible (though maybe it's not possible) from its embedding in the culture of commoditization and mass-unitized response. The reduction of the elevated imagery of 'composer', 'virtuoso', 'maestro', 'expert'; the recognition of the participatory relevance of actually present listeners on actually happening occasions—an adaptation of a deep aspect of black blues culture into the terms of modern urban life— the irreverence toward such symbolic intra-musical etiquettes as: stylistic purity, sonic elegance, or any other kind of surface hygiene, in favor of a radical expressive pragmatism going for nasty, or whatever could be deployed to get the point right—the modern relevance of modern instruments played by modern-looking people in modern styles of stance, movement, and idioms of address, and maybe even the escalation of the reference-volume level of music to approximate and maybe cope with what's coming at people from the everyday world they live in—take away the surface-musical invariants of 'rock 'n' roll' that only provide the instant recognition that maybe is essential only to commoditization, substitute the possibility of not even knowing what kind of music you're going to make until you discover what's materializing out of your necessities, open up all the possible configurations of people in which music might be meaningfully made, exchanged, experienced, and you might have a revolutionary sociomusical tool available if you have purposes for which it might be valuable. I think the realtime improvisational soundmaking and allmedia textmaking sessions, from solitary meditations to multiperson interactions, exemplified by the INTER/PLAY cassette documents, are a direct exploitation of benefits made available by the structure and sensibility of the rock medium—having, actually, almost nothing directly to do with the surface particulars of rock music itself—though we in no way rule out any of those particulars from the range of musicmaking possibility.

Now from what I've said up to here, you might have inferred that reality is what I perceive and look for in music. And reality is what I want to retrieve from it. Reality from reality. That's my musical intuition. And all my music practices all my life have been focussed on that issue. What's really going on here, below the bullshit: that's been the urgent issue I'm always straining to get hold of. Bullshit's the main enemy, music's the main resource to see through it with, to penetrate beneath it, to give me a shot at functioning at a more believable level, in touch with my own base nature. What's that base nature? Not likely I could claim any authority of rigor, so as to give you an assured answer. But *I* need to take a crack at *some* view of that issue so *I* can think about it. And I think Ludwig Wittgenstein understood that the more rigorous a discourse, the tighter the web that it weaves, the more likely it is that the universe it covers like a blanket would fit on the head of a pin. I think that's how come a lot of discourse these days, at the entropic endstage of an age for which rigor and technochops have become the leading metaphors, can only talk *about* texts, among texts. But rigorous discourse, and purely intertextual discourse, are going to squeeze out a lot of the swarm of details, particulars, insights, issues, that are indispensible and compelling to think about and talk about and do something about. So I'm going to talk nonrigorously and nonintertextually, more in the spirit of Sigmund Freud than in the manner of Jacques Derrida, more by introspection than by detached objectification, about the circumstances of our existential predicament.

Along that line, I would say something like this: it seems that it is our primal nature to be suspended, permanently for life, between powerful but irreconcilable contradictories. Primally, our pendulum of innerness swings between the extremes of each of our bi-polarities. From which issues violence, our innate violence. Following René Girard, I would say that violence is ritualized, made symbolic, to regiment society, enabling a human collective to form, evolving a culture. But at the personal level, in a post-physical-survival world, collectivized culture, symbolic ritualization, itself becomes a problematic, not a resource. In such a cultural environment, *creativity*, understood simply as such, individuates the process of ritualizing violence. Creativity is, for us, at present, the most powerful tool we have to use in striving to harmonize being among our contradictories. Though futility seems to be ultimately our fate—existence is, evidently, a deficit operation—we still have to deal with being alive: it is, precisely, what it is we have, to deal with, and what we need in order to survive as far as we can survive is what we call our sanity.

Different people have different ways of dealing, musically or otherwise, with their reality/existence problem. A long time ago I would have felt that a valuable outcome of my ideas would be that they would be appropriated widely by other people—not necessarily in my name, but at least on their own account (I wasn't so aware of the hegemonic activism implicit in this aspiration). But now I believe—with no sense of retreat, but more a sense of advance from that old place—that the main value of my ideas is rather to create a space within which I, perhaps, can survive, alongside of everyone else working out their survival in their own ways. Survival and sanity make a lot more sense as aspirations to cultivate for my mental health than do hegemony or dominance. Not just that hegemony is not required for the value and significance of my music and my ideas—it is positively counterproductive to their value and significance in a world I can imagine surviving in, where my example is an example of being responsible for myself, for working out my own issues and strategies, not a model for what issues should be worked out by everyone else, and with what strategies. I have two friends, with whom I've interacted in soundmaking sessions, to our perceived mutual gratification. But each of these people approaches the problem of harmonizing existence and experience in a radically different way, radically different from my desire to retrieve reality from reality, and radically different from one another. The young one's way is to derive transcendent fantasy from grungy reality: everywhere he goes in the world, he experiences the ordinary or extraordinary data of experience fully and meaningfully as an imaginary life of an imagined creature in a transcendental world. No accident that he adheres to religious practices which stem from the perception that the external senseworld is illusory, and which posit another world, unsensable except through strenuous detachment, discipline, and visioning, as real. The older one creates an intense reality of his own for himself, creates himself as himself in intense real experience, out of a white-hot processing of grungy bits of fantasy material: in a cleared-out hermetic space, mostly contained within the space of his own house, transactions with a sound, a thought, an image, a dog, a teddybear, become transformed into deep and transcendent realities, can create experience to be experienced as and by who he, himself as himself, really is. For me, it's different. I come into every situation in my own name, on my own account, as my actual normal self, as myself experiencing sound, experiencing you, as yourself, and discovering with you what, unexpectingly, we each can really be, and what we can actually be for one another.

The crucial point is that as far as I am concerned there is no way that their habits are not as right for them, as rational and demanding of acknowledgment and support, as mine are for me. Nor does any of our ways have anything implicitly to do with energies of hegemony, or selling anything within commodity culture. Moreover, the medium of interactive sessions seems to enable all of us, concurrently and interactively, to pursue our divergent agendas in mutual harmony and even with mutual support. This is the most acute and particular principle I have taken to guide my activities as a maker of social structures for music doing, thinking, and learning. It is the main guiding principle of Music Program Zero, our program of holistic music study at Bard College. It precludes judgment. It precludes predetermination of content, style, and direction of energy flow. It precludes hierarchization of persons and the enforcement of authority or status. When I ask what kind of a world I want to live in, and how my music, and what kind of music it is, relates to and contributes to building some kind of a world, I know clearly that I should be using particular rather than universal pronouns, first person and second person singular and plural: me, you, us. For the sense I am making, if I am going to make any sense, depends crucially on exactly who—what real, individual persons, that is—I am directly implicating in my attention, and addressing with my thoughts.

I end with a videotape, which documents one recent configuration of sociotextual occasionmaking structure:

Though it happened in a public place, it wasn't a performance.

There is no composer.

What it is is a setup for an occasion of interaction: four people given a stimulus space for realtime painting, a way of responding to, interacting with, listening to, some sound on tape. The initial tapesound is a solo session done on piano in my house, thinking about and imaging Sarah Vaughan right after I heard she had died.

The videotape was made at Bowling Green State University in Ohio last week: three of the people painting are from Bard College (members of the Bard Composers' Ensemble); one is a student, one is an alumna, one is a professor; the other painter is an art therapist who works in Bowling Green.

ON BEING A COMPOSER

Four eminent composers, Milton Babbitt, John Cage, Iannis Xenakis, and Robert Erickson, discuss their experiences as people who are composers. Babbitt's article was written for a forum in *Perspectives of New Music* called "Being a Composer in America"; hence its wry title. Babbitt is, of course, the leader of American Serialism and a brilliant music theorist and polymath whose thinking and teaching have had an enormous influence on the development of art music in America, especially during the 1950s, 1960s, and 1970s. Cage invented a kind of Zen, non-music music, or "chance" music, from which the intention of the composer is to be eliminated. His brilliant figure, full of fascinating contradictions, ensured a lasting presence for the traditions of Dada and Zen in American and European music. Xenakis uses chance in his compositions in an entirely different way. Coming from a background in engineering and architecture, Xenakis initially set up a realm of mathematically controlled stochastic music in the 1950s as a reaction against serialism. In more recent years, he has emphasized the role of music inspiration and creativity in the composition of even the most mathematical of musics. Erickson is an American composer, something of a maverick, whose approach to music includes a focus on sound timbre and speech sounds.

For those who may be stimulated to learn more about these composers, *Perspectives of New Music* has published special forums on Babbitt ("Sounds and Words" in vol. 14, no. 2 and 15, no. 1), on Cage ("In Memoriam," beginning with vol. 31, no. 2), on Xenakis (vol. 25), and on Erickson (vol. 26, no. 2), in addition to numerous articles outside these special forums.

On Having Been
and Still Being
an American Composer

Milton Babbitt

IF COMPOSERS OF a certain age, who began to come of age during the dark age of the nineteen-thirties, are less disinclined to think of themselves as American composers, except as a matter of birth or citizenship, than they were half a century ago, at that time-point even innocent invocations of nationalism carried frightening intimations of the violent irrationalities which threatened to destroy the musical world and—even—the unmusical world. While we could understand the feelings of resentment and frustration of the generation of composers just preceding ours, induced by the range of professional indignities to which they were exposed, from patronization to injustice, such extremes of xenophobia as that reflected by Wallingford Riegger's declaration that he would not shake hands with Stravinsky because, according to Riegger, were it not for the publicity (presumably unwarranted) showered upon Stravinsky, in Riegger's words: "my friend, John J. Becker would be recognized as the great twentieth-century neo-classic composer," seemed a bit excessive. More characteristic was the response of such composers as Walter Piston and Virgil Thomson to the question "What is American Music?," a response meant to defuse and dismiss; it was, simply, that American music was music (any music) written by an American. The expected, even suggested, responses that "American music" was "syncopated" (as if Jonny Brahms hadn't *spielt auf*) or "optimistic" (although we had been led to believe that happy days already were here again) survived only in the linguistic limbo of journalism.

The presence of ever increasing numbers of European musicians among us deprovincialized us by their presence and denationalized us by our awareness of the causes of this presence, even though even some of them transported such already familiar depreciations of American music as: "Of course, Gershwin is the best American composer; of course, he's not *really* a composer, but that's American music for you." And this proposition has persisted down through the intervening decades, with only the composer's name changed to protect the insult's contemporaneity. But the newly arrived composers had their own moments of apprehension in the face of an inadvertent nationalism when "The Composers Organize. A Proclamation" appeared in *Modern Music* in 1938, and began: "The American Composer of Serious Music...." At that time, the word "serious" apparently offended no-one, but the word "American" suggested to some a nationalistic protectionism designed to exclude. It was not so intended, but rather was designed to create a shared community of needs and interests, not of musical dispositions or national origins. The word "organize" did smack of the politics to which some paid lip service, but which was scarcely an American phenomenon and hardly as unanimous as retrospective reporting would have one (and I hope no more than one) believe. Even I have suffered an embarrassing misrepresentation in this regard, to the point of my having considered suing, for defamation of musical character, the publisher of *Serenading the Reluctant Eagle,* whose author states on page 52): "In 1941, Milton Babbitt received the Bearns Prize for his *Music for the Masses.*" In pursuit of his ideological thesis, the author quotes me accurately as having written: "This work was a *pièce d'occasion* which embodied idiomatic conservatism...." But the correct title of the work in question is *Music for the Mass,* an *a capella* setting of sections of the Ordinary (does this make it proletarian?) of the Mass, and the only political influence and intent were academic politics. In a slightly different vein, but one not unrelated to the present issue, the volume in question (the questionable volume) continues: "In the fifties, when composers like Carter and Babbitt would hold sway, a new internationalism replaced the commitment to things American." Would that I had known over whom or what I held sway, for I surely couldn't infer it from the number or venues of my performances, publications, or recordings, or my inability to secure a mere Guggenheim fellowship. However, I should add that I have decided to abstain from legal action since the publisher of this volume also has published the English translation of Schenker's *Counterpoint*, and Schenker's proletarian sympathies were minimal. And the offending book does reprint the observation of Richard Franko Goldman that a "piece needs, for a smashing success in our concert halls, an admixture of witlessness and vulgarity . . . ," which provides at least one reason why I never undertook a "Music for the Masses."

Perhaps the composer who is least likely to be mindful of or at least needs to be reminded of his Americanism is one who grew up and (since so much of what we are is what we were) had his musical personality forever formed far from the metropolitan centers of official musical cultures, in faraway places where the music worlds of Chopin and Stravinsky were no more or less exotic or foreign or even chronologically removed than the Broadway or Hollywood of Ray Henderson and Harry Warren. And so, later, the composers from abroad seemed little more foreign than their American counterparts; often, even their English seemed only a bit less native. But the differences between our American and their European relation to music, to musical composition, particularly to those of the past, were just substantial, sobering, and gratifying enough to remind us that forces of formal and informal conditioning, no less decisive and complex than those which determine language habits and differences—internalized and externalized—and their Whorfian consequences, shape our musical dispositions and behaviour. If the number and heterogeneity of our sources of musical education, formal and informal, produce less attitudinal uniformity than that of—say—Great Britain, so many of whose composers for so long regarded at least the affectation of amateurism and dilettantism as the only proper posture for a gentleman or a would-be gentleman (I can vouch for the persistence of this position only until 1969, when my weekend in London involved nightly panels with senior and junior British composers who, within a matter of minutes, made my presence embarrassingly superfluous as they heatedly accused each other of "typical British dilettantism"), or of the French, who—according to the recently published account by Jacques Monod—responded to his accusations (in his native French) of ignorance of other musics, other languages, other thinking about music with the reassurance that they were happy and satisfied with their lot; in other words, they were telling him: "We're all right, Jacques." I know few American composers who are superciliously casual or provincially smug. But there are more than a few of us who, not paradoxically, came to feel more "American" by becoming, both by propinquity and propensity, a participant in the ongoing primary practice of contemporary musical creation which had immigrated and become so assimilated that, after our participation had been abrupted, interrupted, and disrupted for a long, long time, we attempted to pick up the pieces, to relearn what we once had known, to reconnect with all of the past and our past as a path to the future, and to forget only how much time we had lost.

But on the Continent the more comfortable strategy was to view the history of, at least, contemporary music as a *tabula rasa*, with its history beginning with them, and the dozen years preceding the end of World War II simply never happened, particularly since what happened in music necessarily happened mainly in the United States. This attitude never has changed, as witness the "critical" notes of an always eager to collaborate Dutch writer who dismisses Schönberg's American years as those of "increasing scholasticism," a scholasticism which, naturally, was environmentally induced, and unquestionably undesirable.

So it was, in word or deed, with the Continental composers at Darmstadt in 1964. The music of the past, any past, was viewed only as a competitor of their music for places on concert programs. Discourse about music, like the compositions themselves, was a vehicle of polemic and propaganda; it was dogma eat dogma, with the discovery procedure that of attempting to discover what was to be the shape of musical things to come for the year ahead by discovering what Universal or Schott publications were to be heard around the world, so that one, as soon as possible, could follow in their wake. The methodological madness took such forms, at that time of ideological transition, as: "if you don't know as much mathematics as I do, you aren't a composer; if you know more, you aren't an artist" or "if you don't know as much mathematics as I do, you're naive; if you know more, you're academic." I was led constantly to remember the remark that the only difference between an American critic and a German critic was that the German critic began every review with a quotation from Goethe, for then, even as now, the only utterances that professed to be "analytical" were sentences from Adorno, characteristically unintelligible or unbelievable. I was obliged to recall the Wiesengrund-Adorno who lived on Sheridan Square in 1938, corresponding exactly to the description of him later supplied by Alfred Ayer in writing of Adorno's stay in Oxford in 1934: "He seemed to me a comic figure, with his dandified manner and appearance, and his anxiety to discover whether other refugees had been accorded the privilege, which he so far had not obtained, of dining at High Table." After his variously documented stay in California, following his New York interval, Adorno returned in triumph to Frankfurt, not far from Darmstadt, where he surely dined high on the hog. And so was the professional disjunction between the Continent and us closely comparable with that between Continental and Anglo-American philosophy; in both domains there had been a few attempted and publicly successful crossovers, but the decisive differences in matters and manners remain.

Almost all American composers act in accord with or react against a "thinking about" music, a "knowing that" whose diversity yet defines a common domain, while the Continental composers share common aspirations, shaped not by educational orientation and institutions, but by "real world" political and public institutions. The Continental composer may be obliged to court program directors of radio stations, but also he can expect to encounter even conductors—for example—who not only share his nationality and cultural background but have the authority and professional ambition to perform works other than the riff-raffish displays of evanescently flashy timbral patinas which make life easy for the American conductor, his performers, his audience, and his employers, and yet are permitted to count as a generous gesture to contemporary music.

The European composer even can expect to find a devoted publisher to relieve him of many of all those onerous and demeaning tasks and obligations which attend the preparation of a composition for performance and publication. Any American composer who anticipates the time when, if not just for eminence at least for advanced age, he may receive such treatment, is very likely to be disappointed. Yankee "ingenuity" has bred those parasitic "publishers" who, with their "reprints" and "anthologies" have usurped, from those genuine publishers who gambled on Beethovens in order to be able to gamble on the present, the fragile rewards of their risks and concerns. These venal profiteers have no interest in publishing music, but only in printing and taking from the plates of others.

The Continental composer may guide his professional behavior with a view to enjoying the material rewards of genuine celebrity; the American composer of highly "cultivated" music, with no illusions as to who are the cultural heroes in a people's cultural democracy, may attain bush-league celebrity, with many of the disadvantages of materially genuine celebrity and but few of the advantages. Our most egalitarian of countries has produced, almost necessarily by way of self-preservation, the most remarkable of elites in all realms of creative intellection, and in music—so micro and yet so completely messy a sub-realm—the defensive strategies of survival of its elite have to be applied on many fronts: against that coercive coalition, that union of journalists, media meddlers, performers, and even (some) music historians who perpetuate the axiological illogic of the European ("the best American composer is ...") with "the best contemporary music is...," and when the shocked demurrer takes the form of "but that music is simply silly," the satisfied response is: "of course it's silly, but that's contemporary music for you. The best—as identified by me (us), without any derivation from the analytical through the normative—is silly." Underlying this illicit "is—ought" conversion is the unmistakable implication that they, particularly the music historians, possess so superior an overview and—even—"aesthetic sense" that they *know* that "non-silly" music of any consequence cannot be written in our time, for if it could they would be the ones to write it. So we who attempt to do just that are kidding ourselves; we should be grateful that we, in our lack of superior historic perspective, are more to be pitied than censured. But still we can only wonder how those, no matter how highly developed their aesthetic and historical sensibilities, who presumably no longer depend upon McGuffey's Eclectic Readers for their literary satisfaction, hail its musical clone as music suitable for adult consumption, and, if their words of appreciation of these works are the most interesting things they can find to say about them, how they possibly can find the works themselves interesting. One can recognize a sense of frustration and wonderment similar to mine in the first sentence of Clark Glymour's *Theory and Evidence*: "If it is true that there are but two kinds of people in the world—the logical positivists and the god-damned English professors—then I suppose I am a logical positivist." The reader is free to substitute for "English professors" the suitable musical profession.

In attempting to survive the "cultural revolution" enforced by the aforementioned gang of many and private and public bureaucrats, we hardly can anticipate even moral support from the most recent self-appointed custodians of culture. Allan Bloom, in his Platonic mastery of musical ontology, appears more concerned that rock music "provides premature ecstasy" than that it is rudimentary, mindless music, and he provides as his contribution to musical culture the revelation that now, as was unnecessary in the past, he "introduces" his "good students" "to Mozart." He doesn't bother to identify the works with which he initiates his youthful epoptae; presumably any work of Mozart, as an historically certified masterpiece, is appropriate, since Bloom's characterization of anything which is not "rock" or "popular" is "classical," and never contemporary. In his documentation of the decline of the West (or, at least, the University of Chicago) he asserts: " . . . formerly my students usually knew much more classical music than I did." And probably also the semi-classical, and the hemi-demi-semi-classical. In *Cultural Literacy*, E. D. Hirsch, Jr. affirms: "What Literate Americans Know," in the form of a modestly subtitled "Preliminary List" prepared by Professor Hirsch and his cultured collaborators. On it you can find Prokofiev but not Schönberg, and—naturally—no American "serious composers." You will encounter Will Rogers, but no Roger Sessions; Hank Aaron, but no Aaron Copland; Jimmy Carter but no Elliott Carter; Babbitt (title) but no. . . . So, I am sadly obliged to conclude that if you scratch a cultural moralist or a self-proclaimed "intellectual neo-conservative" you find another populist, a cultural Luddite, an intellectual Philistine.

I am no more prepared to be termed a musical dotard for suggesting that much music has retreated from the rich, complex resources and intriguing challenges which have yet to be realized and resolved than I am to be called an enemy of the people because I question that morality which suggests that it is more virtuous to stoop to attempt to conquer the masses than to attempt to create a standard to which they might aspire.

If I feel that I am confined to a populist concentration camp under the dictatorship of the mental proletariat, I also often feel that we (I can only hope that this is not an editorial "we") composers in America are in the position of Israel in the "family" of nations; I think particularly of that moment during the "Yom Kippur" War when tens of thousands of denizens of Cairo poured into the streets screaming with hysterical joy in response to the report (false) that the Weizmann Institute had been levelled by Egyptian planes. Why this elation at such destruction? Because the Weizmann Institute represented that scientific, intellectual achievement which the Egyptians could not equal, or even comprehend. In Egypt as in America, there is nothing a no-nothing resents more than someone who knows something; he knows plenty of nothing and nothing's plenty for him.

When asked to identify the audience for whom he composed, the American composer Igor Stravinsky replied: "The Hypothetical Other." I—who have been obliged too often to confess that I try to write the music which I would most like to hear, and then am accused of self-indulgence, eliciting the ready admission that there are few whom I would rather indulge—I am prepared to confess that I, too, have composed for a Hypothetical Other, but—to paraphrase another American thinker—I have met my Hypothetical Other, and he is I.

Tokyo Lecture

and

Three Mesostics

John Cage

The following texts were given as a lecture in Tokyo on 5 December,
1986 at the new Suntory Hall. I had been asked to speak about my
life and work. On the 8th of December a concert was given of works
chosen by me. The program was *Exercises 24 & 25* by Christian Wolff,
Socrate by Erik Satie, *Symphony* Op. 21 by Anton Webern, and my
own *Etcetera 2 / 4 Orchestras*. The *Songs for C.W.* first appeared in *ex
tempore* 3, no. 2.

THE FIRST TIME I saw the *I Ching* was in the San Francisco Public
Library circa 1936. Lou Harrison introduced me to it. I did not use it
at that time in any way other than to glance at it. Later in 1950 Christian
Wolff gave me the Bollingen two-volume edition of the English translation

by Cary F. Baynes of Richard Wilhelm's German translation with the introduction by C. G. Jung. This time I was struck immediately by the possibility of using the *I Ching* as a means for answering questions that had to do with numbers. There were, it seems to me, two reasons for my being so immediately struck.

The first was that I had heard a lecture by Suzuki Daisetz, with whom I was studying the philosophy of Zen Buddhism, on the structure of the Mind. He had gone to the blackboard and had drawn an oval shape. Halfway up the left-hand side he put two parallel lines. He said the top of the oval was the world of relativity, the bottom was the Absolute, what Eckhart called the Ground. The two parallel lines were the ego or mind (with a little m). The whole drawing was the structure of the Mind. He then said that the ego had the capacity to cut itself off from its experiences whether they come from the world of relativity through the sense perceptions or from the Absolute through the dreams. Or it could free itself from its likes and dislikes, taste and memory, and flow with Mind with a capital M. Suzuki said that this latter choice was what Zen wanted. I then decided not to give up the writing of music and discipline my ego by sitting cross-legged but to find a means of writing music as strict with respect to my ego as sitting cross-legged.

I chose the Magic Square as a means of changing my responsibility from that of making choices to that of making moves on a chart that had not numbers but sounds on it. Two other composers did likewise at the same time (the idea was in the air): one of them was Wyschnegradsky in Paris. So that when Christian Wolff brought me the *I Ching* with its square of sixty-four hexagrams I was immediately struck and quickly outlined the composing means for the *Music of Changes*. My responsibility had become the asking of questions. I was able to relate any number of answers to the sixty-four numbers of the *I Ching*.

I became free by means of the *I Ching* from the notion of 2 (relationship). Or you could say I saw that all things *are* related. We don't have to bring about relationships.

I use the *I Ching* whenever I am engaged in an activity which is free of goal-seeking, pleasure giving, or discriminating between good and evil. That is to say, when writing poetry or music, or when making graphic works. But I do not use it when crossing a street, playing a game of chess, making love, or working in the field of world improvement. I also use the *I Ching* as a book of wisdom, but infrequently, and not as often as formerly.

The way the *I Ching* works as a computer musically is to tell me for instance how many sound events take place in what length of time, at what points in time, on which instruments, having what loudnesses, etc. And in my writing it lets me continue in a variety of ways my search for a means which comes from ideas but is not about them but nevertheless produces them free of my intentions.

To repeat, the *I Ching* is a discipline of the ego. It facilitates self-altera-
tion and weakens self-expression. I never compose without it: even when I
follow other "metal balls" (rolling ahead of me on the path I am taking)
such as maps of the stars in the space outside of us, or imperfections in the
paper upon which I happen to be writing (how many spots? how many
stars? etcetera).

At one point during my last visit to Japan (invited then as now by Tohru
Takemitsu), I gave a lecture called "Composition in Retrospect." It
appears in my last book from Wesleyan University Press called *X*. Since *X*,
"Mushrooms et Variationes" was published by Burning Books in Oakland,
California as part of a collection of texts by six composers called *The Guests
Go In To Supper*. And *The First Meeting of the Satie Society*, a collection of
materials conceived as presents to Eric Satie from me, Henry David Tho-
reau, Marcel Duchamp, Marshall McLuhan, Chris Mann, and James
Joyce, can now be accessed on the ArtCom Electronic Network carried by
the Whole Earth 'Lectronic Link, San Francisco. "Composition in Retrospect" has twelve short sections on what seemed to me in 1981 to be the
principles of my musical works from their beginnings in the early thirties to
more recent times. The first sections were mesostics on the words Method,
Structure, and Intention (my intention being, of course, nonintention).
The next three were on the word Discipline, discipline conceived as a
means of sobering and quieting the mind, freeing that mind from its likes
and dislikes, taste and memory, making it subject to the Mind outside it.
The following six sections were on Notation, Indeterminacy, Interpenetra-
tion, Imitation, Devotion, and Circumstances. This was the history of a
mind that had changed, from, among other things, a concern with structure to a concern with process, from a whole having parts to something not
characterized by a beginning, middle, or ending. Five years or so have
passed. If I were to continue "Composition in Retrospect" what would be
the words for the new sections? Thinking of my *Thirty Pieces for Five
Orchestras*, the *Thirty Pieces for String Quartet*, and the *Music for   *, a
work in progress for the rest of my life (which began as *Music for Six* but
this next year will have fourteen parts), I would make a new section on the
word Structure or the words Flexible Structure. Parts, no score, periods of
time that can vary in length, a music, you might say, that is earthquake-
proof. And then thinking of the percussion accompaniment for *Ryoanji*, the
conducted orchestral parts of *Etcetera 2 / 4 Orchestras*, and the percussion
piece in memoriam Jean Arp, I would make a new section on the word
Experience or Nonunderstanding, for I have become devoted to tempi so
slow that they cannot be heard or felt as tempi. There should also be a section on the word Contingency. I am thinking of *Inlets*, and even, also the
numbering rather than naming of percussion instruments in *Music for
      *. Making the connection between cause and effect inoperative.

Surely there should be a section on the word Inconsistency. This characterizes both *Etcetera* and *Etcetera 2 / 4 Orchestras*. In the earlier piece the
musicians begin playing as soloists, but move in an ambience of country
sounds if they wish to stations where they will be conducted when those
stations are filled. The present *Etcetera* begins with the musicians being conducted, but in an ambience of urban sound. They may move whenever
they wish to stations where they are soloists, providing those stations are
not already filled. The opposites coexisting. And the other day I finished a
new piece called *Hymnkus*. It is made up of the solos of *Etcetera 2* all
reduced to the same eight-note chromatic range and repeated as are the
verses of hymns but at slightly different speeds. Perhaps this will be like *A
Collection of Rocks*, another recent piece for which I wrote the following
introduction:

> In 1982 I was asked by André Dimanche to design a cover for Pierre Lar-
> tigue's translation of my *Mushroom Book*. This is a part of his series of fifteen
> books called Editions Ryoan-ji, all of which are paperbacked with a paper
> that reminds one of raked sand. My suggestion for the cover of my book
> that I draw around fifteen stones (fifteen is the number of stones in the
> Ryoan-ji garden in Kyoto) placed at *I Ching*—determined points on a grid
> the size of the cover plus the flaps was accepted.
>
> In January of 1983 when I went to the Crown Point Press to make etch-
> ings I took the same fifteen stones with me, but soon found that what can
> be done with pencil on paper cannot be done with needle on copper. The
> mystery produced by pencils disappeared, reappearing only on copper when
> the number of stones was multiplied ($225:15 \times 15$; $3375:15 \times 15 \times 15$).
>
> I have had for some years a large indoor garden in New York. I was
> encouraged by a 20×20 foot pyramidal skylight and eleven large windows
> on the east and south. There are now over two hundred plants of various
> kinds and in among them I have placed rocks large and small brought by me
> from my tours or brought sometimes in a car from the New River in Vir-
> ginia by Ray Kass or from the Duke Forest in North Carolina by Irwin
> Kremen, after I had chosen them *in situ*. Though when I was younger I
> couldn't live with sculpture, now I find that I love the immobility and calm
> of a stone in place.
>
> Outside the eleven windows are the noises of Sixth Avenue. They
> continue all night. I have found a way of translating burglar alarms (a con-
> stant unchanging insistent sound in New York) into Brancusi-like images
> while I am sleeping. This has led me to find pleasure not only as I long have
> in the unpredictable ever-changing sounds of metropolitan traffic, but also
> in the immobile never-stopping sounds associated with modern convenience
> and comfort (the refrigerator, the humidifier, the computer, feedback, etc.).
>
> Picking up *Salt Seller, the Writings of Marcel Duchamp*, I read: Musical

Sculpture: Sounds lasting and leaving from different places and forming a sounding sculpture which lasts. That is what I mean *A Collection of Rocks* to be. It is for Marcel Duchamp that we never forget him who, as he said, must have been fifty years ahead of his time.

There are fifteen rocks. Each is made up of three, four, or five sounds. There are sixty-five points in the performing space. There are twenty-two different sound-producing groups of musicians, each group divided into two parts so that a tone can be made to last, the second group spelling the first when the first is losing its breath. There are no conductors, each group has two chronometers. Each group performs three times from three different points in space. The piece lasts twenty minutes. Versions may be performed which last for a longer time (1½, 2, 2½, 3 times as long as the present version). The musicians must move in order to play from a different position. The audience is free to move about. We are back in the world of traffic, at home, that is to say, in our own time.

Is this another section? And what is the word for it? Sculpture? Immobility? Technology?

My paying attention to slow tempi began, I think, with the accompaniment for the solos called *Ryoanji*, sometimes performed as a percussion solo, sometimes by a chamber orchestra. What I did was, given a metronome reading of 60, to establish a series of measures having twelve to fifteen beats, only five of which would be heard. Finding this direction fascinating I decided in *Etcetera 2 / 4 Orchestras* to go further: I increased the measure lengths from twelve to fifteen beats to measure lengths from twenty-seven to thirty-six beats, keeping the number five as the number of beats that would be heard in a single measure. I also changed the space between single beats from sixty to five for the first orchestra, five and three-quarters for the fourth orchestra, seven and a half for the second orchestra and ten for the third orchestra. Had I kept my notations conventional the conductors would have been obliged to count at a metronome reading of sixty up to twelve between beats for the first orchestra, eleven for the fourth, eight for the second and six for the third. I decided to simplify the notation and make it chronometric rather than conventionally musical.

The solos of *Etcetera 2 / 4 Orchestras* are indeterminate. They consist of one to five repeated tones and another auxiliary tone which may but need not be repeated. I give only the voice leading. The musicians have been asked to choose their own tones but to remember them rather than writing them down. Each solo has seventeen events in proportional notation, space suggesting time, but on unspecified time.

I had the idea for this work for quite awhile before I was able to write it. I knew that a musician would begin by being conducted, would leave that circumstance in order to play a solo. How would he know where he was in his part when he came back to the group he had left? Then in Ljubljana after a performance in Zagreb of *A Collection of Rocks* it occurred to me one morning that there could be a music stand shared by two players. If one of them left to play a solo, the second one could remain until the other returned being able as a result to point out to him where he was in the part. It was this practical idea that got me started writing. As time went on I no longer needed that initiating idea, for the notation became chronometric. But it wasn't chronometric to begin with.

I would like to finish this talk by reading my first autoku and then my most recent one and, finally, *Songs for C. W.*, since the program on Monday includes Christian Wolff's *Exercises 24 & 25* for orchestra. I wrote these mesostics by establishing for each letter of the name a gamut of six full and six empty words and then asking the question, which of the twelve is to be used? An autoku is a mesostic limited to its own words: the string upon which it is written provides all of the wing words that go off to the left or the right. In this case it is in French and the words are those by Marcel Duchamp cited above. My most recent autoku is on a sentence in *Silence* from my "Lecture on Nothing": I have nothing to say and I am saying it and that is poetry as I need it.

Creativity

Iannis Xenakis

THE SOURCE OF THE HUMAN EXPERIENCE

First proposition: rules can only be imposed by the work itself.

—One always comes back to the same question—what is true or what is false in artistic matters?—or to the only response worth considering, to refuse all rules outside the work is to refuse to be crippled, blind, and deaf.

—All philosophical thought, all rules are provided in an original way by the actor, by the artist. We touch here upon the foundation of art: what is originality?

—The analysis will certainly bring us back to genetics. It suffices already to remark that though man's original acts are numerous (as in daily life, the event of walking. . .), the more they are rare and symbolic the stronger is their degree of originality.

Second Proposition: nothing is born from nothing.

—To speak of our originality is to speak of our constitution, and as a consequence of the making of the universe and of its process. It is the same for art as for the destiny of humans and of the universe. The preoccupations of the musician join those of the astrophysicist.

—For centuries, scientific tradition has predicted that nothing can come from nothing. It has viewed the universe as an automation, continuing to exist without a point of return, without a new creation. Suddenly in 1973, a professor from New York University put forth an opposing hypothesis: All the matter and energy in the observable universe could have emerged from nothing.

—I am not an astrophysicist, but, for a long time, I have thought that music is nothing but a path among others, permitting humankind first to imagine, then, after long generations, to lead the existing universe to another, entirely created by humanity.

—Since 1958, I have been writing on the subject of the originality of art and music:

$$\tau\grave{o} \ \gamma\grave{a}\rho \ a\grave{v}\tau\grave{o} \ \nu o\epsilon\hat{\iota}\nu \ \dot{\epsilon}\sigma\tau\acute{\iota}\nu \ \tau\epsilon \ \kappa a\grave{\iota} \ \epsilon\hat{\iota}\nu a\iota$$
$$\tau\grave{o} \ \gamma\grave{a}\rho \ a\grave{v}\tau\grave{o} \ \epsilon\hat{\iota}\nu a\iota \ \dot{\epsilon}\sigma\tau\acute{\iota}\nu \ \tau\epsilon \ \kappa a\grave{\iota} \ o\grave{v}\kappa \ \epsilon\hat{\iota}\nu a\iota$$

"For it is the same to think as to be" (Poem by Parmenides); and my paraphrase, "For it is the same to be as not to be." In a universe of nothingness. A brief train of waves, so brief that its end and beginning coincide (time in nothingness) disengaging itself endlessly.

Nothingness resorbs, creates. It engenders being.

—Still today, through lack of conceptual and suitable experimental tools, astrophysicists are unable to respond to this question, to this captivating notion of a universe open to spontaneous creation, which could form or disappear without respite, in a truly creative vortex. From *nothingness*. A disappearance into nothing.

Third Proposition: the universe is in perpetual creation.

Plato already fought, on a more religious level, against the theory of a continuously extended universe. According to him, God creates the universe, builds it and leaves it. The automaton deregulates itself and becomes increasingly chaotic (this could be the current epoch. . .), to the point where the Creator takes it in hand again and reconstructs the universe.

Transcribed to a scientific level, the anecdote assumes its true force: Because of gravitation, the universe could stop dilating and could commence to contract until it becomes an implosion towards nothingness. This pendulum movement creates the state of perpetual creation.

Again, we are referred back to the foundation of art. You often hear it said: To construct, it is necessary to destroy. In my opinion, this assertion is false. It suffices to put the proposition: The contribution of an individual depends on his originality, his own distinctiveness, even though he is caught in a global and general flux. Einstein would not exist without the breakthroughs of Lorentz. We could extrapolate forever.

Thus opens before us the reason for certain remarkable works, sorts of unsurpassable paradigms (for example the Egyptian bas reliefs. . .); what is done is an absolute. Likewise in music, the architecture of a work, its performance, depend on technique, but also on factors which are impossible to name—the life of him who composes it, of him who performs it, the instrument, the acoustics. Richness elaborates upon itself by stages, to the point of the highest universal preoccupations.

Thought is nothing but a part of doing, whence the absence of archetypes, and a different existence each time. That is, in effect, at least partly, the theory of probabilities: a flux of aleatoric functions.

*   *   *

It is in fact the inner initiative, the transfer to a deed which engenders fulfilment. I am not speaking of happiness, which is a myth, for nothing is absolute. They exist, of course, the joys, the tears. But that is not what should count: They are nothing but epiphenomena of that which one does, suffers, or lives. Death, for example, a supreme misfortune, is a part of life. We sense it, we anticipate it. But we prudently avoid speaking about it, as if it were a guest that we must avoid. Nevertheless, it is there, omnipresent, at our sides. Our organism, degenerating every second, knows it. Now, this definitive disappearance can be transposed in the domain of work: the choices that I make when I compose music, for example. They are distressing, for they imply renouncing something. Creation thus passes through torture. But a torture which is sane and natural. That is what is most beautiful: to decide at any moment, to act, to renounce, to propose something else. It's great. The joy is the fulfilment of living. That's what it means to live.

This tormented life is necessary. Everywhere, at all times. Only, one does not live with it, one refuses it. We surround ourselves with references, politeness, taboos, ethics, for ourselves as well as for others. Or, as a last resort, we spread butter on the psychoanalyst's bread, but what a myth it is to believe that in remembering something, we delve more profoundly into ourselves! The subconscious also forgets. Like memory, it is putrescible. It is not a veil one can lift from the shadow cast by a long abandoned planet. A sort of Hades from Antiquity. In our life, there are entire patches of the past which have completely disappeared, or that we will never find again. It is illusory to think that the subconscious can retain the fantastic quantity of impressions, of suggestions, of fascinations experienced at such and such a moment in our existence.

I can nevertheless ponder: Is it because I no longer remember it that a particular thing no longer exists? The fact that I do not remember it does not mean that the thing no longer exists in my subconscious, certainly. However, I cannot maintain that these memories exist, since they are inaccessible. And if anyone claims that they are accessible, I would very much like to possess the methods for access to them. Because it would be fascinating to explore them, if only in order to turn one's past into a cinema.

The inaccessibility of this memory thus implies that we cannot prove its existence. That is the theory. In addition, practically speaking, it is unthinkable, impossible that the human brain conserve intact, and not degraded, traces or prints of the past. Which are extremely fine and subtle. Let's take the example of our most recent recollections. When we remove them from memory's drawer, we damage them like pinned butterflies. In fact, we replace them with others. And, if we go back further, we realize that memory, if it still exists somewhere, is still more inaccessible, tucked away more deeply. Because it is covered with new traces. Starting from the oldest, yes, but completely restructured. We are speaking of a theoretical view. For me, psychoanalysis is a subconscious view. Moreover (just as other disciplines) it has suffered from an abusive extrapolation; people have wanted to see it as a panacea.

Paleontologist, geneticist, biologist, physician, chemist, mathematician, historian and expert in human sciences. These qualifications comprise the identification card of tomorrow's musician. Of him whom I call the conceiving artist. Who searches after the secret order that rules the universal apparent disorder. Who considers a new relation between art and science, notably between art and mathematics. Since Greek Antiquity and right up to our twentieth century, moreover, certain conquests in music and several discoveries in mathematics spring forth almost at the same moment. And, contrary to what we often think, there have been interactions, osmosis, reciprocal influences. In 500 B.C., for example, the relation between the pitches and the lengths of strings had been established. Music thus gives a serious impetus to the theory of numbers (positive rational) and to geometry. Later (eleventh century), the bi-dimensional spatial representation of pitches as a function of time by the use of staves and *puncta* undoubtedly influenced Descartes' analytical geometry, proposed six centuries later. Direct influence? I do not know, not knowing Descartes in person at all! But ideas cross one another like currents of air. And sometimes very little suffices for the spark to burst forth.

Another interesting example: the fugue. A fixed structure, and fixed if there ever was one, when speaking of school work, the fugue is an abstract automatism, which was utilized two centuries before the birth of the theory of abstract automata. It was the first automaton. And what is an automaton if not the expression of mankind's profound need to reproduce? To project worlds, universes, to create himself in his proper image?

In constructing robots, man took the place of gods. For he felt that the latter were nothing but his own reflection. And now, we are constructing biological robots which tomorrow will give birth to little robots: The dreams of the gods are materialized!

Yet, we always live in the shadow of Sisyphus and Tantalus. Because everything around us moves, shifts, is in constant turmoil. We are not moving through an epoch of certitudes: Cosmonauts in a swarm, we navigate in the provisional, we must reconsider each thought at every instant. This isn't all bad, moreover, for our life thereby becomes much more complicated, more complex, more alive, finds itself all the more enriched. We live more intensely when we must confront swarms of problems, when we must decipher this growing complexity, which is here, before our eyes, hieratic, even if we try to ignore it. That which we live is a bloody hand-to-hand with nature. Which engenders anguish. But, luckily, when we are afraid of something, when it becomes bitter, acidic, we immediately erect defenses. We cannot live without defenses, anyway, at the risk of being immediately annihilated. And our defense is to refuse to see, is to deny the complexity that surrounds us. It is also to create beliefs, myths, good or bad gods. Or elegant theories of physics, which structure our spiritual environment and reassure us, be they legitimate or not. These are our bunkers, our mental machines, veritable automata interconnected with our defensive tactics, with our lines of conduct, with our physical and mental self-protection. So that we can act, know how to act and what to do.

I was about to forget memory, which is forgettable, we all know that. Fortunately. It is even made to be forgotten, it is perishable. For, if we should remember, what with the acuity of reality, of all the past instants, marvels and transformations, we could never take the shock. Memory, nothing but the trace of these instants, equalizes, cushions, lulls. Another self-defense.

But in other respects, one must avoid the trap of becoming imprisoned in memory. It is good to look around, to risk shock, to keep a critical spirit, a power of constant renewal. In brief, a fresh outlook. This risk, for there is one, comprises a part of our existence, just as defense, survival. It is our fate to be destiny.

Society, which stifles us, constitutes an additional risk. It is thus in self-defense that we try to participate as little as possible. So that we can judge it from the exterior. For it rubs off on us, just as history taints the present. Thus, I would rather be outside—putting on the decals—than within—being plastered with decals. Everyone of us tries, according to our ability, to pull away from society and from the work it implies. Work which, for many, is synonymous with slavery. Yet another proof—if one were wanting—that servitude always exists. For if one does not find in his work the possibility of being oneself, the joy—or anguish—of existing, then one is enslaved. And one buys moments of release time—but which are not free—liquified instants of real life, which one doesn't know how to live anyway. Because one doesn't know, one no longer knows.

In his *Republic*, Plato says that a society is just when its citizens do what they like to do. This amounts to saying that all present societies are unjust. In spite of social or socializing theories which seek to liberate humans, to render them creative, to lead them to make decisions in their own interior solitude. And not to impose them from the outside. If only that were practiced since childhood! When I was at school, we were set one against the other, creating an idiotically competitive spirit, a superficial emulation. For what reason? Perhaps one day to obtain recompenses, glory, fortune, privileges . . . material things. Thus, from the very beginning, we do not act according to our own, profound individuality. We must recognize that this aberration, that this false route is a powerful arm of society.

The force of a work is in its truth. And truth is that which can exist without crutches. Those crutches which are often sentimentality, sensitivity, "emotional filth," as Kundera says. Sentiments, understood in this sense, are the alibi of cruelty, of barbarity, of blackmail. Me, I again find myself in that which I do. In movements outside of creation, in the strings which hold it as if in perpetual expectation. Movements of clouds, of galaxies, of crowds, of ourselves within ourselves. All truly creative people escape this foolish side of a work, the exaltation of sentiments. They are to be discarded like the fat surrounding meat before it is cooked. This blubber which envelops the work can also be secreted by our own way of seeing, now: Thus, when one listens to the "Ride of the Valkyries," for example, we should make an effort to abstract ourselves from all the mythology which surrounds these viragos, from all that which Wagner and his crowd have found to say about this music. So as to listen only to the music, to have it within us. That is what confers its value, its perenniality, independently of the sentiments of the time. That is also why we listen to it.

It is the same for African, Hindu, Chinese, or Egyptian art. Why am I so sensitive to them without ever having studied them? Because I appreciate them just as I appreciate the curl of a leaf, the photograph of a galaxy or of a cosmic dust cloud lighted by the stars. For in these sorts of things there exist signs made by mankind. Signs that we must see, not as representations, but as relations among them, without any romanticism. If these relations are sufficiently rich, necessary, and elegant, then the piece is a work of art.

The greatest work is thus that which invokes the highest level of abstraction. That which presents the fewest possible references to representation. In this sense, Altdorfer's *The Battle of Alexander*, with its myriads of soldiers advancing under the vault of heaven, immense, is a much more abstract painting than a Mondrian or a Malevitch, because it implies an effort of abstraction on our part, of enormous reduction to nothingness. We must cleanse it from the historical time that clogs it. There is the true festival of the imaginary: to construct abstractions from that which is the most scrupulously concrete. There also is the force of humanity, which is in its power of generalization, of universality. To see reality with new eyes, that is reality, that is life itself.

Composing Music

Robert Erickson

I ALWAYS SEEM TO NEED time between pieces to do something other than compose, though in truth I would rather be composing. When my head is not filled with music boredom creeps inward and I begin to wonder what to do until the music comes. Those are times of clearing out and codifying, and one of the activities that has filled in the time between pieces is writing. After thoroughly chewing over familiar ideas it is easier to let them go in favor of new notions. If they were not worked over, examined, shuffled, and analysed they could not be given up so easily. But once put into some order—thought about and written about—these used-up thoughts form a platform, a steppingstone from which to launch a new piece of music. Although there may not be many new musical flickerings at the outset, room has been made for anything that might arise.

This piece of writing is a clearing out too, only I find myself approaching it very shyly. There is a fear, primitive and powerful, about examining my composing. What if writing about it might make it disappear? I cannot believe that will happen, because all of my experience until now has been that clearing out, building platforms, trying to understand what I have done in the past, has opened the way for new pieces. It appears that I must periodically get the rationalizing and intellectualizing out of my system, so that musical, rather than verbal, ideas have room in which to move. If the ideas are worked over enough to be packaged as prose then all the better, for in the process of writing they will be carefully scrutinized. The time between pieces—the empty, amorphous, floppy chunks of time, the waiting time—needs filling, and in my case it needs to be filled in a way that invites the next piece or pieces of music. The most important thing about composing is this waiting—waiting in the right way, without fidgeting, respecting the unconscious interior chemistry that will one day fizz up as the decision to compose.

That decision is almost always triggered by something heard, occasionally a musical sound, but more often an intriguing natural sound, something in the environment. In playing with this sound, working out how to make analogues or variations of it with musical instruments, or imagining it in various musical contexts, I may find that it attracts other sounds to it, until a little snowball of sounds has started to roll, and with it the beginnings of a new composition.

I have wondered a lot about this. Other composers seem to find beginnings in themes, motives, forms, ideas about contrapuntal combination; and I have tried to start pieces in that way, without much success. On occasion I have fiddled with theme and motive until I have "heard something," but the sounds that intensely and immediately excite me come from outside. These environmental sounds—traffic, animals, ocean, trains, wind, leaves, airplanes, household sounds, and hundreds more—are, in an exact sense, inspirations and, in a broad sense, the raw materials of my compositions. For I believe that what composers most generally do is to compose their environments. From music's very beginning we have put into order the sounds we have heard, therefore the sounds of our environments. This is as true of the dialogue between the forest and an African Pygmy community as it is of today's one-hundred-and-ten-man symphony orchestra in its superdome, performing for an audience of thousands. If that orchestra is so large, one of the reasons is that the world is noisier than it used to be. Significant sounds compete with louder environmental sounds. The industrial age is loud, and our music reflects it.

I do not wish to give the impression that I try to make my music by imitating the sounds of nature. I have no interest in that. It is the transformations of natural sounds which make them interesting to me. In my composition, *Pacific Sirens*, I started with a tape recording of ocean waves, but the ocean sounds were completely rebuilt, reconstituted into pitch bands, given new wave rhythms, worked upon in many ways to transport the natural world into the world of music. The relation between sounds heard and music composed is less obvious in other compositions. Sometimes the transformations are more extreme, so that there is no possibility of recognizing the natural origin of the sounds used in the music. Rarely are there direct cues such as in *Pacific Sirens* and *Nine and a Half for Henry*. The fact that I need to "hear something" before my compositional chemistry begins to fizz does not imply that a listener ought to be able to spot the environmental sources of my music. On the contrary, he should listen to my music just like any other. If the sounds of nature get me going, like the grain of sand in the oyster shell, that is my concern, not something of importance to the listener, even though I may feel, as I do, that beginning with something heard brings something extra (because external to me) to my music.

If that little group of sounds that I have called a snowball seems to have cohered in some mysterious way, without any particular effort on my part, and without any particular plan or thought of consequences, there is even more mystery to come. As the composing process continues I feel as though I have in my head a cloud of sounds, of which the snowball might be a nucleus or an outrider. Composing the piece is condensing that cloud. At first the cloud is hardly anything more than cloudy. There follows a period of clouds forming and reforming, constantly changing shape—all of this without paper and pencil—until, sooner or later, there is a beginning, a notation. When the first note is written a large part of the composing—the most important part?—has already been done.

How much of my activity is conscious and how much unconscious? It is hard to read my tracks. I feel that I am sleepwalking (daydreaming really, because I am awake) my way into a composition, in the sense that I am not consciously moving in this or that direction. On the other hand there must be some conscious, or partly conscious, control of direction, if I seem able to lose interest in one musical daydream in favor of another. Nevertheless, there is a great deal of groping around, much of it to no apparent purpose, and this implies rather loose reins on conscious activity. I fully expect to get any really new ideas from this kind of play rather than from more conscious and directed actions.

But my thinking hasn't shut down, either. Over the years an accommodation has come about between intuition and thought; they complement each other instead of jostling and interfering. I feel that I am living with at least two persons, the composer and the I who works with him. There may be three of us, if I count the observer who is trying to describe this family group. The thinking part of me has the craftsmanship and the musical cunning. He is the one who looks ahead, tries to decide whether an imagined sound can be converted to practical music making, and he is of course the expert in musical notation, the editor. He meets the world. The composer has no time for that; he is continuously at play among his favorite sounds; in fact he could not create a composition without the full cooperation of the craftsman/editor. But there is no question about who leads.

In my teens, twenties, and thirties I had some tense times over this. I had been brought up to believe that I was the master of my life, that I could direct my actions (and my feelings, this was the false part) in whatever direction I wished. Will power was invoked: it was the key to eating less, practicing harder, learning algebra, and running faster. Believing all this I later tried, when stuck, to compose out of will alone, treating myself as an employee, if not a slave. That didn't work, of course. The playful, intuitive, hardly conscious self that was the composer cared not a damn for my whip, and stopped sending up messages. Without communications to the interior there was no possibility of composed music, and very slowly I began to understand who was the real boss of my compositional enterprise. Nowadays I am strict about letting intuition lead, even to the extent that whenever I have a bright idea about a piece or part of a piece, I send it down to intuition for reworking and assessment.

It may seem odd to allow oneself to be led by such an inefficient, groping, persistently playful entity. I certainly would not drive my car or pay my bills intuitively, only disaster could come of that. But in composing music one's intuition must lead. There is no other way. The job of my rational part, the knowledgeable one, is to make intuition useable and meaningful for the world.

From time to time, often after composing a large work, there is a crack-up. My insides seem to dissolve. Ideas have nowhere to come from. I am a prey to depression. The simplest musical truths seem doubtful, theory ludicrous. Believables evaporate into mist and fog. There is nothing to do but wait it out, but while I am in the midst of it I often feel that I am waiting for life's end rather than for something to run its course.

Fortunately these times last only weeks or months, but a few have run on. Most painful was a period between 1953 and 1956, when for almost three years I wrote nothing. The silence was finally breached by a string quartet—in a rather different idiom than my earlier music—with a special emphasis on color and texture. My scattered parts had somehow knitted together, but differently, and beyond my notice.

I have always been aware of the cracking up, but never yet have I had any sense of the mending, or reorganization, or whatever it is. The cracking is notable for its painful sense of loss. The bottom has dropped out of a familiar mental world. Mending may proceed so unconsciously that one can't notice. In pain, pained, it is hard to distinguish between slightly more and slightly less. There never is a feeling of convalescence either. Malaise seems general, a habit. The only signal that I can count on is when I notice that I am losing interest in serious reading and intellectual tasks. When I find myself drifting toward light reading—spy stories and detective stories—I know that soon I shall be feeling the compositional urges, notions, flickerings of sound that tell me another piece is on its way.

I have even dallied over finishing a composition, fearing that crack-up would follow; and I have tried to compose during this disassociated time, without success. There was nothing to compose with. As I came to appreciate the positive effects—refreshing differences in the mended me, readiness for a fresh start, old baggage jettisoned—I suffered with less struggle, in recent years even with a lively curiosity. Each mending is like a little rebirth, where everything can start afresh, and if I seem to be throwing out old beliefs, old composing methods, old ideas of how I want my music to sound, I am also more open to changes, new beliefs and new varieties of music.

I have led off with a discussion of the intuitive side of my composing because I believe that without intuition any music I might compose would be of no consequence, finger exercises. I believe that a composer must compose better than he knows how. It takes more than brains, or more than the front part of our brain. There is a mystery about that other-than-rational part of composing music, and I would not presume to try to explain it away. But I don't want to surround musical composition with mystification, either. It may take more than brains and intellect, but it does take every bit of those that we can muster.

My kind of composing takes a good memory. I do have an accurate and capacious memory for particular sounds, and the details of the sounds of musical instruments throughout their ranges. My memory for music, even my own, is poor. I have heard recordings of my music at times, even admired or criticised it, without recognizing it as my own. My memory for musical classics is far worse than most musicians', although this deficiency has turned out to be a boon in my teaching, because the music never fails to be fresh for me. The mesh of my memory somehow lets most of the music pass through, trapping only certain details of the sounds used. The sounds do stay in my memory. There seems to be a filing system where they are tucked away until needed, and there is an excellent retrieval system. I know very well why they are so easy for me to remember—I think about sounds a great deal of my waking time. I need to say it differently: I think *sounds* (not *about* sounds). Therefore, the sounds that interest me are constantly brought to consciousness (cognitive psychologists call it rehearsal), listened to, compared with other sounds in memory, put into groups of sounds, and combined with other sounds into textures. I put them into classes and categories, balance them against each other in terms of tone quality or loudness or pitch or some other characteristic. I find myself doing this even when I have no composition under way. In fact I seem to do it for the fun of it. I certainly have my ears open for unusual sounds, and my interest in pawing over the sounds I have in memory may be little more than raking through the gravel heaps of our sound world, searching for the bright one that calls insistently for notice. But I claim that there is more to it than that. The sounds are material to be thought about, yes, but they are also, and probably more importantly, material to be thought *with*. I believe that when I am imagining, combining, categorizing, and comparing sounds I am mentally doing something very like thinking. When engaged in this work and play with sounds I use words very sparingly, though I do end up with conclusions of a sort. At the end of a work/play sequence there is a kind of resolution, a settling into place, not too different in character from the sort of conclusiveness one sometimes feels as the satisfying end to a sequence of verbal mental maneuvers. Neither words nor visual images are necessary. Everything is done with remembered sounds.

The memories must be quite sharp and clear to be of any use, almost as intense as sound perceived. The auditory image one erects needs to be a realistic one, not an abstraction of a sound. If I am interested in a sound I want to have memories of how it sounds close up and far away, in various conditions of ambient noise, at every loudness, and throughout its whole range of variability. I want crowds of examples of that sound in my memory, not some "typical instance" of it.

A portable tape recorder is a marvelous aid to anyone engaged in thinking sounds, not only because it can act as extra memory, certainly an enormous help, but also because it can record sounds under a wide variety of conditions, sounds that can later be compared and studied at leisure. It has another valuable trait—it hears differently than I do. Its microphones are not really very much like my ears, and I can often get help in thinking *about* sounds by being aware of the differences. The tape recorder has become an essential tool for me. I may hardly ever touch my piano—it hasn't even been tuned for years, and I could get along nicely without it—but I keep my tape recorders in good playing condition, because they are essential to my study of sounds. My tape library reflects this. My studio is lined with tape recordings, floor to ceiling, but only a few are recorded musical compositions. The vast majority are recordings of natural sounds or recordings of demonstrations of musical instruments made for me by performers I have happened to be working with—dozens of reels each of Edwin Harkins, Stuart Dempster, Bernhard Batschelet, Peter Middleton, Ronald George, playing trumpet, trombone, flute, and percussion instruments, and several reels each of other common instruments. They may contain demonstrations, conversations about a sound I am trying to find, attempts at producing that sound, the performance of example material I have written—trial runs—with a view to discovering some interesting possibility for the instrument, and a great many wonderfully fruitful mistakes. I have a quick ear for these, for with practice they can usually be controlled, and they often have an astonishing range of musical usability. Once on tape the player can be asked to explore a new sound further. One can name the sound and discuss it as something actually heard. I have my own names for some of the more unusual sounds— "dirty old man," "continuous garbage"—names soon superseded when papers and books are written, but forever my favored usage. Much of the modern extended techniques of today's instrumental virtuosi is no more than the bringing of yesterday's mistakes under smooth, conscious, "on demand" control.

Whenever I compose music using extended techniques or new combinations of sounds I like to pretest the result. Many an idea that seems brilliant falls flat in practice, sometimes through some insufficiency in the player, more often because of miscalculation by the composer. Sketching out bits, which can then be rehearsed and discussed with the performer, can insure the composer against the worst of his errors, and may suggest ways in which he can immeasurably improve a so-so passage. I learned the value of such pretesting when I worked closely with Stuart Dempster in 1965 to compose the *Ricercar à 5* for him. I not only recorded all the sounds to be used, I actually made a tape mockup of the piece before I did the final notation. I gained so much assurance, and was so full of trombone ideas during this collaboration with Stuart and my tape recorder, that I have continued to try to work in that way whenever the opportunity presented itself.

When, in 1977 and 1978, I composed *Kryl* and *Night Music*, two works that are deeply involved with the trumpet and trumpet playing, I had the benefit of a marvelously fruitful collaboration with Edwin Harkins. After years of working in this collaborative way I had acquired some skill in asking technical questions, and in making suggestions about possible sounds, but I was lucky to be working with a musician who was just as interested in new sounds as I was, who often anticipated my suggestions, and elaborated them with possibilities I hadn't imagined.

When I compose solo pieces I like to tailor them to the special talents and idiosyncracies of the player, and Harkins had some very special musical abilities. He had a large repertory of vocal sounds, many of them noise-like, and he could sing strong, accurate pitches through the horn, with or without adding the buzzed lip sound. Furthermore, we were both interested in the pedal-tone range of the instrument, and I was determined to see what kind of music I could get out of microtonal ornaments. There is a considerable range within which alternate fingerings are available for almost every pitch, so that fast microtonal passages require mostly the learning of some special fingerings, although occasionally the third valve slide is used too. Fingering requirements are more radical for the last section of *Kryl*, which is played with the first valve slide entirely removed from the instrument. This completely alters its tuning, and gives more variety in tone color, because with the slide out some of the sounds will come out of the bell of the trumpet and some will come out of one of the pipes at the back. With a fingering chart and recorded sketches I worked my ears into this very bent sound world, certain that what I wrote (I had to notate the proper fingerings) could be played and would be heard.

As I composed *Kryl* I presented Harkins with chunks of the piece for approval or criticism, and I am still amazed at his courage in allowing some of the very difficult moments to stand. Our plan was to run *Kryl* through several performances and, if the very difficult places could not be brought under control, we could then rewrite. In fact, there was very little rewriting after the first performances, mostly rhythmic and articulatory details, nothing substantive. There is even a long microtonal passage that stands as originally written, though when I composed it I forgot to consult my fingering chart, and brought the microtones to a range far lower than usual techniques allowed. Harkins worked out how it could be played using special fingerings in conjunction with a very active third valve slide.

I have tried other kinds of pretesting too. Some instrumental hocket experiments that I made with six players in 1974 were recently carried into a piece for orchestra, *East of the Beach*, and extended in various ways. In turn, this same composition is the proving ground for a kind of texture that I call simultaneous variation, something I plan to use far more extensively in an upcoming orchestra piece.

I have occasionally found a cooperative group of musicians who will run through my sketches even when the notes are hard to read and make only a minimum of sense; and sometimes a group, usually a smaller one, will carry out a directed improvisation. These directed improvisations are wonderful for the composer because he is saved the effort of many hours of copying parts, and because no matter how precise his instructions to a group, it is certain that he will hear some unexpected things. If he is lucky he may even get a completely novel notion about some musical combination of texture or nuance. Because it has been pretested in the recorded improvisation, the composer need only work out how to write it down.

Notation is probably the most conscious, most rational of compositional tasks. There are some personal quirks in mine, but I see notation generally as a simple (sometimes not so simple) matter of communication between composer and performer. It must clearly reveal to the player what he is expected to do, without becoming so full of detail that it holds him in a vise, so I usually feel that I must balance my urge to give a lot of advice with my desire to get all the help I can from the player. The player wants clear directions, the composer wants (or ought to want) the same thing. But there is a difficulty—the music may need to look one way to be clear to the composer, and another very different way to produce the same feeling in the player.

That is why the editing process is so important. It is there that the music written in the composer's notation can be rewritten into performer notation. Sometimes the changes are slight. When players complain about notation the cause is usually a stubborn composer who cannot give up his picture of how it should look. I have occasionally written a piece out twice, once for each of us.

I claim no special talent for, or knowledge about, musical notation. I put no great store by notation that is as meticulously drawn as a medieval manuscript, nor am I impressed by the "artistic" sort of graphic notation that was prevalent a few years ago—visually interesting maybe, but very difficult to read as music. Often these arty-looking scores carried most of their musical information in symbols, created (by whim, is my guess) by the composer for his own dark reasons. Communication is certainly not enhanced by such private musical codes, and players are likely to invent their own meanings for the symbols, or to improvise.

My goals for notation are extremely modest: I want the player to know what I want him to do, and I want my notation to imply the character and quality of my music, while retaining a simple, easy-to-read look. I rarely succeed at living up to this ideal, mostly because it is more rewarding to write new pieces than to edit old ones. There is also a quirk in my notating side that is persistently playful. When I am composing for a particular person I tend to write a tailored-to-measure notation, meaningful for the two of us, not necessarily clear to anyone else. This is a fault, I know, but nothing will get me to change—there is too much pleasure in that player/composer sense of community—and anyhow, I only indulge my frivolities in solo compositions. Amazingly, I have not had any complaints about works such as *High Flyer* and *General Speech*, each of which has a plateful of jokes, puns, and other funning, and perhaps this means that communication is at least partly open and free, or even that what I had written as person-to-person injokes are less hermetic than I thought.

Knowing my limitations in notational skill I tend to write my compositions in stages or states whenever that is possible. In practice this means that a final score is likely to wait until many performances have brought out any problems in the notation. In time, largely through suggestions by performers, the editing makes reasonably good sense, and this well-worked-over version can be fair copied and offered for publication.

There may seem to be something paradoxical about the gulf that separates the hardheaded thinking involved in notating and editing music and the intuitive side that seems to be immune to conscious control. On the one hand I feel that I should be practical; I must do everything possible to make a composition work—come off in performance. I need to be conscious of all the musical problems involved, and good at inventing solutions to those problems. Simultaneously, I work entirely by intuition—it sparks me, fuels me, and drives me. I have learned to move smoothly from one kind of mental activity to the other without clashing mental gears; in fact intuiting and thinking are so intermixed and integrated that they cannot easily be separated, except for the need to talk about them separately here.

The way any artist works seems quite mysterious, and music is more mysterious than other arts, because the produce cannot be seen or handled. For most people the intuitive part of the activity has most of the mystery. There is a mystery, I would be the last to deny it, but there is also less mystery than one might think. When I say to questioners that musical ideas come to me as they are needed I am not trying to make more mystery, nor am I trying to be flippant. After hearing four-year-old children make music everywhere, in buses, at nursery school, at every kind of play, in any and all circumstances—some of it music of astonishing quality—I have come to believe that musical ideas come as they are needed (or at least they came when we were four years old) to all of us. Most people can get along without these individualized musical ideas as they grow older; other needs are stronger than musical ones. A few of us keep on having musical ideas all the way into adult life; we do not give it up, we become specialists—composers. Something may have happened to us that kept the music going; something genetic, the dispositions and desires of parents, or other pressures, other experiences—who can say what reason. Some of us kept doing it while some (most) of us gave it up, but the real mystery is how easily people are able to forget that there was a time when they composed too, when musical ideas came to them as needed, when making music was as natural and ordinary as eating and sleeping.

ENVIRONMENT, CONSCIOUSNESS, AND MAGIC

Apart from categories such as the public, society, politics, and the economy, we wonder about music in wider, more speculative, or more spiritual contexts. David Dunn, in his "Speculations: On the Evolutionary Continuity of Music and Animal Communication Behavior" and the interview "Environment, Consciousness, and Magic," connects music with larger systems—ecosystems and biosystems—in a way that reinserts the issues of ethics and religion, but in different positions and different contexts from their place in Adorno. Robert Duisberg ("On the Role of Affect in Artificial Intelligence and Music") relates to the Dunn articles, attempting to make sense of two disparate systems—human and cybernetic—in terms of one another. Duisberg summarizes the state of research in modeling emotions by computer, as of a few years ago, and makes a strong plea for the inclusion of the affective in any computer system that is involved in making (or helping to make) musical decisions. In her "Four Texts," Elaine Barkin discusses a book about the composer Pauline Oliveros, then goes on to talk about the music of Oliveros, which is concerned with many of the issues raised by Dunn (and in section three by J. K. Randall and Benjamin Boretz). Barkin's "four texts" are her own four passes through this conceptual area, processings that are serial in time but parallel in area, each written in a different style. Taken as a whole, the texts exemplify a kind of nonhierarchical, interactional, improvisational thinking and writing that is closely related to the music reviewed, though as different from it as Barkin is from Oliveros.

Speculations:
On the Evolutionary Continuity
of Music and Animal
Communication Behavior

David Dunn

DEFINITIONS FOR LANGUAGE devised by linguists have generally relegated paralinguistic phenomena to a trivial status. Thus, much of the rich variety of human and animal expression is pared down to "essential" characteristics suitable for analysis by the wielders of Ockham's razor. The narrow boundaries such definitions impose have not only shaped our current understanding of systems of communication between other life forms but adversely impose limits upon our understanding of so-called artificially generated human communication systems such as music. Ironically there may be significant similarities between these systems that could contribute to our understanding of "language," while challenging current definitions of it. The importance of such an interaction between the study of music and the study of animal communication signals addresses the very issue of what might distinguish human consciousness from that of other animals. While this question has been central to the foundations of science and philosophy, understanding of how music may specifically contribute to its elucidation remains to be articulated.

There is something particularly ironic about trying to prove the "species specificness" of human language through human language. Is it possible to use the very tool through which we construct reality to imagine any other outside of it? Ethology attempts to draw inferences about human behavior from observation of animal behavior but to some extent all behavior attributed to animals becomes a mirroring of the human if we cannot step outside of the innate "bioprogram" of our descriptive language. Even though the rationalist view of Chomsky is correct in stating that human language is species specific (grammar as an innate manifestation of biological structure), the same argument is somewhat applicable to the unique communication structures of any species. A unique 'grammar' is intrinsic to a *particular* biological structure and "cognitive domain."[1] This is an oversimplification of something akin to the "innate release mechanism" of Lorenz. Briefly stated, an IRM is an evolved sensory mechanism which pre-disposes an individual organism to respond to specific patterns of stimulation from its external environment. Marler has proposed that such mechanisms served an important role in the evolution of human speech and that something similar to the modifiable auditory templates of birds was involved in both our speech and motor development. How this is similar to IRM can be seen from the fact that infants as young as four months process speech sounds in essentially the same fashion as adults: that is they process it segmentally according to certain identifiable morphologies of phonation. Furthermore, Marler suggests that they can process such speech formations without prior exposure to them.[2] Can such innate properties of human speech imply its connection to an evolutionary continuity of animal communication behavior, and what characteristics might such a continuity exhibit as a more general structural pattern?

The concept of a self-referential consciousness is analogous, in cybernetic terms, to more comprehensive feedback loops ensuring the organism greater stability. The extraordinary flexibility of human speech as a productive system is specifically bound to such self-referential feedback. Since greater complexity results in greater feedback and stability within biological systems, the evolutionary push seems to have been toward self-consciousness. While the recent product of this process has been the increase of self-awareness in individuals within our species, it seems probable that similar levels of complexity, resulting from interaction within networks of individuals of less complex organisms, could achieve an analogous form of self-reference. In such a circumstance the so-called social organization would correspond to a "self." To define complex systems comparable to those of human language would require linguistic analysis of complex ecosystems or social organizations within a species, and not just its isolated member.

Distinctions between human language and the communication patterns of other animals reside in the form of information exchanged in the sense that our language is primarily *digital* compared to the simpler *analogic* structures of animals.[3] It is logical to assume that the more complex the organism, the greater is the need for a more diverse set of communication skills and patterns. In animal kinesics, the magnitude of a signal often corresponds to the magnitude of the referent in relationship to the animal. In human speech the magnitude can not only be arbitrary but irrelevant, and depends upon units of speech that can generate an infinitely productive system. Thus, evidence of a sophisticated linguistic structure originating from an ecosystem or social organization would most likely exhibit such a "digital" structure whereby emphasis is shifted from the discrete signal of an individual organism to the interactive patterns that yield a composite structure. For instance, James L. Gould has discovered that foraging honeybees apparently possess sophisticated powers of extrapolation and can arrive at a conclusion based upon an assumption of pattern deduced from past experience.[4] Such abilities can hardly be explained with simple reference to the current definitions of consciousness and language, or to the interdependence of both. Nor can the isolated mental capacity of a single bee support such complexity. We must either dismiss the role of language in consciousness or look for evidence of a linguistic structure within the complex interaction of a species' social organization or larger ecosystem. The total communicative vocabulary of an individual might be regarded as latent "bits" of a larger logic resident in these interactive patterns, and similar in structure to the productive capacity of human speech. In other words, while the isolated calls of a single wolf are not comparable to the complex speech of an individual human, perhaps the interactive vocal pattern of the pack is and might be regarded as the self-referential evidence of a comparable mental structure. To isolate and study only the individual's calls is analogous to focusing only on the separate phonemes of human language and not its grammar.

To unravel the linguistic code of a cybernetic logic as large as a species' social organization, let alone the overwhelming complexity of an ecosystem, seems a ludicrous proposition. Given the difficult task that acquisition of a foreign human language represents, it seems absurd to contemplate language on a level of multi-species interaction. To further compound the problematics, we may once more ask the basic question: what 'grammars' could such linguistic structures exhibit that might be recognizable as such by humans? This question, however, shifts emphasis from a more fundamental issue. It assumes an impossible objective stance in relationship to an environment from which human observers cannot extricate themselves. Thus, the assumption is not that evidence of such structures should be sought in order to render the intelligence of another life form translatable; rather, such evidence is only part of the ongoing process of discovering the larger mental system within which we are also participants. The creation of interactive languages is not only appropriate, it is essential. Recognition of the language of the observed is only groundwork from which intrinsic interplay may proceed. We must begin with interaction in order to infer language instead of assuming it. It must be invented within the context. Entering into interaction is to begin generation of orienting behavior that includes the other organism. If such orienting behavior eventually permits self-description of its interacting components, such that these organisms can orient to each other and themselves, then a resultant consciousness is immanent through recursive description. As Maturana says:

> Consciousness, then, is not a neurophysiological phenomenon, it is an epiphenomenon of orienting behavior that lies entirely in the linguistic domain.[5]

Gregory Bateson provides cogent insight into the communication structure of dolphins by pointing out that they may communicate information about the patterns of relationship digitally whereas land based mammals fundamentally perform this task through analogic kinesics.[6] While humans utilize spoken language to communicate most things, we in large part allow the gestures of our paralinguistics to express these patterns of relationship also. He asserts that cetaceans, like other mammals, are preoccupied with such patterns but must have encoded the communication of them into their vocal emissions because of the nature of their anatomy and environment. Even though such a communication system would probably appear bewildering to terrestrial mammals, Bateson outlines a research plan for its investigation. This plan parenthetically includes a hunch that this system would not so much resemble the spoken language of humans but rather our music. John C. Lilly also seems to share this intuition,[7] and the idea has even found its way into "pop" consciousness. Every year hordes of tourists descend upon the spawning territories of the California Grey Whale to serenade them. Despite such trivialities this intuition about the potential for music as an interactive language is an appropriate one.

To comprehend the possible similarities between music and cetacean "speech" we must understand the structure of music as similar to a Markov Chain. A Markov Chain is a special kind of stochastic process where the sequence of symbols produced by a system is not only determined by certain probabilities but those probabilities depend upon previous events in the sequence. As a Markov Chain unfolds, its information decreases as a function of the decrease of uncertainty in the pattern. Music deviates from this in the sense that composers continue to insert uncertain elements into the structure as pattern probability increases: continuous elements of the pattern remain highly redundant while new elements are information rich. In what ways can cetacean vocal emissions resemble music and still convey information about patterns of relationship? My guess is that levels of pattern hierarchies exist that also resemble a Markov Chain. In certain of these levels redundancies are assumed that, when deviated from, convey specific information about changes in relationship patterns. Such levels would be reserved for this function while others in the overall waveform could serve to convey more abstract data with less assumed redundancy. The complexity of such a waveform would of course be astounding, and it is just that feature that resembles music. In both systems the complex interplay between highly redundant levels of the structure and others of low probability generate a contrapuntal structure.

The complexity of dolphin signals is further compounded by a possibility posed by Kenneth Norris. He has theorized that emotional reactions between dolphins may be read through echolocating each other's internal anatomy and that they may have evolved such that these concepts take on importance as internalized kinesics.[8] This, however, does not rule out the potential for abstract communication since the complexity of their vocal emissions persists. Therefore, this is another possibility that must be added to the overall communicative waveform in ways that are analogous to the interaction between human speech and kinesics. A further speculation is that dolphins may actually "think" in terms of sonic images derived from these echolocating skills. This may be similar to the ability of musicians to actually think in sound "images" in order to improvise or recall a compositional structure from memory.

The language acquisition skills of the congenitally deaf have shown the lack of dependence of language on speech. Consciousness is obviously not hopelessly linked to the speech channel yet it is very difficult for language "speakers" to imagine what thought could consist of

without its speech associations. Likewise it has been nearly impossible
for us to imagine an ability to think without words. The gap between
human and animal intelligence remains defined by this supposed inca-
pacity even though the deep structure of other communication systems
may show similarities on levels exclusive of words, yet remain sufficiently productive to generate "thinking" processes. Donald Griffin uses
the concept of "mental imagery" to describe a similar idea:

> Mental images obviously vary widely in the fidelity with which
> they represent the actual surrounding universe, but they exist in
> some form for any conscious organism.[9]

Such mental images also seem to be an essential characteristic of creative thinking in humans as if regression to such a pre-verbal mentality
were necessary to disassemble the fixed assumptions of our
word/speech constrained realities. This regression to less inhibited levels
of mentality is what Arthur Koestler has termed "draw-back-to-leap." It
appears not only to be a recurrent pattern of human thought but also
an intrinsic process in biological evolution as well. "Disintegration and
reintegration, dissociation and bisociation reflect the same pattern."[10]
Intellectual and natural history share a common deep structure.

A similar concept forms the basis of Derek Bickerton's theory to explain transformations in human language. He proposes that the origin
of Hawaiian Creole was a creative product of immigrant children who
within a generation synthesized the diverse languages of their parents
into a new tongue.[11] Obviously the non-rigidified mental play of children forms an important part of their language acquisition skills and
may have always played a major role in the evolution of language
throughout human history. Perhaps it is also possible that each individual retraces the mental history of humanity in the same way that onto-
geny recapitulates phylogeny. At some point in the individual's growth,
"cognitive" branchings may occur that either reaffirm a consensual
mind/language path or allow for creative mental play though these
same disintegration/reintegration patterns.

Music as a discipline may serve such a "play" function within the cultural context. While the assumption has been that creative thinking precedes the actual physical evidence of music making, it is also true that
the unique cognitive demands of music as language acquisition generate
an environment for creative dissociation on a cultural level. Music has
long been split between being regarded as a "higher" product of consciousness or a vestige of primitive impulse. It seems more likely that
music requires a broad range of cerebral activity where "thinking" is not

merely limited to verbal constructs. Such integration of mental components into a mental whole is also a *conscious* reaching back into more archaic levels of mind. This may also represent a flexible potential to reinvestigate states of awareness that we share with other life forms. As a potential for interactive language, the model of musical improvisation is useful since it is intricately complex, and yet the rules for its structure evolve within the context of interaction. Once again the Markov Chain comparison is appropriate. It is the specific lack of meaning prior to the context that is essential in the sense that what is assumed are only the general criteria for pattern making, and not signification for those patterns until redundancy establishes the decrease of uncertainty.

The current popularization of hemispheric brain research has spread certain assumptions about the localization of musical perception. Misconceptions seem to have resulted from researchers simply asking the wrong questions while grossly misunderstanding the phenomena they wished to observe. Current terminology such as analytic versus holistic has confused the essential issues. Justine Sergent has designed studies that suggest that both brain hemispheres analyze and that both perceive wholes.[12] The essential differences reside in the realm of data resolution, the left having a capacity for higher frequency information while the right favors lower. The result is a complementary dissociation between hemispheres that is not necessarily based on the type of information perceived (i.e., music versus speech). These resolution capacities signify an evolutionary shift from predominantly analogic systems of communication to digital ones necessitated by the faster perceptual rates of speech.

Julian Jaynes has proposed the term "bicameralism" to describe a preconscious stage of our evolutionary history.[13] This state consisted of linguistic constructs channeled into awareness as aural hallucinations imagined as emanating from an external source. While Jaynes explains this in terms of certain brain-hemispheric-dominance theories (a transition from appositional/right to verbal/left), I find the idea more consistent with a transition from analogic to digital language locatable at an evolutionary stage of gradual dissociation from an *ecosystemic mind*. Jaynes also considers music, poetry, and schizophrenia as throwbacks to the bicameral state. Research showing the beneficial effects of wilderness on recalcitrant schizophrenics implies a similar connection.

Complex ecosystems such as a climax rainforest signify the push toward stable diversification where the multi-faceted interaction of life forms ensures maintenance of the total system. Ecologist Howard T. Odum describes the relationship of early man to these systems:

When man was a tiny part of the stable complex forest, his faith
was in an umbrella-like energy system with God identified as the
intelligence within the mechanisms of forest control, the system.
Primitive forest peoples such as the early Druids of Europe had
religious faith in the forest as a network of gods operating with intelligence. A stable forest actually is a system of compartments
with networks, flows, and logic circuits that do constitute a form
of intelligence beyond that of its individual humans.[14]

Before the shift from analogic to digital communication, hominid intelligence must have filled an intrinsic niche in the cybernetic "mind"
complexity of such networks. A variety of recurrent myths from diverse
cultures express a sense of communion generated by the composite
mentality of these interactions. Such an "archaic" mentality may still be
vestigial in our brain physiology. The need to revisit particular wilderness habitats may arise from these components along with a persistent
fascination for tribal human/animal myths. Could such myths be a descriptive memory of a sense of participation in some larger mental
structure before the human mind developed sufficient self-referential
linguistic complexity to become individually conscious?

   If it is possible that mental structures are generated from complex interactions where new characteristics emerge from the interplay of two
or more existent systems, then I find it quite conceivable that the idea
of the human cognitive apparatus as a unique event in nature is only
true in so far as it applies to individuation within a species, and that this
is only one of the possible outcomes of the more general evolutionary
pattern and necessity for communicative behavior. Is it not possible that
evolutionary "strategies" involved co-existent trajectories where the
push toward more complex mental structures not only resulted in spe-
ciation and individualized mentation, but also in larger mental systems
resident in the interactive dynamics between component species? Furthermore such co-existent trajectories could conceivably result in a serious problematic, which we may now be observing. If an individual species developed sufficient self-referential complexity (i.e., the cognitive
domain of the conscious human mind) to escape the "orbital influence"
of the larger mental structure within which it was resident, conflict
might arise. Unless balanced patterns of interaction are retained that
allow for "linkup" between the individualized consciousness and the
ecosystemic mind, the individualized mind could forget itself as a component and begin to behaviorally subvert the larger structure. Such a
separate mental system might, however, retain elements susceptible to
influence from the ecosystemic structure and continue to exhibit behavior reminiscent of its more archaic function as a mental component.

This behavior could appear intermittently and mostly outside of the conscious mind's window of awareness. Mosaic patterns of mentality could also arise from the potential for components of a cybernetic system to rearrange into different mental configurations. In addition to consciousness being resident in a fixed manner within the interaction of consistent variables, there could exist forms of consciousness that are intermittent resulting from cyclic variables. This would be akin to the non-interactive identities of multiple personality disorders where mental components are not integrated, and separate minds with independent access to specific memories result within a shared physiology. Such mosaic patterns of mentality may explain a variety of supernatural phenomena and persistent belief in localized "spirit" forms. Certainly the agricultural achievements of Findhorn's devas resemble this notion, as do legends of power places and geographic energy points.

Any search to verify the existence of such a form of consciousness must result in a denial of objective status. Since the observer's presence is a further component of the total mental system under observation, interaction is not a matter of choice. The issue becomes: how shall the quality of interaction proceed such that the observer's awareness of the inclusive system is also self-referential for all components? The limitation of most interspecies communication research derives from a denial of this interactive imperative. Attempts to teach another life form human language constructs quickly become ludicrous outside of the higher primates. Likewise, science has only provided small clues to how we might emulate the communication logics of other life forms: animals too often behave in accordance with the controlled expectations of the laboratory. This itself suggests our inseparability from the larger mental structures we attempt to observe. If evidence of the alien mind of another species is to be respected, then every communicative instance demands a unique system appropriate to the demands of its unique context. Science denies the methodology of interaction in its pursuit of objectivity but science cannot be the only form of verity to which we supplicate our knowings. Even science shares a common origin in other mythologies that based their knowledge upon an interactive foundation. The deep recesses of the individual mind were felt to be shared by both the collective tribe and animal spirits whose lives were intermeshed into the daily fabric of life. There are of course diverse cultural examples where belief in possession by and communication with animals and their spirits is a dominant reality. As Gary Snyder points out:

> One religious tradition of this communion with nature which has survived into historic Western times is what has been called Witchcraft. The antlered and pelted figure on the cave wall of

Trois Freres, a shaman-dancer-poet, is a prototype of both Shiva and the Devil.[15]

These religious traditions are evidence of something more than remnants of a naive descriptive language for the overwhelming power of these realities. They are more than desperate attempts to make sense of an awesome world. Such mythologies are the linguistic tracings of the larger mental structures through which we have collectively wandered. Science and philosophy merely added another level to that spiral. Religion, science, philosophy, and art all emerged from a common origin in the interconnected transformations of speech, tool making, and hunting magic.

If there is an evolutionary continuity to communication behavior then the uniqueness of human speech may have arisen from the prototypical seeds of a progenitor primate. This is precisely what John Gribbin and Jeremy Cherfas have proposed from analysis of the research into comparative molecular genetics performed by Vincent Sarich and Allan Wilson.[16] Gribbin and Cherfas demonstrate that the genetic similarities between apes, chimpanzees, and humans suggest that they all branched from a common ancestor that may have been quite man-like. Thus, the peculiar cognitive abilities of humans, resultant from our speech capability, are an elaboration of traits resident in this now-extinct primate. The experiments of Premarck, Patterson, Terrace, Rumbaugh, and the Gardners, which demonstrate the communicative and potential language acquisition skills of various apes, may actually be "plugging" into vestigial traits from this same primate ancestor. These particular characteristics probably proved less useful for the environmental adaptations that the other apes were forced to evolve but were especially advantageous for continuation of the hominid line.

Gordon Hewes has speculated that even though Neanderthals lacked a vocal tract capable of all the articulations of modern speech they nevertheless managed tasks requiring productive language such as social hunting, tool making, and burial of the dead.[17] One explanation is that they utilized gestural languages of sufficient complexity to qualify as a productive system. This raises the possibility that speech evolved from gesture and certainly the recent research into apes acquiring sign language reinforces the supposition that early hominids possessed sufficient mental prowess to develop language before the actual physical ability of speech.

Bronowski has suggested that the inability of the higher primates to oxidize uric acid from our brain cells may have resulted in the lengthening of some direct response paths.[18] The consequent delay in response to stimuli may be responsible for a greater capacity to give attention to detail and for generalized curiosity. Since uric acid is a by-product of the digestion of nucleo-proteins, the increased consumption of animal protein might have pushed this acid accumulation beyond that of the other primates. This event would have gone hand-in-hand with the language evolution necessitated by social hunting pushing us into the realm of a speech modulated reality with its consequent compression of self-referential feedback loops. The carnivorous impulse may be intimately connected to our "speech alienation" from the ecosystemic mind.

Robert Eisler's classic study of Lycanthropy suggests something similar to explain some forms of aberrant human violence and psychosis. He proposed that radical dietary changes in early hominids from herbivorous to omnivorous came about through changes in climate and terrain. A resultant psychic scarring retained in our "ancestral memories" generated a sense of guilt at having to kill to survive. Eisler documents in great detail the archetypal myths of werewolves in cultures throughout the world. He further explains Lycanthropy as "throwbacks to atavistic behavior" where the ancestral memory bursts forth to dominate individual or group behavior.[19]

These ideas in some ways anticipate the MacLean-Papez theory of emotions, which states that insufficient neural wiring between the human neo-cortex and the more archaic mammalian and reptilian brain parts has resulted in a 'schizophysiology': three separate mental structures vying for control of the human organism.[20] If the pre-conscious mammalian component of a larger ecosystemic mind remains intact within us then perhaps its drive toward reunion with that mental structure also remains intact. It may also function intermittently and unpredictably in the sense of Eisler's atavistic throwbacks. The current wholesale destruction of our wilderness environment is also a destruction of such ecosystemic minds that our pre-conscious physiology yearns for. What can no longer be fulfilled through interaction with other life forms is fulfilled through the multiple interaction of such mammalian components (i.e., between individual humans) to generate the pack instinct of crowd consciousness. Fear of such irrational potential within ourselves has forced attempts to "tame the beast" through self-domestication and the eradication of these ecosystemic mental structures. It is denial of the components of our physiology that "call" us back to our reptilian and mammalian origins. We attempt to destroy what we fear inside us by destroying what is outside us. Not only has this poisoned the whole system but our drive to domesticate ourselves and our environment has destroyed the habitat for a part of ourselves that still surges forth to live. The demonic reasserts itself wherever it is sub-limated and each time its "bloodlust" is only more desperate.

Is it possible to establish new "neural mappings" that allow for greater interaction between these levels of the mind, widening the nar-row channel of consciousness to include a comprehensive understanding of our animal side? This is both an internal and external awakening. Communication with animals is not merely for the sake of deciphering communication codes between species. It is a reconciliation with the animal parts of ourselves that persist within the deep structure of our physiology. Learning not to fear that part of ourselves is also a learning of tolerance and love for other life forms. It is allowing the "beast" to coexist in peace and intrinsic beauty.

The desire to acknowledge this beauty has also been an integral part of our cultural history. Attempts to offset our carnivorous guilt with the need to feel a more complete identity with the hunted can be seen as the intuitive balancing of the emerging individual systemic mind with the ecosystemic mind. Hunting magic probably originated from the wearing of pelts for camouflage. The hunt's efficiency could be in-creased by the closer proximity achieved to the prey, but this increase in the hunter's prowess could not diminish the hunter's guilt at having to kill. The donning of the hunted animal's skin thus took on other more mythically potent functions including ritual emulation and communion with the animal's spirit. It is this same process of rationalization that gave impetus to art-making through miming of animal sounds and movement. The flexible capability of the human vocal apparatus to mimic sounds from the environment, including other species, suggests that some sort of onomatopoeic interaction was seminal in the evolu-tion of human speech. Imitative processes are still resident in the com-municative vocabularies of a variety of tribal peoples where the sounds of birds and other animals are not only used to manipulate the envi-ronment, but also as a part of daily interpersonal communication and music making. Obviously in such realities the aural sensory channel must be highly refined even to a point of dominance. However, with the dramatic cultural changes necessitated by alphabetic writing came a shift from aural to visual dominance, which permanently altered our re-lationship to both the external physical environment and our own bod-ies.

Along with this shift, music/dance were relegated to vestiges of a now irrelevant hunting magic. The animal components of our mental structure, however, still required sensory stimulation analogous to the interconnectedness to wilderness now left behind. The old adage, "music soothes the savage beast" [sic] is more in reference to our physiological makeup and the need to allow integration of these other levels of mind into our social and communicative spheres. For generations music has been used to both sublimate and inflame our animal states, but more recently has evolved to attempt integration with our speech modulated realities: widening the window of consciousness to include these other levels of mind.

As these speech realities evolved, consciousness became adept at suppressing other aspects of the systemic mind and in constraining use of the body for communication. Music has reinforced, if even subliminally, a wider use of the body for communication behavior through its contrapuntalness and expressivity. It has kept alive certain neural mappings for these speech-suppressed components of the systemic mind. As an escape valve it has channeled the overflow of our body expressivity into a communicative act, which allows other levels of the mental structure to be resonated. Musicians have generated interactive mental structures analogous to the now truncated ecosystemic mind which may also fulfill a similar function within the deep structure of our individual physiologies.

This function also seems to have been readily exploited by a variety of social and political structures throughout history. The alliance of patronage and music, in a variety of guises, seems intimately connected to the fact that wealth and prestige generally guarantee satisfaction of needs associated with our instinctual nature. The consumer status of current popular music can also be seen in this light but with a slight reversal of function. The profits secured by disseminating essentially redundant sensory data that assuage the need for reinforcement of the systemic mind, are funneled into corporate structures with vested interests in maintaining cultural stasis. Thus, in the eyes of these structures the highly redundant "products" of the music business must retain their role as cultural outputs feeding societal needs in ways that do not allow us to know their consumptive purpose. Since commercial music is a manifested output of this corporate/cultural collusion, it can be used as a symptomatic barometer of current manifestations of how components of the systemic mind are manipulated. I certainly do not believe that industry executives are explicitly aware of this process but I do think that there is evidence to support the contention that it is precisely these mental components that are being fed for the purpose of maintaining a consumer base. Since the adolescent crowd ferment of many rock concerts certainly resembles the pre-verbal frenzy of other primate group interactions, it seems reasonable to assume that socially sanctioned outlets for a certain kind of usually suppressed physicality would be highly profitable.

The actual context of much commercial music betrays a more general cultural trend that has itself become explicit subject matter for a variety of popular musicians. Fascination with images associated with demonic archetypes points to this same need to stimulate archaic mental structures. This may also signify an en masse manifestation of cognitive regression first intuited by general trends of twentieth century art: surrealism has found its way into the market place.

The typical audience response to the complexities of recent experimental musics as "meaningless" is an expected consequence of the more general incomprehensibility that art in this century has pushed toward. The edge of the cultural transformation upon which we are perched can be no less unsettling for a musical audience when predominate compositional ideologies, generally posed in opposition (i.e., serialism versus indeterminacy), move toward the same statistical unintelligibility. More specifically the incomprehensibility of later twentieth-century art to which I refer has much to do with its breakdown of syntactically assumed/speech-modulated language constructs. For instance, the intermittent disassembling of syntactical structures in Joyce's *Finnegan's Wake* achieves a mythic reality as a developmental consequence of his earlier attempts to describe the richness of language embedded in daily mental process. The transition from early to late Joyce is an ever-deepening exploration of an individual's larger systemic mind. *Finnegan's Wake* begins to emulate music the deeper it penetrates the non-syntactical recesses of that mind. The result is a persistent challenge not only to the way we perceive literary structures but also to the familiar way in which the brain actually processes information.

Warren Burt has suggested that this same kind of confusing of primary sound classifiers in the brain (i.e., speech, environmental sound, and music) has become the major issue of experimental music.[21] In this sense experimental music can be contrasted with the "cultural glue" function of commercial music only if it resides at the cutting edge of our perceptual capabilities. Temporary stimulation of the systemic mind by commercial musics seems to provide a limited distraction from our cultural repression but it is this aspect that is specifically exploited so as to maintain the equilibrium of the status quo. However, the challenge to familiar syntactical realities offered by experimental work is thus an invitation to organization of radically different cultural organisms.

How these ideas actually function in the work of contemporary composers is best exemplified by two major figures who, while pursuing very different philosophical paths, have nevertheless explored quite similar regions of ideation. Kenneth Gaburo has tenaciously explored "language as music/music as language," focusing in depth upon the interaction of speech, music, and gesture. Indicating his regard for the mind/body as a contrapuntal whole-system, he states:

> First, no single mode of expression satisfies all that a particular idea requires, . . . I cannot express visually what I can acoustically. But suppose an idea requires both? Since I find it untenable that each could simply pursue a parallel course within a specific compositional space, my task would be to "blur" their 'distinctiveness,' . . . their 'separateness' in favor of a more complex 'distinction' which *includes both*.[22]

In a statement acknowledging his debt to oriental poetry and Joyce, John Cage discusses his own work as a composer/poet exploring the possible dissolution of syntax:

> Syntax, according to Norman O. Brown, is the arrangement of the army. As we move away from it, we demilitarize language. This demilitarization of language is conducted in many ways: a single language is pulverized; the boundaries between two or more languages are crossed; elements not strictly linguistic (graphic, musical) are introduced; etc.[23]

I am fascinated by this similar interest in the breakdown of familiar linguistic structures and disciplines expressed by two vanguard composers generally associated with apposed compositional viewpoints. Since Cage is usually typified as attempting to reject human-made structures through indeterminate processes or by focusing on the sounds of the environment, in what ways can his concerns be connected to Gaburo's intense interest in self-expression and human-made systems? Ultimately both men are passionately concerned with art as a phenomenon that truly resides in the world and not as a distraction from it. This demands that art be respected as a vehicle for social change that grows as a participatory transforming agent from that society as a whole. Foremost in that transformation is the responsibility of the individual to creatively and actively put forth alternatives to the existing order. Regardless of their definite philosophical differences (which I do not mean to trivialize), both Gaburo and Cage address this issue of expanding our linguistic resources as a means to expand our perceptual and social realities. They are leaders in the continuation of a more general trend toward reaffirming the total systemic mentality latent in our imaginative potential.

I do not wish to imply that our partial regression from syntactical speech should result in its abandonment. It is precisely syntax that enabled the productive capacity of our digital speech and consciousness. But I want to point out that we have approached a condition similar to

Koestler's "draw-back-to-leap" where such a regression may be evidence of some next evolutionary change. We can hope that the result will be a resonant interconnection of the multiple levels of mind where consciousness reflects upon the wholeness of this larger mental system. As William Irwin Thompson says:

> Ontogeny recapitulates phylogeny, and before we can go on to the next level of evolution, we must go over in full consciousness the places we have travelled in unconsciousness.[24]

Because it necessitates the interaction of multiple levels of mind, I submit that music-making remains one of our most powerful tools for self-investigation: consciousness and unconsciousness resonantly "aware"; but it is also true that this awareness contributes to an understanding of how "self" dissolves into the external pathways of a *larger* mental structure. Inclusive in this system are other forms of life with which, embedded in the physiological traces of an evolutionary continuity, we share a mutual dependence for survival of the whole *and* its parts.

NOTES

1. Humberto R. Maturana, *Neurophysiology of Cognition,* Collection Two Catalogue (Lingua Press, 1970).

2. Peter Marler, "On the Origin of Speech from Animal Sounds," in *The Role of Speech in Language,* ed. by James F. Kavanagh and James E. Cutting (Cambridge, Mass.: MIT Press, 1975).

3. Gregory Bateson, *Steps to an Ecology of Mind* (New York: Ballantine Books, 1973).

4. B. Webster, "Are Clever Animals Actually Thinking," *New York Times,* 31 May 1983.

5. H. Maturana, *op. cit.*

6. G. Bateson, *op cit.*

7. John Cuningham Lilly, *The Mind of the Dolphin* (Garden City, N.Y.: Doubleday, 1967).

8. Flora Davis, *Eloquent Animals* (New York: Coward, McCann, and Geoghegan, 1978).

9. Donald R. Griffin, *The Question of Animal Awareness* (New York: Rockefeller University Press, 1976).

10. Arthur Koestler, *Janus* (New York: Random House, 1978).

11. Derek Bickerton, *Roots of Language* (Ann Arbor, Mich.: Karoma, 1981).

12. *Brain/Mind Bulletin* 8, no. 7 (28 March 1983).

13. Julian Jaynes, *The Origin of Consciousness in the Breakdown of the Bicameral Mind* (Boston: Houghton Mifflin Company, 1976).

14. Howard T. Odum, *Environment, Power, and Society* (New York: Wiley-Interscience, 1971).

15. Gary Snyder, *Earth House Hold* (New York: New Directions, 1969).

16. John Gribbin and Jeremy Cherfas, *The Monkey Puzzle* (New York: Pantheon Books, 1982).

17. F. Davis, *op cit.*

18. Jacob Bronowski, "Human and Animal Languages," in *A Sense of the Future* (Cambridge, Mass.: MIT Press, 1977).

19. Robert Eisler, *Man Into Wolf* (Ross-Erikson, Inc., 1978).

20. Paul D. MacLean, *A Triune Concept of the Brain and Behavior* (Toronto: University of Toronto Press, 1973).

21. Warren Burt, *Musical Perception and Exploratory Music,* Art & Text, vol. 5 (Australia, 1982).

22. David Dunn and Kenneth Gaburo, *Collaboration Two: Publishing As Eco-System* (Lingua Press, 1983).

23. John Cage, *M,* (Middletown, Conn.: Wesleyan University Press, 1974).

24. William Irwin Thompson, *Darkness and Scattered Light* (Garden City, N.Y.: Anchor Books, 1978).

Four Texts

spec*[ifics]s*   :

The Music of Pauline Oliveros
by Heidi Von Gunden

Two days after

On the way

Elaine Barkin

spec[ific]*s*   :   a glossy, firm yet slender, comfortable 8 × 8

larger than life black&white front cover photo   :

    hair strands dark and lightening
    furrowed forehead
    bushy eyebrows

inside cover white   black   black   white-on-black title
white-on-black publishers info   black   black
white-thanks-on-black   black   white-on-black title&collaborators
black   three-page Becky Cohen white-on-black foreword
thirteen b&w l.h. pages of dream text
        thirteen b&w r.h. pages of dream photo images
black   Pauline Oliveros white-on-black afterword   black
white-on-black printing info   black   black   black   black   black

larger than life black&white back cover photo   :

    back of head   highlighted hair
    boxed blurb   :

   "A vivid dream of passage narrated by experimental composer
   Pauline Oliveros and realized through the exploratory
   photographs of Becky Cohen. The book carries us deeply
   and graphically into the world of ritual and meditation
   that is integral to Oliveros' life and art."*

White to see with, to read by, to make black blacker.

Black for unknown, for eyes closed, for night, for dreamtimeworld (that under world not invariably mirrored above in which "Our footfalls echo on its vaults below . . . [where there] is an opening downward within each moment, an unconscious reverberation, like the thin thread of the dream that we awaken with in our hands each morning leading back and down into the images of the dark."), for our visit with the "psychic inhabitants of the underworld".**

Yet though that World of dreams is unreal to some, Dreams are real   :   we have them, we are affected by them, we try to recapture or forget or understand or analyze or revisit them; their rhythms float and bump and crawl and rush by: they may be our most genuine extemporizations.

On the thirteen l.h. pages, in Oliveros' hand, on lined notebook paper, a dream is recorded. Had the dream text been reproduced in its original length, four and one-third pages (of thirteen lines each) would have sufficed, i.e. & e.g., on seven pages twelve lines have appeared on the previous page, the top or bottom line alone is a new line; on three pages all lines are new. On each page a short stretch of text has been yellowishly highlit. If one chooses to read each page in its entirety, a nagging (haven't you already been read?), stammering rhythm ensues.

Becky Cohen's photographic images ((hands, feet, bodies, Pauline, fingers, indoors & outdoors) (blown-up, reduced, cropped, fuzzy, sharp)), sampled from an enactment, with a cast and props, of Oliveros' dream, bleed off the thirteen r.h. pages. Each photograph refers—subtly, obviously, obliquely, somehow— to the facing highlit text stretch.

Oliveros' dreamscape is filled with her life and day residues; awake she "feel[s] the sensations from the [dream] ceremony and [acupuncture] treatment all day". Cohen's sensitivity to dreamworld evocation is evident on each page.

Read and viewed scroll-like, taking some doing, is a way in; parts of prior images (text or photo) stay in view, a rapid turn we meet a fresh image.

Read and viewed literally for the true story of the dream, l.h. & r.h. facing pages unmysteriously pertain one to the other.

Read and viewed randomly—flip the pages, scrutinize a foot, a hand, a finger, a sentence, a line, a letter—the plot thins, the yield is surreal, all obligations vanish.

Readers of English are but plagued with the reading of English: how neither to read the text nor view the photos in 'story' mode, how to unread to savor essence?

(Or has the idea been too squarely materialized?, a neat well-produced art work, it infrangibly sits there yielding not as much to dream on and be carried deeply into as I had hoped for.)

A misreckoning, perhaps, that Becky Cohen's foreword—the story of *I D* 's occasion (Oliveros' request to have a dream photographed, audacious, egocentric yet an idea not so different from asking someone to play your piece) and its realization (Cohen's process and concerns about interpretation and literality)—precedes the slender book's body. To've been plunged headlong into a mystery world would've been a welcome stroke; save the explanatory remarks for later (or elsewhere).

Yet as both Cohen and Oliveros—in their fore&after words—reflect on their collaboration as forceful and satisfying, ultimately providing each with an entree into the other's world (my critical comments notwithstanding), I opine   :   how salutary were more of us more often to likewise venture.

October 1984

*INITIATION DREAM by Pauline Oliveros and Becky Cohen
Los Angeles   :   Astro Artz, 1981

**from James Hillman's *The Dream and the Underworld*, New York: Harper & Row, 1979, p. 67 & p. 96

The Music of Pauline Oliveros by Heidi Von Gunden
Metuchen, N.J.   :   Scarecrow Press, 1983

"Pauline Oliveros is a disconcerting figure to a great many people."
(Foreword by Ben Johnston, University of Illinois professor emeritus)

"Pauline Oliveros, an internationally known American composer, has been
in the forefront of music since the late 1950s"
(Preface by Heidi Von Gunden, member of the University of Illinois theory/
composition faculty)

Known of and wondered about since the early 1960s; unmet and unheard
until the mid-late 1970s. Albeit Pauline Oliveros puzzles me still, Heidi Von
Gunden's newsy study has hit a spot and filled some gaps. By way of an
exhaustive catalog (comprising instrumentation, manuscript/publication,
premiere, review, and commissioning or dedication information) I am now
aware of Oliveros'

> four works for piano solo   1951-54
> four works for accordion   1957-66
> four vocal works   1957-68
> nine works for small chamber ensembles   1951-61
> six works for dancers   1964-69
> fourteen scores for films and plays   1958-76
> twenty-five tape pieces   1961-70
> twenty-two theater pieces   1964-70
> twenty-seven improvisations   1963-81
> seventeen sonic meditations and ceremonial pieces   1970- 81
> seven "miscellaneous" pieces   1959-80

(the wit and eccentricities of the composer evident in such titles as *Duo for
Accordion and Bandoneon with Possible Mynah Bird Obligato (sic), Seesaw
Version* (1965), *The Day I Disconnected the Erase Head and Forgot to Recon-
nect It* (1966), *Why Don't You Write a Short Piece* (1970), *Unnatural Acts
Between Consenting Adults* (1975) and *Music for T'ai Chi* (1970), *Meditation
on the Points of the Compass* (1970), *Crow Two—A Ceremonial Opera* (1974),
Tashi Gomang (1981)), only six of which—out of a total of one hundred thirty-
nine—are available on disc.[1]

Not to be construed as an indictment of the recording industry. Rather, as
the recognition of my ignorance of Oliveros' prolificness over the past three
decades, my belated knowledge limited to four of the recorded works, two

participations as audience member of "Environmental Dialogue" (in New York City, 1981)[2] and of *Angels and Demons* (at UCSD, 1981), and recent explorations of her *Sonic Meditations*[3] with a group at UCLA.

More than half of her work is conceived with and clamors for live you-are-there presence. The nature of the beast. Or try it yourself. Or read Von Gunden's evocative re-creations, many described from a sensitive and imaginative reading of the score and of performance requisites (e.g., *Pieces of Eight*), many retold from (presumably) first-hand experience (e.g., *To Valerie Solanas and Marilyn Monroe—in Recognition of their Desperation* and *Willowbrook Generations and Reflections*). Retold with a curious mix of matter-of-factness, conversational-teacher mode (maddening at times, flecked intermittently with unpertinencies), a touch of lean language, never either uninvolved or uncritically enthusiastic (Von Gunden, erstwhile student of Oliveros, is no dogmatic adherent), an inevitable touch of hype (why bother writing about someone you have no feel for?), toward the clarification of Oliveros' work and thought, a sincere sell. As if to place the "bizarre", the unconventional (within the context of alleged mainstream Western music), special interests—dreams, imagery, T'ai Chi, consciousness studies, karate, ceremonies, audiences, mandalas, secular meditation—into a permissible (which of course they are) realm, undismissible as yet just more of that inscrutable, transcultural West Coast mishegas.

Motivic constituents in the early works (up to ca. 1961), technical aspects of the tape pieces (how loops, delays, and aspects of the real world were incorporated), level(s) of difficulty for performers and audience, physical layout and performer activity, an idea of the sonic imagery wanted and received, ways in which varieties of "local and global awareness and attention" are realized compositionally are all assiduously attended to (in tandem with biographical data). Strictness of form and the necessities and existence of connections between seemingly random or unrelated (as in dreamtime) events, sounds, props, actions, and format are demonstrated; data enumerating Oliveros' grants, prizes, reputation, and status is proferred; and some "untrue and damaging information about the composer's feminist philosophy" is set straight.

In the prefatory remarks Von Gunden compares Oliveros with Stockhausen since their careers and concerns are "parallel ... in many respects ... yet Oliveros frequently preceded Stockhausen with innovative ideas about music and composition" (is an old predating-originality score being settled?). The final comparisons with Cage, Ives ("but unlike Ives... her works are performed soon after they are composed and are noticed by the press"), and Partch are apt insofar as all four preoccupied themselves with a re-evaluation of Western/European concert music and its tradition. For surely, the model of the Western concert ritual is not the only one worth maintaining and re-creating, an attitude embraced early on by accordion and French horn-playing Texan maverick Oliveros.

Curiously blending the conventional with the mystical, as if to tame (either) one to allow its coexistence with the other, seems to come naturally to Von Gunden. Perhaps a bit more humor or the evocation of a smile that I've experienced as listener to *Bye Bye Butterfly* and *I of IV*, and as participant of *Angels and Demons* would have unbent the unremitting sobriety. Nonetheless, Oliveros' outrageous yet crafty behavior (her *Cheap Commissions*, her self-consciousness, her varied memberships) emerges as part of the picture as does her careerlong interest in the mix of improvisational and instructional activity, in getting others to focus and listen and meditate as she does (and as they might). She found a place in her head that felt good, a way to be a composer, and we with Von Gunden as guide are enabled to learn how she's been working it out.

October 1984

[1]that was, as of 1981
[2]see Nona Yarden's "A Meditation," *Perspectives of New Music* 19 (1980/81): 449ff.
[3]wonderfully documented by Von Gunden on pp. 108–10.

Two days after I'd finished the review of Von Gunden's book I attended a concert of recent music for solo accordion conceived and performed by Pauline Oliveros (the concert was part of "Sounds American"—subtitled "A Week of Amazingly Smart Music"—held at the Joyce Theater in New York City during the week of October 23 . . . 1984), a concert evidencing no re-evaluation of convention or practice apart from the championing of the accordion.

You paid your money ($10), you sat down (anywhere in this reno- vated former art-movie house (the Elgin then)), you listened first to a brief introduction by someone connected with WNCN or WNYC and then—soon after Oliveros appeared onstage, acknowledged the small audience, wheezed the accordion silently (meditatively?) for several moments—you listened to four works for accordion (two of which were for amplified accordion and effects . . . digital delay) (Oliveros dedicated the first work to Susan in the hope that "she would get her grant"). You may or may not have applauded after each piece concluded; you noticed her bare feet manipulating the pedal controls during the electronically amplified works; and you may have heard just how it is that in order for the accordion to sound it needs constantly to be sounding (more and more like any electric keyboard with sustain, amplification, delay capabilities) and heard that slippery fingered right hand playing up and down the white keys mostly of the keyboard while the left hand pushed the drone buttons and the body squeezed the bellowbox.

Titles are as evocative as ever (*Rattlesnake Mountain, Letting Go, The Seventh Mansion: From the Interior Castle, Waking the Heart*); the works were distinguishable one from the other yet each ended in a lingering dissolve (listen to the air you might have thought Oliveros might have said had she said anything other than dedicate the first piece and briefly check with the engineer to ascertain the amplifica- tion setting); each was serious; the concert was real and serious; there was no intermission; it began at 9:45 (pm) and ended at 10:50; you left the theater feeling silent and unaffected; it felt good to be on Eighth Avenue.

What to do, I wondered as I wandered back downtown, when you've gotten to admire aspects of the work of someone and then

discover that you've confused yourself insofar as you've made equiv-
alents of incompatibles. But to backtrack.
A conception of Oliveros' work had priorly begun to take shape
in my head, a conception predicated on hearsay, on willingness and
desire to believe in liberating qualities—and to believe in its especial
relevance for me at this time in my life—a conception which ignored
totally the didacticism and thus confused directed group practice
with autonomous participatory interaction. And furthermore
(mis)interpreted preoccupations with rituals, dreams, meditation,
et alia as the signalling of attitudes toward an alternative music culture whereas such preoccupations have (here) ultimately resolved
themselves into familiar compliance with convention (a concert
is a concert) (or perhaps no outlet or outcome other than com-
poser-performer-audience ambiances (regardless of content or
format: "audience participation" does not guarantee interaction)
seems no longer worth pursuing or was ever intended).

Thus a misreading rather than an accusation.
For whatever I might have during a brief awakening of interest in
Oliveros' work experienced and imagined as not business as usual
(i.e., desire for acceptance, fame, respectability, "making it" as
a composer (in which world—up-or-downtown, East-or-West-
CoastSide)—matters not) was misperceived   :   novel content was
mistaken for re-evaluative intent. Somehow to have beguiled myself
into a misreading of identity.

Several weeks after the completion of the above two reviews I read
through Oliveros' recently published collection of articles (which
span two decades, 1963-1982), *Software for People* (ineluctable programming image tells us much).

Surface after surface.
My soles in the shoal; no need to tread water.
No well-meaning, folksy, artless word is unprosaic.
No article wants returning to.

November 1984

On the way to becoming we most of us try others on. Not
whole bodies. Those parts whose fit might still enable pores
to breathe. Ultra tight fits unintentionally wanted by some
constrain, intentionally put upon also constrain. The longer
the wear the less the bind feels. Wanting fitness at first is all.
Itself gets used to. Until. The want to become again revives.
We cast off second hands exposing our remaining rawness,
selfness. Ourselves becoming again consolidated. Refit.
Until. Awareness momently that superficies may become
our real thing. Fitness is no longer all. When unawareness of
prosthetic appliance environs us we are not us. Then to
divest to unbecome to become. And reinvest ourselves with
discards of now our own former molting. Or refashion from
some scratch never wholly unloosed of old fits. Or invent
new starts. Or even as it were to unbecomingly flounder.
And reimage ourselves barely unjointedly as we reimagine
fitting ourselves all out. Conjoining our unbound first hands.
Until.

December 1984

On the Role of Affect in Artificial Intelligence and Music

Robert Duisberg

LE COEUR *a ses raisons,*
que la raison ne connait point.
—Blaise Pascal

1. INTRODUCTION

1.1 WHY MUSIC IN AI?

Artificial Intelligence is a field rich in potential for both science and industry. But the very name of the field, whatever one may mean by it, engenders controversy of a profound and metaphysical sort, often associated in philosophical circles with the Mind-Body Problem or the Physicalist/Spiritualist debate (Searle 1980; Dennet 1978). The problem apparently revolves around the personal character we associate with our conscious experience of our own minds, and certain apprehensions we have regarding the embodiment of such things, again whatever they may be, in physical structures other than organic ones like ourselves. The intent here is not to debate the Mind-Body Problem, nor to discuss the locus of the soul. It is rather to consider the implications of taking seriously the apparent goal of AI, to construct the closest thing we can to an artificially intelligent machine.

Many useful insights into how a mind could be modeled in AI may be gained from a knowledge of our own minds, and thus AI and Cognitive Psychology interact increasingly. Most of the notable work in the field has, reasonably, concentrated on the aspects of thought amenable to logical analysis, subject to a clean syntax.

However, it is clear that much of our conscious intellectual life, indeed its fundamental motivations, are based in urges, drives and emotions that are less appropriately considered under such a logical regimen: "only the surface of reason is rational" (Minsky 1981, 28). The very act of knowing involves the ordering of sensory input according to conceptual frameworks, but the development and application of appropriate concept networks is necessarily a creative and intuitive act. "Aesthetic sensibility plays the part of the delicate sieve" (Wechsler 1978, 1) in appraising the efficacy of such application.

It is an aberration of recent western culture that has so polarized the concepts of Science versus Art, rational versus aesthetic, so as to render them mutually incommensurable, when they are clearly and necessarily interacting parts of a complex whole.

> . . . The prevailing conception of science, based on the disjunction of subjectivity and objectivity, seeks—and must seek at all costs—to eliminate from science such passionate, personal, human appraisals of theories, or at least to minimize their function . . . [But] the act of knowing includes an appraisal; and this personal coefficient, which shapes all factual knowledge, bridges in doing so the disjunction between subjectivity and objectivity (Polanyi 1958, 15–17).

An epistemology which incorporates such passionate appraisal into the heart of factual knowledge suggests itself as an important feature of any realistic mind model that would avoid a specious rational/intuitive dichotomy.

As artists and scientists, if we honestly profess to study the mind, we must try to understand the structure of feeling, for it is only by and with such feelings as wonder and love that we grow to create within our own individual mental lives the world as we interpret it, and it is through such structures that we apprehend our physical and social surroundings.

First one must gain an understanding of how concepts come to be formed in the mind, and model how sensory patterns come to be ordered into structured concepts.

> First, facts are not data. They are mental artifacts, selected by human concerns and abstracted from experience by filtering through a screen of schemata. Second, this screen is necessarily tacit; we infer its nature only from observing its operations, but our inferences can never be complete or up to date. Third, the screen is itself a product of the process which it mediates and, though tacit, can be developed by deliberately exposing it to what we want to influence it. (This is the essence of education.) (Wechsler 1978, 152)

Now music is a fertile field for such modeling, for to understand any piece of music involves recognizing its salient structures, always in its own terms, in order to appreciate how they are manipulated. Minsky likens a sonata to a "teaching machine" in which material is presented in the exposition and its meanings subsequently explored (indeed established) by displaying the material in varied forms, contexts, and elaborations. The suggestion is clear that if one could model how a listener decides what is important or salient or interesting in a piece of music, where there is no predetermined "vocabulary," then one might have a reasonable model of how minds go about apprehending significant structure in superficially chaotic environments. He suggests the possibility of "future simulations that grow artificial musical semantic networks, perhaps by 'raising' simulated infants in traditional musical cultures" (Minsky 1981, 35).

Furthermore music seems to span an interesting middle ground, highly structured formally and numerically on the one hand and indisputably evocative of emotion on the other. Its structure lends it to quantitative study and yet its semantic content is reflective of our emotional intuitions. An effort to understand the deep and semantic structure of music, the structure of the emotional meanings so precisely expressible in music, may pay off in a better understanding of the mind with respect to its motivational underpinnings in feeling. This broad issue will be discussed in the context of the central theme of this paper, that affect may in some useful sense be considered the *driver* of concept formation. This intuition is supported by Papert's suggestion of "an applied genetic epistemology beyond Piaget's cognitive emphasis to include a concern with the affective" in child development (Papert 1980, vii). Higher level concept formation may also be so conceived in view of numerous corroborative statements by the great mathematicians and physicists of being led to their theories by aesthetic intuitions and emotions, the rigorous proofs only coming later (Hardy 1967; Poincaré 1963; Pais 1983). "I maintain that attitudes do really precede propositions, feelings come before facts. This seems strange only because we cannot remember what we knew in infancy" (Minsky 1979, 5).

1.2 EXPRESSION AND DENOTATION

Music communicates meaningfully, without question. But there are at least two modes in which such communication is commonly appreciated, which may as well be called Apollonian and Dionysian. This is again, perhaps, a needless dichotomy but it is historically manifest in abundant aesthetic debates such as that of Formal versus Program Music or Brahms versus Wagner (Hanslick 1957), Classicism versus Romanticism, etc. The first mode has to do with the recognition of structure, and is akin in this respect to the apprehension of mathematical beauty.

> We bear in mind the feeling of mathematical beauty, of the harmony of numbers and forms and of geometric elegance. It's a real aesthetic feeling that all mathematicians recognize, and this is truly sensibility ... The useful combinations are precisely the most beautiful ... (Poincaré 1958, 15).

The forms and objects that partake in the structures so perceived in music are essentially syntactic in character. In this mode it therefore makes fair sense to speak of "Form without Content" or "Symbol without Referent," and we are motivated to bring to bear all the technology of phrase structure, generative and systemic grammars used in parsing of the structured languages used in computing (Roads 1979; Lerdahl 1983). This mode of appreciation lends itself to formal and computational models of which Terry Winograd's work discussed in the next section is a classic example.

But the Apollonian mode cannot be the whole story any more than mere syntax can be adequate to encompass natural language. Syntax tells little about meaning.

The second mode of appreciation requires consideration of music not so much as one would consider a mathematical theorem but more as one would consider expressions in a kind of language. Musical events, be they rhythmic, harmonic, melodic, or whatever, can scarcely be said to denote in the way words do in a verbal language. But musical symbols may properly be said to *express* things other than themselves, and thus it becomes important to clarify the distinction between denotation and expression.

The logical structure of denotation is relatively straightforward. Computationally the denotation of a referent by a symbol may be thought of as a pointer from the symbol to the referent. Thus words have pointers to their

denotata and text can be "understood" by performing table-lookups of definitions. Furthermore such association is typically established through convention as in verbal language.

Now consider a slow rubato passage in the minor mode played by 'cello
solo expressing great sadness. This description gives information of two kinds,
saying something about the properties the passage possesses as well as what
feelings it expresses. The first kind is clear; the passage is a concrete instance of
slow 'cello sound in minor mode and free rhythm. But instead of saying that
the melody expresses sadness one might say simply it is a sad melody. Is it sad,
then, in the same way that it is slow? Whereas the passage literally possesses
slowness and it literally belongs to the class of 'cello sounds, only figuratively
does it possess sadness or belong to the class of sad things.

> What is expressed is metaphorically exemplified. What expresses sad-
> ness is metaphorically sad. And what is metaphorically sad is actually but
> not literally sad, i.e., comes under a transferred application of some label
> coextensive with "sad." Thus what is expressed is possessed (Goodman
> 1976, 85).

If expression is seen to be the possession of a set of attributes, then determination of what is expressed is like a recognition problem achieved by measuring a
match or fit between the strictly musical properties (i.e., pitch structure,
rhythmic structure, etc.) of the expressive object and the properties of the
emotion which the object possesses and expresses.

1.3 AFFECTIVE MEANING, MEMORY AND HEURISTICS

This suggests that cognitive appreciation of musical semantics requires *a
priori* knowledge of the emotional world, that is, a known set of expressible
emotional properties, in the same way that understanding stories and text in
natural language requires knowledge of the world in the form of scripts or
some other template (Schank 1978). Of the Yale centered group doing
research in natural language processing, Wendy Lehnert's work on narrative
comprehension and summarization succeeds remarkably well by being driven
by a system of "affect state" relations. The emotional states and motivations
of characters are the structural nodes in a network which comes to represent
the meaning of the text. From her striking empirical demonstration of how
cleanly the concepts imparted by a narrative text can be organized by simple
affect structures it is a short step to envisioning such affective structures as
actual generators of concepts. Her affect-driven knowledge representation is
highly suggestive and could be extended to an application to music.

The notion that the meaning of a narrative can be embodied in a graphic network of connected affect nodes, and that useful summarization and question answering can be achieved by means of traversal of such a graph is similar to Minsky's idea that meaning arises out of a kind of network of associations. "Something has a 'meaning' only when it has a few; if we understood something just one way we would not understand it at all. That is why the seekers of the 'real' meanings never find them" (Minsky 1981, 29). Minsky is one of very few authors willing to address the question directly, and comes to describe the networked character of a mental state by the metaphor of a "society" of mental "agents," with memories described as partial traces of the network (K-lines) (Minsky 1979). Agents are seen to exist in a hierarchy being driven by requests from above and responses from below. *"The recognition of what events should be considered 'memorable' . . . must usually be made by some other agency that has engaged the present one for a purpose"* (Minsky's italics). The "other agency" could be a "feeling agent" expressing our disposition toward a given configuration of the network, that is, whether a situation is worth remembering.

Affect would function, then, as a system of heuristics regarding the appropriateness of executing storage and abstraction operations. In a graphic and geometric visualization, one might think of an affect state as a temporal and "spatial" pattern (where "spatial" dimensions may correspond to appropriate parameters such as "tension," "activity," "direction," or "weight") whose form could be recognized, in the same way that the emotional referents expressed by music might be recognized. This structure corresponds in some clear way to the configuration of the network representing the overall mental state, and in a crude first model could be derived by some simple transform. The abstraction involved in such a transform arises almost automatically out of Minsky's "Level-band Principle" and is related to the function of metaphorical transference as described in the process of musical expression.

Once abstracted from the network representing the mental state and recognized, the feeling state, functioning like a "hunch" or a "gut feeling," figures prominently into the preconditions of any heuristic to determine appropriate subsequent action, in particular actions pertaining to laying down memory traces or forming new concepts. So it seems natural in conclusion to consider how such "feeling heuristics" apply to machine learning and concept formation. Doug Lenat's work on the nature of heuristics (Lenat 1983a; Lenat 1983b) yields remarkably successful learning behavior as demonstrated by the undeniably creative concept formation performed by his EURISKO and AM programs. His work will be discussed in the final section of this paper with an eye to what insights might be gained from acknowledging the prominence of emotions in guiding human heuristic behavior and how structural modeling of emotions, guided by what we learn from musical structure, relates to his "heuristics about heuristics."

2. WINOGRAD: SYNTACTIC AND SEMANTIC INTERACTION

Terry Winograd's program to analyze tonal harmony has the virtue of restricting its domain to a tractable subproblem within music theory while demonstrating the power of a methodology with much broader applicability. Indeed, much of a vastly more complete and detailed current theory of music is acknowledged to have analogs in such methodology (Lerdahl and Jackendoff 1983).

2.1 A TERSE OUTLINE OF SYSTEMIC GRAMMAR

The type of grammar chosen to represent and analyze harmony is known as *systemic* and is apparently not common in computer science applications. Systemic grammar differs from phrase-structure and transformational grammar both in the history of its development and its intent, which is reflected in its formal structure. It is an outgrowth of concerns in anthropology and sociology (Halliday 1981; Halliday 1978; Kress 1976; deJoia and Stenton 1980) rather than mathematics or formal logic. Its motivations lie in consideration of language as a social activity, to which concerns about the nature of grammaticality are adjunct.

Systemic grammar is based on the notion of choice embodied in the concept of a *system*, which is a set of choices of *features* together with a condition of entry, and is notated graphically in two dimensions by a *system network* (see figure 2-1). Any sentence or item in the language may be described by the set of choices that have been selected in its realization. A set of *realization rules* is associated with each feature choice, pertaining to what functions and categories must be present when a given feature is chosen as well as requirements of agreement and ordering of constituents. These rules are less precise and formal than the generative rules of immediate constituent and transformational grammars, being more of the character of consistency checks than actual effective production rules. The features chosen are said to be realized as structures represented by the linear sequence of constituents.

> Since systemic grammar is not centered on a concern with formal rules, the general attitude is that it is better to say something less precise about an important aspect of language than to ignore it completely because it does not yield to the available formal tools. It is possible to provide descriptions that are structured (i.e., they include formal representations like system networks, not just descriptive text) but that are not generative in the strong sense of providing rigorous rules. Much of systemic grammar follows this course (Winograd 1983, 277–78).

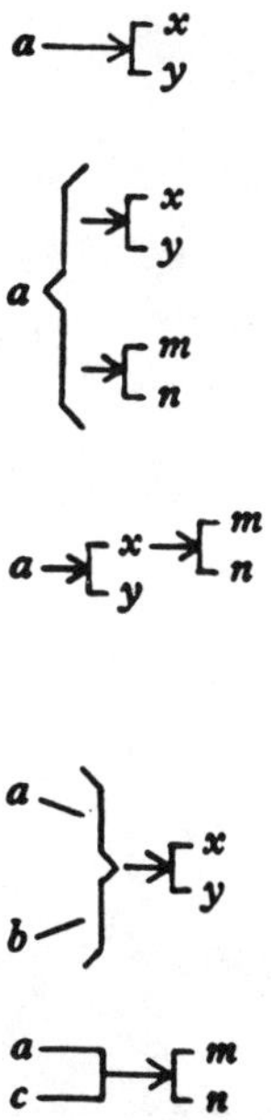

$a \longrightarrow \begin{bmatrix} x \\ y \end{bmatrix}$

there is a system x/y with entry condition a (if a, then either x or y)

$a \begin{cases} \rightarrow \begin{bmatrix} x \\ y \end{bmatrix} \\ \\ \rightarrow \begin{bmatrix} m \\ n \end{bmatrix} \end{cases}$

there are two simultaneous systems x/y and m/n, both having entry condition a (if a, then both either x or y and, independently, either m or n)

$a \rightarrow \begin{bmatrix} x \\ y \end{bmatrix} \rightarrow \begin{bmatrix} m \\ n \end{bmatrix}$

there are two systems x/y and m/n, ordered in dependence so that m/n has entry condition x and x/y has entry condition a (if a then either x or y, and if x, then either m or n)

$\left. \begin{matrix} a \diagdown \\ \\ b \diagup \end{matrix} \right\} \rightarrow \begin{bmatrix} x \\ y \end{bmatrix}$

there is a system x/y with compound entry condition, conjunction of a and b (if both a and b then either x or y)

$\begin{matrix} a \\ c \end{matrix} \rightarrow \begin{bmatrix} m \\ n \end{bmatrix}$

there is a system m/n with two possible entry conditions, union of a and c (if either a or c, or both, then either m or n) .

FIGURE 2-1: NOTATIONAL CONVENTIONS IN A SYSTEM NETWORK
(KRESS 1976)

The power of systemic grammar lies in its recognition that the form of a sentence may be the result of choices made within several systems operating simultaneously in orthogonal dimensions, as contrasted to the usual generative grammar in which a constituent is associated with exactly one path in the derivation tree. (Even though in a transformational grammar the role of a constituent may change under transformation, still at any point in the derivation all relationships are taken to be inferable from the single constituent tree structure at that point.) The advantage of this type of grammar is in the close connection between the syntax and semantics, as some choices along certain dimensions can correspond closely to the meaning of the sentence.

2.2 A SYSTEMIC GRAMMAR FOR TONAL HARMONY

The grammar consists of five ranks of system networks: Composition, Tonality, Chord Group, Chord, and Note. The system networks and realization rules for Tonality and Chord are reproduced in figures 2-2 and 2-3 by way of

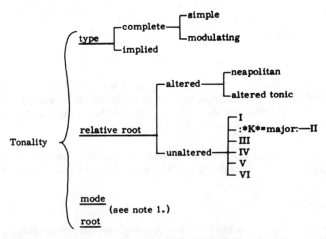

Note 1. The choice of features in the mode and root systems are dependent in a complex way on the choice of relative root and on *K*. This dependence is most easily expressed in the form of a table, Table I, but the status in the grammar is the same as dependencies indicated with lines and brackets.

Realizations:

Tonality : : +dominant; +(sec). . .(sec); (sec)⌒dominant
complete : : +tonic; dominant⌒tonic
simple : : tonic⌒¥
modulating : : +sec₂⌒(sec₂)⌒. . .⌒(sec₂); tonic⌒sec₂
implied : : +domprep; domprep dominant; dominant ≜Chord Group direct
relative root,   The realizations of the relative root system act through
mode, root : : the connections with the mode and root systems to pro-
                duce *K* as indicated in Table I.

Constituents:

dominant : : Tonality$_{simple, V}$ or Chord Group$_{V \text{ or } VII}$
sec : : Tonality or Chord Group
tonic : : Chord Group$_{I, direct}$
sec₂ : : Tonality$_{simple \text{ or } implied}$ or Chord Group
domprep : : Chord Group$_{II \text{ or } IV \text{ or } VI}$

FIGURE 2-2: SYSTEM NETWORK AND REALIZATION RULES FOR A TONALITY
(WINOGRAD 1968)

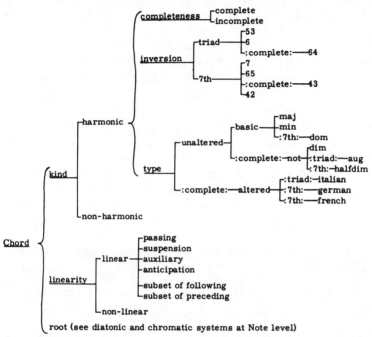

Realizations:

    completeness, inversion, type : : These three systems are realized jointly in the specification of notes which serve in the constituent structure. Completeness and inversion function together to determine the diatonic values of these notes. The realization is a list of diatonic intervals above the bass, where each note must form one of these intervals, and there must be at least one representative for each interval. This pair of systems also specifies which note has the subscript root, by specifying its interval above the bass. The details of these facts are included in Table III. All three systems jointly determine the set of chromatic intervals in the chord in the same way. The facts are included in Table IV, where empty entries appear wherever the particular combination of features is precluded by the system network.

    non-harmonic : : This is a default term, realized by the presence of a structure which cannot be produced by any combination of features depending on harmonic.

    linear : : This is a context-sensitive realization, which limits the notes according to the notes of the following (FOL) and preceding (PREC) chords. Details are in Table V.

    non-linear : : A default term.

    root : : The selection of features is passed down to the constituent $\text{Note}_{\text{root}}$ as a restriction.

Constituents:

    N : : Note

FIGURE 2-3: SYSTEM NETWORK AND REALIZATION RULES FOR A CHORD
(WINOGRAD 1968)

example. Within the grammar though, it is clear that the structures so described are ambiguous at every level, and it is this that makes the problem interesting. For example a chord sequence vi $\to$ V^6 $\to$ I in C-major might also be ii $\to$ I^6 $\to$ IV in G-major or I $\to$ III in a-minor with a passing lowered-VII^6. The only way to resolve such multiplicities of interpretation is in the context of the entire piece without which the full relative function of the chords cannot be known. A music theorist in rendering a "reading" of a composition that he feels expresses its basic logic is guided by considerations of clarity and economy of the parse (where an economic parsing would have a minimum average depth of nesting of secondary tonalities throughout the composition). For the purposes of this implementation, Winograd combined all such considerations into a very rough numerical value associated with a given parsing he calls a "plausibility value." An integer value is assigned to each possible sequence of two adjacent harmonies according to the following arbitrary scheme.

> 0: authentic cadence, opening progression, dominant preparation, dominant substitution
>
> 1: fifth progression, plagal cadence, deceptive cadence, triadic outline
>
> 3: for any chord interpreted as a linear or passing chord
>
> 5: confusion of tonal structure, that is, anything other than V or IV going to I
>
> 4: anything not covered above.

The rules are ordered so that if anything higher in the list applies the others are ignored. Clearly the lower values imply a more "plausible" parse and the intuition is that the progressions associated with values 0 and 1 are the progressions with clear structural functions that tend to establish a tonal center.

As the parsing proceeds, a separate "path" is constructed for each of the different possible parsings of the string encountered up to that point. That is, in the spirit of the systemic grammar a number of different tonal systems are considered in parallel. A disadvantage is that the number of paths considered can grow exponentially in the length of the string. In order to limit this growth, advantage is taken of the fact that modulatory progressions are rare compared to complete cadences, so the string is scanned in reverse order from right to left, and preparations are preferentially considered in terms of where they arrive. Further reductions are achieved by eliminating parse trees that are redundant in the sense that they arrive at the same analysis via different paths, and trees which seem to be "doing badly" in that they are coming up with plausibility values that are too high.

Overall the program implementing this grammar and parsing strategy gives sophisticated "readings" such as one might expect in an undergraduate harmony class. It is admittedly limited in being able to deal only with a direct sequence of chords as the input, and thus is applicable to music with the simplest rhythmic structure, and overlooks the structural effects of melodic and contrapuntal ideas, without reference to which harmonic structure can sometimes not be adequately explained. Moreover, little effort was spent on dealing with nonharmonic or linear chords. But these shortcomings are the result of deliberate restriction of the problem, and are not structural shortcomings of the methodology. The structures resulting from realizations in a systemic grammar need not be one-dimensional but may have several different dimensions, as the result of independently-operating systems. Also the resulting structure need not be segmented in one way but may have several constituent structures, even within the same dimension, and music abounds with such nonexclusive groupings, as in melodic groupings, phrase groupings, harmonic groupings, etc. There appears to be no limitation in principle why the systemic approach could not be extended to embrace such additional dimensions.

I would take issue with but one point. Winograd describes his system as being driven by "semantic heuristics," assigning a level of "meaningfulness" to any parsing, and thus it is able to choose the "best" parse of all considered. When it is revealed that the heart of the system's "semantics" is his ad hoc plausibility value, it appears to be a curious use of the term, if it is taken to mean "the study dealing with the relations between signs and what they refer to" (Webster's 3rd Int'l, 1961). These values associated with pairs of chords reflect the role of the progression in the context of the string of chords, but it is essentially a syntactic role, and has no bearing on what the chord string may *refer* to extramusically. Be it granted that the function of a chord is a higher-level syntactic category reflecting a larger context than its local lexical identification (spelling), still it confuses the issue to suggest that this is the meaning of the chord; one must look further for that.

Though beyond the scope of this paper, such a further look should lead to a "grammar of the emotions," and it seems worth digressing briefly to mention a detailed "Structural Theory of the Emotions," by Joseph deRivera. The theory postulates a "matrix of emotions" (see figure 2-4) describing "the particular emotions as movements in a three dimensional interpersonal space," which "suggests that any particular emotion is the outcome of a pattern of 'choices' that organize our relationship with the other" (deRivera 1977, 71). The structural similarity between this description and the form of systemic grammar is intriguing and suggests the plausible application of such a grammar to the "parsing" of emotional states based on "interpersonal motion." The theory describes emotions primarily in terms of their relations to each other and to externally observable interpersonal movement, rather than the internal structure and form of the emotion itself, so it is not directly applicable to modeling of subjective affect states. But an ability to parse a man-machine interaction into an appropriate affect state could lead to more sensible or to at least "friendly" machine responses.

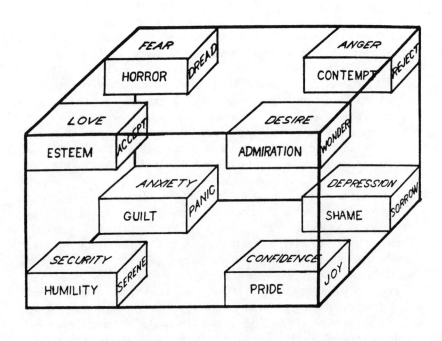

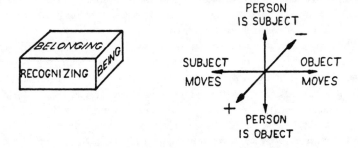

FIGURE 2-4: THE MATRIX OF EMOTIONS (DE RIVERA 1977)

3. LEHNERT: AFFECT STATE PATTERNS

Wendy Lehnert's approach to the problem of comprehension of an utterance is typical of the "Yale School" of natural language processing in that there is little concern for the actual surface form of the utterance, the emphasis being instead on the nature of the structures created in memory in response to the text. The paradigm for exploring such memory representations is to ask the reader to summarize the narrative text, and the summarization behavior is taken to reveal what sorts of inferences, causal-chains, and integration of information into knowledge structures has occurred.

> When a reader is asked to summarize a story, vast amounts of information within the memory representation are selectively ignored in order to produce a distilled version of the original narrative. This process of simplification relies on a global structuring of memory that allows search procedures to concentrate on central elements of the story while ignoring peripheral details (Lehnert 1982, 376).

In her system the mechanism of such global structuring is built out of remarkably simple affect states which combine to form *plot units* of greater complexity. In fact, affect states of only three kinds are posited:

- events that please (notated + in diagrams)
- events that displease (−)
- mental states with neutral affect (M).

The neutral M-states are usually associated with intentions or goals. Patterns are in turn comprised of a number of such primitive states connected by arcs or "links." Links are of various types. Links between affect states involving a single character are called *causal links* since they relate to causes of mental states and intentionalities behind events. There are four labeled kinds of causal links:

- Motivational links (m) from an affective event to the mental state it causes
- Actualization links (a) from an intentional mental state to a resultant affective event
- Termination links (t) from one event or mental state back to another whose affective impact has been thereby supplanted or displaced
- Equivalence links (e) between distinct affective responses to the same event or mental state (i.e., resulting from a change in perspective).

Not all 36 pair-wise configurations are possible but legal configurations are constrained as follows:

- m-links must point to a mental state
- a-links must point from a mental state to an event
- t- and e-links must point:
  □ from a mental state to a mental state, or
  □ from an event to an event.

3.1 PLOT UNITS

The fifteen legal pair-wise combinations form the set of *primitive plot units* and each is referred to by name as in figure 3-1.

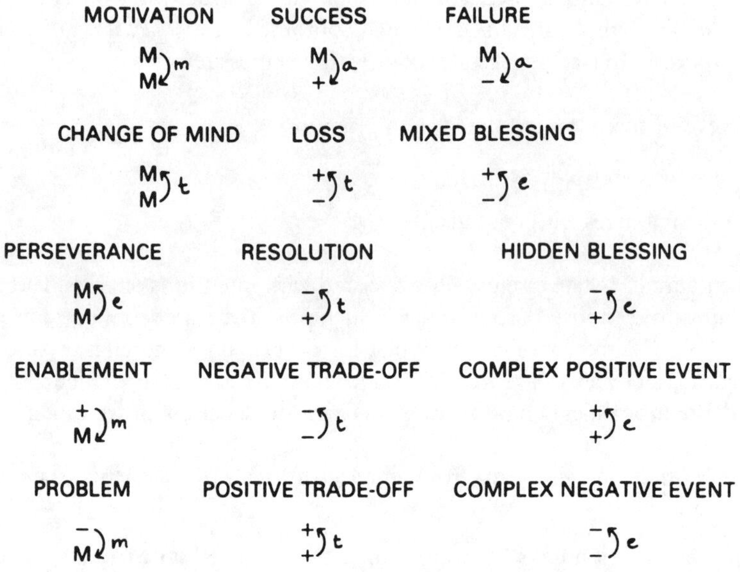

FIGURE 3-1: PRIMITIVE PLOT UNITS (LEHNERT 1982)

The graphic convention is that states involving a single character are aligned vertically and that time flows down the page. These primitive plot units can be combined into complex plot units such as in figure 3-2.

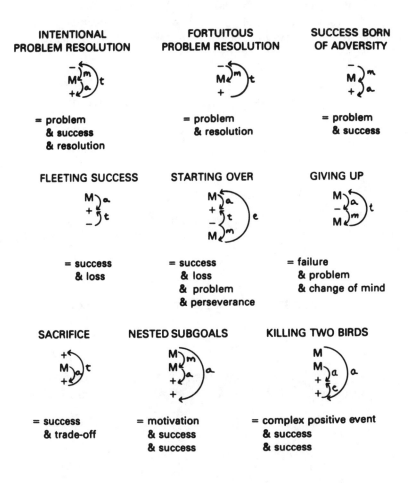

FIGURE 3-2: SOME COMPLEX PLOT UNITS (LEHNERT 1982)

In addition, narratives involving more than one character involve cross-character links, notated with diagonal segments between affect states where the higher state precedes the lower in time. Such links can occur between any pair of states and their interpretation is as in figure 3-3.

With these relatively simple elements then, many configurations of great complexity and subtlety arise, of which just a few are shown in figure 3-4.

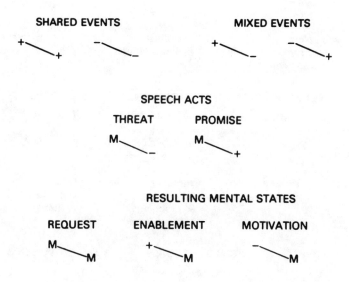

FIGURE 3-3: SOME CROSS-CHARACTER LINKS (LEHNERT 1982)

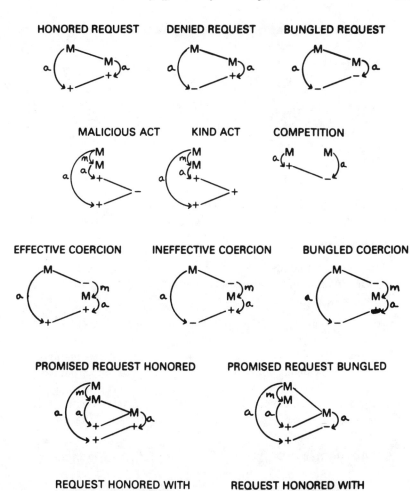

FIGURE 3-4: SOME COMPLEX PLOT UNITS INVOLVING TWO CHARACTERS
(LEHNERT 1982)

3.2 CONNECTIVITY AND NARRATIVE COHESION

A set of precise definitions are given concerning graphical connectivity of plot units, among them:

- Two plot units A and B are *related* iff they share a common affect state.

- A is *connected* to B iff*

  1. $A = B$.

  2. A is related to B.

  3. There exists a sequence of intervening plot units $U_1, \ldots, U_n$ such that A is related to U_1, U_i is related to U_{i+1}, and U_n is related to B.

- A *family* around A is the set of plot units related to A.

- F is a maximal family in K iff F is a family contained in K and the number of units in F is greater than or equal to the number in G for all families G contained in K.

- A is a *pivotal unit* in K iff the family around A is maximal in K.

It is noted that stories that yield highly-connected plot-unit graphs correspond naturally to highly cohesive narratives, and it is claimed that narrative cohesion is an important factor for effective memory retention, and furthermore, the information expressed in a pivotal unit tends to be a central part of a general summary.

3.3 SUMMARIZATION

A summary is then generated by the following algorithm:

1. Extract all top-level plot units from narrative text. (This issue is not central to her current analysis, and is handled by mechanisms employed in an earlier story comprehension system, BORIS.)

2. Derive the plot unit graph structure.

3. Identify the pivotal unit P.

4. Generate a *base-line summary* from a frame for P.

5. Augment base-line summary with information from plot units related to P.

---

*Iff = if and only if.

Step 4 is accomplished by associating with each plot unit a frame structure from which a natural language description of the content of the unit can be generated. For example, a general frame for a Retaliation unit might read: "Because X's [?] caused a [−] for Y, Y tried to [+] to cause a [−] for X."

The fairly elaborate formalism outlined here becomes convincing in view of abundant examples provided and empirical comparison of the kind of summarizations that people construct in response to a given story to those derived via the system.

Some of the limits of such analysis are clear and acknowledged. Since affect states reflect information about personal goals, plans and intentions, they are not applicable to texts that contain no information along these lines, for example, expository or purely descriptive writing. Still the most striking feature of the analysis is how even such an extremely coarse modeling of affect can so effectively organize information of this kind.

In thinking of an application of this paradigm to music the kind of summary one typically finds in concert program notes immediately comes to mind. The attempt to write a "music appreciation program" that would try to write such summaries in response to musical input is likely to yield insight into possible cognitive structures involved in music listening, in the same way that narrative summarization suggests strategies to structure stories. To pursue the analogy a little further one could imagine, corresponding to affect states or events, musical events, mapped probably not onto a single affective dimension (− , 0, +) but several. For example, within a particular musical style, descending minor appoggiaturas might map onto one end, and major-scale passage work onto the other end of a "happy/sad" dimension, presto/pizzicato and lento/legato onto two ends of an "activity" dimension, piccolo with string-harmonics and triangle on one end, and tuba with trombones and timpani on the other of a "weight" dimension, etc. One might then imagine primitive "plot units" like "Imitation" (with several distinct subtypes, i.e., direct, sequential, altered, inverted, etc.) or "Juxtaposition" (which might include contrasting and similar) or "Transformation" (including rhythmic and melodic augmentation and diminution, modulation, extension, dissection, concatenation, etc.) and others. Such smaller units then would fit together into sections and finally the standard large-scale musical forms.

4. MINSKY: MEMORY, METAPHOR AND MEANING

Minsky's K-line theory offers an extremely simple graphic model which, in spite of its simplicity, nonetheless yields neat, almost procedural descriptions of such fuzzy phenomena as analogy and metaphor.

4.1 A BRIEF SUMMARY OF THE K-THEORY

A state of mind is envisioned as a great hierarchical lattice of *agents*, the partially autonomous individuals in a "society of mind," each embodying an active idea or concept. Information moves upward in the lattice so that any given agent receives input from a roughly pyramidal hierarchy of agents beneath him. Most agents are grouped into small "cross-exclusion" arrangements, each having inhibitory connections to others in the group so that only one in the group may be active at a time, and further resulting in a built-in short-term memory. This is rather like object-oriented data abstraction taken to its logical conclusion.

When a memory is formed a *K-line* is created for it, which is thought of as a "wire" with potential connections to any agent, and a *K-node* at the end whose activation in turn activates the connected agents. Memorizing a particular state of mind creates excitatory attachments to agents currently active in that state. The crucial issue is that actually only a subset of currently active agents can really afford to be reactivated in evocation of a memory. "It is *not* the goal of Memory to produce a perfect hallucination . . . *A memory should induce a state through which we see current reality as an instance of the remembered event*" (Minsky 1979, 8). To obtain the desired metaphorical function he proposes his *Level-Band Principle*. Simply stated, it says that when an agent A forms a memory, the K-line it creates should only attach to active agents in the current state of mind which lie "within an intermediate band of levels" somewhere in the hierarchy beneath A, not too high and not too low. This is so that in evocation, current goals which are likely to be represented by agents higher up will not be overwritten by the forced excitation of the activated K-line, and the particular contingencies of the current situation will not be lost by forcing the states of the lower-level perceptual agents.

The theory is elaborated by proposing the recursive notion of connecting K-lines to other K-nodes as well in accordance with the Level-Band Principle, which is just to say that new memories are clearly built on earlier remembrances. Graphically then K-nodes grow into a structure with connections echoing those in the agent hierarchy, except that information flows the other way: agents pass their information to their superiors, but K-nodes activate other K-nodes and agents below them.

It's interesting to see how abstraction happens almost automatically in such a network. Consider an agent encountering a problem in the current situation. If the agent activates a memory of a similar situation, but the mind-state of this memory differs in some detail from some current situation, then the agencies involved in the conflicting details will tend to become inactive because of the cross-exclusion connections. Thus the common, nonconflicting properties are automatically extracted, and this is the essence of abstraction and metaphor. If the resulting state of mind leads ultimately to resolution of the problem, this combination of earlier K-node and current activations could be remembered as a new K-node representing a new generalized concept.

4.2 LEARNING

Minsky is vague on the crucial subject of how learning is accomplished in his model except that he postulates the operation of a third agency network which controls the formation and linkage of K-nodes to other K-nodes and agents. He is forced to make this assumption, which is dangerously suggestive of infinite recursion (What agent controls the agent which controls . . . the formation of K-nodes?), since he rejects the behaviorist reinforcement theory of learning as being too simplistic. Reinforcement theories rely on "recency" to determine which strategies should be remembered when a goal is finally successfully achieved. This is considered inadequate since longer-range strategies are often involved and one would also like to forget more recent blind alleys and failures. Thus, he concludes that different scales of tactics, strategies and goals are segregated and kept track of in a separate web of agencies.

In order to break the recursion an agent at some level up in the control hierarchy will have to have enough information available to make a judgment on the "relevance" of active agents under its control. This judgment must be intuitive in character, as such judgments are in humans, that is, based on incomplete information and by means of metaphorical associations with other memories. Clearly we tend to "notice" percepts and states of mind associated with a strong affective response, and the link between emotion and memory is certainly profound; memories tend to carry with them their own emotional tone, and may be evoked by a similar emotion in the present. Thus an extension to the theory may be to think of K-lines as something more complex than a mere excitatory wire. Rather, think of a three-dimensional K-matrix, where entries correspond to agents in the intermediate Level-Band which may be active or not. Further, the entries may not necessarily be simple black or white, inactive or active, but may be "colored pixels" encoding a little more of the agent's state or "mood." The spatial form of this pattern may match, in ways previously described, a recognizable emotion. In this way one might imagine the control agent capable of recognizing an active agent configuration in some level-band under its jurisdiction, which corresponds to a strong emotion, which would then trigger the creation of a K-matrix for that configuration. The form and formation of that memory is then intimately connected to its emotional associations.

5. LENAT: HEURISTICS

Among the most interesting attempts to "raise an intelligence" is the EURISKO heuristic learning program, whose education now spans tens of thousands of hours of CPU time on a Xerox 1100. Types of learning are considered to lie on a spectrum from rote memorization in which the learner is relatively passive, through concept formation, theory formation and discovery, in which the learner is progressively more autonomous and responsible for the resultant representation of the knowledge. Doug Lenat's concern is for the extreme end of this latter region, motivated by the observation that knowledge acquisition from human experts is the bottleneck in building intelligent expert systems today, and "the neck of the bottle is narrow indeed for those fields in which there is as yet no human expert." And furthermore, "the world is too complex to be modeled deeply in any formal way, but a dynamically-growing body of heuristics might suffice" (Lenat 1983a, 36–37).

He proposes then an "Accretion Model of Theory Formation" in which a body of heuristics concerning a specific domain grows upon itself through observation and experimentation in the domain. The model is described by a set of not entirely sequential steps.

1. Given a set of definitions, objects, operations, and rules, gather data about them: find examples of definitions, apply rules and operations, etc.

2. As this proceeds look for patterns in the data gathered.

3. Build hypotheses upon patterns observed, and design and execute experiments to test these.

4. Make new definitions as the body of hypotheses develops, to make the statements of the most useful conjectures more concise, and go back to step 1.

5. From time to time, as the above loop proceeds, create some new heuristics, "by compiling the learner's hindsight."

6. Even more rarely, augment or shift the representation in which the domain knowledge is encoded, as necessary.

The pervading philosophy is that a dynamic collection of informal heuristics is sufficient to drive and direct the model, *even steps 5 and 6*!

Many assumptions are implicit in the model. The first step assumes that the learner is able to make direct observations, which immediately limits the accessible domains, essentially to the fields of mathematics, games and programming. The second rule implies the availability of a large store of known patterns to recognize, and the programs are provided with sets of general domain-independent low-level pattern-noticing rules. And it is emphasized that it is only a working assumption that such rules are indeed domain independent. The third step requires some rules in the initial body of heuristics that will allow the program to generalize meaningfully from the observed patterns, followed by specialization to new specific questions and test cases, and "deeply embedded into this point is a set of metaphysical assumptions about the world: most phomena [*sic*] should be explainable by a small set of simple laws or regularities, knowledge comes from rational inquiry, causality is inviolable, coincidences have meaning, etc." (Lenat 1983a, 38).

The fifth and sixth steps constitute the major design idea that distinguishes EURISKO from the more limited model used in AM. They assume that both heuristics and aspects of the representation language can be synthesized, modified, and evaluated just like any other domain object. The consequence for the implementation is that heuristics suggesting operations on heuristics and frame structures, which one might well be tempted to treat specially as metaheuristics, are in fact distinguished in no way at all.

Heuristics themselves are stated informally in a way similar to a typical production system rule: a set of preconditions followed by consequent action. But the fact that these are represented in a form identical to that used for domain concepts allows the program to learn about and alter its own knowledge base.

5.1 THE REPRESENTATION LANGUAGE FOR CONCEPTS

The basic representation in the system employs frame-like units with slots, and this is applied uniformly to domain concepts, heuristic rules, and system concepts as well. Each slot with its name may be considered as a unary function, which, when given that name returns the value in the slot, and thus rules need not distinguish slots from functions. Each slot also has its own unit describing the slot, including such information as the types of legal entries in the slot, what units such a slot is legally a part of, etc. (see for example figure 5-1). Using such information the program may alter its own representation; if it is noticed that certain slots and values are never used they may be eliminated or, more often, new slots created for values that have been computed repeatedly on the fly or, if entries on a given slot become too numerous, the program will search for specializations so that the slot can be split. Since concepts are related to each other through Generalizations, Specializations, IsA, and Examples slots, knowledge becomes organized in a huge generalization/specialization hierarchy. This is true of the heuristic rules as well, with the general so-called "Weak Methods" (generate and test, hill-climbing, etc.) at the top and hundreds of domain-specific judgments near the bottom. One of the principle stated goals of the research is to get a grasp on the structure of this "space of heuristics."

NAME: IsA, Isa, Is-a, ISA, IS-A
   Informally: is, element-of, is-in
DOMAIN/RANGE: $\langle$Units $\rightarrow$ SetOfUnits$\rangle$
IS-A: Sot
FilledWithA: Set
EachEntryMustBeA: Unit representing a set
Inverse: Examples
UsedByInheritanceModes: InheritAlongIsAs
MakesSenseFor: Anything
MyIsA: Eurisko unit
MySize: 500 words
MyCreator: D. Lenat
MyTimeOfCreation: 4/4/79 12:01
Generalizations: AKindOf
Specializations: MemberOf, ExtremumOf
Worth: 600
Cache: Always
English: The slot which tells which classes a unit belongs to.
ALGORITHMS:
   Nonrecursive Slow PossiblyLooping: λ (u) $\{c \in$ Concepts $|$ c.Defn$(u)\}$
DEFINITIONS:
   Nonrecursive Fast PossiblyLooping: λ (u,c) c.Defn(u)

FIGURE 5-1: FRAME UNIT REPRESENTING THE CONCEPT OF AN "IsA" SLOT
(LENAT 1983B)

5.2 THE CONTROL STRUCTURE

The control algorithm as well is represented in EURISKO as a set of concepts with the intention that the program be able to meaningfully alter its own control code, but this has always resulted in bugs. Basically the structure consists of three nested Select-Execute-PostMortem loops: select and work on a topic; given a topic, select and work on a promising task; given a task, select and obey a relevant heuristic rule. Each topic in the system (e.g., NumberTheory, Games, DevicePhysics, Aesthetics) has a slot called Agenda containing a list of tasks pertaining to that topic and its specializations. When the execution of a heuristic suggests a new task involving, say PalindromicNumbers, EURISKO then searches up along Generalizations links (e.g., through

Numbers and SymmetricConstructs) until it finds topics (ultimately, NumberTheory and Aesthetics) and a pointer to the task is put on the agenda in each topic encountered. But note that these topics are represented, like any other concept, in a frame unit, and there are rules that can operate on them, to split and specialize a topic if it has too many tasks piling up on its agenda, or else when an agenda becomes too small, to merge it into all appropriate immediate generalizations' agendas. "In such cases, the general agendas should adopt (a little of) the small agenda's aesthetics, values, heuristics, reasons, goals, open problems, points of view" (Lenat 1983b, 68), though in the current implementation, only the tasks are inherited.

Task selection is based on ratings which are constantly updated during the post-mortem phase of actions. When a task fails it is likely to be put back on the agenda along with new tasks which might enable this one to succeed. If the subtasks in turn succeed, then their post-mortem should raise the rating of the original task.

Once a task is chosen a body of potentially relevant heuristic rules are collected that may help to satisfy it. There are in fact a number of different ways that a rule may be interpreted depending on space and time bounds, how many rules are applicable (whether they should be ordered first), whether the interpreter must check whether some new rules become relevant during the course of rule execution, and so on, and of course there are heuristics that govern these choices. The post-mortem phase of an individual rule execution involves bookkeeping information about time and space used, new units created, tasks placed on agendas, etc.

5.3 HUMAN INTERFACE

There is a high frequency with which EURISKO generates "new" concepts that are effectively equivalent to already existing ones. The problem of recognizing this equivalence is serious and difficult, and the program, as one might expect, has some heuristic tools to try to detect this. Each unit has slots which are specified as "criterial" and which define it. The description of each such slot, in turn, describes the way it makes sense to do matching. For example, for concepts that are defined logically in terms of others, one might recur on the boolean subexpressions, or if the concepts are of algorithms, one might evaluate the functions on test arguments to see if they yield the same results. But this is one area in which human supervision is most helpful in practice to keep things from bogging down. Lenat admits to considerable intervention and "hand smoothing" of newly-generated concepts.

There is also some elementary user modeling in order to accommodate the varied expectations of users from differing fields from whom the program is expected to learn. Each group of people and the set AllPeople get their own concept frames, which are arranged in a hierarchy with the concepts of individual users at the bottom. These concepts influence what kinds of topics and tasks are chosen to work on, and what is chosen to be explained in what depth. "EURISKO does learn simple models of each new user, but there are at present very few psychological and societal heuristics for building up (and testing!) such models. Based on our model of theory formation we are not surprised that only minimal sorts of learning were achieved without a deep model of the domain" (Lenat 1983b, 73). This is clearly an area where development of some emotional modeling could be important and useful.

5.4 CONCLUSIONS

Certain criteria emerge concerning appropriate domains for mechanized discovery, chiefly:

- The search space should be immense and largely unexplored by humans (as in three-dimensional VLSI* design, or the Traveller Trillion Credit Squadron naval fleet design wargame).

- There must be ways to simulate or directly carry out experiments.

- The domain should be rich in heuristic structure with no good algorithms, as in a very complex domain where precise inference is unmanageable or impossible, raising the utility of plausible inexact reasoning.

Once one gets past the impressive success of the program in performing genuinely innovative discovery, one begins to recognize the "personality" of the program as that of a tireless monomaniac focused entirely on this task of search and synthesis. In a more general application, or in the context of a more general intelligence, it is clear that this kind of activity should be rather occasional, if for no other reason than that it is so extremely costly.

Thus one is brought back again to the question of what should initiate this kind of search. Within the present discussion, the answer is that it should be the recognition of an emotional state that initiates the search in order to displace the emotion (or augment it in the case of a positive state).

Consider, for example, a computer employed in a mundane task, say general accounting, in an environment of computer non-sophisticates, say in an insurance office, in which users can largely be expected to want to use the

---

*Very Large-Scale Integration; the technology for densely packing circuits containing hundreds of thousands of electronic components on a single computer chip.

machine and access its data through a natural language interface. Now one can also expect a user to occasionally express his displeasure with the machine when it misinterprets some request in English and doesn't give him what he wants. It makes good sense then for the machine to respond to this expression appropriately by "parsing" it as a motion in the Emotional Matrix of Interpersonal Space (see figure 2-4) corresponding to a motion of the "object" (user) away from the "person" (machine) and the "person" (machine) is the object of the emotion, along the dimension of recognition. This position in the matrix reads out "shame." If this happens often the rating of the shame frame will increase until it demands the attention an intense emotion does, by achieving a high priority on a task agenda. The unit representing shame can then be expected to suggest appropriate actions, the first of which is probably to apologize, and subsequently to "think about it," try to form a concept of what the misunderstanding is and why it comes about, and to try to create some heuristics relevant to avoiding the misunderstanding in the future, augment the user models by noting that people like this get upset about such things, and finally to seek a little reassuring confirmation from the user that these surmises are reasonable, not to mention a little pat on the CRT.

The potential for Artificial Intelligence is certainly enormous, but already applications based exclusively on formal logical inference face bottlenecks and limitations. In our efforts to be practical and precise in our thinking, let us not forget the heart and "its reasons," because there are very good reasons indeed that our emotional lives are as rich and commanding as they are, for affect and aesthetics are the very basis for knowledge, even purely factual knowledge. Whatever our minds—or any minds we create—may achieve must owe much in the end to the influence of such reasons of the heart.

BIBLIOGRAPHY

deJoia, Alex, and Adrian Stenton. 1980. *Terms in Systemic Linguistics: A Guide to Halliday.* London: Batsford Academic and Educational Inc.

Dennet, Daniel C. 1978. *Brainstorms: Philosophical Essays on Mind and Psychology.* Montgomery, Vt.: Bradford Books.

deRivera, Joseph. 1977. *A Structural Theory of the Emotions.* Psychological Issues, Monograph 40. New York: International Universities Press.

Goodman, Nelson. 1976. *Languages of Art, an Approach to a Theory of Symbols.* Indianapolis: Hackett.

Halliday, M. A. K. 1978. *Language as a Social Semiotic.* Baltimore, Md.: University Park Press.

Halliday, M. A. K., and J. R. Martin, eds. 1981. *Readings in Systemic Linguistics.* London: Batsford Academic and Educational Inc.

Hanslick, Eduard. 1957. *The Beautiful in Music.* New York: Liberal Arts Press.

Hardy, Godfrey Harold. 1967. *A Mathematician's Apology.* London: Cambridge University Press.

Kress, G. R. 1976. *Halliday: System and Function in Language.* London: Oxford University Press.

Lehnert, Wendy. 1982. "Plot Units: A Narrative Summarization Strategy." In *Strategies for Natural Language Processing.* Hillsdale N.J.: Erlbaum Associates.

Lenat, Douglas B. 1983. Theory Formation by Heuristic Search; The Nature of Heuristics, II: Background and Examples. *Arificial Intelligence,* 21(1): 31–59.

Lenat, Douglas B. 1983. EURISKO: A Program that Learns New Heuristics and Domain Concepts; The Nature of Heuristics, III: Program Design and Results. *Artificial Intelligence,* 21(1): 61–98.

Lerdahl, Fred, and Ray Jackendoff. 1983. *A Generative Theory of Tonal Music.* Cambridge, Mass.: MIT Press.

Minsky, Marvin. 1979. K-Lines: A Theory of Memory. *MIT Al Memo 516* (June, 1979): 1–35.

Minsky, Marvin. 1981. Music, Mind, and Meaning. *Computer Music Journal* 5(3): 28–44.

Pais, Abraham. 1982. *Subtle is the Lord. . .: The Science and Life of Albert Einstein*. London: Oxford University Press.

Papert, Seymour. 1980. *Mindstorms: Children, Computers, and Powerful Ideas*. New York: Basic Books, 1980.

Poincaré, Henri. Translated by Halstead, G.B. 1958. *Science and Method*. New York: Dover.

Poincaré, Henri. Translated by Bolduc, John W. 1963. *Mathematics and Science: Last Essays (Dernières Pensées)*. New York: Dover.

Polanyi, Michael. 1958. *Personal Knowledge, Towards a Post-Critical Philosophy*. Chicago: University of Chicago Press.

Roads, Curtis. 1979. Grammars as Representations for Music. *Computer Music Journal* 3(1): 48–55.

Schank, Roger C., and Robert P. Abelson. 1978. *Scripts, Plans, Goals and Understanding: an Inquiry into Human Knowledge Structures*. Hillsdale, N.J.: Erlbaum Assoc.

Searle, John R. 1980. ''Minds, Brains, and Programs.'' In *The Behavioral and Brain Sciences*. London: Cambridge University Press.

Wechsler, Judith, ed. 1978. *On Aesthetics in Science*. Cambridge, Mass.: MIT Press.

Winograd, Terry. 1968. ''Linguistics and the Computer Analysis of Tonal Harmony.'' *Journal of Music Theory* 12(1): 2–50.

Winograd, Terry. 1983. *Language as a Cognitive Process: Syntax*. Reading, Mass.: Addison-Wesley.

Environment, Consciousness, and Magic: An Interview with David Dunn*

Michael R. Lampert

*E*XPERIMENTAL COMPOSER *and interdisciplinary theorist David Dunn has worked in a variety of sonic media, including traditional instruments, tape music, and live electroacoustic performance, as well as developing a variety of interactive environmental structures. For approximately fifteen years his work has explored the interrelationships between a variety of geophysical phenomena, environmental sound, and music. The connection of this work to nonmusical disciplines such as experimental linguistics, cognitive ethology, cybernetics, and systems philosophy has expanded his creative activities to include philosophical writings and media projects within a broad domain. During the course of this investigation he has moved progressively from activities which transcend musical composition per se towards the embracing of the idea of artists as* whole-systems *consultants and inte-*

*David Dunn, Michael R. Lampert, 5 May 1987.

grators. Most specifically this progression can be seen in his environmental projects where an initial interest in interspecies communication has been expanded to include the idea of mind as an emergent property of the environment at large. Mr. Dunn's compositions include Position as Argument *(with Chris Mann, 1982),* Entrainments 2 *(1985) and* Sonic Mirror: Simulation 1 *(1987). His book* Skydrift *is published by Lingua Press.* Music, Language and Environment, *a collection of selected scores and writings, was recently published as a private edition. His article "Speculations: On the Evolutionary Continuity of Music and Animal Communication Behavior" and composition* Nexus I *were published in* Perspectives of New Music, *vol. 22. He is currently President of the International Synergy Institute, a nonprofit think tank and interdisciplinary publishing house based in Santa Fe, New Mexico.*

For a composer to arrive at the point where you are today, it would be a very long journey if you started from a traditional European background. Your background appears to be different, since you started studying with Harry Partch at a young age.

Actually, my initial training was classically oriented: I started out studying the violin as a child. I probably started composing in a serious manner at the age of fourteen.

My interests, even in the very beginning of my compositional career, have always been fairly eccentric. Even though I was writing serial music and Stravinsky imitations, I was always doing "oddball" things at the same time, which led to an interest in electronics and tape music. I also developed an interest in Partch's music at that time. When I was seventeen years old, I made the point of going to a particular university with the specific intention of connecting with Partch. I really wasn't interested in the university per se, but Partch's main assistant taught there, so I enrolled in his theory class. Within the first year of college I began working with Partch and studying his music.

How did Partch's use of pitch materials interact with your work in the electronic medium?

Perhaps it did in an indirect way. Probably the first coherent style that I tried to work in was serialism. I wrote a twelve-tone string quartet at age sixteen and tape music came immediately after that. I was mostly working with *musique concrète* at that time, taking sounds from instruments and the environment and transforming them into short tape pieces. The association with Partch was inspiration to think beyond these established ways of making music.

How long were you associated with Harry Partch?

I was an assistant to him and worked intensively with him for the last four years of his life, from 1970 to 1974 when he died. I performed with him primarily for the film *The Dreamer That Remains*. I was living in the basement of his house, assisting him in the process of preparing and tuning his instruments. He was quite ill at this time. Under his tutelage I was primarily serving as an instrument technician, but I was also working as an assistant on a variety of levels. He called me his "factotum."

After Harry died, I continued to be very involved in performing his music until 1980, which was the last public performance which I took part in. This was a series of performances we did for the Berlin Festival, and a live broadcast on West German Radio of Partch's composition *The Bewitched*, a dance-theater work.

How did this powerful early contact with Partch influence the way you thought about music?

That's a good question. It certainly influenced me in a way that I would not have considered at the time. I was passionately interested in Harry's music, yet my work bears very little semblance to his except on the level of a sort of "rugged individualism." It has to do with experiencing Partch's dynamic personality and imagination at an early age. I not only saw the beauty of that, but also the pain and suffering that can come with that type of gift. I couldn't be very naive after having seen what Partch's work meant to him, both the beauty and accomplishment it represented, contrasted against the extreme difficulties that Harry encountered during his lifetime. His particular path was unique: it was neither popular nor academic, and it never really had a place in the world to reside within.

Harry's support system was always ad hoc. He could never really count on anything or anyone, with the exception of a certain amount of patronage that was given very generously by Betty Freeman, at the end of his life. Except for that, he received some small grants and support from a few private foundations and academic institutions in a very limited way. Oddly enough, it often wasn't the music departments which helped him. At certain points his work was supported by linguistic departments, engineering departments, et cetera, at odd numbers of different universities. For the most part, Harry supported himself his entire life doing menial work. He had been a migrant farm worker, a newspaper proofreader, and during the Depression he was a hobo. So he really didn't have a support system and he really didn't want one if it meant compromising his work. He wouldn't have turned down support but it had to come in a form that he felt was honest. He never made his work conform to a pattern that was academically or popularly acceptable. This was certainly a very interesting role model for me. The only way that I could be authentically influenced by him was by making the choice to strike out on my own, whatever that meant.

My music is not like Partch's—I'm not involved in the same issues that he was, except in a peripheral way. In any case, I operate under a different set of criteria, to the point where so much of what I do today strikes out beyond the boundaries of music per se. However, while it is outside of what many people consider to be music, I certainly see it as connected to a lineage or tradition of music-making. At this point, I am more interested in seeing how music informs a transdisciplinary perspective.

Experimental music is very often a synonym for avant-garde music, yet your music seems to be truly experimental in the sense that you are actually conducting experiments in the sonic medium. Does the term "experimental" fit your music, and how do you feel about the term in general?

I think that it refers to a school of thought that has tried to differentiate itself from what was previously known as the avant-garde, and after that was known as "new music." For the most part, new music is now part of a traditional perspective, and is largely academically acceptable. It comes out of a school of thought that was popular in the sixties and seventies which has now become quite influential, even in terms of popular music. A composer like Philip Glass has a tremendous popular following, equivalent to someone like Aaron Copland or Leonard Bernstein during their respective generations.

Socially acceptable . . .

Yes, and while I'm not particularly a fan of any of these composers, it is evident that their appeal is quite broad-based. Glass appeals to a very diverse public, one that listens to rock and roll, new-age music, even jazz, in addition to the ethnic music that has gained in popular interest during the last decade. Leonard Bernstein had a similar appeal, certainly with a piece like *West Side Story*, which was concerned with very diverse musical idioms.

I feel that the new-music community has purposively moved into that realm. I see the New Music America Festival as an attempt to try and establish a more broad-based support and interest for the kind of music that was considered very fringe during the sixties and seventies. It's a very diverse set of musics that fit in with that: experimental jazz for instance, or the music composed by Pauline Oliveros, Alvin Lucier, and Robert Ashley. Much of this parallels the continuation of integral or total serialism, in addition to other types of music that were associated with academic institutions on the east coast or in Europe. All of these distinctions are now a bit blurred. I see my work as somewhat outside of these traditions, even though I was influenced by all of them.

What I specifically mean by the term "experimental music" is similar to what experimental refers to in the scientific sense. I'm not making a claim for "doing" science, but I am making a claim for the relevancy of certain activities within the domain of an experiential exploration of sound and consciousness from a transdisciplinary perspective. What I see as experimental is that I'm actually trying to create experimental situations, the outcomes of which are uncertain. This is not John Cage's indeterminacy where partially controlled situations allow for certain kinds of musical results. His results may or may not be predictable, but there is a certain kind of gestalt which is predictable, a certain type of mannerism towards shaping sound which is characteristic of Cage's work. His musicality is amazingly sensitive and consistent.

In my work I set up an interaction with the environment, using sound as the vehicle or the medium by which the interaction unfolds. I do not know what the outcomes of these interactions will be. This process has been accused of being unmusical and that may very well be true. However, for me, the final outcome is the area of main interest. I'm interested in gaining information from an experimental situation that can't be arrived at otherwise.

You also studied with Kenneth Gaburo.

I consider Kenneth to be my main teacher.

As I understand it, Gaburo's work is often involved with linguistic theory, the interplay of acoustic and electronic sounds, as well as other concerns, all coming from a composer with a traditional background, yet experimental in a certain sense. How does this inform your work?

The major focus of Kenneth's work, to give a very brief synopsis, has been the interrelationship of music and language. He attempts to explore what the boundaries are, while trying not to make assumptions about any dichotomy between these two phenomena. He often specifies a multiplicity of languages, musical and otherwise, that are contrapuntal in their organization, thereby creating a synergetic resonance that is expressive. This influenced me a great deal, and I was interested in studying with Kenneth so that I could have access to his thinking about language and music. I felt that there was a specific gap that I needed to fill concerning my interest about the physical environment and music. The assumption was that there were certain connections between language and the sounds of the wilderness as a linguistic phenomenon. Studying with Kenneth helped me to formulate some more concrete directions regarding the exploration of this relationship.

Kenneth Gaburo's work, while very experimental, is still presented within a more traditional "concert" setting. On the other hand, your music is tending more toward the sacred domain of pure science. Do you believe that music may be able to intuitively "pre-create" the results of more rigorously scientific experimentation, and how does this relate to your current work?

Xenakis has made claims that musicians haven't really known what they were working with, in the sense that certain kinds of formal mathematical concepts were worked out intuitively by musicians long before they were actually mathematically formulated. I have a feeling that certain kinds of intuitive leaps can be made within the boundaries of what I'd call art that are relevant for science. In this case, I mean art as a way of engendering an exploratory perception of the world. I think there is now a general feeling of constraint with the traditional roles of both science and art. They are looking to each other out of desperation.

Part of science's particular problem is its assumption of objectivity, trying to posit a world that is nonparticipatory, where the scientist is trying to diminish or negate himself from the process of observation. I've been interested in systems that involve what historian Morris Berman has termed "participatory consciousness," referring to a distinction between the world views of the Middle Ages and the modern world. What differentiates most cultural views prior to the seventeenth century is that they rested upon an assumption that the observer was not separate from the thing observed. This is a very old tradition and the most active continuation of it is occult science.

Does art then offer an alternate view of reality?

Not really. I operate under the assumption that these things aren't separate. For me, the aesthetic response is what Gregory Bateson referred to when he said, "beauty is the pattern that connects." I interpret that to mean that the aesthetic response, the perception and apprehension of beauty, becomes a sort of resonance: we see and feel our own individuated mind expand to include something that we previously didn't assume to be part of us.

Referring to the larger Self as the pattern that connects, I can see a certain continuity in your thought regarding the identification of this larger state of resonance with the environment. In Cage's work, the emphasis has been shifting from the smaller self as composer to the larger Self as a participant in and creator of larger structures that dwarf the individual. Does your work fall within this Cage-inspired lineage?

There is a certain American tradition that is connected with Cage's indeterminate processes. I certainly see that what I'm interested in would not have been possible without Cage's contributions. Cage wasn't alone in this, he has been a major figure in the movement to expand the use of musical and sonic resources to include an emancipation of all sound. But in this idea's articulation, there's still the feeling that these sounds are merely materials to be used for composition. Cage wanted to abstract the sounds and allow the sounds to be themselves. I'm interested in understanding a sound *and* its context as part of a purposeful, living system with attributes of mind.

For certain composers, their interest is in taking these sources as raw material for manipulation. I'm interested in regarding these as conscious living systems with which I'm interacting. It isn't to manipulate the sources and create "groovy" sounds that no one has ever heard before. I want to regard these sources as sentient beings and their sounds as the evidence of complex-minded systems. The compositions then become a process of setting up an interactive situation in order to create a collaborative work that is evocative and representative of a larger system of mind inclusive of myself and other living systems.

Such as in your composition Mimus Polyglottus *(1976)?*

Yes. In that project I worked with a single species. I spent a year studying the mockingbird, *Mimus polyglottus*, which is indigenous to the southern United States. These birds are extraordinary mimics and will often change the sounds they are imitating in seemingly creative ways. I've even heard them mimic automobile engines and washing machines. The compositional process was to find a stimulus that would be close enough to the bird's own song yet challenge the bird's ability to mimic. I used an electronic sound source and recorded the interaction in realtime. I regard it as a successful composition because it was a coherent language construct that creatively included the bird's cognitive apparatus.

David, in your compositions there has been a very interesting progression of notations used. Starting with mostly standard electronic diagrams as in Mimus Polyglottus, *you changed to large, semideterminate spiral structures such as those used in* Ring of Bone *(1981), and then in* Entrainments 2 *(1985) you used topographical maps with oscillator, microphone, and performer placements designated. This seems to be a largely indeterminate type of notation.*

Actually, this was mainly a descriptive type of notation, a recollection of something that was largely word-of-mouth. In some sense the environment specified this notation. The score itself is a way of representing the structure that unfolded interactively.

Is notation adequate for the type of work that you're doing now?

It depends on the project. The chronological sequence that you refer to was not a conscious exploration of notation itself. The notations reflect different ways of working with the environment or language over a number of years.

Some of these pieces that you refer to, *Ring of Bone* for example, have these spectacular scores that result from a sort of "genetic engineering" of language, a recombinant linguistic DNA constructed of phonemes. I analyzed a text in precise detail and then constructed the composition out of pattern relationships embedded in macro- and microlevels of structure. There's no traditional way of notating those kinds of complexities, and I'm a firm believer in the idea that the process of composition should determine the notation. These pieces aren't about twelve tones to the octave, or anything like that.

Yet you use vertical structures to represent pitch and horizontal to represent time.

Not necessarily. In *Position as Argument*, for text recitation, violin, and tape, the violin part can be entered into at any point, top or bottom, right or left. However, there are very specific rules as to how you can proceed. It's almost like a subway map and the pathway is up to you. At the same time there are severe constraints. While you can explore any path you choose, over the course of the piece you have to exhaust all of the possible pathways. It combines determinate and indeterminate aspects.

In Position as Argument, *the violin part was derived from a verbal text, using an analysis of the information as the basis for your derivation. What method did you use?*

This involved taking the text and breaking it up into its phonetic components, and then analyzing the structural relationships between all the available phenomena for an entire segment of text. I then traced these out and assigned a carefully chosen equivalent violin sound for each individual phoneme. After that, I created a matrix by tracing the unfolding of a particular pattern. For example, where you would see a particular word in the text, you could also find the same word in a different time domain, imbedded throughout the text and distributed in a manner that was previously invisible.

So the words are found, matched with violin analogs to the phonemes, and distributed like a crossword puzzle throughout the text, up and down, backwards, and so on?

Sometimes. Any particular word within the text falls within a linear order. It has a syntactical sequence. Most of the words in the text could also be discovered by connecting the phonemes between the words. Take the word "the." If it occurs three times in the text in its normal sequence, you may also be able to find the various phonemes which make up the word imbedded in other words. The sequence of those imbedded phonemes seemed to be meaningful because of the patterns that would pop out of the texture.

And by using the analogs, the patterns become more discernible?

Yes. It's also a way of structuring the composition as intrinsic commentary on the text.

Yet the use of phonemes in this composition is different than in Madrigal *(1980), for example.*

Yes. In *Madrigal* I was using phonetic notation for a different purpose. I recorded one minute of environmental sound and transcribed it through learning to articulate each sound vocally: birds, insects, airplanes, and whatever else took place during that one minute. After finding a way to reproduce each sound with my vocal apparatus, I'd transcribe that sound into English phonetic symbols, with additional signs. I then organized a piece of music for voices that consisted entirely of that transcribed source combined with electronic transformations of the original environmental recording.

The use of the term madrigal for the composition's title is certainly appropriate given the propensity of the early English madrigalists to use the sounds of birds and other animals within their vocal compositions.

I certainly saw that piece as a continuation of that tradition.

In listening to your latest composition Sonic Mirror: Simulation I, *I was per-plexed with the overall steady-state soundscape, juxtaposed with a highly unpredict-able interaction of sound sources. How and why did you create this piece?*

I'm involved in creating a set of simulations for a very large utopian proj-ect. This is an expansion beyond the level of interaction with large eco-systems that has occupied me: connecting ecosystems with other eco-systems and applying telecommunications technology to the nonhuman world. What *Sonic Mirror* will ultimately be is an expansion of the interac-tive digital technology that I've been involved with on a limited scale. I want to create a stationary cybernetic sound sculpture which will be satel-lite-uplinked to similar sculptures in other locations. The idea is that such systems would function as sonic mirrors processing electromagnetic data from a particular environment. The sculpture might function as an autono-mous entity that interacts within an autonomous environmental intel-ligence. What interests me is this process of interactive reflection back into the environment. I think of it as applying current technology toward the rediscovery of natural magic. This is a great tradition that uses elementals as a ground of power. In my case it is a marriage of music and electronic tech-nology which serves to invoke an archaic relationship to nature.

Now that's a pretty wild idea, right? [He laughs.] Since I feel a sense of responsibility about this, I've started by creating simulations of these tech-nological-environmental-human interactions. I've used recordings of the environment in a studio situation where I've had sufficient technology to work with. Eventually this technology will be made portable so that it can be used outdoors in the environmental context. The recording you heard was the first simulation that I've done. This involved taking a recording from the Cuyamaca Mountains in San Diego County and running that through electronic devices (analog and digital) to create a series of pattern tracings which are entirely determined by the environment itself. In a sense, I'm trying to remove myself from the situation as much as possible, allowing the audio recording of the environment to control the sound tech-nology. I then interacted with these patternings in realtime using another computer system and digital sampling device.

Were the sounds that the environment triggered chosen by you?

I programmed the timbres.

Do you plan to interface these systems with others?

Well, these are really study pieces that are being developed in order to play with possible techniques. Ultimately, one ecosystem will interact with another ecosystem, using satellite or balloon transponder technology.

Is the concept of mind really applicable to the environment or is this the superim-position of human concepts upon nonhuman entities?

One of the consistent assumptions of certain so-called primitive societies, the Pygmies for example, is that the environment is a living, cognitive entity. The rainforest is the support structure for a complex intelligence. The control mechanisms of the forest—what we now call an ecology—they saw as a deity. The Pygmies call the forest "mother" and regard themselves as part of this more inclusive consciousness. There are very old models for this kind of thinking.

This concept of mind is also related to current scientific investigations in the fields of systems theory and cybernetics, not to mention the ecological philosophy of Gregory Bateson. We know that in a climax rainforest, for example, there are very involved homeostatic processes of self-regulation at work. This can be thought of as a coherent system in the same way that an individual human organism can be regarded as a complex ecology of sub-systems, often with their own autonomy. It's hard to look at films of cellular activity in the human body and not have some sense that each cell has its own autonomous purpose. We are like corporate entities made of all these cellular communities.

The question of mind and the Cartesian assumption which negates it in other living systems is, for me, completely untenable. A new branch of science, known as cognitive ethology, rigorously makes the case for complex attributes of mind amongst animal life. Studies on bees imply that they exhibit complex patterns of behavior and communication that approach a high level of intelligence, or at least an intelligence far exceeding what we have previously imagined.

And this holds true for vegetation also?

There's certainly evidence that trees communicate through chemical signals. What that may mean in the larger scheme of these issues is still an open question.

You've written about music being an unconscious replacement for destroyed ecosystems. For instance, there is a correlation between the rise of industrialization in Western Europe and the development of increasingly complex musical forms from monophony to massive symphonic structures.

I've speculated that there may be a relationship between these two phenomena. I've wondered if there is some connection between the loss of environmental complexity brought on by the rise of industrialization and the increased complexity of Western music as an attempt to recapture a lost complexity of environmental sensation.

My assumption has been that music is a very important activity, something that is pervasive amongst all cultures. My interest has been in seeing music as an archaic form of language, perhaps preverbal. There appears to be some connection between music and animal communication behavior that is very suggestive of an evolutionary continuity. One of my intuitions is that music is, in many ways, a holdover from our mammalian and reptilian identities. The model that I'm using here is Paul MacLean's triune brain theory. He hypothesized that new brain structures have subsumed previous ones throughout the course of evolution. His theory is that, within the human brain, interactions between the reptilian, mammalian, and neo-cortex are somewhat insufficient. We may behave as if we have three differ-ent kinds of brains vying for control of the organism.

To think about music in this light is interesting. Perhaps music is a ves-tigial means of connection between our mammalian identity and our more rational cognitive apparatus. Perhaps it is a remnant of some commu-nicative behavior appropriate for interaction with these larger ecological sys-tems of mind. It might be a means to reaffirm that continuity.

We consist of these subsystems, each of which may require a certain range of environmental conditions in order to maintain a stable identity. The biospheric disequilibrium which industrialization has engendered, through destruction of environmental complexity, must be sensed inter-nally by individuals. As we've increasingly become creatures of the urban milieu, perhaps we have used music as one of the means to stabilize these archaic aspects of the human mind. It becomes a compensation for our alienation.

Does the evolution of your music from Mimus Polyglottus *to* Entrainments 2 *signify a reintegration into these systems that we are disassociated from, via the con-scious manipulation of sound?*

Possibly. The shift of emphasis has been a progressive expansion of con-text: moving from interactions with a single member of another species towards interactions with complex environments. I've tried to expand the sense of "mindedness" that I've been working with. *Entrainments 2* was the first one of my projects that had an audience in the traditional sense— with approximately fifty people present at the performance. It also involved a wide variety of life forms and human interaction with the environment. There were people moving through the space with electronic sound gener-ators and a computer set up to process the environmental sounds in a cyclical manner.

It was also influenced by the ancient Chinese geomantic art of *Feng-shui*. Geomancy was used throughout the world as a process of articulating a bal-anced relationship between humanity and the environment. The Chinese believed that the Earth has lines of energy flow throughout its body in a manner similar to the acupuncture meridians mapped in the human body. I'm very interested in these archaic systems of understanding environmen-tal balance: seeing ourselves as an intrinsic part of larger systems. I would be happy if my work serves no other purpose than to suggest ways in which we might rediscover this sense of fundamental connectedness.

Your work suggests that it may be possible to understand and communicate with the environment through the use of technology and linguistic systems.

Well, I don't see it in terms which are that cut-and-dried. I'm not making any claims for being able to take an environmental recording and decode it for hidden messages. I'm probably closer to the ancient Greek oracles whose messages came in very ambiguous forms. I feel that we have to redefine our relationship to the environment in a way that is life-enhancing. This is not just for the sake of wilderness preservation. It is also a very human issue because our lives depend on the maintenance of the whole system. This idea of environmental language isn't really language in the sense that there's a code that needs to be broken. I'm referring to language in the sense that we're engaged in a coevolutionary scenario. We need to compose processes of interaction which will help reestablish a saner balance of humanity within the biosphere. The language I'm envisioning is an experiential, dynamic process that explores whatever tools and metaphors are available in that direction.

And this would include music and music composition, with the types of intuitive thinking which may be engendered by those activities?

Sure. All of these may provide clues. I have no desire to go back to archaic forms of music in order to reestablish this balance, just as I have no desire to go back to archaic forms of religion. Given who we are in the twentieth century, and the peculiar perspective that we have as residents of this century, we wouldn't be satisfied with returning to archaic ways of behaving. But there are clues provided by all of these things, and I think that it's necessary to examine them, and whatever else we have to find our way out of the mess we're in.

Gregory Bateson's statement that "the experiment to live without religion has failed" is a very profound one. To me that doesn't mean we should go back and embrace old forms unconsciously. I think it means that we have to create a religion appropriate to the circumstances that we are living in.

And the same for music?

Yes. What I'm really expressing is a spiritual and ethical imperative. The point is not whether someone is making "good" music. The question is: to what use can we put music that is life-enhancing? That may mean not making music in the manner that we're used to. It may mean dropping music altogether. In either case, within this immense cultural history which we call music there may be clues for our continued survival on this planet which only music may provide. My intuition is that music does offer clues towards our survival, and I'm much more interested in that than in being a composer.

MUSIC AND LITERATURE

Music's relation to literature can be as distant as the application of a critical technique from literature to music, or vice versa; or closer, such as construing music as literature or literature as music, or perhaps setting a text in a song or opera; or intimately entwined, such as creating hybrid music/literature/critical objects, such as J. K. Randall's "Compose yourself" series, or Kenneth Gaburo's "LA," given here. In the "Symposium: The Nature of Music," which Arthur Berger commissioned, the Aristotelian philosopher Herbert Schwartz, the distinguished poet Delmore Schwartz, and the noted composer Arthur Berger address in concert some basic philosophical and aesthetic questions about music. Arthur Nestrovski's article, "Joyce's Critique of Music," takes some material that might initially seem unpromising to a musician (musical references in Joyce) and weaves it together with material that always tantalizes a musician (the text-counterpoint of *Finnegans Wake*) to come up at the last with a surprising and stimulating conclusion. Finally, Clayton Eshleman's poem sheds a human light on the pioneering American composer James Tenney.

Joyce's Critique of Music

Arthur Nestrovski

JOYCE'S CRITIQUE IS THREEFOLD: it comprehends an anatomy of musical value, a critique of the production and circulation of musical works, and the adaptation of compositional tropes for the development of his own writing techniques. To these three aspects correspond, respectively, the signaling presence of musical allusions (increasingly insistent from *Chamber Music* to *Finnegans Wake*), the portrayal of musicians, paramusicians and musical events (in all his works), and the evolution of combinatorial, serial thinking (both more and less apparent in his last book, as we will see). Joyce was an active amateur singer throughout his life, and he often spoke about music; most of what he said was trivial and arrogantly conservative. His true critique is in his fiction, and I will argue that it is as much a function of the writing as the writing itself is informed by musical concerns. Joyce's views on music are neither as sensitive as Proust's nor as insightful as

Mann's, but the effect of music on his writing has in turn been more influential to contemporary composers than either *La Recherche* or *Doktor Faustus*. Once subjected to the exigencies of style, Joyce's treatment of music—often highly sentimental on the surface—becomes charged with a political meaning that is not always apparent thematically. Joyce's style owes a great deal to his ideas about music, but these are not necessarily of capital importance: it is as a political praxis that Joyce's writing is able to capture irony, and it is through this circuitous route that his own ideas, as well as everybody else's, are systematically and ironically exposed. If music confidently feeds the writing at one end, it comes out the other end considerably less certain of its powers, usurped and deconstructed by the writing. It is this writing which has been important to those composers that matter today, and it is both symptomatic and ironic that they should owe so much to the greatest bad musician of the time.

ALLUSIONS, CITATIONS, PASTICHE

Musical allusions in Joyce's writings may be listed under two headings: allusions through citation (direct or implied), and allusions through parody or pastiche. By far most of the published accounts of music in Joyce's books are concerned with tracing, cataloguing and briefly describing the presence of citational allusions. Every one of Joyce's works alludes to music: to Irish ballads, Elizabethan airs, minstrel songs, music-hall numbers, bawdy catches, nursery rhymes, Gregorian chant, Renaissance and Classical Masses, semi-classical melodies and scenes from operetta and opera. Every one of these references is ideologically and institutionally marked: as Joyce makes clear, no act of composition can be ideologically neutral, just as no act of performing or listening can be. In Joyce's texts, music is systematically exposed for its roles in the hegemonic arena of (Irish) culture; not accidentally, it is often, if not always, coupled with sexuality, as we will see.

My major concern in this essay is the last of the three critiques mentioned above, that is, the mimetic adaptation of compositional tropes in Joyce's prose. But I want to examine a few examples of his treatment of allusions and of his social mapping of music as well. Underlining these is the question of whether a coherent aesthetics of music can be found in Joyce's writings, and if so in which respects it might relate to the general theory of aesthetics first expounded by Joyce himself in the Paris and Pola notebooks[1] and then, in its final form, by Stephen Dedalus in chapter 5 of *A Portrait of the Artist as a Young Man*.

My first example concerns a group of recurring allusions to Elizabethan music, particularly Dowland. References to Dowland are to be found quite prominently in *Portrait* and *Ulysses*; they are also present in *Finnegans Wake*,

Stephen Hero and the Triestine vignette *Giacomo Joyce*, and Dowland's settings can be heard as an undersong to virtually every poem in *Chamber Music*. As a young man, Joyce himself was fond of singing Dowland; years later, when he came to write his self-portrait-with-a-difference, this rare taste was placed at the center of Stephen Dedalus' agonistic, authorial search for character. Threatened by sexual jealousy and the prospect of failing friendship, Stephen

> allowed his mind to summon back to itself the ages of Dowland and Byrd and Nash.
>
> Eyes, opening from the darkness of desire, eyes that dimmed the breaking east. What was their languid grace but the softness of chambering? And what was their shimmer but the shimmer of the scum that mantled the cesspool of the court of a slobbering Stuart. And he tasted in the language of memory ambered wines, dying fallings of sweet airs, the proud pavan: and saw with the eyes of memory kind gentlewomen in Covent Garden wooing from their balconies with sucking mouths and the poxfouled wenches of the taverns and young wives that, gaily yielding to their ravishers, clipped and clipped again. (p.233)

Occurring very near the end of the book, this richly stylized paragraph, more than pastiche but certainly no parody, is a key exercise in the forging of Stephen's conscience, an epiphany of the epiphanist encountering for the millionth time a reality of experience which is all the more real as it registers the pressures of representation itself. This "spell of arms and voices," detached from its surroundings by an all too noticeable artifice of imagery and vocabulary, yet activating a much stronger, much livelier form of reading, is a manifest emblem of music as poised between physical drive and metaphor, at once the most mediated and the most immediate form of language. The frequent metamorphic and allegoric crossings between music and sexuality in Joyce's fiction have their ground on this dialectics of style and the posited image of a style-less, immediate physicality. So far this brief passage has been Stephen's greatest achievement; imaginary and fragmentary as it is, it is a much more personal statement than the villanelle inspired by Emma: there the virtuosity was derivative in a weak sense, as the budding Stephen claimed (to himself) to be a poet, but could only bring himself to emulate, not fully consciously, the *risqué* lyrics of Wilde, D'Annunzio or Arthur Symons. The Elizabethan paragraph, on the contrary, is a model of wilful misprision; it is made up of those images which, by an ironic turn, it will disabuse as literary, idealized and beautiful. It is essential for this very purpose that the pastiche be good, that the beauty of the manipulation be suspended before our eyes in all its exhilarating artistry: and Joyce is always exhilarating when he does that. Stephen, nevertheless, dismisses the exercise as mere "old phrases, sweet only with a disinterred sweetness ..." What Stephen is searching for is the means without means to express unrest of blood, as exemplified in his next sentence: "Yes, it was her body he smelt: a wild and languid smell: the tepid limbs over which his music had flowed desirously and the secret soft linen upon which her flesh distilled odour and dew." The motifs are essentially the same, and the sentence amounts to a translation to the present and the personal of what before was in the past and general. The irony, however, is that Stephen here is piteously reaching for Life, phenomenal and urgent, while unwittingly rewriting *Sweets of Sin*. But this irony is not Stephen's, it is Joyce's, and it is only Stephen's in so far as in this autobiography of style he returns as Joyce to imitate—to repeat ironically—his own early gestures of fire and weak bold misprision.[2]

One effect of stylized allusions of this kind is to expose the illusion of natural discourse, natural life; it follows as a corollary that the stylization will place (or displace) what is alluded to in a critical culturescape. The question we must then ask is: Where is Joyce himself? Who grants him immunity of vision? Or, to reverse Nietzsche's formulation: Who is the author, and what power does he seek to gain over the text? In a work where all words are borrowed words, "one world burrowing on another" (*FW* 275.06), which words are Joyce's own, if any? Is *Ulysses* really an epic of the writer-subject as Everyman, as we have so often been told? Is *Portrait* then the education of this ecumenic apostle? I, for one, do not read either book as an *Apologia Pro Vita Sua*, and least of all as a blessing. In the closed, repetitive, institutionalized structure of borrowed life that constitutes Joyce's vision, there can be no privileged position, no outside and no outsider. If Joyce cannot be unambiguously found in his own texts, it is because he has disappeared therein, along with every other representation of omniscient authorship and stable identity. Do we ever hear Joyce's voice in *Ulysses* or *Finnegans Wake*? I am not sure. His Hitchcockian brief appearances, if such they are, would, besides, be liable to the same charges of stylization directed against any other of his characters.[3] It is not for nothing that Joyce's work has been particularly stimulating to Bakhtinian analysts: dialogism is its very subject, heteroglossia its language.[4] This is as abundantly evident in *Finnegans Wake* as, with only a little less show, in the early works. Throughout *Portrait*, for instance, we are always made aware of a gap between Stephen himself as the memorialist writing and an (other) author painting him in the act. Parallel to Stephen's sentimental and political education, what *Portrait* portrays is a series of transfers that take Stephen from one Jamesonian prisonhouse to another, and it describes him according to corresponding stages of linguistic constraint, since for Joyce (though not yet for Stephen) there is no unconstrained vantage point from which to write. The role of allusions must be understood from this perspective: if they are there for the sake of satisfying a high modernist encyclopedic impulse—as the humanist tradition of Joycean scholarship has stressed again and again—it is also true that the encyclopedia is treated in a stricter etymological sense, as a "circle of knowledge" (*kyklos* + *paideia*), a closed circle, or more accurately a series of concentric circles, mirroring one another within the circumscribing frame of *Finnegans Wake*.[5]

Every allusion is a marker: for us, readers of Stephen, his allusions are the signposts of his erudition, his hereticism, his hermeticism, his confusion, his aloofness, his aspirations, his efforts to withstand the symbolic as well as the very material pressures of fatherland, home, church, language, gender, capital and art. For Stephen himself they are active elements of an unrepresentable motion of difference, or of forging, as he says, while alluding to Ibsen (*Brand*), Blake (Los) and Wagner (Siegfried). His allusion to "the age of Dowland, Byrd and Nash" is a defensive behaviour just as much in *Portrait* as in *Eumaeus*, when he resists Bloom's entrepreneurial aesthetics with

> praises of Shakespeare's songs, at least of in or about that period, the lutenist Dowland who lived in Fetter lane near Gerard the herbalist, who *annos ludendo hausi, Doulandus*, an instrument he was contemplating purchasing from Mr Arnold Dolmetsch, whom B. did not quite recall though the name certainly sounded familiar, for sixtyfive guineas and Farnaby and son with their *dux* and *comes* conceits and Byrd (William) who played the virginals, he said, in the Queen's chapel or anywhere else he found them and one Tomkins who made toys or airs and John Bull. (*U* 16.1761–69)

Joyce's mimetic feat here is something of a stylization to the fourth degree; these are Stephen's words, Stephen's borrowed words, as reported by Bloom in Bloom's attempted literary style. Allusions proliferate: Stephen has read enough about Dowland to know that Fetter lane was the address of the lutenist's family in London—a detail which now brings to mind his discussion of Hamlet, earlier in *Scylla and Charybdis*, when he had thought of "a rosery of Fetter lane of Gerard, herbalist" (*U* 9.651). He knows, and quotes—to Bloom, of all people—Ralph Sander's Latin anagram, *Johannes Doulandus Annos Ludendo Hausi* ("playing I used up my years"). Consistently troping on music-making as love-making, he makes a pun on Byrd laying the virginals. We still do not know what Stephen *hears* in this music, but he is clearly attracted by the poetic aura of old "conceits," as much as by the old names and old words: lutenist, herbalist, *dux*, *comes*, Tomkins, John Bull, Farnaby and son, toys, airs. What seems more significant, though, is that Stephen here is playing off his knowledge and his taste against Bloom's. Just as Joyce's characters inhabit an integrally tabulated universe, where everything displays an exchange value and everything speaks in pounds, shillings and dimes, and just as they are constantly made to tabulate their small budgets (notice the sixtyfive guineas), so there is also instituted a semiotic commerce of allusions, where every reference commands its price in symbolic exchange. This is dramatized by Bloom's immediate imaginary canvassing of Stephen's talents; he is ready to capitalize on the young man with "a phenomenally beautiful tenor voice like that" and "with his university degree of B.A. (a huge ad in its way)." While Stephen is singing Johannes Jeep's *Dulcia dum loquitur*,[6] Bloom reflects that "original music like that, different from the conventional rut, would rapidly have a great vogue," and that Stephen "had a capital opening to make a name for himself," as well as "causing a slight flutter in the dovecotes of the fair sex." We know, however, that Bloom will never realize any of his great managerial enterprises, and the passage is comic because, as with a different case later in *Ithaca*, *we* know that Bloom knows that Stephen knows this is foreclosed: everyone is perfectly clear and perfectly hopeless about it. The association of music with an economically determined symbolic status is as inevitable and constant in Joyce's works as is its relationship with sex; I will return to this point below, when we read some excerpts from *Dubliners*.

Before leaving this passage, though, I must comment briefly on Stephen's reference to Arnold Dolmetsch. Dolmetsch, from whom Stephen (like Joyce himself)[7] was contemplating purchasing a lute, was, of course, the grand pioneer of the early music movement. "Early music" in this context, however, must be understood for what it was then, and not for what it has become today; that is, a strong appropriation, or fictionalization of the past, signalized by the inauthenticity of its very name, and conducted in accord with a recuperative project characteristic of most, if not all Modernisms. For Stephen, then, early music, or more specifically Elizabethan music, still retains at this time something akin to what Arnaut or Cavalcanti once meant to Pound: a liberation of reading, an attempt to control history, and a practice of negativity, or resistance. It is in view of this that Stephen's realization of the music, as constructed in the texts, seems so disappointing.

It could not be otherwise: misreading is Joyce's psychopolitics of everyday life. Similarly to Freud in his treatment of the parapraxes, the Joycean critique has its focus on the identity of reading and misreading, which for Joyce (though not for Freud) becomes itself a metonymy for the relations between repression and (cultural) overdetermination. What is revealing, however, is that Stephen at this stage is still misreading *weakly*, ventriloquising communal paradigms. In the middle of writing his villanelle, he probes his memory for images with which to continue. He sees himself singing to Emma

one of his curious songs ["curious" is Emma's epithet], sitting at the
old piano, striking chords softly from its speckled keys and singing . . .
to her who leaned beside the mantlepiece a dainty song of the Elizabethans, a sad and sweet loth to depart [old piano, softly, dainty,
sad and sweet, beside the mantlepiece—is this John Dowland's music
or Burt Baccarach's?] . . . While he sang and she listened, or feigned
to listen, his heart was at rest but when the quaint old songs had
ended . . . ["quaint" is close to "curious," but it is Stephen's
word] he remembered his own sarcasm . . . (P 219).

Stephen's choice of the Elizabethans, as of Sweelinck and Jeep in *Eumaeus*,
is a partly wilful and partly intuitive cultural deviation, but this is not yet
kenosis[8]: his sentimentalization will be undone by what is sentimentalized:
his reading is hardly his, and reveals more about its own deficiencies than
anything it might do to Byrd or Dowland. The evidence is scant, but what
we see of the narrator in *Giacomo Joyce*, playing "lightly and softly singing,
John Dowland's languid song," (p. 9) and what we hear of Stephen's
performances in *Portrait* and *Ulysses* point toward highly sentimentalized
renderings, confounded by trite late nineteenth-century fixations, as well as
quite personal ones.[9] Elizabethan song, for this sensitive adolescent undergoing sexual crisis as well as authorial anxiety and financial duress, may be a
personal terrain from which to conduct his poetic warfare, but it is also,
and perhaps predominantly, an allegoric substitution for (his inability to
engage in) sexual love—and Stephen's daydreaming will develop symp-
tomatically in that direction: "She passed now dancing lightly across his
memory as she had been that night at the carnival ball . . . At the pause in
the chain of hands her hand had lain in his an instant, a soft merchandise."
All the elements for a sexual-economic critique of music are here, but they
are not to be articulated by Stephen in any coherent way. What is ironically
represented is the fact that music, for Stephen, has charms that go beyond
rhetorical persuasion, indeed cannot be read rhetorically, which must mean
they cannot be read at all, but somehow bodily taken in. It is the symptomatic portrait of a subjectivity in flight, unable to command Romantic
irony and reduced to the weary "broken cries and mournful lays" of an
overflowing yet unfulfilled disenchantment.

EVELINE AND THE BOARDING HOUSE

To these images of song as the scene of seduction, there correspond the
counter-scenes of listening as interrogation and rogation. Before addressing
these, however, I must complement the first group with some brief examples drawn from *Dubliners*. I purposely choose them from stories other

than *The Dead*, in which music is most conspicuously a central theme, at once the symbol and the ambience of life and of death. Joyce's treatment of music in *Eveline* is no less significant: it marks every modulation of circumstance and feeling in the story. As the "broken harmonium" is an emblem for the family's economic and moral disaster, so is the street organ's "melancholy air of Italy" a sounding icon of mourning in release, the coincidental tolling of Eveline's mother's death, resounding now at a moment when she unconsciously and unsuccessfully construes the death of her father. ("He would miss her," she thinks—a defensive projection for the fact that *she* will wish/miss him dead.) The "black mass" of the boat pursues this deadly allegory to the sounds of "a mournful whistle into the mist" and "a bell [that] clanged upon her heart." Eveline's unassailable motionlessness is a triumph of the death drive over the erotic alternative offered her by Frank's courtship. She yields momentarily to Frank as she yields to Eros under the sign of music:

> He took her to see *The Bohemian Girl* and she felt elated as she sat in an unaccustomed part of the theatre with him. He was awfully fond of music and sang a little. People knew that they were courting and, when he sang about the lass that loves a sailor, she always felt pleasantly confused. (p.39)

What is evidenced here, as in countless other similar occasions, is that music for Joyce cannot be understood outside of an erotic, endlessly mediated zone: something that Eveline intuits as well, though ideological censoring makes it impossible for her to verbalize it, either to herself or to others—and something that Stephen Dedalus will learn to distinguish in a "dainty song of the Elizabethans" no less than in the bought, "frank uplifted eyes" (*P* 101) of a first providential whore. Beyond this, which might by now have been expected, the excerpt also exemplifies an attendant observation: that all music is inconstant and equal to its specific location, that is, to its socially, therefore symbolically burdened space. Eveline felt elated "as she sat in an unaccustomed part of the theatre"—the erotic attraction of capital playing as important a part in this as the capital appeal of a wishfully "frank"[10] romance. This same point is unwittingly made by the narrator in *Cyclops*, who speaks of "a duet in the opera" (*U* 12.704)—where the colloquial, symptomatic "the" allows for a telling ambiguity. Synecdochic substitutions of place or dress for song abound in Joyce's works. This is the sense, for instance, of Leopold Bloom's (Henry Flower's) Orphic appearance in *Circe*, theatrically garmented with "dark mantle and drooping plumed sombrero," carrying his orientalized dulcimer and a longstemmed pipe whose bowl is fashioned as a female head, with "dark velvet hose and silverbuckled pumps," the romantic Saviour's face with flowing locks and the "spindlelegs and sparrow feet" of Mario the tenor (*U* 15.2478–90).[11] The substitution in this case is circular; costume stands for song as song stands for conventionalized sexual-economic drives, one of whose prime forms of representation is, precisely, the theatrical conventions of the day.[12] Such sequences always depend on a posited identity between, on the one hand, music, sexuality and capital and, on the other, performing locations as ritual, socially accepted spaces for the incestuous interplay between the former three.

Eveline is a tale of the return of the repressed, but here the repressed and the repressive coincide: in musical experiences, for instance, at once figures of fullness and submission. Turn-of-the-century Dublin was, by all accounts, an extraordinarily active musical city, and the signs and effects of music are accordingly chronicled in virtually every story in *Dubliners*. The following passage comes from *The Boarding House*:

> Mrs Mooney's young men paid fifteen shillings a week for board and lodgings (beer or stout at dinner excluded). They shared in common tastes and occupations and for this reason they were very chummy with one another. ... Jack Mooney, the Madam's son, who was clerk to a commission agent ... had always a good one to tell them and he was always sure to be on to a good thing—that is to say, a likely horse or a likely *artiste*. He was also handy with the mits and sang comic songs. On Sunday nights there would often be a reunion in Mrs Mooney's front drawing-room. The music-hall *artistes* would oblige; and Sheridan played waltzes and polkas and vamped accompaniments. Polly Mooney, the Madam's daughter, would also sing. She sang:
>
> > *I'm a ... naughty girl.*
> > *You needn't sham:*
> > *You know I am.*

Everything that has been discussed so far is represented in this extract: composition of place as the social placing of composition, commoditiza-tion[13] of song in symbolic and sexual exchange, authorial use of borrowed idiolect and disintegration of the monophonic voice ("young men" is Mrs Mooney's expression, "very chummy" is the young men's own, "a good one to tell" Jack Mooney's, etc.). The story as a whole, however, will also serve to introduce two more characteristics of Joyce's fiction; namely, the use of song-lyrics as myth and the reflexive nature of Joyce's major texts, always rewriting one another.

After *Finnegans Wake* has taught us how to read, it is difficult not to reread Joyce's other works as if they were part of it. Conversely, a return to the earlier texts may also expose aspects of his last book so far unnoticed—as is the case with *The Boarding House*. To read it as an intimation of episodes as well as techniques associated with *Finnegans Wake* means that, on one level, special attention might be payed to the onomastic punning going on, and on another, to the set, paradigmatic characterization, which suggests some underlying matrix likely to have been exploited by the story. Having thus been alerted by such names as "Mooney" (combining money and moon—a recurrent Joycean figure for woman, menstrual cycle, lunacy), or "Polly" (an avatar of the *poules* in *Finnegans Wake*—of which more anon—as well as a metem-psychotic Polly Peacham), or even "Hardwicke" Street (the address of the "Madam's" establishment), and having considered this description of a Sunday night's musical procuring, it will now be the name of Mr Doran—one of Mrs Mooney's tenants, a clerk seduced by Polly Mooney and like her trapped into marriage obligations miserable to both— that will provide the strongest indication of where and what to search for. "Bob Doran" reappears a few times in *Ulysses*; in *Cyclops*, for instance, the narrator observes the pitiful drunkard by the counter and then imagines him "of a Sunday with his little concubine of a wife, and she wagging her tail up the aisle of the chapel ... doing the little lady.... And the old prostitute of a mother procuring rooms to street couples. Gob, Jack made him toe the line. Told him if he didn't patch up the pot, Jesus, he'd kick the shite out of him" (*U* 12.811–16). The name appears yet again in *Finnegans Wake*; it is the surname of the hen Biddy Doran, who finds Anna Livia Plurabelle's letter in a rubbish heap, and who simultaneously doubles as one of ALP's multiple images. "Biddy Doran" has been variously glossed as relating to Brigid (the pagan goddess of poetry and fertility), St. Bridget (a Christian version of Brigid, and as such the female patron of Ireland), Biddy O'Brien (a mourning friend of Tim Finnegan, in the Ballad of "Finnegan's Wake") and, by way of Greek *doron*, meaning "gift," to Pandora (the Greek Eve, whose "box" contained "all ills flesh is heir to") and Dora (not only Freud's patient, but also D.O.R.A., the Defense of the Realm Act, a censoring device). Since she is once called "Belinda," both Roland McHugh and Adaline Glasheen[14] link her to Pope's Belinda, in *The Rape of the Lock*; and for other reasons, which need not be discussed, Biddy Doran is also seen as more indirectly having to do with Charlotte Brook (the eighteenth-century compiler of an anthology of Irish verse) and Sheridan's Lydia Languish (from *The Rivals*). All these annotations are, nevertheless, not entirely convincing. As it so often happens, the glosses, though extensive, still seem somewhat insufficient, accessory, they too like hens pecking around a rubbish mound for an indistinguishable letter. One of the most idiosyncratic effects of *Finnegans Wake* is to induce such an unmitigating, half-blind hunger for glosses, which can turn us all into pecking, cackling hens; it is just one of the ways in which Joycean scholars are made to reproduce the very structure of knowledge caricatured and

undermined by the text. It is another typically Joycean joke that in this case
not only does a better explanation, a central reference around which all the
others have their orbit, actually exist, but it had already been used by Joyce
himself, in *Ulysses*.

I am referring to the "Ballad of Doran's Ass," alluded to by another
Madam, Bello, while chastising Leopold Bloom in *Circe*: "I'll teach you to
behave like a jinkleman! . . . Aha! By the ass of the Dorans you'll find I'm a
martinet" (*U* 15.3023–25). According to Gifford and Seidman,[15]
"Doran's Ass" is an Irish ballad about one Paddy Doyle who, drunk one
night, mistakes Doran's jackass for his sweetheart, Biddy Tool, and copu-
lates with the ass. Suddenly realizing what he has just done, Paddy then
rushes back to Biddy:

> *He told her the story mighty civil*
> *While she prepared a whiskey glass:*
> *How he hugged and smugged the hairy divil*
> *"Go long," says she, "'twas Doran's ass!"*
> *"I know it was, my Biddy darling."*
> *They both got married the very next day,*
> *But he never got back his ould straw-hat*
> *That the jackass ate up on the way.*

There can be no doubt that this is the principal source for Joyce's Biddy
Doran. What is particularly striking then is the fact that Joyce has mingled
the girl and the ass in a single name: this in itself defines Joyce's par-
onomasic, anal reading of the ballad as centered upon a metamorphic pun
on "ass." Paronomasia and anality are, of course, two fundamental elements in the writing of *Finnegans Wake*, and also, or so it would now seem
in retrospect, of *A Boarding House*. Both have to do with Joyce's mimetic
representation of the unconscious (though it must always be made clear that
this is a reified, stylized kind of mimesis). The puns are similar to the
dream-work in that the relationship between incompatible and simultaneous signifieds is often more significant than the signifieds themselves.
Anality, or more narrowly anal sex—which is non-gender defined—
constitutes an instinctual challenge to many assumptions sustained by the
id concerning both female and male sexual determination. So anality is
related to the confusion of gender that will plague Joyce's characters with
increasing force in each succeeding work. And anality performs yet another
role for Joyce: it is a manifestation of his overtly anti-Catholic stance on the
issues of contraception and preservatives, much debated during the first
decades of this century.[16] The "ould straw-hat" in the ballad, like the
"white hat"—or "caoutchouc kepi," or "rubberised inverness," or more
simply "gum"—which the characters of *Finnegans Wake* are often begged to

take off (to the tune of a celebrated music-hall refrain) are all metaphors for the condom, Joyce's prime symbol of sex for pleasure, not for reproduction. Anal fixations and scatophilia are equally important, especially in connection with literary and artistic self-expression, but these need not be of concern to us at this point. The question that must be addressed is what the role of this ballad may be in structuring narrative patterns in *Finnegans Wake* as well as in Joyce's earlier fiction, and what significance the choice of music, or more specifically of song-lyrics, may have had in this.

Beyond anality and punning, the ballad of "Doran's Ass" offers a demotic Irish version of an old topos: a young man seduced by a young woman and (both) forced by a parental figure, as representative of a double-faced, quick-witted law, into what turns out to be a convenient marriage, at least for the latter. Variations of this set are also possible: the young man may be the seductor, rather than the seduced, the mother or father may be substituted by the young woman's brother (a Jack Mooney), etc., but the basic structure of relationships, the allocation of fixed functions for characters in one or another position remains the same. It is only within the tradition of this model that the abrupt leap between the fifth and the sixth lines of the ballad can be accepted, a drunken bawdy scene of sodomy being followed, without transition, by rushed nuptials "the very next day." The ellipsis is made possible because in a sense the story is already all too well known; it is less an individual, "original" tale than the retelling of an archetypical matrix, for which indeed there can be no origin, no first source, but only the synchronic multiplicity of versions that is characteristic of myth. I do not refer to myth by mere analogy: if anality and puns are thematic and technical representations of the unconscious, myth too stands for Joyce as the collective equivalent of individual neurosis, a thematic replication of structural laws which both derive from the unconscious and are imposed upon it by institutional repetitive pressure, itself the result in part of such unconscious circumscription.[17] (It must also be noted that the dream images developed by Joyce replicate universal oneiric themes which repeat mythology themselves.) Many such tale-patterns are reduplicated in Joyce's work, the stories of Odysseus and the ballad of "Finnegan's Wake" being only the most notorious examples. The assumed strategy of withstanding the historical incubus by seemingly standing outside it, suspended above supercycles of mythical repetition, is a commonplace of Modernist scholarship. Joyce's use of the ballad of "Doran's Ass" in *The Boarding House* would seem clear enough from this perspective; only this fails to acknowledge that what Joyce is really and characteristically registering is the violence of mythical representation itself. As employed and modified by Joyce, mythical narrative always performs a triple function: it is a means of containing the proliferation of details, so important for the surface of his prose; it makes of every tale a doubling, one more actualization in an infinite, Nietzschean series of repetition in difference; and it delivers itself as an arbitrary, cultural liquidation of experience, though one whose determining gesture bears a would-be natural signature. In what concerns the use of the ballad of "Doran's Ass" in *Finnegans Wake*, given the binary oppositions that permeate its text, and bearing in mind that there are also plenty of suggestions of a hasty wedding between HCE and ALP, particularly in connection with the story of the Norwegian captain (in chapter II.3), not to speak of the blatant association of the Porters' pub with a brothel, it is perhaps not too fanciful to conceive of "Doran's Ass" as a counterpart to the ballad of "Finnegan's Wake." If the latter retells the myth of the Fall and (sexual) Second Coming, "Doran's Ass" represents Joyce's first myth of music itself, as the conflictual realm of physical love and social constraint, immediacy and ideology. To posit this ballad as thematically essential to the book would, for one thing, make us reconsider Joyce's perhaps not so naive assertion that *Finnegans Wake* was "pure music,"[18] although with regard to this other factors too must be involved. As for the possible objection (which I have encountered in seminar rooms) that this ballad cannot be seen explicitly in the text, I am not moved to greater eloquence than simply to remind the objectors that "explicit" language is hardly Joyce's favored mode, and that, in the context afforded by his late work, no allusion need be more explicit than the name Biddy Doran already is.

It is, in any case, significant that "Doran's Ass" and "Finnegan's Wake," like many other of Joyce's narrative scenarios (including the texts of "*La ci darem la mano*," "*Tutto è sciolto*," or "At Trinity Church I Met my Doom," the latter being closely related to "Doran's Ass") are not purely literary texts, but song-settings: in other words, there is here an ostensible association between Joyce's treatment of music and of myth. Two reasons are likely, as I see it, for this recurrent coupling: one is the structural homology obtaining between musical compositions and the organization of myths, something that has not yet been examined, but which will be of concern to us when we discuss the presence of etymological clusters in *Finnegans Wake*; the other is thematic, and has to do with Joyce's mythology of music as such, in its affinity to some of the sexual and economic myths often repeated in his fiction. The text of these ballads is amenable to mythical treatment in so far as they provide a set of traditionally fixed character-functions allowing for potentially infinite reduplication. Hearing these texts as music, though, and not simply as poetry—a fallacy the critics have often incurred—may transform our reading of them in previously unsuspected ways. In the case of *The Boarding House*, for example, it would oblige us to view the story as a Chinese-box of musical portrayals, the Sunday night episode re-enacting the tale of music as the scene of seduction, encapsulated by a larger, doubling narrative that is itself derived from its musical version as a ballad, which is borrowed by the story as a whole. *The Boarding House* dramatizes—perhaps over-dramatizes—an image of music whose effects Joyce (at first) resisted both by exposure and aesthetic theorization. The similarly interactive pattern of micro and macro narrative patterns operating in *Finnegans Wake* provides for an altogether different response, which I take to be Joyce's final and most mature critique of music. More ground has to be covered, however, before it can be properly assessed.

"REAL CLASSICAL"

Joyce's repertory of musical allusions could in itself be the subject of a much longer study than this one. My purpose so far has been merely to map out (in as general a manner as possible, while analysing specific examples) the strategic dissemination of musical references and musical imagery through-out Joyce's major writings, and to relate it briefly to some other fundamental issues at work in the text. A particularly important element that would need to be further explored is the subtly emphatic way in which musical taste helps to define, if not all, then at least the large majority of Joyce's characters, in terms that go beyond aesthetic appreciation to the semiotic over-determinations characteristic of an emerging late-capitalist world. Contrary to the received opinion, much debated but recently on the rise again,[19] that Joyce's characters are super-tangible, more-than-human portrayals from life, it seems to me that they are better perceived either as conventionalized theatrical hyperboles (and there is much to be said for accounts of both *Ulysses* and *Finnegans Wake* in terms of theater) or else as Daumier-like caricatures of the Dublin bourgeoisie and working-class, but in any case as points of magnified definition in an ideological force-field. If they then appear to be so viscerally human, it is exactly because "humanity" may be much closer to such stereotypical, restrictive staged forms than what is proposed by the (embarrassingly reactionary) humanist idealism of those, mostly American, critics who might be collectively described as the Joycean New Age. The mimetic abandonment of Joyce's writing is, if anything, an abandonment to reification, an attempt to discard illusion through reflexive stylistic exposure (a characteristic feature of all modernisms, as Theodor Adorno has shown). What has been said of music above must be understood from this larger perspective: the point is that Joyce's characters' musical horizon is determined by ideological closure, and that their ways of experiencing music, as given in the text, must seem almost obligatory, in light of what Marx (and Joyce) views as the structural limits imposed upon thought by class positioning within the social totality. If Joyce's work charts "the crisis of liberal capitalism," as Franco Moretti has said of *Ulysses*,[20] and as could also be argued of every other of his books, then it is only to be expected that his treatment of music should isolate that same vision of cultural superfluity, industrial control and inflationary, universal commoditization which accompanies the material and epistemic shifts characteristic of modernity. (This is one aspect of Joyce's sociology of music which I intend to take up on another occasion.) For now, to complete this bird's-eye view of musical allusions in Joyce's works, I only want to mention something that might be seen as a massive allusion by default, the quite conspicuous absence of references to instrumental music in these texts. With a few, isolated exceptions—such as Stephen's citation of Sweelinck's variations, in *Eumaeus* (these too being a set of variations on what is for him a highly symbolic song), or the brief and metaphoric descriptions of a street harpist (an image of Ireland) and a street-organ player (a harbinger of death; see above), in *Dubliners*—all music alluded to by Joyce is vocal, ranging from song-settings to Mass and operatic arias. One simple reason for this is the not so simple equation between types of musical listening and a complex of institutionalized musical customs in the public sphere. In what concerns instrumental music, a somewhat moribund, but still exploitable Romantic legacy has it that this is the highest mode of musical expression, the very embodiment of music as an intelligible, though transcendental language, a language comprehensible solely in its own terms, and therefore to be reputed as superior to all other, less indirect forms of representation. This idea, however, is less a legacy of Romantic music proper than of twentieth-century misinterpretations of early nineteenth-century theories about eighteenth-century music. It is true that an image of music can be distinguished behind the ambitions of much nineteenth-century poetry, and Symbolist poetry in particular (which was considerably important for Joyce), but "music" there is invoked primarily for its *textual* nature, and as part of a continued battle between the poetic and the (quite literally) instrumental reason. I will elaborate on this point at the end of this essay; for now, I only want to stress the distinction between the idea of instrumental music in, say, Rousseau, or Keats, or Hegel, and the modern industrial representations of so-called "classical" music, and their sacralization in vernacular language. This is, for instance, the underlying sense of such colloquial, and therefore significant remarks as those of Miss Douce in *Sirens*: "The tuner was in today ... and I never heard such an exquisite player ... The real classical, you know" (*U* 11.277–80). "Real classical" is high praise, and from Miss Douce's point of view—which is a paradigm of common sense—it clearly elevates the piano tuner above his assumed class-image and his physical handicap. Instrumental music is associated to poetic feeling *and* to intellectual complexity: therefore to high-breeding, or high culture: therefore to potential economic solvency. If this sounds reductive, it is because the progression itself *is* reductive, like any other instance of ideological syllogism. A non-paradoxical contradiction of such false reasoning is the also widespread and distorting trivialization of High Romantic music aesthetics represented by the figure of music—specially music without words—as a universal, immediately accessible language. On the one hand, instrumental music is made to stand for the distant and the high poetic; on the other, it is assumed to be an irrational, but transparent form of communication, "the speech of the soul," as the narrator says in *Giacomo Joyce* (p.16). It is at once a Hermetic code and the Adamic *reine Sprache*. Nevertheless, it is also true that no amount of social critique could ever be enough to indict the aesthetics of instrumental music today, as the only available modern aesthetics of musical intelligibility, as well as of musical intelligence. For Joyce too, it must have had this weight: but if the void left by the disappearance of instrumental music from his writings is to be understood, it must be considered against his own formulation of an aesthetic theory in the Paris and Pola notebooks, and its fictional elaboration in the words of Stephen Dedalus in *Portrait*.

APPLIED AQUINAS

The Paris notebook was written in 1903; it was complemented by a shorter set of speculations collected in the Pola notebook, of 1904. In conjunction with some earlier essays, these were then employed by Joyce as a source for the discussion of aesthetics in *Stephen Hero*, which in its turn would be rewritten ten years later, with considerable alterations, for inclusion in chapter 5 of *Portrait* (pp. 204–215). It is important to bear in mind the successive dates of composition of this material; for whereas there is no reason to doubt that the early notebooks represent a distillation of Joyce's own thoughts at the time, there is evidence everywhere in the text of *Portrait* (not to speak of the works that followed) to suggest that his aesthetic theory had undergone very definite changes in the intervening years. I mention this because the subject is still too often discussed from a perspective that tends to equate the late, published texts of Joyce with his earliest manuscript sketches, just as the perspective is made to resolve upon a single fugal point, binding the author, his signature, his past life, his person, and his fictional character as one. Yet what there is here is another of those typically Joycean junctures where the very notion of identity is put in check. The inside-outside of Thomist philosophy in Joyce can only be read as a form of textual conflict, even when, as in this case, the conflict is a theoretical one concerning the text's production. In what follows, I have tried to summarize, as briefly as possible, only those points which have a bearing on Joyce's account of music; it is not by any means an exhaustive review of Joyce's ideas on aesthetics. It will be seen that the difficult slippage obtaining between authorial and character voices has not a little to do with a theory of music.

The Paris notebook begins by differentiating aesthetic emotion, which is static,[21] from active feelings of desire and loathing, which urge us to go to or from something. "All art ... is static, for the feelings of terror and pity [inspired by tragedy] on the one hand and of joy [inspired by comedy] on the other hand are feelings which arrest us." The end of all art is "the apprehension of the beautiful," which depends on this rest to be properly presented and properly seen by us. Art is defined as "the human disposition of sensible or intelligible matter for an aesthetic end."

The Pola notebook develops the argument, then, with the definition of the beautiful and the act of apprehension. The beautiful, like the true, is spiritually possessed (it is not an immanent quality of the object); it is desired by the "aesthetic appetite [Aquinas's *appetitus*, the inclination of a thing toward some good] which is appeased by the most satisfying relations of the sensible," as the intellectual appetite is appeased by the most satisfying relations of the intelligible (remember that, according to the formulation above, both sensible and intelligible matter may be so disposed as to serve an aesthetic end). "Those things are beautiful the apprehension of which pleases"—a translation of Aquinas's *Pulchra sunt quae visa placent*, identifying *visio* with *apprehensio*, and thus stressing the effect of beauty on the subject. Apprehension implies three activities: simple perception, or cognition; recognition ("there is no activity of simple perception to which there does not succeed in whatsoever measure the activity of recognition," which is judgmental); and, finally, satisfaction, "the nature, degree and duration of the satisfaction resultant from the apprehension of any sensible object ..."

Stephen's dialogue with Cranly in *Stephen Hero* equates this theory of apprehension with Aquinas's three conditions of beauty: *integritas*, *consonantia*, and *claritas*. These are translated as "wholeness," seeing the thing as *one* thing, "symmetry," seeing the thing as a *thing*, and "radiance," seeing that it is *that* thing which it is (pp. 212–13). As rewritten in *Portrait*, symmetry is changed to "harmony," Cranly becomes Lynch, but more importantly, the earlier explanation of *claritas* as the moment of "epiphany," when the soul of the object "leaps to us from the vestment of its appearance," is now restricted to the self-signifying proportion of the whole, the *quidditas*, or whatness of a thing, the "supreme quality of the aesthetic image," apprehended in the "luminous silent stasis of esthetic pleasure." (Joyce would never use the term "epiphany" again, unless disparagingly; its connotations were clearly embarrassing to him.) The dialogue ends with Stephen's classification of lyrical form, where the artist "is more conscious of the instant of emotion than of himself as feeling emotion"; epical form, where "the centre of emotional gravity is equidistant from the artist himself and from others"; and dramatic form—which is the highest—where "the personality of the artist . . . finally refines itself out of existence, impersonalises itself . . . [so that, as with Flaubert] the esthetic image . . . is life purified in and reprojected from the human imagination."

There are three questions I want to consider with regard to this carefully articulated theory: what kind of theory is it; in which ways does it inform its own textual practice; and, finally, how does it relate to Joyce's treatment of music? The first two questions must be considered together, since the circumstances of its exposition affect the content of the theory and its value. What kind of theory is it, then? Contrary to most views (of Joyce's no less than Aquinas's aesthetics) I think it is a formal theory of the object, not the celebration of an aesthetically inspired viewer.[22] The substitution of the three stages of the act of apprehension (cognition, recognition, satisfaction), as presented in *Stephen Hero*, by Aquinas's objective conditions of beauty (*integritas, consonantia, claritas*), as it appears in *Portrait* already gives this away. The point is that the *visa placent* of Aquinas's proposition implies for Joyce not only a subjective element, but also an object whose constitution must *a priori* stimulate the aesthetic appetite. When Joyce says that anything can be aesthetically perceived, he is not by any means stating that any and everything in the world is art—the mock catechetical questions in the Paris notebook as well as in *Portrait* argue strongly against it—but rather that *for the artist* anything can be conceived or transformed into an aesthetic object, which is for Joyce not so much, or not only an aestheticist, but rather a Nietzschean outlook on the world. On the other hand, neither can the aesthetic particular be apprehended without the senses, nor can the intelligible in the sensible be grasped without an act of abstraction. The "self-signifying proportion" of the whole (the apperception of "wholeness" and "harmony") must be both experienced in the particular and understood in the general, a non-simultaneous double vision which constitutes *claritas*, as the dialectics of aesthetic apprehension. (Joyce is here closer to the reflexivity of the late Rousseau than to his more direct precursor, Pater.) What the theory propounds is not an account of aesthetic appreciation as epiphanic drunkenness, but rather a kind of second immediacy of the subject, who both gives himself to the object and resists it. "Dramatic form" is the exponential realization of such an aesthesis at the level of the author. At this point, however, the theory turns against itself: its pre-history is disavowed, and it appears to us as an aesthetic object itself, *Stephen's* thoughts on aesthetics, typically allusive and stylized. In biting its own tail, the narrative here presents a theoretical argument which both reflexively comments on the elaboration of the prose and, by its positioning within this text and even more so within the entire corpus of Joyce's work, deconstructs it as well. Besides, this same text has already sounded the death-knell of Stephen's theory in the event of Lynch's single authentic interruption of Stephen's speech, his "soft and solemn" rendition of Venantius Fortunatus' hymn, *Vexilla Regis* (a Crucifixion hymn!). It is a curious, embarrassing moment, both for Stephen, for us, and for the text: just as his theory is ultimately incapable of touching the art in art, and can only systematize around it, so the dead words on the page cannot even begin to make this "Great music!" heard, and can only mutely point at it. But just as Stephen had been previously rescued from a priestly life by "a quartet of young men . . . striding along . . . and stepping to the agile melody of their leader's concertina" (*P* 160), so now the text is rescued from an impossibly ambitious, self-defeating full mimesis by the silent admission of its own misprisions and the assertion of (aesthetic) non-identity. Stephen's theory must always fail before a simple evidence of song: "*Mulier cantat*," notes Cranly at a later passage, and the "soft beauty of the Latin word" seems truly "more persuading than the touch of music or a woman's hand" (*P* 244), since music and sexuality will always, to a fundamental degree, evade any discourse that is not ideologically articulate, and therefore partial, whereas the "Latin word" is an accent whose overtones are much more adequate for reading. A fuller listening than is given in these texts would be impossible for Joyce (though it was not so for Proust). To a certain extent the writing itself must substitute for it; and as for the rest, all that Joyce can reproduce is trivialized music's relentless assault on institutionally trivialized listeners. All that Joyce can say about music is that it is institutionally censored and institutionally censoring; and this is what his texts repeat again and again, as we have seen. Beyond this, however, they can *show* what they cannot say: the intangible quality of lived experience as aesthesis—something that may seem to be no less institutionally marked, but that contains in itself essential seeds of contradiction. Politicizing art for Joyce is always an aestheticizing politics of this kind; and there are two ways in which the texts enable us to see it: either by the distancing effect of stylization, or else through their own internal structure, and its demands upon the reader. There is always in Joyce's writing a contradiction between what the text says and what it is actually doing; I do not mean only the ironic exposure of stylistic repression, but a further turn against its own accusations in so far as they are divested of the individual, non-identical structure of any particular text. You cannot read one without the other: Joyce's "return to the body" is always an aesthetic return to the material form of the text as an object as well. There is, therefore, a real sense in which his prose asks to be read as music—but this is not what is usually referred to as the "musicality" of his language, since this "musicality" is a literary trope which really has very little to do with music—but rather a sense of tone and overtones, of colour and detail, which stares at us in the same way music does, from its seemingly impenetrable self-containment.

Nowhere is this shown better than in the *Sirens* chapter of *Ulysses*, Joyce's most extensive critique of music up to *Finnegans Wake*. Commentators, of late, have rightly reacted against the traditional assignment of a greatly overstated preeminence to the musical themes and techniques employed in the episode, but this seems to me a rather extreme and opposite manifestation of theoretical blindness (in the productive sense defined by de Man)—it disfigures what is ostensibly the meeting-point of all musical currents in Joyce so far, and does so in order to say precisely what could have been said about it from a musical perspective anyway, provided this went beyond the mere identification of analogies.[23] I have written on *Sirens* elsewhere,[24] and I take this as an opportunity to avoid further enlarging a paper that already seems in danger of overstepping reasonable limits; in any case, after what has been discussed above, to engage in a detailed reading of *Sirens* would be repetitive, although a few significant novel points are brought to the argument. I will restrict myself to the two most important ones.

The first is the double failure of theory, epitomized by Bloom's fart and by the narrative impasses in the face of music. Bloom's exit is the subject of a later note (for *Finnegans Wake?*) to be found in a small scrap of paper now reproduced in facsimile as page 141 of Notebook VI.B.11–2 of the James Joyce Archive. It reads: "theory ends by an impromptu fart." The question we must ask is *whose* theory ends in gas—unless we too, like Bloom, prefer to fizzle away as an answer. Bloom is certainly not my image of the great wise empirical sage, let alone a theorist of practical life. His response to music as sublimation and seduction is curiously ambiguous; on the one hand, it is a sign of resistance; on the other, it is a signal of elusion too, and of his inability to engage in listening in any way other than the most mortifying surrender. The *Sirens* episode, from this point of view, is a recital of the reality principle as the realm of simulation and of death—as indicated by Joyce's preceding annotation on the Archive sheet: "Simulacra hominis: dolls, mummies, dummies, shapes, reflections, shadows, ghosts, corpses. Doubles." The operatic act becomes a no-exit play of the consciousness unable to apprehend material life, either through the senses or through theorization, the two complementary stages of *claritas*, or lucidity. His fart is not the chapter's answer to music; it is more like music's counter-exposure of Bloom. But here once again, the theory turns against itself, since both the music that is read-as-heard in the Ormond bar and the posited figure of Bloom-as-a-real-person must transcend the limitations of commentary. The semiotic world of the signifier is also the world of signifying aesthesis, which the text reproduces almost in spite of itself. Here too, as Deleuze says of Proust's *Recherche*, "there is no Logos, there are only hieroglyphs,"[25] the text itself being the most tantalizing hieroglyph of all, confounding essence and translation, sign and meaning, in an exemplary way. This, and not Bloom's fart, is the chapter's response to music, and this, if anything, is *Joyce le symptôme*.[26] Bloom's fart, on the contrary, his farting over the "*Done*" that ends Ben Dollard's song, quite apart from the censure it passes on national virility, is both an end to the chapter and a final punctuation of Stephen's telegram to Mulligan: "*The sentimentalist is he who would enjoy without incurring the immense debtorship for the thing done*" (*U* 9.550).[27] This debtorship is incurred by Joyce against and above Bloom's fart, through its representation. But even this seems not enough, which brings us to the second point I wanted to make. It is not enough, because for Joyce his writing had not yet progressed as much as he knew it could in this direction; and it is this that for me explains his often quoted letter to Harriet Weaver, of July 1919, in which he tells her that having finished writing *Sirens*, he now found it "impossible to listen to music of any kind." His image of burned fields left behind the writing of each chapter similarly implies not only the mastery of the other but a recurring aporia of the same. To the double failure of theory is therefore added the triple failure of writing—although calling this chapter a failure would be mad, were it not for the work that followed it. If it fails, it fails because the objectification exerted by the kind of direct interpretive reading which this writing demands is necessarily at odds with what Adorno calls "the dimension in nature which speaks meaningfully" (*Aesthetic Theory*, p. 102) and which, as with works of art, can only be fully perceptible in *temps durée*. It is this temporal mode which Joyce's writing had not yet captured, a time that must be invented as the time of writing proper, not of mimesis. Music, for Adorno as for Joyce, is the pivotal model of aesthetic perception because it both implies pure immediacy, through an appropriation of time, and resists it too, that is to say, spatializes it, through an analytical reflection that must define the listening as more than mere spontaneity. "Composition" is this rational articulation of a temporal excess, a reconstruction of time which simultaneously designs its form and goes beyond its means, speaking to the non-rational, aesthetic ear. If *Ulysses* charts "the crisis of liberal capitalism," it is no less by its ideological subversions than by the assertion through art of this qualified, but irreducible form of irrationalism, which in the manner of Borges' reversed lineages might be called the Foucauldian element in Joyce. If then for the writer it does not go far enough—as Joyce must have detected while considering the comments that *Ulysses*-in-progress had elicited, from public as well as private critics—it was at any rate the crossing of the waters; and by this time, having completed *Sirens* and now moving more and more towards a different kind of writing for the remaining seven chapters of the book, he was already involved with another, much more ambitious project.

FINNEGANS WAKE: GENESIS

The genealogy of *Finnegans Wake* itself has something to do with what I have just said. Thanks to the thirty-six volumes of notebooks, typescripts, galleyproofs and odd manuscript notes now available in facsimile in the James Joyce Archive, it is possible to have a fairly comprehensive view of the evolution of the text as well as of some of its compositional principles. Indeed, there is no doubt that Joyce intended this material to be published eventually, saving every little scrap of paper and mailing notebook after notebook to his benefactress, Harriet Weaver. The writing process of *Finnegans Wake* is as much a part of the book's content as anything else,[28] and was clearly seen by Joyce as such, a fact which gives a distinct, less prosaic significance to the much abused expression "work in progress." Two questions in particular interest me here. One is posed by Joyce's immense, prolonged effort to jot down daily the ramblings of his mind, whether directly relevant to the book at this stage or not, making records of incidental images, reflections on all his previous works as well as this on-going one, free associations, dreams, personal finances, domestic trivialities, isolated words and expressions, vocabulary lists in several idioms, trial portmanteaus and puns, numbers, sums, titles, names, short sentences, etc. Much of this material was then left aside to be employed as found-objects ten, even fifteen years later in some cases. I know of no other book written in this fashion, remorselessly and systematically exploiting the author's own past verbalizations. The allusion machine feeds on these notes also, which on the whole are treated like reified bits of the culture's consciousness. The problem of writing, then, becomes a problem of framing, of finding the means to contain such an incessant flow of *materia prima*—in its double sense, as both primal and raw material. This is the issue I now want to examine, since it involves some musical techniques. What has to be addressed is not so much the function of the larger schemes in the text—Viconian cycles, internal symmetries, the main thrust of the Earwicker plot, the repetitions of the park incident as a founding scene—though these too must be dealt with later; it is rather the development of the prose itself, at a localized level.

The matter can be seen from two complementary points of view: one, genetic; and the other, structural, or as Joyce calls it, rhythmical. Genetic approaches may present their case most forcefully by comparing Joyce's earliest prose pieces, the *Epiphanies*, with this, his last book, *Finnegans Wake*, and then inquiring into the quite astounding evolution of his style over these three decades. Briefly put, there is to be seen in the latter text a bewildering proliferation of detail, which is accommodated by a no less bewildering expansion of the syntax; the question, then, is to gain insights into the technical bases that made this possible. An examination of pre-publication sources lays open the fundamental importance of troping for the growth of the text; and I mean "trope" not only in its current, rhetorical sense—which is, of course, relevant too—but also in the more restricted, medieval (and musical) sense of trope as a composition by interpolation, by addition of new material to a given old work. To a large extent, *Finnegans Wake* is a trope of this kind: it grew inside out, through the multiplication of inner clauses (even whole paragraphs, or sections) in between the relatively straightforward segments with which the text began. Proliferation and interpolation are the two most evident syntactic devices that can be discerned while reading early and late versions of the manuscript side by side. At a larger level, the accomplished units were then submitted to piecemeal, mosaic-like juxtaposition, sentence, section or episodic fusion and other such formal contrivances, as David Hayman has shown in his analysis of Joyce's drafts.[29] It should be clearer now how it was possible for Joyce to go back to old notebooks and select entries almost at random for inclusion in the text, since it is made to accommodate all, by a seemingly endless capacity for amplification. What this does not illuminate, however, is the underlying pattern of cohesion that is felt to be operative between adjacent—and sometimes even widely separate—sections of prose, an uncanny feeling of underlying unity, cutting across diverse thematic material, which more extended readings of the book always provide. In order to examine one of such binding mechanisms, it is first necessary to introduce Joyce's idea of rhythm, together with some of its fictional realizations.

RHYTHM

A definition of rhythm appears in the Paris notebook and also, slightly reworded, in *Portrait*: "Rhythm, said Stephen, is the first formal esthetic relation of part to part in any esthetic whole or of an esthetic whole to its part or parts or of any part to the esthetic whole of which it is a part" (p.206). Once again, the text demands to be read reflexively: on the one hand, this is a general definition, one that attempts to differentiate form— what happens every instant, at the smallest meaningful division of a work— from frame, the larger scaffolding of the parts of parts, and to relate them to each other; on the other hand, it is also saying something about itself, and about its relations to other parts of *Portrait* as an esthetic whole and *Portrait* as a part of the larger whole constituted by Joyce's entire oeuvre. It stands out for comparison with both earlier and later memorable images of rhythm: for example, close to the beginning of the book, while suffering his first experiences at Clongowes Wood College, the child Stephen

> thought that he was sick in his heart if you could be sick in that place. [...] He wanted to cry. He leaned his elbows on the table and shut and opened the flaps of his ears. Then he heard the noise of the refectory every time he opened the flaps of his ears. It made a roar like

a train at night. And when he closed the flaps the roar was shut off like a train going into a tunnel. That night at Dalkey the train had roared like that and then, when it went into the tunnel, the roar stopped. He closed his eyes and the train went on, roaring and then stopping. It was nice to hear it roar and stop and then roar out of the tunnel again and then stop. (p.13)

This image is repeated, with an additional analogy, only a few pages later:

First came the vacation and then the next term and then vacation again and then again another term and then again the vacation. It was like a train going in and out of tunnels and that was like the noise of the boys eating in the refectory when you opened and closed the flaps of the ears. Term, vacation; tunnel, out; noise, stop. (p.17)

Together, the two passages inaugurate a long procession of simulative figures of rhythm as interrogation, which for Stephen will come full circle in *Nestor*:

A poor soul gone to heaven: and on a heath beneath winking stars a fox, red reek of rapine in his fur, with merciless bright eyes scraped in the earth, listened, scraped up the earth, listened, scraped and scraped. (*U* 2.147–50)

Stephen's (silent) commentary elaborates on the riddle he has just proposed to his students, at the end of a history class—meaning both the goal and the disintegration of his talk. The funereal fox is Joyce's heraldic device of rhythm, a bend sinister, decorated on one side by ensigns of motherhood and recollections of his mother's death, and on the other, by fatherhood and the burial of fathers and precursors. This inevitable, rhythmical return to Dalkey and to yet another boys' school will propitiate Stephen's thoughts of poetic aimlessness and willed self-generation, of an artificial semination of the self in writing. Stephen's work and progress have been arrested at mid-point, with this riddler inquisitor-as-artist suspended between an early, overcome mute inquirer and a posited, not yet engendered artist-as-questioner, an artist as self-questioner, a self-voyeur, whose exemplary narcissism must be so formalized as to reflect everyone else's own. On the basis of what is stated in the Paris notebook, that the parts "constitute a whole in so far as they have a common end," it would therefore seem a legitimate critical task to set this last trope of rhythmical, vital questioning against the other earlier images from *Portrait*, and to ask what the sense of their rhythmical opposition may be, so as to approach the more largely significant question of their common end, as both the goal and the disintegration of Joyce's rhythmical talk, his talk on history, and history's talk to him.

Stephen's analogic exercise in the refectory is his first acknowledged fabulation of listening; it has been preceded, however, by one other questioning of sound, the "little song" of the gas in the school's corridor (*P* 12). The little song itself follows two primal recollections of song and dance, associated respectively with himself and his mother, and included in the eight epiphanies of early childhood with which the book begins. There is a difference, though, between the initial two impressions and the little song of the gas, in as much as the latter is already a poetic construction and a querying. Beyond the immediate, symmetrical affective relationships of his very early infancy, all listening is bound to be reflexive, asymmetrical and transitive; all listening will become, first, analogy, and later metaphor, but in either case a form of hermeneutics: it is precisely the evolution of Stephen's structure of interrogation that is represented, as well as conditioned by the succession of his linguistic and musical metamorphoses.

The riddle of the roar-and-stop is akin to the riddle of the fox in that they both imply for Stephen an urge to translate—to translate the untranslatable—just as all of Joyce's figures of rhythm beg us to do the same. This is why the anxiety of translation, which is the strongest form of the anxiety of reading, is epitomized in the text by images of listening, since sound cannot be translated without metaphor and without reduction. Musical listening in particular serves to highlight the difficult superposition of spatial metaphors upon time: the relation of parts to whole in music is primarily temporal—"what is audible is presented in time, what is visible is presented in space" (*P* 212)—but it is also spatial in so far as listening involves memory and the knowledge of form. The *nacheinander* is only inexactly the musical mode, since this is also analytically, that is to say, spatially informed; rhythm in Joyce's work is similarly playing upon that dialectics of visual and audible, spatial and temporal modalities which forms the subject of Stephen's meditation in *Proteus*, as well as of innumerable passages in *Finnegans Wake*, and most ostensibly of all the fable of the Mookse and the Gripes in chapter I.6.

A subtle inversion, however, has taken place between Stephen's early substitution of noise for trains for school terms, and his later, mock-professorial, unanswerable riddle in *Nestor*: in the first case, as a child he is surprised and mystified by the questions posed to him by his analogy; in the second, it is he who challenges the school children with what must seem to them like a question, though *it is in effect an answer*—just as his early analogy had been. What is common between the two tropes is, precisely, the *aesthetic* figuration of rhythm as a structure of transitive binary oppositions, which demands interpretation and yet cannot be interpreted, since the gesture of attribution bears the signature of Nature, "all things I am here to read." Such binarisms are to be endlessly re-enacted before Stephen's mind's eye: holly and ivy, green and red, Protestants and Catholics, male and female, England and Ireland, the rise and fall of waves, white roses and red roses, York and Lancaster, chastity and sin, etc. In the space of the imagination, all of these become interchangeable, by analogy or metonymy for the child, by metaphor for the adolescent poet. Later, however, once inscribed within the irrational non-geometry, the non-spatial thought of *Finnegans Wake*, this dialectics of rhythm must be seen to crumble, either because there are supplementary and unaccountable terms to it, or else because the oppositions are playfully, punningly exposed as one more fiction of identity. The contradiction between a listening which opens up to fantasy—through the well-worn, conventional paths of logocentric thought, to be sure—while simultaneously closing itself to the object is at the very center of Joyce's dissection of listening. At least until *Finnegans Wake*, there seems to be no viable way out in Joyce's fiction: either the form is heard as space, obliterating time and lived experience; or else the time of listening turns into the imaginative, fantastic time of metaphor and ideology. Stephen's riddle in *Nestor*, like his "Parable of the Plums" in *Aeolus*, signalizes a deconstructive motion of withdrawal from, rather than penetration into the gnostic depths of sight and sound as cabalistic enigmas; as such it introduces a typically Joycean approach to history which reverts to the original sense of the word as an inquiry, and can only respond to it with the imposition of violently artificial, borrowed frames, such as Viconian cycles, Homeric narratives or other rhetorical devices. It will be seen, however, that in the process of rhythmically controlling his prose, Joyce arrived at a solution that simultaneously allows for the textual surface to assert this critical identity and contradict it through understated, underlying, barely credible yet powerful figures of evasion.

LEITMOTIVES

Rhythm and memory of the text are activated by leitmotivic technique. Leaving aside the park incident and such other recurring elements as the letter, the wake, or the battle—more properly thematic than motivic—there is still a large collection of isolated words and sentences whose function is motivic, as has long been noticed.[30] The use of these motifs in *Finnegans Wake*, and to a lesser extent in *Ulysses* as well, is both a response to and a swerving away from Wagner's most notable music-dramatic method. As with Wagner, so Joyce's texts employ motifs dramatically, as conducting guidelines for the narrative surface. In this respect they are equivalent to textbook accounts of the Wagnerian leitmotive, which tend to reduce it to such a rather naive role; and some criticism of Joyce falls prey to the same reduction, even when its ambitions are considerably more sophisticated. In either case what we get is a weak adaptation of Debussy's famous *bon mot*—about Wagner's characters always having to present their card before they sing—now stripped of its belated irony and self-protective cruelty. Debussy's music itself, not only *Pelléas* but even more so *Jeux* and the other late works, is, like Joyce's *Finnegans Wake*, a much more cogent and much more destructive critique of that monstrous ancestor. Beyond their ancillary but all too apparent effects in providing character (and more generally thematic) identification, Wagner's motifs perform a triple function: they are a means for the text to comment on itself reflexively, suggesting the presence of elements that are not to be seen on stage but which explain, confirm or undermine the action; they constitute among themselves a complex symbolic matrix, in which derivation and kinship are all important (as has been well-known since Lorenz's analyses were discussed by Lévi-Strauss in *Le cru et le cuit*); and lastly, but even more fundamentally, they are the very stuff out of which Wagner's music is made. It is true that the motifs are occasionally heard in direct, blatant association with the stage drama, but they are *always*, though less spectacularly, to be heard in the orchestral fabric. Motifs are everywhere and not only for symbolic reasons: the leitmotive was Wagner's technical solution to the problem of writing extensive works in a language that is both harmonically unstable and non-periodic. The motivic nature of Wagner's music is serial and combinatory: once there is established a large enough collection of small elements, the work can proceed forever through their combination and recombination: in this it already bears the precept of the open-work, which is where Joyce's modernism finds its most Romantic inspiration.[31] The Sublime in Wagner is grounded on the mechanical, counter-sublime of this leitmotivic technique. It is self-generating, freed from chronology, and allowing for potentially infinite recombination, and so potentially greater even than the image of death, the sublimated limit of sublimity. Joyce's *Finnegans Wake* is similar to Wagner's music-dramas in this respect as well: it is his most assertive, though also most ironically deflated work on the Romantic Sublime mode—a deflation strong enough to project it into the productive spheres of modernism and beyond—and it is, of all his books, the one most burdened with mortality. Joyce's leitmotivic technique too operates on both narrative and structural levels simultaneously; but contrary to Wagner's practice, in *Finnegans Wake* the "rhythmical" play of the leitmotives is a negative motion, a non-dialectical contradiction, a saying-against that works to disrupt, not confirm the surface of the text.

ETYMOLOGICAL CLUSTERS

One of the ways in which this happens is through the etymological clusters
that crisscross the undertext of the book like an invisible system, present
(nearly) everywhere yet nowhere made explicit.[32] Etymologies in *Finnegans
Wake* are as much of a threat to the book's linear coherence as the portmanteaus and puns: no-one can tell where the line may be drawn to stop the
words' dissemination of meaning, and this applies as much to phonetic
short-circuiting and interlingual semantics as to the accumulation of past
signifieds within the individual signifier. The nature of this text is such that
all available signifieds can be made plausible by context, so that the identity
of the signifier too is put in check, as its historical phantoms wake to walk
uncertainly through strange and unnatural terms. At this point I can only
describe how a few of these clusters work; I perceive evidence of others in
the text, even though I cannot yet fully explain them, and I have no doubt
that there are many more I cannot see at all. Since the clusters are not
gradually introduced, but rather implied as a given from the very first page
of the book, I will begin by simply presenting one of them, and then
proceed to demonstrate how it is to be found and how it functions. This is
what I have called the "clock cluster:"

CLOCK/CLUCK/BELL/*BELLE*/*POULE*/
HEN/WHORE/*HORA*/CLOCK

The first reason for grouping these words is that they recur often in the
book; *Finnegans Wake* must have a record number of words used no more
than once in the text—Joyce's habit of crossing out words in the notebooks
once they had been transcribed to the manuscript, in order to avoid
repeating them, is a genetic proof for this trend—so that, when common
words like "clock" or "cluck" are to be seen reappearing time and again,
they are bound to be specially significant, and the question is to discover
why. A short answer is that it is because they are all interrelated
etymologically—though in a way that is only meaningful within the context
of the book. That clock and cluck are etymologically related is acknowledged by the text: "to kick the time off the clucklock lucklock" (531.24);
both can be related to Dutch *klok*, a bell (*klokken*, to cluck, is echoic), and
bell is also in the root line of clock through Old French *cloque* (whence
modern *cloche*). This is the kind of relation that informs such critical
passages as the meeting of HCE with the cad in chapter I.2: "could he tell
him how much a clock it was that the clock struck had he any idea by cock's
luck as his watch was bradys.... The Earwicker ... prodooced from his
gunpocket his Jurgensen's shrapnel waterbury ... but, on the same stroke,

hearing above the skirling of harsh Mother East old Fox Goodman, the bellmaster . . ." (35.18–30)—where "clock," "cock" and "bell" are telling their own story under and against the narrative tide. For a "bell" is phonetically equivalent to a "belle," a figure much used in connection with HCE's daughter Issy, or Isabel—or "is a bell" (433.03). And Isabel, as ALP's daughter, assumes Ovidian forms as both the chick, the hen, and French *poule*, hen, belle or whore. The hen, as ALP, Kate, or Issy-as-ALP, is the one who finds the letter—perhaps *Finnegans Wake* itself—in the rubbish mound: "until I lerryn Anna Livia's cushingloo, that was writ by one and rede by two and trouved by a poule in the parco!" (200.36–201.02). Scottish "hen," ALP as a whore, and Issy as the two girls who HCE (the incestuous father and pimp) meets in the park are all implicated in such statements as "while you were ringing his belle" (515.02), or "he married his markets, cheap by foul" (215.19). Clock, cluck and hen are to be read together on many occasions; I give only one more example: "my litigimate was well to wrenn tigtag cackling about it, like the sally berd she is" (364.30), where "sally" is an allusion to "Sally/Christine Beauchamp," a case of divided personality that was used by Joyce as a source for the character Issy (I am referring to personalized characters, rather than the *sigla* roles defined in the drafts, for the sake of convenience; the explanation is difficult enough to follow without this attending complication, though the book is harder still). But if a "clock" can lead to a "hen," through a series of transitive relations, the hen as "whore" can lead back to "clock" through the Old Norse *hora*, provided it is read as the Latin *hora*, or "hour," that completes the cluster.

To save space here I will merely mention three other of the most important clusters:

DEAF/DUMB/DEAD/DEW/*ROS*/*ROSS*/HORSE

BOSS/*BOSSE*/BUMP/BUSH/COW/CABBAGE

BALL/PHALLUS/BALLAD/*BALLEIN*/BAIL/BILL/BULL

I will skip here the laborious derivation of these clusters, but before I discuss the relevance of an etymological associative reading of this kind, I want to amass further evidence by presenting at least one more cluster in detail:

COD/BUCKLE/HEARING/HEAP/EAR/ARSE/SWIFT/FOX/**BEND**

cod: HCE as Finnegan/Finn MacCool associated to "fin": cod, salmon, herring, trout; "cod" is also a fool—"Hoo was the C.O.D.? Bum! . . . The Fin" (102.35); "cash on delivery;" a "pod" (a word I will return to); the scrotum. < IE *geu-*, to bend.

buckle: anal/scatological fragment frequently repeated, "the story of how Buckley shot the Russian General;" "buckle" also means to bend (< Du *bukken*).

hearing: with "heard," two of the most frequent words in the book (over 100 entries); < IE *keu-*, to notice or observe, also to arch or bend (in this sense equivalent to *geu-*). Thematically related to ear/ OE *ears*, the buttocks/ ME *ars*, arse/L *ars*, art. *keu- also the root for "heap" (rubbish heap where the letter is found). Both "bend" and "arse" and "ear" are components of Earwicker's name: Ear/*ars* + wicker, < Sw *vica*, bend. Similarly, "earwig" < OE *earwicga*, *eare*, *ear* + *wicga*, worm, < IE *weik-*, to bend. "Earwicker" also related to Vico, through L *vicus*, group of houses, whence "wick," a town (cf. first sentence of the book); to "clock," through G *Wecker*, alarm-clock; and figuratively, through (bending) "wick" to the penis.

swift: < IE *swei-*, bend; whence "swift"—Jonathan Swift and Lawrence Sterne doubles of Shem and Shaun, and Swift's Stella and Vanessa doubles of Issy as the two girls. "Swift" also a small fox; "fox" alludes to Parnell (one of his aliases); fox hunts throughout the book, alluding both to Parnell and Oscar Wilde (doubles of HCE); as a verb, "to fox," the staining of book leaves with yellowish discolorations—letter stained with a "teastain," or "pee ess" (111.20, 111.18).

bend: Notice that, as opposed to all other clusters, which are developed by association, this one is formed by rooting: every word in it *means* "bend" at a more or less removed etymological layer. From *Stephen Hero* we know that Skeat's Etymological Dictionary was Stephen's "treasure-house" of words (p.30); Joyce too "read Skeat's *Etymological Dictionary* by the hour," (p.26) so it is quite startling to find that "*band, bind, bend, bund*" is Skeat's first example of vowel change in Anglo-Saxon languages (A Concise Etymological Dictionary of the English Language. Perigee edition, 1980; p.x). In *Finnegans Wake*, this appears, slightly transformed and in capital letters on p.379: "BENK! ... BINK ... BUNK ... BENK BANK BONK." This etymological big bang may well have given rise (figuratively, and as may be seen perhaps not so figuratively) to the entire mass of words in *Finnegans Wake*, "the chords of all [linking] back" etymologically, as Stephen reflects in *Proteus* (U 3.37). At any rate, and whatever its ultimate significance, "bend," with its deviating, daemonic potential must be one of the most crucial words in the book, and one that Joyce has strategically placed in its first line ("from swerve of shore to bend of bay") and—since "along" can be derived from the IE root *lenk-*, meaning bend—also in the last.

Am I justified in reading etymological associations of this kind? Does the text allow for such a reading? Quite apart from the problem posed by etymological overdetermination, it is a distinctive feature of *Finnegans Wake* that the latter question cannot be answered in any positive sense. Any reading that can be made to relate coherently to the text is justified. It cannot be known for certain whether etymological clusters were intended by Joyce; they could be, and it seems likely that they were, but they could equally well be accidents resulting from this characteristically laminated prose. With language that is so voluminous, you can always find underground relations if you excavate deep enough, although the relations might belong to language, not to literature. The point, however, is that Joyce's text forces us to confront this very indecisiveness as the uncertainty principle of all reading, whose claims must always arbitrate against the uncertainty of the signifier. Ante-Joycean reading has its grounds on universally recognized conventions; once, however, these are exposed and disavowed, as here, then there is no apodeictic intelligence that can be self-justified without a trial. In this case, the truly critical task becomes not so much one of validation (since the validation is given *a priori*), but rather of discerning the use such a reading may have, the way it affects our previous readings and the way it can be seen to act, from the text, upon the text.

What is an etymological cluster for? It re-defines the text in many ways: it allows for counter-narratives that run subjacent to the surface—in the case of the meeting between HCE and the cad, for instance, it implies a sexual sale of the daughter—and it opposes the directional progress of the book by an experience akin to the Benjaminian "shock": once a cluster is known, the reading stops every time one of its words returns, cutting across the thickness of the book to form alternative patterns of quasi-narrative. Cluster words are also articulating, half-cadential points for Joyce's "musical prose," by which I mean his appropriation of Wagner's motivic technique, the essential factor of rhythmic organization once traditional periodic structures have been dismantled. Each word simultaneously interrupts the text, as it communicates with its own and other etymological exchange centers, and propels it forward with the energy thus gained. To read *Finnegans Wake* with an eye for etymological clusters means to perceive embedded in the prose a sequence of scattered matrixes, that can themselves be turned into narrative orders by the reader, once a certain fluency with the elements and workings of the text has been acquired. These underplots are systematically integrated; they suggest the operations of an unconscious that is truly the text's own, the etymological unconscious of the words themselves, now made apparent by a schizoid split of which Issy is the darkest muse—the same split whose global, institutional effects have been studied by Deleuze and Guattari in *Anti-Oedipus*. Etymology is the hypogram[33] of *Finnegans Wake*: it defines a region of latent meaning where language always signifies something other than what it says, and then doubles on itself as aesthetically self-signifying. Joyce's etymological hypograms *depend* on this essential undecidability: it undermines not the role of the clusters themselves but the more spontaneously assumed readings of the text as a whole, whose foundations on the autonomy of the signifier-to-signified relationship are here revealed as a matter not only of convention (as with Saussure, who could not finally contemplate his own theory of the hypogram in Latin poetry[34]), but as a coming-together that can always disband on its own volition—only there is no volition, and no one to will. Overdetermination, as Paul de Man once said,[35] is a symptom of despair as well as of control, and Joyce is not exactly the author who will make it easier to decide between these alternatives. For this is at the very heart of Joyce's subversions of writing, which not for nothing were contemporary (more or less) with Freud's psychoanalytic hypogram on the one hand and, on the other, the analytic philosophy of Wittgenstein, who was equally aware of the hermeneutic *Angst* even when he decided that it was not up to philosophy to confront it.

Moreover, it is not only through etymologies that this decentered, motivic, anarchic drive is realized in *Finnegans Wake*: even the individual letter can be an agent of counter-memory and symbolic practice. This is the case, for instance, with the letters *T* and *O*—standing for the male and female genitals[36]—or the *p* and its doubles, *q*, *b* and *d*—standing for the two girls, "the subligate sisters, P. and Q." (508.23), "as alike as two peas in a pod," or two printed pees, mythologized in the *prankquean* story (21.05–23.15) and then reappearing throughout the book in thematic guises, as "peace," "peas" or "piss," as well as their typographic icons—bid, pod, pip, dud, pub, pop, etc—all of which exploit the manifold, combinatorial "peequuliar talonts" (606.30) of this linguistic split.

It is the hypogram, thus, that alters most decisively the temporality of Joyce's work: here at last is a writing that has captured a time that is not mimetic, a time that is the writing's time as inalienably as that of music is of music. This time's modality, however, is as much a psychologizing of space—epitomized negatively by the resisting materiality of the book, as we flip pages back and forth to find our way—as it is the repetitive time of compulsion and of myth, of repetition as a symptom, or the compulsion to repeat as the tendency towards an absolute, deathly discharge. In this too, Joyce's hypogrammatic book stands as his work of revelation, as imbued with the apocalyptic tone recently adopted by philosophy as with the compulsive serial time of Viennese atonality. Yet to Schönberg's unifying model of the series, "*einziger, ewiger, algegenwärtiger*"—only one, eternal, omnipresent—Joyce substitutes, on the larger scale, a counterpoint of superimposed frames, and on the smaller scale, an irrational, unrepresentable heterophony by contrary motion that can never be resolved upon one single time signature. *Finnegans Wake* is an open work in more senses than one: it cycles back forever onto itself, it is technically open to, and suggests infinite recombination (against the arbitrariness of the self-contained, completed art-work), and it construes a daemonizing, writerly, supremely ironic bending of time which is both the expression of Joyce's art and its most fatal designation.

THE TWO CRITIQUES

I must now improve on my initial statement, so as to correct the balance between the posited divisions of Joyce's critique of music. As we have seen, there are, as it were, *two* critiques of music in Joyce's work. One is a critique of practical music, Joyce's not so dialogical theory of what might be termed listener-response, and which comprehends both a map of mishearing and a construction of the aesthetic in the age of mechanical production. The other is a critique of pure (or instrumental) music, centered upon the appropriation and transformation of musical time, and which resolves upon a counter-sublime of repetition and seriality. If Joyce's writing, especially the late works, can then be said to be "musical," it is only in view of the latter sense, which is how, paradoxically, the writing most fully comes into its own literary determination. This is not to dismiss the evidence of an unabashed sonorous language and an ostensive play of leitmotives, counterpoint and other musical devices. My point is that the most apparent handling of such musical elements does not, at the formal level, progress beyond the use of a literary, not musical, rhetoric of tropes. What is most musical in Joyce's writing does not necessarily coincide with what is thematically *about* music; yet this distinction has only rarely been made.[37]

It is also important to recognize the extraordinarily advanced conception of music offered by Joyce's late prose. For the fact is that, in spite of the (for us) misleading references to Wagner, Mozart, Italian opera, popular songs, etc., the "musical" organization of a work like *Finnegans Wake* does not correspond to any music written before Joyce; if there is a repertoire that can at least in part respond to it, it is the work of post-serial composers like Boulez or Berio.[38] "Response," in fact, is too meek a term to describe their relation to Joyce; it would be more accurate to say that we only read Joyce the way we do *because* of their music. Post-serial music owes a great deal to Joyce; "Joyce," however, or at least the normative post-structuralist Joyce, is an invention of the composers, so that the source becomes indistinguishable from the shadow. The process of influence here is hard to follow, partly on account of the reversed invention of Joyce by Boulez and his contemporaries, partly because of all these works' "interdisciplinary" predicament, and partly because reflexivity in such belated times has become defensive to

the point of warpness, an unrelieved *vertige de l'hyperbole*, where hyperbole
is another name for language. So Joyce's writing, the most self-consciously
literary language imaginable, is found to have a source in music, or more
precisely, in the patterns of assimilation and resistance between music and
language that have been a characteristic of all modernisms since Rousseau
and Beethoven. What is unusual, and remarkable, is that in his agonic reenactment of this conflict he should have almost literally invented the music
which would, in its turn, teach us how to read him in the first place.[39]

There is, therefore, a critique of judgement (of sorts), to complement the
other two critiques: it is the reading exercised by post-war composition
upon its great literary precursor. An essay such as this one, on Joyce and
music, ought to be followed by another one, on music and Joyce, since,
although contained by *Finnegans Wake*, post-serial music will do what
violence it can to reappropriate its usurped autonomy. To place Joyce as a
crucial figure in the history of mid-twentieth-century music will sound like
a polemical statement, yet it is only meant as an accurate factual observation. Similarly, I do not mean to be polemical when I say that, with regard
to this repertoire, music analysis has repeatedly shied away from its responsibility, which is to interpret works of music—meaning that it must force its
way beyond formalism. Given the resistance to theory, or more precisely,
the resistance *of* theory—music theory—to an interpretive project that
would move beyond its foundation in analysis, it is not all that surprising,
but still ironic, that it should be Joyce again who would force a re-
examination of his re-examiners. My intention in this essay was primarily to
describe, as comprehensively but as succinctly as possible, the mixture of
aesthetic, formal and political discourses on music that can be found
throughout Joyce's writings. This is of importance to an understanding of
Joyce's writing in itself, particularly with regard to the coordination
between immanent, formal disruption (as was the case with the etymological clusters) and a more explicit representation of the texts of
culture. The assimilation of figural language to historical totalization stands
at the center of Joyce's critique; and we have seen how music, for Joyce,
can suggest a way out of rhetorical—which is the same as ideological—
overdetermination.[40] What becomes an issue for composition after Joyce,
what is still an issue for contemporary composers is the way in which
literature (*not* "language") can suggest a way out of aesthetic ideology. This
essay will have fulfilled its purpose if it may serve as a preliminary step
toward an integrative, critical study of the central mid-century compositional canon, a study that must come to terms with Joyce's work in more
than just cursory terms. This, in its turn, would entail a rhetorical analysis
of musical compositions. And when so much appropriation and recupera-
tion has already taken place, it would be only fitting for such a study to

appropriate those very literary strategies which have once defended literature from music, and which now must work to explicate how the musical
has come to mean the same as the textual identity of music, and how
textual troping of this complexity can generate music, and its history.

NOTES

1. Cf. *The Critical Writings of James Joyce*, ed. by E. Mason and R.
Ellmann (New York: The Viking Press, 1959), 141–8.

2. Who is writing the book becomes ambiguous in such moments, since
we cannot claim with any certainty that Stephen in the future will be
Joyce remembering Stephen, unless it be by some Lacanian
substitution.

3. It is significant that in the notebooks for *Finnegans Wake*, Joyce does
not write in the first person, but always refers to himself as "J.J.," one
more *siglum* incorporated into the system of signs he employed for
identifying character-functions. Cf. Roland McHugh, *The Sigla of
Finnegans Wake* (London: Edward Arnold, 1976).

4. For a recent, sustained Bakhtinian analysis of the role of popular
culture in Joyce's earlier works, see R. B. Kershner, *Joyce, Bakhtin, and
Popular Literature: Chronicles of Disorder* (Chapel Hill: The University
of North Carolina Press, 1989). As Kershner writes, "[Joyce's]
authorial voice sounds only dialogically . . . never wholly separate from
the inner voices of the protagonists" (p. 109).

5. Margot Norris has recently proposed a view of Joyce's books as a
whole following "the arc of Vico's cycles of personal history," with
Portrait, *Ulysses* and *Finnegans Wake* itself corresponding to youth,
maturity and old age, and *Dubliners* as the *ricorso* (cf. "Mixing
Memory and Desire": The "Tristan and Iseult" Chapter in *Finnegans*

Wake, in M.Beja, P.Herring, M.Harmon and D.Norris, eds., *James Joyce: The Centennial Symposium*. [Urbana and Chicago: University of Illinois Press, 1986], 132). Such a mirrored layering of thematic images would be characteristic of Joyce, and it is plausible that he himself may have conceived of his oeuvre as one more of these superimposed circles—one whose completion materializes as his figure of death, circling out of *Finnegans Wake*, circling back to Switzerland, and to the impossible demand of yet another circle: "Yes, I think I'll write something very simple and very short" (cited in Richard Ellmann, *James Joyce* [New York: Oxford University Press, 1982], 731).

6. Annotators have dutifully glossed Johannes Jeep as an early seventeenth-century German composer, but they have failed to indicate how little known he is, outside of specialized musicological circles. For Stephen to quote from Jeep's *Studentengärtlein* is as subtly idiosyncratic an act as it has been for him to parody Joachim Abbas' *Vaticinia Pontificum* in *Proteus* (*U* 3.113), or to invoke Brunetto's "basilisk" in the library episode (9.374).

7. Cf. Ellmann, *James Joyce*, 154.

8. Here as elsewhere I am indebted to Harold Bloom's poetics of influence. "Kenosis" is the dark third stage, the middle point in Bloom's account of the revisionary, self-engendering swerve of a later poet away from the crippling power of a precursor. It is a breaking device, similar to the psychological defense mechanisms against repetition compulsions. It is a movement towards discontinuity with the precursor, and it is marked by the poet's apparent emptying out of himself, *as well as* of the ruling earlier figure. Only after kenosis can the reversal of influence begin to take place in the later poet's work. Cf. Bloom's *The Anxiety of Influence* (New York: Oxford University Press, 1973), as well as *A Map of Misreading* (New York: Oxford University Press, 1975), and, among his many other books, two of the most recent ones, *Poetics of Influence* (New Haven: Henry Schwab, 1988) and *Ruin the Sacred Truths* (Cambridge, Mass.: Harvard University Press, 1989).

9. It is not difficult to imagine Stephen's "soft" piano accompaniments to his own singing, and the brutal disfigurations attending the use of that vile, equal-tempered, pedalled, high-strung instrument: a "coffin of music."

10. The insistent punning on "frank" is Joyce's, not mine; it recurs throughout his works, most notably in *Finnegans Wake*, where Shaun is often described as/identified with frank/Frank, "otherwise frank Shaun" (413.30).

11. A reference to the Italian tenor Mario, *il Cavaliere de Candia*, has already been made in *Aeolus*, when Red Murray comments that "Mario was said to be the picture of Our Saviour," and Bloom thinks of "Jesusmario with rougy cheeks, doublet and spindle legs. Hand on his heart. In *Martha*" (*U* 7.55–58). The two passages read together constitute a complex net of allusions, involving Bloom's Martha, Bloom as Mario in *Martha*, Bloom and Martha in a fictionalized opera-like real-life *Martha*, and even an image of Jesus as the artist. Joyce will rewrite the scene from *Circe* in *Finnegans Wake*, where "Nomario!" tenor Jaun, with "naughtingerls juckjucking benight" him, boasts of his "singasongapiccolo to pipe musicall airs on numberous fairyaciodes"—the old "whatdoyoucallit dulcimer" now more explicitly associated with a "whatyoumacormack [John McCormack, tenor] in the latcher part of [Jaun's] throughers" (*FW* 450.19–26). Joyce's Location Law of music is given here its most succinct and malicious formulation, in the words of Jaun the tenor preaching to the twenty-nine girls: "Birdsnests is birdsnests."

12. On theatrical conventions as agents of institutional pressure, see Cheryl Herr, *Joyce's Anatomy of Culture* (Urbana and Chicago: University of Illinois Press, 1986), specially chapters 3, 4 and 5.

13. Throughout this essay I employ "commoditization," rather than the other, more familiar, barbaric form of the word.

14. Roland McHugh, *Annotations to* Finnegans Wake (Baltimore and London: The Johns Hopkins University Press, 1980), 111. Adaline Glasheen, *Third Census of* Finnegans Wake (Berkeley: University of California Press, 1977), 27.

15. Don Gifford with Robert Seidman, *Notes for Joyce* (New York: Dutton, 1974).

16. Cf. Richard Brown, *James Joyce and Sexuality* (Cambridge: Cambridge University Press, 1985).

17. On the roles of myth in *Finnegans Wake*, see Margot Norris, *The Decentered Universe of* Finnegans Wake. *A Structuralist Analysis* (Baltimore and London: Johns Hopkins University Press, 1976), specially chapter 2. See also John Bishop, *Joyce's Book of the Dark* (Madison: The University of Wisconsin Press, 1986), chapter 7, and Norman O. Brown, *Closing Time* (New York: Random, 1973), for two rather different accounts of Viconian mythology in *Finnegans Wake*.

18. Cf. Ellmann, op.cit., p.703.

19. A somewhat surprising and somewhat alarming nostalgia for conservative models of intepretation is evident in such recent works as Zack Bowen, *"Ulysses" as a Comic Novel* (Syracuse, NY: Syracuse University Press, 1989), or Theoharis C. Theoharis, *Joyce's* Ulysses: *An Anatomy of the Soul* (Chapel Hill: University of North Carolina Press, 1988). Alternative views are represented by, among others, Cheryl Herr's very different kind of anatomy (cf. note 12 above), Lorraine Weir, *Writing Joyce—A Semiotics of the Joyce System* (Bloomington: Indiana University Press, 1989), Vicki Mahaffey, *Reauthorizing Joyce* (Cambridge: Cambridge University Press, 1988), Jacques Derrida, *Ulysse gramophone—deux mots pour Joyce* (Paris: Galilée, 1987), or Bernard Benstock, ed., *James Joyce: The Augmented Ninth* (Syracuse, NY: Syracuse University Press, 1988), which includes a translation of one of Derrida's texts (the other is in *Post-Structuralist Joyce*, see note 23 below).

20. Franco Moretti, *Signs Taken for Wonders*, Revised edition (London and New York: Verso, 1988), chapter 7, 182–208.

21. The reference here is not only to Aristotle's *Poetics*, but also to Kant's primary differentiation between the sublime and the beautiful, in the *Critique of Judgement* (paragraphs 24 and 27).

22. Although my approach differs in some important points from his, I am fundamentally in accord with Eco's discussion of Aquinas and Joyce in *The Aesthetics of Aquinas* (Cambridge, Mass.: Harvard University Press, 1988) and *Le Poetiche di Joyce* (Milano: Bompiani, 1982).

23. Cf. for example the sequence of essays on *Sirens* in Attridge and Ferrer, eds., *Post-Structuralist Joyce: Essays from the French* (Cambridge: Cambridge University Press, 1984).

24. "Blindness and Inwit: James Joyce and the Sirens." *The Iowa Review*, vol. 18, no.1 (Winter 1988).

25. Gilles Deleuze, *Proust et les Signes* (Paris: P.U.F.: 1964). English translation by Richard Howard (New York: George Brazillier, 1972), 167.

26. Cf. Jacques Lacan, *Joyce le symptôme*, in Jacques Aubert, ed., *Joyce avec Lacan* (Paris: Navarin, 1987).

27. This play on the final "done" of the sentimentalist will recur throughout the book; I cite only two of the most striking examples: "O, he did. Into her. She did. Done" (13.849); "A

NOBLEWOMAN (*nobly*) All that man has seen! / A FEMINIST (*masculinely*) And done!'' (15.1465).

28. For a collection of studies on this subject, see Claude Jacquet, ed. *Genèse de Babel—Joyce et la Création* (Paris: Editions du C.N.R.S., 1985) and also, by the same editor, *Genèse et Metamorphoses du Texte Joycien* (Paris: Publications de la Sorbonne, 1985).

29. Cf. David Hayman, *A First-Draft Version of* Finnegans Wake (Austin: University of Texas Press, 1963). As Hayman says, "Joyce often doubled or tripled the length of passages by the time he finished reworking the first draft. A single manuscript page usually reflects between four and ten separate revisions of the draft. Consequently there are not only additions but also additions to and changes in additions; there are not only changes but changes in and additions to changes'' (p.10).

30. Cf. specially Clive Hart, *Structure and Motif in* Finnegans Wake (Evanston: Northwestern University Press, 1962).

31. My reading of Wagner is the reading made possible *by* Joyce, as well as by the music of Boulez, Berio, Nono and other post-serial composers. It is somewhat perverse that post-modern Wagner should find a better theorist in Dahlhaus than in Adorno, which may still prove to be an indictment of the former. For Adorno, the leitmotive is an allegorical, not symbolic element: the motiv transmits "congealed meaning"; expression "does not present itself, but is itself the object of the presentation." His critique of the leitmotive is congruent with his views on the "permanent regression," the constant flow into the already known in Wagner's music. In Joyce, however, allegory is inseparable from deconstruction, and the leitmotive itself becomes part of a dynamic structure of recombination and reinterpretation, as will be seen below. For Adorno's most extensive discussion of Wagner, see his *Versuch über Wagner*, transfigured into English as *In Search of Wagner* (London: NLB, 1981).

32. "Etymological clusters" is a convenient, though not entirely accurate term. Although, as will be seen, the association between the words in a cluster is usually triggered by, and always involves etymology, it may also involve semantic or phonetic elements. "Word clusters" would be better, were it not for the fact that there are also groups of words associated thematically on the surface of the text, and that the two cases must be distinguished.

33. "Hypogram" is one of Saussure's terms for the underlying anagrammatic patterns he believed he had discovered as an

organizational principle of representative Latin poems. The difficulty he himself experienced in accepting his theory was the fact that, given the patterns of repetition implied by the limited repertoire of phonemes in the language, one can never be sure whether such "anagrams" are intentional or accidental. In other words, there may be signifying processes working beneath or alongside the manifest signs of the text. This means that there may be forms of patterning working without prior conventions or readers' recognition, or alternatively, that there may be meaningful patterning created *by the reader*, who must then determine what to count as a signifier. Either way, Saussure's own model of language as a system of signs would be under attack. Cf. Jonathan Culler, *Ferdinand de Saussure* (Ithaca: Cornell University Press, 1986), 123–33, and the next note.

34. Cf. Jean Starobinski, *Les mots sous les mots: les anagrammes de Ferdinand de Saussure* (Paris: Gallimard, 1971). English translation (*Words Upon Words*) by Olivia Emmet (New Haven: Yale University Press, 1979).

35. Paul de Man, "Hypogram and Inscription," in *The Resistance to Theory* (Minneapolis: University of Minnesota Press, 1986), 43.

36. Cf. Margaret Solomon, *Eternal Geomater—The Sexual Universe of Finnegans Wake.* (Carbondale and Edwardsville: Southern Illinois University Press, 1969), chapter 5, "T," 59–69.

37. A recent essay that does bring out the difference is Caroline Patey's "La Logica di *Ulysses*: Musica, Mito, Metonimia," in C. de Petris, ed., *Joyce Studies in Italy*, vol. 2 (Roma: Bulzoni, 1988), 173–92. However, like so many other articles on Joyce and music, her discussion too relies on a conception of music that does not, in fact, correspond to the advanced musical ideas taking shape in Joyce's prose. To understand music in Joyce, one must be familiar with Boulez and Berio and other post-serialist composers, since *that* is the music which most closely responds to Joyce's achievement, and which, in retrospect, can teach us to listen more adequately to his work. I will return to this point below.

38. For explicit comments on debt incurred, cf. Boulez's essay, "Sonate, que me veux-tu?," in *Orientations*, translated by Martin Cooper (Cambridge, Mass.: Harvard University Press, 1986), and Luciano Berio (with R. Dalmonte and B. A. Varga), *Two Interviews*, translated and edited by D. Osmond-Smith (New York: Boyars, 1985). Joyce's influence is not, of course, restricted to these two musicians; his sphere of dominance is wide enough to incorporate such diverse composers as Ligeti and Dallapicola, or John Cage and Ferneyhough.

39. Over two hundred years after Rousseau's *Confessions*, I have no intention to harmonize the collected personal statements by Joyce on music with the highly sophisticated arguments to be found in his texts. It is puzzling, to say the least, that the most advanced technician of his age should prefer Othmar Schoeck to Stravinsky, or compare Bellini to Wagner, to the latter's disadvantage: it is not so much the blundering mistake in judgement as the sheer incongruousness of the relations that is shocking. I suspect Joyce was content to play the Irish Joyce for his friends as well as for himself, and played it with gusto; it was if anything an act of bravery, and a positive statement of sorts, to have written what he had and still never let go of this sentimental biddy, though a considerable amount of theatricality must have been assumed by himself, if by none other.

40. On. the relation between (the term is his) "figural" language and history, cf. Paul de Man's works, especially the essays on Nietzsche and Rousseau in *Allegories of Reading* (New Haven: Yale University Press, 1979).

BIBLIOGRAPHY OF JOYCE'S WORKS CITED IN THE TEXT

Dubliners. New York: Viking/Penguin, 1968 and reprints.

A Portrait of the Artist as a Young Man. New York: Viking/Penguin, 1976 and reprints.

Ulysses. Edited by H. W. Gabler. New York: Vintage Books, 1986.

Finnegans Wake. New York: Viking/Penguin, 1967 and reprints.

Stephen Hero. New York: New Directions, 1944 and reprints.

Giacomo Joyce. New York: Viking, 1968.

Epiphanies. Buffalo: University of Buffalo Press, 1956; reprinted by Richard West, 1979.

Letters, vols. I-III. Edited by Stuart Gilbert (I) and Richard Ellmann (II and III). New York: Viking, 1957–66.

The James Joyce Archive. 63 vols., general editor Michael Groden. New York: Garland, 1977–80.

Symposium:
The Nature of Music

Arthur Berger

WHILE I WAS a graduate student in musicology at Harvard in the mid-1930s I edited a periodical called *The Musical Mercury* (for recollections of it see *Perspectives of New Music* 17, no. 1 [Fall–Winter 1978]: 63ff.). It was short-lived (1934–37) and the issues were small. Copies may still be found hidden away on library shelves, but the following discussion seemed to me too fine to deserve the oblivion and there seemed no more apposite place for it to be reprinted than *Perspectives*. For I think it may have been my editorial stint as a student that suggested the idea of a magazine to Benjamin Boretz when he in turn was my student at Brandeis—an idea leading eventually to our founding *Perspectives* together in 1962.

It may seem immodest of me to include my own writing in what I deem worthy of reprinting. My contribution, however, makes its way here on the coattails of the essays by the two Schwartzes. It adapts the Symposium to a

music journal by bringing the discussion around from the realm of general speculation to a realm of the concrete. Indeed, my contribution caused me some
misgivings as I looked back at it in proximity to the other two. Their clarity and
conciseness convinced me that mine needed re-editing before being reprinted.
While doing so I thought of other ways to put things and other things to say, but
since the Symposium might be of interest as a period piece, the emendations and
additions have been separated either by placing them between square brackets or
by placing them in footnotes, none of which appeared with my own article.

The Symposium was spread over two issues, March and June, 1936 (3, nos. 1
and 2). The subsequent articles were not part of the unit formed by the three
printed here from the March issue. Herbert Schwartz was a pianist and Aristotelian who was completing his graduate studies at Columbia. The last I heard of
him he had left the university in discouragement for parts unknown since the
music and philosophy departments, when he submitted his thesis, each claimed
a lack of the expertise to judge what was subsumed under the other's discipline.
Delmore Schwartz was, of course, the noted poet who became something of a
cult figure posthumously and served as model for the writer in Saul Bellow's
novel *Humboldt's Gift*. A biography of Delmore Schwartz by James Atlas
appeared in 1977 (Farrar Straus Giroux) and the letters were collected recently by
Robert Phillips (Ontario Review Press, 1984). Another poet, Paul Goodman,
contributed to the Symposium in June, which prompts me to wonder how
much of the communication we had between musical and literary people exists
today.

It will doubtless be an oddity to look back upon the concern with expression
after so many of us for so many years have occupied ourselves with form.
Stravinsky's notorious disclaimer— "l'expression n'a jamais été la propriété
immanente de la musique"[1]—appeared in 1935 in *Chroniques de ma vie* which I
had not yet seen. But the doctrine of "art for art's sake" was still being debated
and from Vienna we were hearing rumblings of Positivism with its advocacy of
an objectivity inimical to anything so vague as feeling. These were powerful
forces and we had no illusion that we had vanquished them. In a letter dated July
31, 1937 (Phillips collection, 31) Delmore warned me, " . . . the whole thesis of
Expressiveness has to be stated with much more care than Prall,[2] you or I were
aware several months ago and I hope you are continuing to think about it." But
Delmore and I became more and more involved in our separate arts, and never
did go on to develop our philosophy formally. Some of the notions surfaced in
1945 in my article "Form Is Feeling" (*Modern Music* 22, no. 2) and I have continued to live with the reassurance from Herbert Schwartz's carefully reasoned
argument that even our most abstract structural analysis has something significant to do with feeling. As a final word I should like to remind the reader that
Imitation is used here in the Aristotelian sense, and when I had the commonplace meaning in mind, to distinguish it, I used "mimic."

Music and Emotion

Herbert Schwartz

IT IS NATURAL for the layman to think that music is a language of the emotions. It is perhaps just as natural for the musician to think of it as a language of tones. The task of philosophy is to bring layman and musician together, since the common ground of expert and nonexpert is, in a sense, foreign to both.

The layman, of course, does not know what music is, and when he calls it a language of emotions he is saying that he does not know what it is—somewhat elaborately. Neither does the musician know what music is: "A language of tones" means that he is not interested in knowing what it is. His meanings are given by tones, not words.

By "knowing" I mean knowing through ideas and the relations between ideas. There is no intention to disparage either the layman's appreciation or the musician's understanding, and what our hypothetical layman and musician are saying about music, is by no means to be dismissed as irrelevant and meaningless.

Rather, both are to be taken as signs, possibly converging signs, with a not too far distant point of intersection.

Seeking that point, let us assume that music has something to do with emotion just as truly as it has to do with tones. This much follows immediately: if music has anything to do with emotion, there must be relevant and irrelevant emotions; if emotion is the essence of the matter, then different musical compositions must be emotionally distinguishable. Otherwise all music, if not all art and everything besides, would be fused in one pervasive emotional feeling, which suggests an experience more incommunicable even than aesthetic experience. I am making an assumption which may seem to some unwarranted, that everything is not everything else. One thing, then, is not another, and this string quartet by Mozart is not that piano sonata by Beethoven.

Well, if the two are different, and if emotions are essential to their understanding, the emotions will be different. The question is: What accounts for the difference? We must remember that the two compositions are not only different, but that each is unique. What, then, are the unique emotions which characterize each, and how are certain emotions bound up with a definite succession of tones in time?

Let us go over to the musician to see what he finds. Musicians, we discover, have the literal-minded habit of talking about phrases, periods, three and four part forms, etc. From which we might conclude that they look upon a composition, from their limited technical point of view as just that: a composition. And a composition, I take it, is something composed, that is, placed together. It seems reasonable that it is the parts that are placed together.

Are emotions, then, the parts that are put together? They must be if the musician and layman are somehow right. But I suspect that before we are through the layman will be telling the musician something about his technical "parts," and that the musician, on the other hand, will be telling the layman a good deal about his "emotions." They will have to if they are to understand each other.

Let us restrict ourselves to a single part. We will ostensibly be restricting ourselves to a single emotion. Within a single part we find a succession of tones arranged in rhythmic formation. This, unlike the emotion, is directly observable, so it will be better to start with it. It is this arrangement of tones in succession which is associated with some special emotion. The musician will insist that all the tones and each rhythmic pattern is essential. If anything of these is altered, however slight, the musical part is not the same. It follows from our acceptance of both the layman's and musician's opinion that the emotion will be different. To each musical part there must correspond one and only one emotion.

The conclusion need hardly be drawn: A musical part is an emotion, not, certainly, as something on paper, but as something actually heard and experienced. If the musician and the layman are right, we must mean by music what is actually being listened to by someone, a conclusion which should persuade us that we are on the right track.

But apparently one must be a fairly expert listener to grasp the emotional content of a musical composition. The subtlest differences among the relevant emotions are determined somehow by the tones and their relations. And the number of such emotions must be as great as there are distinct musical parts, which is almost as large as you please. If there is anything in the layman's claim, this must be the case; so that the first thing the layman learns about his emotions is that he is capable of having many more than he perhaps realized. He discovers too that his emotions must be more formal than he supposed, for this rhythmic succession of tones is decidedly formal. And if he would find out something more surprising still, he might ask a musician if there is anything which relates one musical part to another. Musicians seem to discover intricate and very important relationships between the parts: the better ones trace transformations and analogies with an insight which might make some mathematicians a bit uneasy, and philosophers too, if they recognized "the same." It seems to be the case, then, that the so-called emotions are not only formal, but that each of them is formally related, or relatable, to the others.

We may now turn to our layman and ask him a few questions about his emotions. Everyday emotions, he will recognize, demand action. Our being angry means our wanting to do something about it. We are not angry in the abstract, but we are angry with someone. And when we do not do something about it we become angrier; the contemporary method of catharsis is contemporarily called "rationalization." If the "emotions" of music were anything like that, music should be a painful experience. Our layman, though, seems to enjoy his musical emotions, so we may conclude that they are not like that. It may not be beside the point to ask why they are not like that.

But first we should perhaps acknowledge what our musician has learned from the layman about his "technical parts." If the emotion is a part, it is just as true to say that the part is the emotion, and to restrict the meaning of music to a bare formal division into parts is to deprive it of its reality in experience. Actual music is not the relation of notes on a staff, but the actual succession of tones within ourselves, and the condition of their being within ourselves is that they be felt, not as practical emotions, as we have seen, but as something like them. The ordering of tones is the ordering of something like emotions. I think that by this time we have been sufficiently embarrassed by the same word for the "emotion" of music and the emotion of practical life to be looking for a word which will distinguish them. What sort of word will, I think, be clear when we have answered the question already proposed.

It seems not too unlikely that the formal quality of the musical emotion is related to the fact that it does not demand action. Approaching the problem from another angle, it seems strange that in the case of music there is no object of our emotion. If we are musically angry, we must somehow or other be angry in general. Certainly we are not angry at the music. This quality of our musical emotion and its formal nature suggest this connection: we do not feel the need to act in musical emotion because we are acting, acting, that is, musically. And our action has its beginning and end in the beginning and end of the musical composition. Our action consists in realizing the implications of the emotions we feel and these implications are in the relatedness of the emotions. The emotions of music work out their own rationalization, or rather we work them out when we really listen to music, and that working out is our action. Whether we state this as the formal relations of a composition, or in terms of our feeling, we are talking about the same thing. The form is felt and the feeling is formal, and that is the he and the she of it. The "he," however, is somewhat more articulate.

The conclusion to which we are forced is that music is not quite as irrational as the layman suggests, nor, on the other hand, as cut and dried as the musician would lead us to believe. Our minds and our feeling get together, and the word we are looking for is suggested by that fact. Suppose we call it "sensibility," that is, the quasi faculty relevant to those acts in which our minds and feelings are united. Those are not exclusively acts of aesthetic perception. The faculty appears to be related to, among other things, ethical conduct, and Plato insinuates on more than one occasion that it is closely akin to philosophic speculation. It is a sense of proportion adaptable to all our activities, and the usefulness of music is its power to develop that sense. Music as such is the teacher of the emotions rather than their expression, teaching them not to take themselves too seriously, to play a sort of dialectic game with each other in the course of which they are hidden and discovered, translated and transformed, examined and re-examined in each others terms until at last they are revealed in their true natures. If it were possible to say what those "true natures" were, music would be a superfluous art. The emotions of music pass humorous comment on the ponderous recitals of psychoanalysis, on the too learned dissections of psychology, and on the composers who, too much concerned with their humanity, abuse them in an effort to force them to express what they steadfastly refuse to express. It is the business of the imitator to know that he is imitating.

In that guise I have been saying a lot of things for the layman and the musician: it is not in the least essential that either should actually claim that what I have said he himself claims. They were simply useful types to refer to. It is dangerous to be even as explicit as that about the "philosopher." It occurred to me several times that the description of the musician was more fitting for the philosopher, but I was thinking of a good musician. At any rate, the two are not far apart in the opinion of certain venerable philosophers who might recognize a variation on their own theme.

Poetry as Imitation

Delmore Schwartz

I INTEND TO USE the art of poetry as an example of how one can speak precisely of the nature of Art. Each statement is to be understood as asserted of each of the arts, in its own terms.

It seems, however, that the effort to describe the nature of art is presumptuous, naive, and romantic. Mr. T. S. Eliot, to use the usual prominent example, has often objected: "Those who indulge in the Essence of Poetry fantasy... Repeated meditation led me to suspect that there are surprisingly few things that can be said about Poetry."[3] On the contrary, notions of what poetry "is" are repeatedly implied in Mr. Eliot's criticisms.[4] I. A. Richards, who is similarly opposed to the notion that poetry is any one thing, similarly asserts that it is one thing, namely, the coordination of impulses and interests: "It is never what a poem says, but what it is that matters. The poet... uses words because the interests which a situation brings into play combine to bring them, just in this form, into his consciousness *as a means of ordering, controlling and consolidating* the whole experience."[5] The implicit assumption that poetry has a definable character is made in other and familiar ways at the present time. Marxians sometimes derive from Tolstoy and announce that art is communication; more often they tend to assert that a poem is the expression of the character of society. This is of course closely related to the historical school of criticism. More examples could be given, but are not necessary. The point is that it is continually assumed that poetry is one thing, not everything, and not any thing.

Now it seems to me that a great deal of instruction about the nature of poetry can be obtained by connecting two statements of Aristotle. One of them is in the *Poetics*, the other in *De Anima*. In the *Poetics* it is said that poetry originates in imitation, a statement which has disturbed many critics because it seems to suggest photography, that is, mere duplication of an original already present. Such critics have responded by interpreting the text, saying, for example, that by imitation is meant the imitation of the creative activity of "Nature." The text itself shows how false such glosses are: "We delight to view the most realistic representations . . . though the objects themselves may be painful to see . . . the forms, for example, of the lowest animals and of dead bodies."

In *De Anima*, on the other hand, Aristotle, in describing the act of knowledge, says that in that act the mind in a way becomes its object: "The mind is in a way all things"; "Actual knowledge is identical with its objects." This seems to me to mean that the mind in knowing mimics, that is, imitates its object (although only insofar as it is intelligible). Thus the act of knowing and the act of making a poem have in common the process of imitation (although what is imitated is obviously not the same). Having recognized this connection, I wish to go further: *The act of making a poem is an act of knowing.* This statement clearly needs qualification and elucidation, but first I wish to point out that this connection is further suggested in the *Poetics*: "it is natural for all to delight in imitation . . . The explanation is to be found in a further fact: to be learning something is the greatest of all pleasures . . . the reason of the delight in a picture is that one is at the same time learning something—gathering the meaning of things."

In order to explain what I mean when I say that the act of writing a poem is an act of knowing, I intend now to advance a metaphor which will, I hope, turn out to be a description rather than a metaphor. The only way in which I can learn what my face is like is by looking in the mirror. This fact is even clearer when I consider the back of my head, which I certainly could not perceive without the aid of the mirror. In exactly that way both the substance and the medium of any art can be explained. As to substance, we recognize that there is a great deal in our lives and in our society which cannot be "seen"—about which neither metaphysics, nor psychology, nor the daily newspaper can tell us very much. But we do find out about our ways of valuing, our half-known assumptions, our disguised motives and emotions, in a work of art—both historical and biographical criticism witness this fact. We have then, in each art, a particular kind of mirror, namely, the medium.

The way in which the medium of poetry mirrors can be briefly indicated, primarily by examples. The first fact about the medium of poetry is the fact of words in meter. Next we observe that the most important part of a poem is its rhythm, not qua rhythm (in the sense of sensuous delight), but in the sense that it is in the rhythm that feelings and even perceptions are most clearly objectified. Many words are inherently imitative to begin with; for example, crack, splash, shout. But imitation in poetry is at much subtler levels. Three simple examples follow:

> The whistling winds already waked the sky;
> Before the whistling winds the vessels fly,
> With rapid swiftness cut the liquid way.
> > (Pope's translation of the *Odyssey*)

Here imitation is still at a sensuous level. In the first tercet of the *Divine Comedy* each verse, and the rhyme in particular, contains the emotion:

> Nel mezzo del cammin di nostra vita
> mi ritrovai per una selva oscura
> che la diritta via era smarrita.

And lastly, in a Shakespearean song a whole attitude is to be found in the meter, in the phrasing of the words and in the sounds and implications of the words themselves (although a prose translation would find them of little meaning):

> When that I was and a little tiny boy,
> > With hey, ho, the wind and the rain,
> A foolish thing was but a toy,
> > For the rain it raineth every day.

Rhythm, as one aspect of the medium of poetry, can be imitative, in the most precise and revealing way primarily because it is an element, at a further remove, in what is being imitated. There is clearly a rhythm in breathing, in walking and riding, in opening and shutting doors, and in hope and desire—that is to say, we exist "in time." Thus the medium has a natural basis which enables it to be that which can mirror.

Now the substance of a poem has been said to be that of which one is scarcely conscious, yet which is basic in one's being; and the medium has been pointed to as capable of the most subtle reflection. What then could be more natural than the repeated discoveries which the poet makes as he writes his poem? He may begin with a general plan and with a long premeditated theme, but actually he finds that the finished work is an unexpected transformation of his intention. Valéry, to use but one of innumerable testimonies to this fact, says: "J'ai l'espoir de quelque imprévu que je désigne . . . Qu'est-ce que le Même, si je le vois à ce point changer d'avis et de parti, dans le cours de mon travail, qu'il le défigure sous mes doigts; si chaque repentir peut apporter des modifications immenses; et si mille accidents de mémoire, d'attention, ou de sensation, qui surviennent à mon esprit, apparaissant enfin, dans mon oeuvre achevé, comme les idées essentielles et les objets originelles de mes efforts."[6] Note that Valéry is describing how the implicit being of the poet enters into his poem (mille accidents de mémoire, d'attention ou de sensation) and *is known only because it is in the poem*. A better instance is music, where, surely, we find that matters are brought to light and made known which could not be known in any other way: indeed this is so much so that it is almost impossible to say what is made known except by pointing, as in the story of Beethoven repeating the composition, when asked for its meaning.

Similarly the spectator can note that he approaches the work of art as an object to be known, if he watches the shift in the nature of his attention when he regards any object as aesthetic. Thus, when I sit at the table and eat, I am aware of the table and its objects only slightly, only insofar as I have to be in order to find what I want to eat and, presumably, continue the dinner conversation. But if I want to enjoy the objects on the table as things seen, I have to sit back, cease to act and merely look (which is of course itself an act): and only by such "looking" can I see the white tablecloth, the round table, the pitcher of water, and the glasses. I must, that is to say, "contemplate" things in order to enjoy them as works of art.[7]

Because of what the substance is and what the medium is, we come to recognize that the fundamental virtues of the poet are (1) mastery of the medium, language, for only by the most capable, most sensitive control of his craft will imitation be possible; and (2) sincerity or honesty (since a kind of knowing is involved): "The peculiarity of all great poetry . . . is merely a peculiar honesty, which in a world too frightened to be honest, is peculiarly terrifying . . . Blake's poetry has the unpleasantness of all great poetry. Nothing that can be called morbid, or abnormal, or perverse, none of the things which exemplify the sickness of an epoch or a fashion, have this quality. Only those things which, by some extraordinary labor of simplification, exhibit the essential strength or sickness of the human soul. *And this honesty never exists without great technical accomplishment*." (My italics)[8]

Having reached this point, we can see how the tortuous problems of poetry and belief, and poetry and propaganda, yield to the doctrine of imitation. Confronted by a work whose beliefs are not our own, we cannot and actually do not condemn the work for its supposed error. If it is an adequate mirroring of beliefs, if through it beliefs as held and felt are made knowable, that is sufficient. We prefer works whose beliefs confirm our own, but we can readily distinguish between such confirmation and enjoying the presentation of the beliefs of the *Iliad*. If this is not so, the many readers of the *Divine Comedy* who are not Thomists must be split personalities.

The problem of poetry and propaganda meets a similar solution. The poet who adequately and sincerely reveals his interests is writing the best propaganda. He is reflecting his age and his social experiences in a thing which will display the character of society most accurately. Someone might object that this presentation will be clear only after a time. The objection is correct only because poetry is not read often nor properly. If it were, it would be obvious that an honest poem, as a *poem*, is likely to make the "facts" clear, while whatever is written with an eye to political persuasion antagonizes, like anything explicitly advertised. What, it might be objected, of the sincere presentation of opposing "class positions"? Again, it can be answered: if these presentations are good as poems, that is, as imitations, then they are in a real sense propaganda for a recognition of the "facts" (e.g., the class positions, insofar as there are class positions). It is precisely for this reason that no Marxist can deny the value of great works which reflect the capitalist and feudal economies.

The distinction between the knowing which is art and other types of knowledge need not be discussed here. Clearly, in knowing what is in a poem we know immediately and not in discursive terms, our knowing being intermediate between a proposition and a sensation, partaking, in a way, of the character of both.

Having recognized that a poem is an imitation in which knowing is essentially involved, we can now admit its auxiliary uses and consequences. A poem does communicate and express experience; it does coordinate impulses and interests (though there is no guarantee in the work itself that it will do so); it does reflect the age. But it does all of these things only because it is an imitation for the sake of knowing. The point to be most remembered is that knowing takes place only in the specific act of imitation, not before it. Or, as E. M. Forster has said (speaking as a novelist): "How can I know what I think before I see what I say?"

Music as Imitation

Arthur Berger

T HE COMMON GROUND between poetry and music is determined by the elements of sound and rhythm.[9] But whereas in poetry the sounds of most words have conventional reference to some particular external objects or activities with which they have no aspect in common, musical symbols bear an intrinsic relationship to that which they may be said, in the broadest sense, to "represent." The musical symbols are comparable to such onomatopoeic words as "crack, splash, shout," cited by Delmore Schwartz. Or let us take a foreign word as it sounds to someone who does not understand it—*schrecklich*, for example. This word strikes the ear with a quality that is marked off from the gentle, the serene.[10] Needless to say, the quality will vary with the intensity, pitch, duration, and timbre of the voice. But the impact of the *sch* followed by the rolled *r* against the hard *ck* is itself determinate.[11] Whether or not this quality is consciously defined the qualitative experience is definitive, and is, moreover, consistent with the conventional meaning (frightful, dreadful), which itself, finally, is unnecessary to the experiencing of the quality.

As long as the listener does not inquire into the conventional meaning and regards the heard effect as sufficient, which is rare, the experience is analogous to that of the musical auditor. The symbol is related to its object causally or, as the psychologists would say, functionally. The relationship is, moreover, in terms of pitch, intensity, duration, and timbre. (Each of these but the last one[12] lies within a natural continuum that in music serves as the basis for systematic treatment yielding higher organization and thus greater variety in imitation.) In both cases (hearing words phonetically and hearing tones) the object that has summoned up the symbol disappears, the symbol itself being sufficient.

In reference to the last point, some exceptions may be disposed of as not being exclusive to the art of music, or as being, when they do occur in music, relatively incidental. These include, first, bugle calls and such, in which a specific series of notes is used as a semaphore or word-substitute for a given object or activity; and second, those instances when the intrinsic relationship between the musical symbol and the thing symbolized is such that they are entirely or scarcely indistinguishable—e.g., literal bird calls, automobile horns, factory noises. If there is to be no difference between the original and the artificial simulation it may be pertinent to ask why the original sources were not used in the first place— as Respighi did via the phonograph in *The Pines of Rome*, Alexander Mossolov with a steel sheet in [an at one time often played Soviet work] *The Iron Foundry* (for factory noises), or Gershwin with actual automobile noises in *An American in Paris*. The logical extremity is a symphony of birds and beasts, a kind of miracle play with Noah, baton in hand, competing with the act of the trained seal.

[Had this been written after the time when *musique concrète* and the song of the whale entered into the picture I think I would have made it clearer that I was berating not the use of everyday sounds in the service of artistic ends but their use for mimicry in the spirit of a comedian's impersonation, though even then I could have cited composers like Antheil and Varèse as representatives of the more dignified approach. Also, had it been known what Messiaen could do with bird calls I would certainly have granted that beyond mimicry there was a role for them as inspiration for a composer in shaping his own imaginative tonal configurations.]

The manner in which musical sound mimics bird calls is not without relation to the more subtle type of imitation which isolates the distinctive inflections of the voice in groans, sighs, laughter, etc. Chromatic scales approximate a wail because they approach the portamento. But chromatic music does not imitate human wails in the same manner that flutes imitate or mimic specific bird calls. It is, rather, the general aura of sorrow or wretchedness that has been distilled from the concrete happening.

If sound mirrors the external indications of human emotions, rhythm may be said to imitate their innermost manifestations—the quickening of the pulse, the felt action of the glands. I do not want to be understood as saying that these *are* the emotions themselves.[13] I merely wish to point out that such bodily processes come closest to making evident the aspects of emotion that are distinct from the practical or intellectual causes. And music in its greater capacity to imitate these bodily processes best embodies the emotion they accompany. [Perhaps I should have included dance.] So that even if music can suggest horses' hooves and the gentle trickling of water, the fact that this art is ahead of other arts in embodying emotions—and these, moreover, divorced from the particular and so directly present to unbiased attention—is reason enough for it to favor doing just this, as it has indeed done, reserving the more obvious types of imitation (mimicry) for an occasional conceit.

Poetry, as Delmore Schwartz indicates, by virtue of its rhythmic component, is also capable of mirroring inner feeling. But there is a sense in which music, in its parameter of rhythm, does so more—shall I say—vividly. Poetry, in its turn, is more capable of directly embodying emotion than prose—the emotion in prose arising, rather, not directly out of the sensuous, the qualitative surface of the medium, but out of our conceptual grasp of the meanings conveyed by the conventional symbols. [I am aware that prose can be more or less rhythmic, but as rhythm becomes more and more important in prose, reaching the level at which we encounter it in Joyce, we are apt to say that it approaches poetry.] Thus, poetry is an intermediate stage between prose and music. The meanings poetry shares with prose enable us to localize the attitudes and feelings conveyed purely by the sound and rhythm.

This is something that can still be accomplished when poetry and music are allied in song. Imitation at the lower level in this genre is not unlike the mimicry of commonplace objects discussed above, but it is less literal and possesses a nobler tradition. I refer, of course, to *word-painting*. Here, as in poetry, the meaning of the words provides a clue to what is symbolized by the music. A composer may be motivated to use an ascending line by any number of things, but in conjunction with a word like "high" or "up" such a line is understood as presenting the directly felt quality of what the word stands for. Bach and his contemporaries were apt to paint a sad word by using chromatics conjunctly whatever the context—as in his Cantata, BWV 66, where the faithful are joyously exhorted to banish sorrow with plaintive measures for the specific words evoking it. [In the latter part of the eighteenth century the *Affektenlehre* went into this whole matter quite seriously.] But word-painting is a harmless indulgence; one should not make too much of it or claim it is there when it is not, after the fashion of the musicologist who found a sixteenth-note figure in the accompaniment of a *Don Giovanni* aria (a common scale pattern) to represent the gracious sweep of that notorious courtier's flowing white plume.[14]

Imitation of contexts, of groups of notes is at a somewhat higher level. I take an example of this from the "Domine Jesu" of Mozart's *Requiem*. Mozart divides the text into phrases and clauses in the manner of the old motet. Observe

Andante (tenors)

Ne ab - sor - be at e - as   tar - ta-rus, ne ca-dant in ob - scu-rum,

EXAMPLE 1: MOZART, *Requiem*, "Domine Jesu," MEASURES 21–23

that at "Libera eas de ore leonis" there is no horrific roar of trombones, only a slight emphasis of "ore leonis," but at the succeeding "ne absorbeat eas Tartarus, ne cadant in obscurum" (Example 1), the distress underlying the larger context is unleashed—distress lest the souls of the faithful be swallowed up by Hell and cast into the abyss. This takes the shape of a fugal exposition in which excitement is conveyed by widely spaced intervals of descending sevenths and ascending sixths. The element of distress or supplication in the sevenths returning by sixths would seem to have some similarity—to pick a random example—to such cries as "*help* I'm *falling*" or "if *only* I *could*," where the italicized syllables are noticeably higher in pitch. (Such epithets as "distress" admittedly convey none of the ramifications of the musically embodied emotion, but are convenient here in marking off the present emotion from the kind that may be subsumed under the rubric "joy.") The seventh resembles the approximate octave of the voice (i.e., registrally) in excitement or longing. Thus, its elevation into an almost unique value in some Schoenberg may account for the unresolved agony, the constant *Weltschmerz* despite the cerebral shroud. [This observation is exceedingly embarrassing to me, especially since sevenths and ninths have become as much a norm in my music as step-wise progression was in Classicism, and yet the sentiment, I daresay, is not at all dark most of the time. We knew too little twelve-tone music to realize that its constructs were separable from an ethos suggestive of gloomy, gas-lit, Viennese attics.]

Another explanation of the melodic skips is more graphic and at the same time fanciful: namely, the steep descent by sevenths may be said to represent the souls being hurled into the abyss. Or again, assimilating human conflict to the conflict of keys or pitch areas, we may distinguish a certain conflict—as of the souls trying to free themselves from the mouth of the lion or the horror of Hell—in the conflict set up between the C-minor pentachord in the higher register and another (overlapping) segment of C minor in the lower register that outlines the lower tetrachord of the relative major, Eb.

Such associations have a strong element of fatuity about them. The highest musical experience does not consist in summoning up images of this sort. We rest content in the quality of the sound as we did in the case of the word *schrecklich* when we contemplated its phonetic surface apart from its semantics. On the other hand, I wonder whether the multiplicity of associations may not have something to do with the pleasure we derive from music even though we do not conceptualize them—or conceptualize them only when we examine them in the separate activity of analysis. Thus, just as the single tone in music to be precisely what it is must consist [when it is not a sine tone] of various overtones which may or may not be directly present to attention, so the musical phrase may be said to have *over-emotions*, so to speak, drawn from various reaches of human experience. It would be an aspect of music remotely related to the practice of poets of choosing words with special reference to their historical accretions—that is to say, to their frequency and variety of occurrence—so that meanings ancillary to the main one may come into play, like overtones, to reinforce or even conflict with it. [William Empson's *Seven types of ambiguity* did not appear until 1939 (New Directions), but the investigations of I.A. Richards into the connotative aspects of words was a fascinating subject to us.]

Since in vocal music the word provides a clue to the emotion, we are more willing to grant its presence and agree on its nature. But even when the word limits the scope, there can be, as we have seen, more than one "meaning" to the music. If such, then, is the case in vocal music, how much more varied and extensive the reference must be when the scope is not thus limited. To be sure, vocal music has properties that instrumental music may not have. But it is a mistake to assume that we require totally different laws to explain what governs it and a totally different aesthetic to determine how in essence it functions. [Think of the instrumental *chansons* of the Netherlands School that were thought for a long time to be vocal or the music "per cantare o sonare."]

The same type of pattern that was observed in the *Requiem* is found in various permutations in Mozart's instrumental music (Example 2). The tension will vary accordingly with these permutations. For example, the passage in the *Requiem* (Example 1) derives special emphasis from starting with the major seventh while in Example 2c we hear the diminished seventh instead of the major.[15] But nothing now motivates us to hear the afterlife of the soul. The tension, such as it is, could have been motivated by anything from the despair of not having money for the next meal to the sudden pang of grief of one who misses a departed friend. But such considerations are beyond the purview of the listener who, should he inquire into them while listening, might find himself moving farther and farther away from the music itself. Yet the feeling inherent in them is no more occluded by removing the text than it was when we heard *schrecklich* without having the dictionary meaning. The feeling is no longer verified by the words, but in some sense it must still be there.

The listener rests content in the musical embodiment of whatever emotion is involved insofar as he does not seek extra-musical aid to justify it. This does not mean that he necessarily basks in the auditory rays of some vague feeling or other. For the effectiveness of Mozart's sequence of sevenths lies not only in its own configuration but also in the way the sequence is related to the other parts of the work. (Remember that Herbert Schwartz has insisted on the "parts.")

None of the passages in Example 2 is of a kind that we normally think of as one of the main events, and we also get the sense (other passages along the way

EXAMPLE 2a: MOZART, SYMPHONY IN E FLAT MAJOR (K. 543) SECOND
MOVEMENT (MEASURES 46-50), STRINGS ONLY

EXAMPLE 2b: MOZART, "DISSONANCE" QUARTET (K. 465),
FIRST MOVEMENT

EXAMPLE. 2c: MOZART, "LINZ" SYMPHONY (K. 425), FOURTH MOVEMENT
(MEASURES 93–116), STRINGS ONLY

may give the same sense) that something unexpected has been superimposed on
continuity that in the immediate vicinity is fairly contained and regular in phrase
structure, harmonic succession (e.g., IV-V-I), interval content, etc. But if there
is an element of the unexpected, even of surprise, I hasten to add, it is not in the
nature of the "nervous thrill" to relieve our "drowsy revery,"[16] or the scream
that pierces the calm of the mystery cinema's dead-of-night. For the sequential
pattern in each case enters quite naturally as counterpoint to a parallel sequence

in the lowest voice based on a motive from the rounded phrase that has just been heard.[17] Yet what transpires injects an element of tension, of adventure, briefly tonicizes the secondary (minor) triads of the scale, and lifts us to a plane at which what has been established as the fundamental plane shines forth in juxtaposition more plainly and persuasively, as if by a sudden shift of attention while we regard an object or activity we momentarily discover a new aspect, or literally a new side.

This notion of discovery should remind us of a point made by Delmore Schwartz: the poet may begin with a general plan, "but actually he finds that the finished work is an unexpected transformation of his intention." For a Classical composer the general plan may have consisted in a body of themes or motives along with other ideas, including the key structure within which all the material will be arranged. To be sure, the plan for a sonata also allows for the "free fantasy" of the development where relatively unexpected events may occur, paradoxically, as if on schedule. But Examples 2b and 2c are each from the second group of an exposition, and 2a which is not from a sonata allegro is in an analogous place in its movement. So-called analysis of the "music-appreciation" variety, in its fixation on first and second themes, is apt to disregard our sequential pattern since it does not fit into either of these categories, though it may flow from them. Such narrowly selective analysis falls woefully short of dealing with what Herbert Schwartz disarmingly calls the "dialectic game"—the drama that goes on, for instance, when a sonata otherwise notable for just pleasing themes and its satisfaction of the minimum requirements of the formula is animated by moments of the kind we have examined.

It is one of the ways the masters have of realizing the implication of the parts (call them emotional or technical)—that is, by allowing them to throw light upon one another, so to speak, by transformation, contrast, combination, etc. This is a kind of active probing—not a passive submission—to reach a vision of the emotions, or as Herbert Schwartz has put it, to unfold their "true natures." Since he reminds us that the "he" (the form) is "more articulate" than the "she" (the feeling), we do well to leave fanciful speculation on this "true nature" to the literary people who are skilled in handling words and images; we should content ourselves with the knowledge that as musicians, when we concern ourselves with the form we are, in a not too easily definable sense, addressing ourselves to the feeling. Whether or not the composer, in unfolding this "true nature," is at the same time the teacher and arbitrator of his discordant emotions, as Herbert Schwartz maintains, I am not prepared to say. It is enough for this discussion that the "true nature" is somehow revealed in the relationship of the parts.

NOTES

1. "... expression has never been an immanent property of music." *Chroniques de ma vie* (Paris: Denoël et Steele, 1935), 1: 116. Stravinsky retracted the statement in *Expositions and Developments*, his collaboration with Robert Craft (New York: Doubleday, 1962), 114: "That overpublicized bit about expression (or non-expression) was simply a way of saying that music is suprapersonal and superreal and as such beyond verbal meanings and verbal descriptions."

2. D.W. Prall was a professor of philosophy at Harvard with whom Delmore and I studied aesthetics and who was a good deal more influential on my thinking than on Delmore's.

3. *The Criterion* 13: 153.

4. For example: "The *genuineness* of poetry is something which we have some warrant for believing that a small number . . . can recognize." (Introduction to *Selected Poems* [New York: Macmillan, 1935], by Marianne Moore.)

5. *Science and Poetry*, 53, and again and again elsewhere.

6. *Variété, A Propos d'Adonis* (Paris: Nouvelle revue française, 1924), 158.

7. For an elucidation of this shift in attention, as well as an analysis of the medium, cf. D. W. Prall. *Aesthetic Judgment* (New York: Thomas Y. Crowell, 1929; Apollo-Crowell, 1967).

8. T. S. Eliot, *Selected Essays* (London: Faber and Faber, 1932), 275.

9. "I think the poet may gain much from the study of music . . . a poem, or a passage of a poem, may tend to realize itself first as a particular rhythm before it reaches expression in words . . ." T.S. Eliot, "The Music of Poetry," *Partisan Review* 9, no. 6 (1942): 465.

10. In trying to verbalize the feeling, whether in music or poetry, we do well to bear in mind Herbert Schwartz's admonition that the "he" (form) is "more articulate" than the "she" (feeling), so that it is easier to say what a feeling is *not* than what it *is*. I return to this notion at the end of the discussion, but I should forewarn the reader that I will be labelling feelings naively later for convenience—fully aware that the particular label chosen is debatable and that the feeling cannot be encapsulated in a single epithet plucked from its context.

11. I recall hearing *Götterdämmerung* in French and being quite taken aback when Brünnhilde, recoiling at the sight of Siegfried disguised by the Tarn-

helm as Gunther, addressed him in the gentle syllables of "Inconnu" where Wagner had written "Schrecklicher."

12. Timbres vary in the same way that tastes and smells do. "Pitches are at definitely apprehended distances . . . How far, on the other hand, and in what dimension in taste, does the taste of pork lie from that of beans and in what direction or recognized dimension is the smell of violets from that of pine needles?" D. W. Prall, *Aesthetic Analysis* (New York: Thomas Y. Crowell, 1936; reprint, Apollo-Crowell, 1967), 18.

13. This precautionary remark was prompted by claims of psychology that emotion is *defined* by the visceral reactions. The nature of emotion raises difficult problems that are not dealt with here. For example, does it make sense to say we can recognize an emotion in music without undergoing it, and how does the emotion change character when it is brought into relationship with other emotions in other parts of the work?

14. I was referring to Hugo Leichtentritt with whom I was doing most of my work at Harvard. On another occasion while examining the same opera he asked the class for the meaning of the D♯ in the overture. Privately amused, I came up with Don Giovanni's "defiance," at which Leichtentritt was positively transported. It is this practice of making a travesty of expression that understandably leads others to deny it entirely and is no doubt what Stravinsky had in mind in his Shakespeare songs in which, at the words "one string husband to another," he has the winds play and the viola rest.

15. Indeed, to appreciate how remarkable it is that through Mozart's reshaping and strategic placement the pattern acquires any tension at all, we have only to consider that with enough honing of the sharper edges we can eliminate tension altogether. What remains is the bland formula that enjoyed such currency in the eighteenth century—as in the following example from a toccata by Alessandro Scarlatti, in which the sevenths can be articulated by suppressing the notes in parentheses:

Observe, incidentally, that the variant in Example 2c returns in the recapitulation with the diminished seventh in the fourth measure replaced by the major seventh that is prescribed by the basic pattern.

16. The allusion is to the way George Santayana somewhere characterized most people's listening: "a drowsy revery relieved by nervous thrills"—though I confess to having dragged this in merely because I was taken by the locution.

17. Note also how in Example 2b our sequential pattern grows out of what precedes it in its own voice: Thus, C–D of measure 63 rhymes with F–E of measure 61 and then goes on to form its own sequence of measures 61–62, with the result that the ascent D to B comes in the form of a prolongation.

For a Friend

Clayton Eshleman

Gentle James Tenney
his words to me 20 years ago
Does she turn you on?
No. *Then you can't live with her.*
Down at the creek 50 yards
from his house where I'd gone
overcharged with LSD to cry
Comfort is rare wine,
& it startles me today to think
how particular nodes of others'
words hang, in the soul,
beautiful dead moments
I can visit. Guanajuato mummies,
arrested still in the cry
of their most acute occasion

Except in that underworld
one can stroke the leathery skull.
Here I can no longer touch
Jim's words other than in
evocation of his kind & generous
character. For he could have waited
until I returned to the house
& then asked me: *what's wrong?*
But he did not. He came down
to what today feels like
"the river" in "shall we gather at
the river" & rocked my
infantile despair briefly in his arms.
And as I looked into my cry
I saw that love & sex were not
to be divided—better be alone
than drape across that fence,
your head over Jeannie Woodring's backyard grass,
your ass facing your parents' bedroom.
So I walked, I think hand in hand,
with Jim back across the New Paltz road
torrid July heat which the acid had stoked into
Edenic roar, like all Edens poised
on the peristaltic waves of a jeweled worm's back.

*　*　*

Late night Matilija Ave., Sherman Oaks, 1970
dancing with Jim Caryl and Christine in our unfurnished living-room to
    "The Friends of Distinction,"
their subtle ecstacy drew the four of us into a shoulder-locked
    4-square dancing,
and a heat began to rise, as if we had become chimney
or some sort of Boschian creature,
close as I've ever been to an utter giving into
    something below,
for it was as if a pit of coals and rain, a spore of living
   orge
was fanning fire & merciful moisture across my body . . .

                          a moment I connect
with Jim's "Rags," his presence in Carolee's "Fuses,"

his willingness to vomit every morning for months in post-Reichian
   therapy,
his ecstacy component, so rare especially
                  given his gentleness—

                  *   *   *

It is not sentimental to affirm
those cutting-through moments that eternalize
a friendship. Very few people
are suddenly of a peculiar size that meets our fantasy of
   our size.
Too often I feel small, or large,
a misfit either way, and know I yearn for those moments of
   reciprocity
in which the air is umbilical about another and myself.
I haven't seen Jim for years.
No matter. A mouth appears around a corner asking,
have you something to say about JT?
   Of course—almost because he's of
my course. In the late 60s/early 70s
   several moments ceased to subtract
themselves, and hold—in that basin from which dryness and
   moisture seem to be in constant flight
—is that the soul?   The energy intoxication taps
              braided on the mobile corral
                   of our linked shoulders & arms

                18 May, Los Angeles—
                29 September, Ypsilanti.
                1986

LA

KENNETH GABURO, 1987

---" I have the sense of listening to
the sound, for itself,   more clearly
for itself, than seems to be possible
in earlier music."   James Tenney

IT IS THE SO MOST TO ME PROBABLY BEAUTIFUL TO PONDER-WONDER ONE'S WAY INTO M
AKING, (I.E., COMPOSITION). SO, ALSO TO SIMPLY DO IT; TO CATCH ONE'S SELF IN
THE ACT, SO-TO-SPEAK. AT ONCE THIS IS SO WHETHER ONE'S MAKING IS OF ONE'S OW
N MAKING, OR OF ANOTHER'S; (IN THE SENSE OF COMING TO KNOW IT).   BUT IT IS
NOT ENOUGH TO SUPPOSE THAT ONE HAS HEARD THE BEAUTY IN ANOTHER'S MAKING, (OR
ONE'S OWN, EITHER), BY MERELY HAVING "HEARD" IT, WITHOR WITHOUT PONDER-WONDE
R; (ALTHOUGH I DO NOT ARGUE AGAINST THIS POSSIBILITY, IF BY "HEARD" ONE IS R
EFERRING TO SOME NEURO-BIOLOGICAL SENSE-FUNCTION AND, OF COURSE, IS PRESUMIN
G NO SEVERE IMPAIRMENT IN THIS REGARD, AS WELL). HOWEVER TO COME TO A POINT
OF PROFOUNDLY HEARING IS, IN FACT, TO HAVE COME TO MAKE (COMPOSE); ONE'S, OR
ANOTHER'S.   STILL,
BEYOND THE LIMITS OF SOMETIMES RECOGNIZABLE MUSIC, (HOWEVER, THE NOT-NECESSA
RILY 'HEARD' MUSIC IN A MORE PROFOUND MANNER THAN THE SIMPLY NEURO-BIOLOGICA
L), MAY OCCASIONALLY BE FOUND THE DEEPERLY IMBEDDED: 'MUSICAL'.   NOW, THIS
OCCASION IS SO, SOMETIMES, EVEN WHEN MUSIC'S SURFACE SIGNS, (E.G., THOSE OF
NOTE, RHYTHM, HARMONY, FORM), ARE NOWHERE TO BE FOUND. SO IT IS HERE, IN THE
SEEMING AWSOME STILLNESS OF ANZO; THIS BORREGO NEAR WHICH I ONCE LIVED, AND
FREQUENTLY RETURN TO; THIS DESERTSPACE WITH WHICH I QUARRELED FOR SO LONG; T
HIS NEITHER TOTALLY VACUOUS NOT FULL FOR ME ONE; THIS ENDLESS PERSISTING, IN
ITS SEEMING TIMELESSNESS AND STILLNESS, ONE. BUT ONE, NOT ALONE;   ONE NOT
MERELY SELF-OCCUPIED. CONTRARILY, UNTOLD LIFE-FORMS ARE HERE; ---SEEN, HEARD
, FELT---; THEYSEEMING MOMENTARY, BUT NOT MINUSCULE. HERE, DELICATE FLOWERIN
GS, (FLUTTER-SOUNDING), WEAVE THEIR TREMOLOS WITH MINIMAL AIR-MOTION; ---APP
EARING AND DISAPPEARING IN WONDERFULLY COMPLETE CYCLES---; UNSTIRRING THE SU
RROUNDING, UNOCCUPIED SAND. HERE, EACH LIFE-FORM PERSISTS IN ITS OWN WAY, WI
THIN THE PERSISTENCE OF TIMELESS, STILL DESERTSPACE.   THERE IS NO SILENCE
HERE, BUT NOT BECAUSE VISITORS ENTER. I AM ONE. IN STATES OF SHADOW A CONSID
ERABLE PART OF THE TIME, I COME OFTEN TO PONDER-WONDER THE QUESTION: COULD
THERE EVER BE ANY CONCILIATION BETWEEN WHAT/HOW I FEEL LIKE WHEN HERE IN THI
S DESERTSPACE, GENERALLY REGARDED AS PRIMITIVE; --- (HEREINAFTER AKA 'PRIMIT'
)---; AND WHAT/HOW I FEEL LIKE WHEN THERE, IN THAT ELSEWHERE WORLD, GENERALL
Y REGARDED AS CULTURED; --- (HEREINAFTER AKA 'CULT')---? BUT WHAT IS THE SENS
E, IF THERE IS ONE, WHICH COULD BRIDGE THE SEEMING INCONGRUITY OF PRIMIT'S'M
USICAL' SAY, WITH, SAY, CULT'S MUSIC; A SENSE WHICH WOULD NOT CAUSE ME TO GO
INTO AT LEAST ACOUSTICAL SPASMS WHENEVER I TRY TO BRING THE ONE INTO THE SPA
CE OF THE OTHER? GOOD GRIEVE, LOQUENDI, ALTHOUGH IT IS NOT THE WEST-EAST CON
FLICT, (COASTS OR CONTINENTS), IT SURE SEEMS SO. IT IS AMAZING TO ME THAT MY
EXTRAORDINARILY LONG PREOCCUPATION WITH PHEMENOLOGY, WHICH I HAVE ASSUMED TO
BE THE HEIGHT OF ELEGANT PHILOSOPHICAL ERUDITION,--- (HAVING, AFTERALL, COME
OUT OF CULT'S GRANDEST MOMENTS)---, IS TAKING ME, INSTEAD(?), TO A KIND OF P
RIMITIVE, (= RADICAL), VIEW; NOT AT ALL SIMPLY 'SOUNDING', SIMPLY 'HEARING',
NOR EASY LISTENING. AT LEAST WHILE IN THE WORLD OF ANZO'S PRIMIT, AND/OR ELS
EWHERE UNDER ITS INFLUENCE, COMPOSITION IN THE SENSE THAT I/WE HAVE COME TO
UNDERSTAND IT AS A WESTERNER'S CULT, IS DEAD. THIS IS SO, PARTICULARLY, IN T
HE SENSE OF ITS OPERATIONAL CONCERNS FOR FORM, TIME, STRUCTURE, PHRASE, LICK
, (ESPECIALLY ITS "LICK"), ET ALIA; NOW ALMOST UNIVERSALLY TRANSFORMS OF TRA

SFORMS OF TRANSFORMS; EMBEDMENTS OF EMBEDMENTS; TRACES OF TRACES OF ALL OF T
HE OTHERS COMING BEFORE AND DURING THE GREAT ABUNDANCE OF CONTEMPORARY PRAXI
S, ET ALIA, SO ABUNDUNDANTLY NOW ENCOURAGED BY GUV AND CORP WHO NEVER SUPPOR
TED ANYTHING UNLESS IN THEIR OWN INTEREST(S), AND IN THEIR OWN IMAGE.   (I
DON'T CALL THIS POLITICAL MUSIC INSPITE OF THE HOWEVER ASSOCIATION).   ALL
CLICHE'.   TAKE SHELTER!
(BUT OF COURSE THIS IS A GREAT AGONY FOR ME AND CERTAIN OTHERS WHO HAVE SEAR
CHED AND FOUND THIS SEEMINGLY ELUSIVE STATE REFERRED TO AS COMPOSITION). BUT
EVEN-IF THE WORKS ARE NOT THE CLICHE' BORN OF COMPOSITIONAL PROCEDURES I SPE
AK OF, THEN THE CONCOMITANT AGONY IS THAT THE MECHANISMS, (e.g., THE "ORCHES
TRA", THE "STRING QUARTET", THE "PIANO", THE "VOICE", ---"WHATEVER"),   ARE.
ONCE, SO REMARKABLY THE CO-CONSPIRITORS IN THE MAKING OF BEAUTIFULLY MADE MU
SIC, NOW, AS THE YET GRAND ENVIRONMENTAL DOMAINS FOR MUSIC, THESE MECHANISMS
NEUTRALIZE THAT WHICH A WORK IS. BY THEIR NATURE, THEY HELP TO DECOMPOSE THE
COMPOSITION THEY CONTAIN. A COMPOSITION CANNOT BE EXPERIMENTAL, TO SAY NOTHI
NG OF RADICAL, IF THE COMPOSITION OF AN ORCHESTRA, SAY, BY ITS NATURE, ISN'T
. THE HEARING OF THE ONE DISABLES LA-HEARING THE OTHER. IN CERTAIN COMPANY C
OMPOSITION IS MORE OR LESS A CONTINUAL RECONFIGURATION OF THE ORCHESTRA'S (O
OTHER MECHANISM'S) CONVENTIONAL STRUCTURE; INSTRUMENTS OUT OF THE USUAL STAG
E-PIT-AUDIENCE, NO MATTER. THEY ARE IN THEIR POWER, BACKED UP BY AGES OF NOW
COMFORTABLE, NON-CONTRAVERSIAL + TODAY'S MUSIC MIMICS, DOING LITTLE MORE THA
N POSTPONING THE DEATH OF IT. BUT MAN, IS IT COSTING PUHLENTY FOR ITS PRESER
VATIVES; DITTO NOW FOR THE LEVEL OF PERFORMANCE, WHICH LIKE SDI, IS MUCH IN
EVIDENCE BUT NOT NECESSARILY WHAT IS NEEDED FOR THE FURTHER ENLIGHTENMENT OF
THE HUMAN SPECIES, TO SAY NOTHING OF A MOTION TO ANOTHER LEVEL OF CONSCIOUS-
NESS. IT IS TRUE, OF COURSE, THERE WILL ALWAYS BE THE NEW, YOUNG, AS-YET UN-
INFORMED GENERATIONS, WHICH, ONCE HAVING DISCOVERED THAT THERE IS SOMETHING
WORTHWHILE ABOUT "SERIOUS" MUSIC,---(MAYBE BECAUSE OF THE FIREWORK DISPLAYS
WHICH SO FREQUENTLY APPEAR TO BE A BASIC REQUIREMENT FOR ITS ILLUMINATION)--
-, WILL BUY IT, SUPPORT IT, CONSUME IT, (I.E., THAT WHICH HAS ALREADY BEEN E
STABLISHED BY EMPHASIS IN INSTITUTIONS OF LOWER LEARNING, METHODS, BOOKS, TH
E REPERTOIRE OF EVERY GROUP, ALL WORKING HAND IN HAND TO MAINTAIN THE VALUE
OF WHICH, ---IF NOT DEAD---, NEEDS NO MORE OF ITS KIND THAN IT ALREADY HAS O
F). IT ALL BEGINS TO SOUND LIKE ONE GRAND MUZACKY. AND, THE INCREDIBLY WELL
OILED, ALL-CONSPIRING MECHANISTIC TECHNOLOGIES WHICH DRIVE IT, IN OVERKILL G
EAR, ---(RIGHT INTO THE BONE MARROW)---, ARE LIKE AGED BEEF; THE GREATER THE
AGEING, ---(THAT IS: WITHIN LIMITS; THERE IS, AFTERALL, SOMETHING TO BE SAID
FOR STYLE)---, AND THE GREATER THE TASTE, ---(THAT IS: THERE IS SOMETHING TO
BE SAID FOR THE MOUTH)---, THEN THE GREATER THE DECOMPOSITION, ---(THAT IS:
DEATH)---, OF THE ONCE LIVING. AS WITH SEEMINGLY INSATIABLE DESIRE FOR FAMIL
IARS, ---(THE "UN"-ONES BEING ONLY WEIRD CURIOSITIES LIKE CIRCUS FREAKS)---,
AND NON-CHARGED CONSISTENCIES, IT ALL SEEMS SO COMFORTABLE. A NEW HIGH.   A
SUPERSONICAMENTE WHILE NEVER LEAVING THE GROUND. AND THE CURRENT NEW WAVE, (
THE WAVE OF THE WEEK, SO-TO-SPEAK), OF CONTINUAL NEW WAVES IS/ARE ALREADY CO
NNECTING UP, ---(ALTHOUGL UNKNOWINGLY, AND UNINTENTIONALLY, I AM SURE)TO THE
FUNERAL MUSIC I HEARD SO OFTEN AS A KID WHEN I PRACTICED THAT ACT: AN ACT AL
READY THEN POLLUTED BY TOO MANY LILIES, AND BY THE SACCRINE MELLOWNESS OF SE
MENLESS ORGAN SWELLS; ---(NO DIFFERENT FROM THE CURRENT RAGE FOR SUBLIMINAL
AUDIO TAPES USED TO OVERCOME IMPOTENCE)---; I USED TO WONDER HOW ANY SPIRIT
COULD LIFT OFF WITH SUCH SMELLINGS OF ITS OWN FORMALDEHYDE, ---(NOT EASILY C
ONCEALED AT CLOSE RANGE)---, BEING RECYCLED WITH ADDITIONALLY FANCY HYPNOTAP
ES. NOW THIS SHIT, ---(WITH GENTLE RAIN-DROPPED ORCHESTRATIONS)---,ABOVE ALL
, I DON'T WANT TO HAVE PIPED INTO MY EARS VIA ESPECIALLY A WALKMAN, WHICH RE
CENTLY MY DENTIST SUGGESTED BEFORE COMMENCING TO BREAKUP THE INSIDE OF MY MO
UTH WITH HIS HIGH-SPEED DRILL, THINKING IT WOULD HELP ME FEEL BETTER.   I
SAID TO HIM I'D RATHER DIG FOR THE INCREDIBLE SONIC-VARIATIONS OF HIS HIGH-S

PEED DRILL INSIDE MY MOUTH ANYDAY, BUT HE COULDN'T QUITE GET BEHIND THIS ANT
I-SOCIAL ATTITUDE BECAUSE HIS CUSTOMERS, ---(SO HE SAYS)---, ALL LOVE HIS WA
LKMAN, EVEN WHEN I SAY I AM A RADICAL COMPOSER GOING FOR SOMETHING ELSE,HE I
S NOT IMPRESSED; ---(SO WHILE I'M GETTING INTO THE ACOUSTICAL SPECTRA OF HIS
DRILL, BEING A POLYPHONIC PERSON, I HAPPENED TO FLASH ON A YOUNG COUI-LE,OVER
-HEARING THEIR INTENSE DISCUSSION ON THE BEAUTY OF B-MINOR WHILE AT LUNCH I
N A SMALL D.C. WASH-BISTRO THE PREVIOUS WEEK;---((NOW MIND YOU LOQUENDI, NOT
EVEN ABOUT THE MASS IN---; BUT SIMPLY "OH HOW THERE'S SOMETHING ABOUT B,   AS
NO OTHER MINOR HAS)) ---; SOUNDING AS-IF THEY WERE ABOUT TO COME ON IT TOGETH
ER; SAYING HOW IT COULD BE TRANSFORMED DIGITALLY; HOW OPERATIONS COULD BE PE
RFORMED DITTO FOR 12T, FOR QUARTER-T AS WELL; HOW THE FINAL DOMINATION OVER
KEY, SCALE, PITCH, ET ALIA, ---IN NO MATTER WHAT SENSE; ---((AS FOR LIKE-PAR
AMETERS)) ---, IS AT HAND, AND BY ANYONE)---; SO, I BEGAN TALKING TO THE DENT
IST AGAIN, INSTEAD, ABOUT HOW I COULD COMPOSE WALKMAN'S MOUTH WITH HIS SPECT
ACULAR DRILL, AND HOW IT IS TIME FOR A GENUINE UNCORRUPTED MACRO-BIOTIC DIET
TO AVOIDE FURTHER MOLAR DECAY. BUT HE DOESN'T SMILE AT THESE MATTERS EITHER,
SINCE HIS DRILLING IS OVER, AND, THAT'S THAT!   STILL,
CULT'S MUSIC WON'T GO DOWN SO EASILY; ---(PARTCH WAS RIGHT: BEGINNING OVER A
GAIN, MEANT, ((MEANS)) , PRECISELY THAT)---; IF NOT BY DEAD COMPOSITIONS, OR
CENSORIAL MECHANISMS, THEN NEITHER BY THOSE STAGNATING PRACTICES OF LANGUAGE
WHICH CORRUPT IT, PERPETRATING ITS DECAY, (AND LOVING IT), WITH BEEFED-UP ST
YROIDS; NOR BY THE SEDUCTIONS OF MIMESIS, ANDROIDS, AI, MODELS, QUOTATIONS,A
NECDOTES, SIMULATIONS, AND SAMPLINGS, WHICH OVERCOME GLORIOUS POSSIBLE LIFT-
OFFS TO IMAGINATION'S WONDERFUL UNIVERSE. ENDLESS PERMUTATIONS AND COMBINATI
ONS OF ALREADY-MADE RESIDUALS ARE PREFERRED. TECH HAS FINALLY BECOME THE PRO
CESSOR OF INHERITANCE OF CULT'S PERHAPS EVER TRUST-DEEDER. CULT FEELS SAFE.
SECURE. IT HAS INVESTED WISELY. BY A KIND OF BLIND SODOMY IT MUST NOT KNOW T
HAT IT IS DYING. NOR, FOR THAT MATTER, DOES IT SEEM TO BE ABLE TO SENSE OTHE
R 'FRINGE' BENEFITS TAKING HOLD, WHICH IT WOULD NOT EASILY WANT TO KNOW ANYW
AY, BECAUSE THESE PUT FORTH NOT MERELY NEW NOTIONS OF COMPOSITION; ---(NOT
CONNECTED TO NOTE LICKING, PER SE: AFTERALL, WHAT IS NOTE A FUNCTION OF?)---;
BUT REQUIRE A NEW WAY OF THINKING, (EVEN OF MUSIC), ALTOGETHER; ---(GOOD GRI
EVE; NOT THAT!). IT IS SOME KIND OF TRAGEDY THAT THE PROFOUND DISCOVERIES OF
THE NEW (NOW OLD) MUSIC IN THIS CENTURY, EVEN AS EXPRESSED BY ITS CONCEPTUAL
LANGUAGE, ---(TRY MORPHIC RESONANCE, OR PARAMETRIC TRANSFERENCE, FOR INSTANC
E)---, REMAIN UNINCORPORATED, SOMETIMES AS-IF THEY NEVER HAPPENED.   (JAMES
TENNEY, HEREINAFTER AKA: JT: "WE GET STUCK, WE GET STUCK. IT'S LIKE WE DON'T
WANT TO GROW. WE WANT TO HAVE THE BENEFITS OF BEING GROWN WITHOUT THE PAIN O
F GROWING,---WE'RE IN A TIME OF BIRTH OF A NEW WORLD AND IT'S REALLY VERY PAI
NFUL---). OF COURSE, BY EVERY STATISTICAL COUNT, WHAT I'M SAYING ABOUT CULT'
S DEATH WOULD SEEM COMPLETELY FALSE. THE CRITERIA, ---THE STUFFED-WITH-PEOPL
E-HALLS---, THE $'S ARE EVERYWHERE IN EVIDENCE. SO ARE ALITA, THE PREYING MA
NTIS', THE PREYING MANTIC, (A PROPHET, ---ONE EFFECTED BY DIVINE MADNESS), T
HE MANTICORE, AND MANTICULATOR. BUT SOME WHO YET-PRACTICE COMPOSITION, ---(W
HICH IS TO BE DISTINGUISHED FROM WRITING "PIECES"; AN INCIDENTAL EXPRESSION
WHICH HAS BEEN DIGNIFIED IN CULT'S WORLD)---, DO SO WITHOUT SUCH FAMILIAR AC
OUTREMENTS. ONE MAY FIND THEM IN ASSORTED CATECOMBS HERE AND THERE, ESPECIAL
LY PRESERVED BY THE NON-ELITE. THEY ARE USUALLY SMILING; AND SAFE.THIS IS SO
, BECAUSE CIA REGARDS THEM AS HARMLESS NUTS. ONE OF MINE IS ANZO.   LOQUENDI
ALSO COMES ALONG. SOMETIMES, TO KEEP ME FROM GOING MAD. BUT SINCE COMING TO
UNDERSTAND PRIMIT BETTER, WE ALSO LOOK FOR LA. SEEKING LA IS A RATHER RECENT
DESIRE. I HAD NO NOTION OF THIS AT THE TIME THE IMPULSE FOR ANTIPHONY IX CAM
E TO ME HERE, DURING ONE OF MY PONDER-WONDERS. (ANTIPHONY IX IS MY FIRST SO-
CALLED ORCHESTRAL WORK IN 28 YEARS. IT BEGAN BY MY PASTING 12 SHEETS OF BLAN
K GRAPH PAPER SUCCESSIVELY ONTO A LONG STRIP OF BUTCHER PAPER. THE ROOM WAS
MADE AS DARK AS POSSIBLE. I SAT AT THE TABLE, PRICKING THE PAPER WITH MY PEN

POINT. I SAT AT THE TABLE, PRICKING THE PAPER WITH MY PEN POINT. MY EYES WER
E CLOSED. I HAD LITTLE SENSE OF DIRECTION, TIME, PAGE SPACE, DISTRIBUTION, O
R MUCH ELSE EXCEPT FOR SOUND MOTION PEN CONTACT + MY ACHING BACK. I   STOPPED
WHEN I FELT I HAD VISITED ALL THE SHEETS. IT'S CALLED: "A DOT"). AS I'VE SAI
D, OTHERS ALSO ENTER PROBABLY FOR DIFFERENT REASONS. WHO KNOWS? THE   DISTANT
SOUND OF A BIKER'S RIG; A CHILD WITH PARENTS ON THE HORIZON; COUPLES   NESTED
IN SOME MINUTELY DIFFERENTIATED SHADED FORMATION. IN ONE WAY OR ANOTHER, ALL
ATTEND TO DESERTSPACE WHILE HERE. MARKED OFF BY EXTRAORDINARILY DIVERSE MOTI
ONS OF COMING AND GOING, DESERTSPACE SEEMS ALWAYS TO BE CHANGING. IT IS ORDE
RLY BUT NOT ORDERED. ITS OTHERWISE STILLNESS AND TIMELESSNESS IS ETCHED BY P
ROVOCATIVE, SEEMINGLY RANDOM GESTURES GIVEN TO IT BY THOSE LIFE-FORMS   WHICH
COMPRISE IT: NOW HERE, NOW THERE; POISED, FLEETING, CYCLIC, DIFFUSED.   I AM
STARTLED. DESERTSPACE IS NEVER QUITE THE SAME. BECAUSE OF THIS, CHANGES APPE
AR ALWAYS TO BE IMMEDIATE AND CONCLUSIVE. BUT THIS IS A DECEPTION. FOR, BOTH
DESERTSPACE AND ITS LIFE-FORMS, ---WHETHER OCCUPANTS OR VISITORS---, ARE CAU
GHT UP IN CONTINUAL STATES OF BECOMING. THIS IS ALSO VERY STRANGE TO LOQUEND
I, BECAUSE NEITHER SEEMS TO CARE THAT IT BECOMES; (LOQUENDI DOES). IT IS USE
LESS TO MAKE PREDICTIONS ABOUT HOW IT WILL BE NEXT TIME, OR TEN MINUTES FROM
NOW, (BY MY TIME). BECOMING IS WHAT DESERTSPACE DOES; SO, ALSO, FOR ITS OCCU
PANTS. IN THIS BECOMING, I HEAR A RATHER INCREDIBLE KIND OF, ---(IN ANTIPHON
Y IX, I WANTED THE ORCHESTRA + CHILDREN TO PERFORM ONE TUTTI VOCAL UTTERANCE
; SOMETHING SINGULAR IN THE MORPHEMIC SENSE, BUT WITH NO OTHER PARTICULAR SI
GNIFICANCE IN MIND AT THE TIME. JUST DAYS BEFORE THE PREMIERE, 'LA' SIMPLY C
AME TO ME. IT SEEMED PARTICULARLY ARESONANT TO ANYTHING I WAS CONSCIOUSLY HE
ARING IN THE WORK. SO, I SIMPLY INCLUDED IT, THINKING I WOULD FIND A WAY TO
MAKE SENSE, (I.E., 'COMPOSE' IT), LATER;   ---((NOW, LA, OF COURSE
, IS A FAIRLY BIG DEAL. IT IS FOUND IN MANY LANGUAGES, IN NUMEROUS SENSES, A
ND HAS A GRAND HISTORY. I MEAN LIKE: LA AS IN GERM THEORY, (((PARTICULARLY F
ERMENTATION))) ; AND FALALA, LALALALA, (((AS IN REFRAINS))) ; AND LA-DIE-DA
, (((AS IN SO-SO; AS IN AN EXPRESSION OF DERISION; AS IN WHAT'S THE BIG DEA
L?; ((((AS IN CHRIS, THE MANN OF FEW WORDS "LA DIE DA" MIND-BLOWING SPLATTTT,
)))) , FOR VOICES))); AND AS A GRAPHIC FOR NO REASON, I ONCE MADE, (((TWO WH
ITE LETTERS, L+A PLACED IN THE SW CORNER OF A SOLID, DENSE SHEET OF BLACK CO
NSTRUCTION PAPER))) ;AND, OF COURSE, AS IN THE SLIGHTLY RIBALD, (((FR., OOH
LA LA))); AND CERTAINLY "E-LA", (((HIGH NOTE IN GUIDO'S BIG SCALE WITH IT'S
ASSOCIATED "GAMUT", ---CONTRACTION OF MED.L.= GAMMA UT, ---WHICH HAS ITS OWN
SUB-COLLECTION OF STRANGE BEDFELLOWS AS IN: " A SOULDIER'S GAMMAUT GOES   FAR
BEYOND E-LA", ((((J.CARUSO: ACT OF WARRE, 1639)))) ; OR "THE SOUNDERS OF THRE
E-FOURTHS OF THE NOTES IN THE WHOLE GAMUT OF CRIME", ((((DICKENS: T.T.CITIES
,1859)))) ; ---OH GUIDO, HOW YOU DO RAMBLE ON))); AND RECENTLY VIA A TENDER N
OTE FROM A DEAR FRIEND, JOHN ALBAUGH, OR PERHAPS, (((WITH SOME LIBERTY))) ,J
OHN LA BAUGH, WHO WRITES: "A BIG LESSON I'VE LAERNED SINCE A RRIVING IN EAST
L.A. FROM IOW A:LIVE FOR THE MOMENT! EVERYTIME I LAEVE ONE P-LACE FOR A-NOTH
ER I LAWAYS THINK A-BOUT HOW GRE-AT IT W-AS IN THE P-LACE I JUST MOVED FROM.
I'M A-VOIDING THE PRESENT BEC-AUSE IT'S TOO H-ARD TO F-ACE SO I P-LAY IT S-A
FE BY LIVING IN THE P-AST A-ND/OR FOR THE FUTURE. SO, EVERYTIME I C-ATCH MYS
ELF DOING TH-AT, I TRY TO DO SOMETHING PRESENT)) ---; A GRAND AFTER-THE-FACT
WAY OF MAKING SENSE COMPOSING); ---A RATHER INCREDIBLE KIND OF PRIMIT; ---(W
HICH I DID WHILE PURSUING MY STUDY OF THE VITALISTS; ---((AND OF COURSE OF L
A: AS AN EXCLAMATION FORMERLY USED TO ACCOMPANY OR INTRODUCE A CONVENTIONAL-
PHRASE, OR ADDRESS, OR TO CALL ATTENTION TO AN EMPHATIC STATEMENT, OR PERSON
SUCH AS "LA NOW", "LA MA'AM", (((LA JT))); AND IN RECENT USAGE, LA AS A MERE
EXPRESSION OF SURPRISE, WHICH IN ANTIPHONY IX TRANSLATED INTO BEING 'STARTLE
D' BY SOMETHING)) ---; IN ORDER TO ENRICH MY SENSE OF THIS NEW PRIMIT I FELT
IMPELLING ME. AND WHILE SIMULTANEOUSLY WORKING ON "ISIT" FOR DAVID DUNN'S IN

TERNATIONAL SYNERGY JOURNAL, I RAN SMACK-BANGO INTO THE EXPRESSION: "KAREN
DOCTRINE OF THE LA"; ---((BY THE WAY, THE EXPRESSION, "DOCTRINE", IS AN ANTH
ROPOLOGICAL ONE, NOT USED BY THE "PRIMITIVE" KARENS WHO KNEW NOT SUCH MATTER
S, ALTHOUGH THEIR'S WAS SURELY A BELIEF SYSTEM OF SOME COMPLEXITY, AND, APPA
RENTLY, A VITALIST ONE)) ---; AND IT IS THIS KAREN SENSE OF LA WHICH FINALLY
BEGINS TO GET TO ME)---; -IVE BREATHING: LIFE-FORMS WHICH PARTICIPATE IN DES
ERTSPACE, ---UNPREDICTABLY MARKING OFF INCREMENTS OF TIME, IN ITS TIMELESSNE
SS; ---(AGAIN: IT COMES UP: VITALISM: EXISTENT; MANIFESTATIONS OF LIFE;   ---
THAT THE PROCESSES OF LIFE ARE NOT SUFFICIENTLY EXPLICATED BY THE LAWS OF PH
YSICS AND CHEMISTRY ALONE); BREATHING; AND MOMENTARILY MASKING ITS STILLNESS
;---(IT IS NOT SO DIFFICULT TO IMAGINE HOW VITALISM, IN ITS GENERALITY, AND
ESPECIALLY IN ANZO, COULD BE, ((COULD HAVE BEEN)) , STRETCHED TO INCLUDE TH
E MORE COMPLEX CONCEPT OF "ANIMISM"; ((E.G., STAHL'S "ANIMA MUNDI", ET ALIA
)) , WHERE ALL SO-CALLED "NATURAL OBJECTS", ---HUMANS, ANIMALS, PLANTS, STONE
S, ((INCLUDING NATURE ITSELF)) , ARE INHABITED BY SOULS, WHICH MAY EXIST IN A
SEPARATE STATE; ---((THE APPARITION OF THE DISEMBODIED SOUL HAS IN ALL AGES,
BEEN THOUGHT TO BEAR A SPECIAL RELATION TO ITS DEPARTURE FROM ITS BODY AFTER
DEATH)) ---;LIFE-FORMS! BREATHING! DESERTSPACE IS LEFT CONSPICUOUS BY THE PRE
SENCE OR ABSENCE, ---COMING AND GOING---, OF ITS LIFE-FORMS. PERSISTENT DESE
RTSPACE CANNOT LEAVE, BUT IT IS NEVER SILENT. IT IS NOT UNALIVE.NOW I DON'T
QUITE KNOW WHAT TO DO WITH THIS ONE. BUT I'M THINKING MY SKEPTICISM OF ANIMI
STIC NOTIONS IS NOT FOR SURETY. PRIMIT SEEMS TO BE SAYING, "BREATHING IS THE
ULSING RATE BETWEEN ABSENCE AND RESENCE; THE COMING AND GOING OF ANZO'S MEMB
ERS". IN THIS SENSE, DESERTSPACE'S STILLNESS MAINTAINS A SUBTLE-SHIFTING AMB
IENCE OF QUIESCENT NOISE; AGAINST WHICH, AND (INDESPENSIBLY) WITH WHICH, THE
ABSORBSION AND REFLECTION OF ALL VIBRATING MATTER IS AUDIBLE. LISTEN.LISTEN.
LISTEN. AVOIDE HOT LIGHT. I CAN FEEL THE SOUND OF BLOOD FLOWING THROUGH MY B
RAIN AT THE EXPERIENCE OF ANZO'S DISEMBODIED SOUNDS. A SOUND APPEARING AFTER
LEAVING ITS TRANSMITTER, THEREBY ANNOUNCES IT. SOUND MOVES BETWEEN TRANSMITT
ERS AND RECEPTORS, ---(AS DOES BODY-GHOST'S PERSONAL LIFE, ((APPEARING AFTER
DEATH)) , ANNOUNCES ITSELF TO A KAREN IN A DREAM). BUT NOW, FOR THIS KIND OF
EXPERIENCE, KARENS WERE REGARDED AS SAVAGES AND BAEBARIANS, AS DISTINCT FROM
THOSE CULTIVATED, CIVILIZED SOCIETIES WHO SO VIEWED THEM IN THIS LIGHT. BUT
WHY NOT THESE SO-CALLED MYTHS, (WHICH PERSIST TO THIS DAY), WHEN HUMANS LIVE
D SO VERY CLOSE TO, SO DIRECTLY WITH, THE PHENOMENA THEY DESCRIBED, AND, NEC
ESSARILY MADE SENSE OF IT IN THE WAY THEY DID?   (TYLOR: "MYTH IS THE
HISTORY OF ITS AUTHORS, NOT OF ITS SUBJECTS"; "PRIMITIVE CULTURE", p.416, v.
1; HENRY HOLT & CO., 1889). LOQUENDI AGREES;(SO DOES LEVI-STRAUSS).   CULT
DOES NOT. AS I GET INTO THE KAREN "MYTHS" I BEGIN TO CONNECT SOUL WITH SOUND
, (AT LEAST THIS FAR I CAN GO). KARENS CONSIDERED THEIR "MYTHS" BY EXPERIENC
ING THEM, THINKING THEM, RITUALIZING THEM. SOUND WAS ALWAYS INVOLVED. IT PRO
VIDED A GRAND CONNECTOR TO INTERNAL AND EXTERNAL MATTER. SOUND; NOT THE LEAS
T EXPRESSED BY THEIR VOCAL LANGUAGE: GESTURE, MIMICRY, EMOTIONAL TONE, INTON
ATIONS, EMPHASIS, FORCE, SPEED, UTTERANCE OF ALL SORTS, (UNIMAGINABLE WITHOU
T THE CO-RELATIVE: "MUSICAL"). SO IT IS WITH ANZO'S DESERTSPACE.   NOTHING
SEEMS TO BE WITHOUT THE SENSE-ASSOCIATION OF SOUND: SEARCHING FOR FOOD; THE
ROARS AND THE SUBLIMINALS; THE OMNI-PRESENT STILLNESS, ITSELF. I'M IN UP TO
MY EARDRUMS MAGNIFYING EVERYTHING. ALL APPARENT. NO, NO, NOT BY SILENCE! (TH
E SILENT UNIVERSE BELIEF IS/WAS A DUMB IDEA; HOW CAN ONE STOP THE SOUND IN O
NE'S HEAD, CF. BECKETT'S "COMPANION")? SUDDENLY, SEEMINGLY FROM NOWHERE, (
ALTHOUGH NOT TRUE), MY UNDERSTANDING OF KAREN'S LA COMES TO ME. IN THAT SO-
CALLED "PRIMITIVE-BARBARIC" CULTURE, "LA" STOOD FOR SOUL, AND, EXTRAORDINARI
LY, SOUL WAS CONNECTED WITH SOUND. IMAGINE THE WONDER OF IT LOQUENDI: LA/
SOUL/SOUND, (HEREINAFTER, SOUL + SOUND AKA: LA). THREE CHEERS; (TWICE MORE).
AND, SINCE THE KAREN'S LA SEEMED TO ENCOMPASS A WELL-MARKED VITALISTIC SYSTE

M, THEIR LAS, ---(BROADLY GROUPED INTO PERSONS, ((KA-LA)) ; OTHER LIVING MATT
ER, ---PLANTS, ANIMALS, ((KE-LAH)) ; AND THOSE INANIMATE KINDS, ---KNIVES, AX
ES, STONES, ET ALIA, ---REFERRED TO AS "OBJECT-((KEH-LA)) SOULS")---; SEEM
ENDLESS.   STILL,
I AM NOT DISMAYED BY ANZO'S APPARENT SPATIAL OPENNESS, (A KIND OF MINIMALISM
), AND, THEREFORE, VULNERABILITY, (ALSO MINE). THERE ARE NOT ENDLESS   CONDO
CLUSTERS OR YAVY NARDS OR WAL-TO-WALL COMBUSTION ENGINES TO GIVE ONE A FALSE
SENSE OF PROTECTION, STRENGTH, AND PRIVACY, ---AND "CULTURE", (ALTHOUGH   IT
CERTAINLY IS 'ONE'). IMAGINE IT: ALL LA SEEM CONTINUALLY POISED HERE. PRIMIT
IS AT HOME. THEIR PRESENCE CAN BE FELT MORE OFTEN BY SOUND THAN BY SIGHT WIT
H TIMBRAL PLAY FROM THE MOST ABOUT-TO-BLOSSOM THRESHOLDS OF THE AUDIBLE,   TO
THE VIOLENCE OF FLASH-FLOODS; (WHAT DO YOU SUPPOSE WOULD HAPPEN IF THE NEW W
AVE WERE TO DISCOVER THE SOUND OF THE BUZZARD?); IT IS NOW EASY FOR ME TO IM
AGINE THAT ANZO, TOO, IS A LA; A VAST PRIMIT DESERTSPACE ENCLOSING COUNTLESS
ONES: THE LA OF A RAINBOW IN THE SKY DRINKING WATER; THE LA OF A MAD BEE; OF
AN EPILEPTIC LIZARD; ---(AND I FLASH ON NOTIONS OF ANIMISM AND THOSE ENDLESS
KAREN TALES OF THE PRESIDING GENII OF NATURE: THE LAS OF CLIFFS AND VOLCANIC
ASH, WHERE NIGHT AND HADES TAKE PERSONAL SHAPE)---; OF A MOUTH OF NIGHT LA;
OF A WIDE-YAWNING, SWALLOWING LA; ON AND ON. EVERY LA IS LOCATED SOMEWHERE ,
BUT WHERE? PRIMIT IS A FLEETING DESERT; AMBIGUOUS, BUT NOT ANONYMOUS. TINGED
. DOES IT MATTER IF ALL THE MEMBERS CANNOT BE IDENTIFIED? I WONDER WHERE THE
SOUNDS GO, BUT WHAT DIFFERENCE WOULD IT MAKE TO KNOW? WHAT DOES IT MEAN   TO
CULT TO REPORT THAT EVERYTHING IS ALIVE HERE? WHAT IN HELL DOES IT MEAN TO A
NALYZE, ---ANALYZE WHAT?---, WHEN THERE'S SO MUCH TO EXPERIENCE WHILE MOVING
THROUGH MASSIVE STRATA OF BREATHING ROCKS WHICH CONTINUALLY KLANG WITH THEIR
OPENING AND SHUTTING LA HERE, LA THERE; RICOCHETTING AROUND GIGANTIC SHADOWY
ROCK FORMATIONS THROUGH PRECIPICES ENCOUNTERING OTHERS: ---(MESSENGERS OF
ANGELS, SO THE KARENS SAY)---; OPENING AND SHUTTING UNSEEM GATES. IN ANZO IS
IT SOUND I'M HEARING SOMETIMES, OR IS IT SOUND ABOUT TO BE BORN?   (IF SO
, THAT'S GETTING REAL CLOSE TO THE CUTTING EDGE OF THINGS OH CULTO);   AWSOME
STILLNESS BEFORE SOMETHING FLUTTERS? (OR DID IT)? THE ULTIMATE   GENTLEMOST,
EVENMOST SUBLIMINAL OF VIBRATING MATTER;   THEN COUNTERED BY CLASHING
THUNDER'S LA, ---(ALSO EMBODIED BY THE MIGHTY THUNDERBIRD FLAPPING AND FLASH
ING IT OFF WITH EAGLE AND VULTURE)---; OR BY THE MIGHTY TORTOISE WHOSE SOUND
SOF MOVING ARE SUPPOSED TO CAUSE EARTHQUAKES: ---(WHAT, IN ANZO?; DUNNO, BUT
MELVILLE'S ENCANTADAS INTRUDE)---; OR DID I?   (PERHAPS)?   BUT
UP IT COMES AGAIN: VITALISM: (D.J.B.HAWKINS, HERINAFTER AKA= DJBH: "HOWEVER
ESSENTIALLY MAN MAY BE A MATERIAL BEING, THE BURDEN OF PROOF IS ON THOSE WHO
WISH TO HOLD THAT HE IS NOTHING ELSE"; p.13, MAN & MORALS, 1960; SHEED AND W
ARD). NOW I PONDER-WONDER IF THERE IS ANY INTRINSIC CONNECTION BETWEEN DJBH'
S HYLOMORPHIC POSIT, ---(AS DISTINCT FROM THE EITHER OF THOROUGHGOING MATERI
ALISM, OR THE CARTESIAN + PLATONIC VIEW THAT THE SOUL IS ESSENTIALLY AN INDE
PENDENT ENTITY WHICH, HOWEVER, INHABITS AND USES THE BODY NOW AND THEN)---;A
ND THE KAREN'S SO-CALLED 19TH CENTURY "PRIMITIVISM"; EACH OF WHICH I FIND CO
NNECTABLE TO MORPHOGENETIC RESONANCE + PRIMARY CAUSATION; ---(E.G., PETER GU
Y MANNERS, HERINAFTER AKA= PGM: "LIFE'S INTEGRATING PHENOMENON: THE PRINCIPL
ES AND PRACTICE OF CYMATIC THERAPY: I.E., PGM'S POSIT: SOUND, "LIFE'S INTEGR
ATING PHENOMENON"; 1980 (?); BRETFORTON HALL CLINIC, WORCESTERSHIRE). "ELL,
ELL", SAYS MY "EVELOPING" PRIMIT, "ESERTSPACE IS A BODYSOUL LIFESOUND;   LA
IS". I'M BEGINNING TO GET INTO IT TOO, AND ALTHOUGH I SHOULD BE THRILLED WIT
HOUT QUESTION, I ALSO FEEL A STARK SADNESS. I SOMETIMES FIND MYSELF VIEWING
IT AS SOME 'REMAIN' FROM WHICH LA DECIDED TO SPLIT AND I'M WATCHING IT HAPP
EN; (AM I THINKING NUKE AGAIN?); SOME REMAIN WHICH, AT ITS END, WAS NOT VERY
MUCH ATTENDED TO?; ANOTHER ALONENESS---; SEPARATED FROM ANYTHING BUT PONDER-
WONDER AS TO HOW IT GOT THIS WAY; PROVOKING A SENSE THAT IT COULDN'T,   OR

CAN'T CARE? (IN THE HEAT I REALIZE I FEEL SO BOMBARDED BY CULT'S JUNK THAT I
T BEGINS TO FEEL LIKE A VIRTUE IN THIS AWSOME-SEEMING ANZO INDIFFERENCE: ESP
ECIALLY WHEN JUNK PROVIDES INCOME FOR BAG PEOPLE. BUT NO, DAMMIT; THE APPEAR
ANCE OF ANZO'S REMAINS ARE DUE TO ITS UNCLUTTEREDNESS!   BRAINWASHED. STILL
, IS SOUND, IN THE SENSE I'VE BEEN EXPERIENCING IT, DISEMBODIED DIFFERENTLY?
WE CARRY IT IN US, TOO. SOUND: TRANSMUTATATIONS ONE INTO ANOTHER AS IT MOVES
OUT; BUT ALSO STAYS. SOUND: AS A SPATIAL MODE OF BEING. SOUND: REMEMBER LOQU
ENDI; ---FIRST MATTER; IN THE BEGINNING WAS---; OR ANYONE? SOUND: CAN YOU
IMAGINE THE BIG BANG GANG WITHOUT IT? SOUND: AS A HYLOMORPHISM: SELF-MAINTAI
NING, SELF-DEVELOPING; ---(INSIDE OUR EARS I CALL IT THE GREAT ORAL TRADITIO
N)---; SELF-REPRODUCING INSIDE OF OTHER BODIES; ---(A SINGLE TRANSMITTED SIG
NAL IS NEVER THE SAME). SOUND: A STRUCTURE WHOSE WONDERS EXCEED THOSE OF ITS
CONSTITUENT 'REMAINS' TAKEN IN ISOLATION; BUT NOT IN THE WAKE OF; BUT NOT IN
THE RETURNED TO A DUST OF; ---(I AM REMINDED OF BRUN'S MAGNIFICENT "DUSTINY"
; IN ITSELF NOT A TRIVIAL COMPUTER-COMPOSITIONAL BANGO!) SOUND: FANTASY AS
SUPERNATURAL EXPERIENCE. CERTAINLY KARENS LAS WERE; RUNNING ABOUT TO CATCH A
SICK MAN'S LA, ---(IN OR OUT OF DESERTSPACE)---; HIS BUTTERFLY!   CAN YOU
BELIEVE IT? A SO-SWEETLY UNDULATING BUTTERFLY IS A SICK MAN'S LA; ---(ALSO
SO-CONSIDERED BY THE NOT SO PRIMIT GREEKS; PERHAPS ONCE THERE WERE NO CULTS)
---, A BEING CALLED IN BY OTHER KAREN LAS, FOR SOME MELLOWSWEETHELPINGCURE ?
AND I FLASH: COMPOSITION CAN STOP POLLUTION! (AND YES, JT'S ARE SO CAREFULLY
WROUGHT; NOW YOU GET THEM; NOW YOU DON'T; ---((JT: "DIFFICULT MUSIC,---BEING
CHALLENGED IS A KIND OF VALUE IN ITSELF; ---COMPLEXITY---IT'S GOING TO TAKE
AWHILE BEFORE THE PEOPLE WHO ARE NOT ASKING QUESTIONS NOW BEGIN THINKING ABO
UT THEM")) ---;NO LIKELY POSSIBILITY FOR SIMPLE SELF-((EVIDENCE))-HERE. BRIDGES
:---((YES, A TITLE; AND AN ACT OF MAKING THEM; COMPOSER TO LISTENER)) ---: BU
T, THERE ARE LAYERS AND LEVELS OF CONCEPT, WITHIN LAYERS AND LEVELS OF PERCE
PT, BETWEEN THIS AND THAT. BARRIERS STOP; (FOR A MOMENT). BUT PLACES TAKE ME
SOONER OR LATER. JT HAS NOTHING TO DO, ---((AS FAR AS I KNOW)) ---WITH ANZO ;
BUT THIS IS WHERE I GO TO STRANGELY MEDITATE FASHION ON WORK; ---MINE, IN TH
IS CASE, JT'S---; OTHERS. THE LAST TIME I WAS HERE, BUT NOT THE LAST TIME. P
ONDER-WONDERING IS WHAT LIES AT THE BASE OF EXPERIMENT, AT THE BASE OF RADIC
: A BOND BETWEEN US; MAKING SOMETHING HAVEN'T SEEN (YET); HAVEN'T HEARD (YET
); HAVEN'T DONE (YET); YETYETYET). PERHAPS THIS WAS A DREAM? BUT NO DREAMS I
AM AWARE OF ARE SILENT. A KAREN'S DREAMS ARE WHAT LA SAW, HEARD, AND EXPERIE
NCED IN ITS JOURNEY WHEN IT LEFT THE BODY ASLEEP (BUT NOT EMPTY). THIS SEEMS
VERY SOPHISTICATED TO A PRIMIT; (CAN WE EVER GET OUT OF OUR SKIN(S) WITHOUTS
, WITHOUT MAKING A SOUND)? IMAGINE: A DREAMING KAREN'S LA VISITED ONLY THOS
E REGIONS WHERE THE BODY IT BELONGED TO HAD BEEN ALREADY. THIS SEEMS VERY CO
NSERVATIVE FOR A PRIMITIVE. LA, THEREFORE, ONLY STRETCHED ITSELF, BUT NEVER
REALLY LEFT. LOQUENDI, DO YOU SUPPOSE THEY HAD SOME SORT OF HYLOMORPHIC SENS
E? THERE WERE OTHER DREAMLANDS TOO, WHERE LAS OF THE LIVING OFTEN WENT TO V
ISIT THE LAS OF THE DEAD. NOW THIS SEEMS MUCH MORE RADIC TO A PRIMIT.   SOUL
-LAND WAS A DREAMLAND IN ITS SHADOWY SPACES. IN FACT, THE KARENS MOST DISTIN
CT AND DIRECT INTERCOURSE WAS HAD WHEN THEY BECAME ACTUALLY PRESENT TO ANOTH
ER LAS SENSES IN DREAMS AND VISIONS. LA TO LA, SO TO SPEAK. (A NATURE SPIRIT
-PROPHET, "WEE", IS SAID TO HAVE ENCOURAGED MATTERS BY SITTING ON THE STOMAC
H OF THE DREAMER,---WITH MINUTE FLUCTUATIONS IN SPEED CAUSING CERTAIN PHASE
CHANGES, WHICH TURNED INTO VERY NERVOUS MOTIONS AND SOUNDS, WHICH TURNED INT
O ACTUAL CONVULSIONS ENABLING LA TO GET TO LA, ---((CULT'S CONTEMPORARY COUN
TERPART ARE SEXY VIDEOTAPES, JERKED OUT OF ONE-NIGHT STANDS IN TELMOS)),---SO
-TO-SPEAK, TO GET STRETCHED, SO-TO-SPEAK! IMAGINE IT: SOUND, VOICE PRINTS, L
IVING, MOVING, AURAL INTERCOURSE; SOUNDS EMBRACING SOUNDS; SIGNALS APPROACHI
NG, MEETING, SWIRLING; FUCKING EACH OTHER WITH METAPHORIC MIXERS, UPING THE
HARMONICS IN GRANDO COPULAS OF COPULATIONS.   OR

IS IT ONLY A LACE SCARF I AM SEEING MELLOW TIME MEANS VERY LITTLE. HAPPILY
, THERE IS NO WAY TO CALL A BOARD OF DIRECTORS AT 10:00 TO DISCUSS THE HIGH
COST OF SIGNAL DISTORTION. ONE IS NEVER PREPARED. ANZO SIMPLY SAYS "ITIS" .
AS IT IS. ONE CAN NEVER BE FOR SURE WHAT IS GOING ON. PREDICTIONS, ---IN WH
ATEVER SENSE THEY HAVE ANY SIGNIFICANT FUNCTION HERE---, MAY PROVIDE SOME V
AGUE NOTION THAT THIS OR THAT WILL LIKELY HAPPEN, BUT NOT WHERE, WHEN, HOW,
OR, IF AT ALL. NOW I'M NOT REFERRING TO WHEN IT WILL GET DARK, OR WHEN THE
SUN COMES UP, BUT TO SOUNDS; TO LA. EVEN HOW ONE WILL FIND THEM, (I.E. THEI
R STATES), AT ANY POINT OF INTRUSION IS ALWAYS TINGED BY SOME MINUTELY DIFF
ERENTIATED, BUT FLEETING, METAPHONIC. IN SOME SENSE, ONE IS NEVER PREPARED,
---(CURTAINS DON'Y OPEN, LIGHTS DON'T DIM)---, AS ONE IS NOT FOR THE AGED;F
OR THE EARTH'S CO_2 HEATING; FOR THE MINDLESSNESS OF RAPACITY. UNCERTAINTY,
IN ANZO, IS IN SPADES. IT IS IN THIS ENVIRONMENT THAT LA RESIDES PARTICULAR
LY WELL. WHERE IT IS, WHAT IT DOES, HOW IT GOES, HAS THE TIMBRE OF UNCERTAI
N. TO BE SURE IT IS CONNECTED TO SOME SOURCE, BUT IT ALSO HAS A LIFE OF ITS
OWN. UNCERTAIN MUSIC: HOW GRANDLY, RADICALLY, MUSICAL! PRIMIT, WHO WALLOWSI
NTHISNOTION, VIA LA, BECOMES A KIND OF LUSTRATION. IT IS FOR ME AN ENVIRONM
ENTAL (COMPOSITIONAL) DISPLACEMENT; FROM PRAGMATIC, MATERIALISTIC, MECHANIS
TIC, STATISTICAL CULT, TO A SYMBOLIC CLEANSING PRIMIT; FROM A REMOVAL OF CE
RTAIN MIND-BODY POLLUTENTS TO A KIND OF LUST-LESS DELIVERANCE. ANZO IS NO
MERE IL/LUSTRATION OF SOMETHING ELSE. IT IS NOT A KIND OF LA-CONTINUANCE WH
ICH HAS CHARAC TERIZED THE SO-CALLED "SAVAGE" FOR TOO SO LONG.   PRIMIT:
(AS IN SIMPLE; BASIC; ROOT, RADICAL). AND RADICAL: (HERINAFTER AKA=RADIC) ; (
ALSO AS IN SIMPLE, BASIC,ROOT,PRIMITIVE); A GRANDO INTERSECTION,   AS IN:
RADICAL:ROOTS; (E.G.,MOISTURE IN PLANTS; ITS PRESENCE BEING NECESSARY FOR T
HEIR VITALITY); AS IN: PRIMITIVE:RADICAL; (E.G., BIOLOGY-ANATOMY; REFERRING
TO A STRUCTURE IN VERY FIRST OR EARLY STAGES OF GROWTH; ---((THIS IS NOT EX
ACTLY WHAT CULT CONJURS UP WHEN THESE EXPRESSIONS ARE USED)) ---; THE EXPRES
SION IS RARELY APPLIED TO A STRUCTURE FROM WHICH SECONDARY STRUCTURES ARISE
BY BRANCHING; ---((E.G., AS IN BIFURCATION)) ---; METAPHORICALLY A PRIMARY P
ROCESS IN CULT COMPOSITION). PRIMIT AND RADIC TRANSLATE SOUND INTO UNCERTAI
NTY; UNCERTAINTY INTO SOUND. SO I CAN'T BE SO SURE A RAINBOW DOESN'T HAVE S
OUND WHEN I KNOW, (REMEMBER LEARNING) THAT A 3/4" X 8' SHEET OF PLYWOOD (FO
R THE MOMENT, SEEMINGLY SOUNDLESS),FLATLY PLACED ON A SOLID SURFACE (SEEMIN
G SOUNDLESS), TO WHICH A CERTAIN WEIGHT-LOAD IS APPLIED (SEEMINGLY SOUNDLES
S), WILL VIBRATE AT ITS MOST RESONANT FREQUENCIES CIRCA 120KHZ, VERY HUMAN-
HEARABLE UNDER SIGNAL DEMODULATORS. BEAUTGRANDO. ONE CAN IMAGINE THAT THE H
ARMONIC SPECTRA, (+ FORMANTS), WITHOUT DEMODULATION, ---THEREFORE "OUT-OF-R
ANGE" OF HUMAN PERCEPTION DIRECTLY---, ARE, NEVERTHELESS THE CONSEQUENCE OF
A KIND OF SPATIAL 'STRETCHING' OF THE PLYWOOD'S BODY. NOW, THIS BODY, TAKEN
AS A FUNDAMENTAL, ---(I.E., 'SIMPLE', 'BASIC', 'ROOT',=PRIMIT-RADIC)---, NE
VER LEAVES THE FLOOR, LITERALLY, BUT IT DOES. IT REACHES OUT AND IDENTIFIES
ITSELF WITH ITS OWN SPECTRA (REMOVED FROM IT AT A CONSIDERABLE DISTANCE). I
TS HARMONIC CONTENT, TIMBRALLY, (AT LEAST), ARE THOSE OF PLYWOOD AT BASE.TO
ME, IT'S A LA. (DO YOU SUPPOSE PLYWOOD MIGHT BE UP THERE MIXING IT UP WITH
SOME KAREN LAS)? IMPALPABLE? I HAD A GUARDIAN ANGEL ONCE. (NO, IT IS NOT LO
QUENDI, WHO NEVERTHELESS, SOESN'T COMPLAIN ABOUT THIS PERHAPS-DISCREPANCY .
NOW I AM NOT MAKING A CASE FOR "OBJECT-SOULS", BUT I AM MORE THAN IMPLYING
THE EXISTENCE OF 'SUBJECT-LAS'. ANYTHING THAT VIBRATES HAS/IS SOUND; SOUND
ASSOCIATED WITH, ENDEMIC TO, IMBEDDED IN, SOME ENTITY:---AND YET CAPABLE OF
'STRETCHING' FROM ITS BASICNESS. SUCH ENTITIES CANNOT BE REDUCED TO SOME ME
RE ELECTRO-MECHANICAL, (+ ACOUSTICAL) FORMULATION, ANYMORE THAN CAN BE SAID
FOR HUMANS. IF IT, ---WHATEVER IT IS, IS IN MOTION-VIBRATING, IT IS IN SOME
SENSE, 'LIVING'; (SO, FOR THE MOMENT I PUT SOME SORT OF RESTRICTION ON THEI
R "LIVINGNESS", BUT NOT AS-IF THEY WERE "BRAIN-DEAD". I POSIT: IT IS POSSIB

LE THAT ALL ENTITIES IN THE UNIVERSE ARE IN VIBRATION; THAT SOUND IS AN INTE
GRATING PHENOMENON; ---(BY THIS, I DO NOT INTEND: "MUSIC IS A UNIVERSAL LANG
UAGE")---; THAT SOUND, IN SOME SENSE, IS A KIND OF TELEOLOGY; ---THAT THE PR
OCESSES OF LIFE ARE DIRECTED TO THE REALIZATION OF CERTAIN NORMAL WHOLES, OR
ENTELECHIES: TO BE COMPLETE; THAT WHICH AN ENTITY IS BY WAY OF ITS FORM;   ((
CF. MORPHIC RESONANCE; SOUND-AS-LIVING)) ; ACTUAL, NOT MERELY POTENTIAL EXIST
ENCE. PERHAPS MUCH SERIOUS 20TH CENTURY MUSIC IS RIGHTLY CRITICIZED FOR   NOT
HAVING ENOUGH LIFE IN IT. I KNOW, LOQUENDI, THINKING OPAQUE, IN SOME SENSE,M
AKES IT SO. OK; BUT THIS IS CRAZY. IF SOUND IS WHAT I'M GOING FOR, ---AS   A
SUBJECT-LA---, IT HAS TO END UP SOMEWHERE. DOESN'T IT? IT CAN'T JUST GO ON A
ND ON WITHOUT A BODY. (IS IT ITS OWN BODY?). NOW PAPER ON WHICH, ---TO THIS
DAY---,IT IS FREQUENTLY INSCRIBED, IS A SOUNDLESS WORLD; ---(THERE'S NOBODY
HERE). FURTHER, WHAT DOES ONE REPRESENT OF SOUND WHEN ONE PUTS IT ON PAPER ?
WHAT DOES SOUND DO WHILE STORED IN PAPER'S 'MEMORY'? WHAT SENSE IS THERE TO
NOTES OR TIME IN DAVID DUNN'S DAY-LONG ENVIRONMENTAL, (ANZO), WORK:SKYDRIFT?
SOUND, ---ANYONE ISSUED---, IS ALWAYS CHANGING, BEING CHANGED, BY THE ENVIRO
NMENT IN WHICH IT IS BEING TRANSMITTED, (INCLUDING: 'ON PAPER'), TO SAY NOTH
ING OF WHAT RECEIVER'S DO TO IT. HOW DOES ONE COMPRESS AN ALL DAY SONIC EVEN
T, (OR MAHLER'S 7TH) INTO SOME MICROSCOPIC SYNAPSE-MEMORY PLACE? WHAT KIND O
F STATE DOES IT BECOME THERE? SURELY IT CAN'T BE THE ONE THAT WAS ON PAPER ?
SURELY IT HAS BEEN 'DISEMBODIED' FROM WHAT IT WAS WHEN IN AIR, (NOW RESIDING
IN SYNAPSE-MEMORY), OR WHEN IT WAS IN COMPOSER'S MIND, (NOW RESIDING IN PAPE
R)? DOES TIME DO ANYTHING WHILE SOUND IS ON PAPER? ISIT ON THE DOLE DURING T
HESE, SO-TO-SPEAK, TIMES? (CULT SAYS: "TIME IS MONEY"). (PRIMIT SAYS: "TIME
IS A HUMAN FABRICATION"). WHAT HAPPENS TO STORED SOUND AS IT IS CALLED FORTH
INTO CONSCIOUSNESS? CAN ONE ASSUME THAT EACH MEMBER OF A CONCERT HALL IS REC
EIVING THE SAME SOUND AS TRANSMITTED, SAY, FROM A SOLO PIANIST? (SOME POETS,
TOO, AGONIZE SO; ---((I HAVE HEARD THIS SAID OF THEM)) ---JERRY, IS THIS TRUE
?). SO WHO OR WHAT GETS THE REAL ONE; THE INTENDED ONE? WHAT INTENDED ONE? (
RADIC ASKS: "WHERE IS TIME OTHER THAN IN THE MATERIALS WHICH SPATIALLY MARK
IT OFF, AND CONTAIN IT")? AND YET SOUND, BEYOND QUESTION, IS EXPERIENCED. WH
EN ONE ENTERS ANZO, IT IS SPACE THAT OVERWHELMS. WHEN I APPROACH ANZO, I LOO
K, BUT CAN'T FIND TIME ANYWHERE. SO, HOW CAN HEARING OR LISTENING IN ANY SEN
SE BE SHARED HERE, IF TIME ISN'T AROUND TO ORGANIZE MATTERS? (LA APPEARS: "I
PROPOSE THE ACT OF LISTENING AS AN ALTERNATIVE TO TIME"). SO, PONDER-WONDERI
NG, SUPPOSE ELEMENTS, (MATTER), IN SPACE EXIST (ONLY) IN SOME STATE(S) OF IN
TERACTION WITH EACH OTHER, ---("AS IS ACTUALLY THE CASE", SAYS LA)---, AND N
OT AT ALL AGAINST A BACKGROUND OF TIME; THAT EACH IS TO THE OTHER IN SOME MA
NNER OF BEING, OR ANOTHER? SO I LEARN THAT ANZO IS FOR LISTENING.   PRIMIT,
RADIC, AND LA, ANNOUNCE TO ME AND LOQUENDI: "NOW HEAR THIS!" MOST GRANDEXTRA
ORDINARILY. IT SEEMS AS-IF WE'VE BEEN CAUGHT IN THE ACT, ---DOING EXACTLY TH
AT. POISED. ATTENTIVE. AWARE. LISTENING. WHEN HERE, ---ALONE WITH MY KA-LA ,
LOQUENDI, PICKING UP ON THE STILLNESS SOUND; OF THE ALWAYS DESERTSPACE RESON
ATING; LISTENING TO THE FEEL OF IT; LISTENING TO TALKING TO ONE'S SELF TALKI
NG TO THE LISTENED TO. THIS IS NOT ASSUMED TO BE A CONDITION OF MADNESS, OR
BAD MANNERS. HERE, BODY MOTION RESPONDS TO SOUND MOTION TO BODY MOTION, NOT
MARKED OFF BY BATON DOWN BEATS APPLAUSE COUGHING PROGRAMS BEING READ SPECTAT
ORS EACH IN THEIR OWN TIME, (OOPS!), THAT IS EACH IN THEIR OWN WAY SHUTTING
UP SOMETIMES NOT SOMETIMES SNORING ANNOUNCES THAT AN UNANTICIPATED EVENT IS
HAPPENING IN ORDER TO ASSUME THE PROPER POSTURE FOR HEARING, (BUT ACTUALLY,I
SUPPOSE, ---MORE FOR SEEING). NO. ANZO IS AT ONCE. WITH IT. ONE IS IN IT. IT
IS NOT JUST IN YOUR FACE BUDDIE. A WONDERFUL AMBISONIC. OR IT SCARES THE HEL
L OUT OF YOU AND ITS SPLITSVILLE FOR YOU KIDDO. I CANNOT REST EASILY UNTIL A
LL NOISE HAS BEEN IDENTIFIED. IMPOSSIBLE; CERTAINLY A VERY DIFFICULT SORT OF
LISTENING. BUT ONE CAN WONDER-PONDER ENDLESSLY ABOUT THIS MARVELOUS KIND OF

'LIVING PHENOMENA'; YOU JUST KNOW ITS BEEN GOING ON BEFORE YOU ENTER, AND IT NEVER ENDS BECAUSE YOU LEAVE, OR WHETHER OR NOT YOU DO; ---(NOT AS IN CULT'S CASE; ---A MOVIE, A CONCERT, A LECTURE, ANNOUNCES ITS OWN ENDING, LIKE IT OR NOT; ONE IS "ASKED" TO LEAVE, OR AT LEAST AN "INVITATION" TO DO SO IS FAIRLY-WELL PRONOUNCED; ---((YOU HAD BETTER, ANYWAY, OR YOU'LL BE SWEPT OUT WITH TH E POPCORN; NO CHANCE TO STAY IN THE PLACE WHICH MIGHT HAVE CAUSED SUCH A WON DERFUL RESPONSE, THAT IT WOULD HAVE BEEN BEAUTIFUL TO LINGER AWHILE; TO HAVE AN AFTERPLAY IN THE SPACE AND RESONANCE OF THE EXPERIENCE)) ---;   TOO SAD. UNDER THE CONDITIONS OF CULT, I AM NOT SURPRISED AT HOW LITTLE IS KNOWN OF T HE EXTRAORDINARY WORK OF THE 20TH CENTURY. UNDER THE CONDITIONS OF PRIMIT, I HAVE LEARNED TO LISTEN WITH EARS ALL OVER MY HEAD AND BODY; SO DO THE CATECO MB DWELLERS I KNOW OF. NOW I'M NOT POOR-MEING YOU BABY, ---ALTHOUGH IT IS A MAJOR COMPLAINT I HAVE, WHICHIS: IT IS VERY MUCH A MATTER OF ALONENESS FOR M WHEN HEARING-LISTENING IS NOT SHARED BETWEEN PEOPLE. IT COULD BE A SHARING O F KNOWING BEYOND CITING OF LITERALLY. BUT, HOW CAN HEARING-LISTENING BE SHAR ED UNDER THE CONDITIONS AND CONVENTIONS OF CULT? YET TO ENTER ANZO IS TO KNO W THERE ARE OTHER WAYS. IN ANZO, LISTENING IS WHAT ONE DOES. THIS IS WHAT AN ZO'S EVERY LIVING CREATURE DOES; I SUPPOSE, FOR SURVIVAL. (WOULDN'T IT BE EV ERSOGRANDELEGANT IF PEOPLE LISTENED TO MUSIC AS-IF THEIR LIVES DEPENDED   ON IT?) CONCEPTUALLY, I THINK MUSIC COMPOSITION, OF THE KIND I REFER TO, IS ENT ERED INTO AN EMPTY SPACE. ONE WHICH IS NOT-YET OCCUPIED BY IT; (E.G., A BLAN K TAPE, OR PAPER IS SUCH, BUT SIMPLY NOT THAT). IN SOME EMPTY PLACE, SPACE , SOMETHING(S) WILL BE ENTERED THEREIN. FOR ME, IT IS SOME KIND OF IMPERATIVE, THEREFORE, TO CONSIDER HOW THAT SPACE WILL BE OCCUPIED, AND WITH WHAT. ((DIT TO)), FOR ANZO.MOST PEOPLE DO AS MUCH WHEN FURNISHING AN EMPTY ROOM. CERTAINL Y, THERE HAS BEEN ALL OF THIS WONDERFUL MUSIC IN CULT'S WORLD, NOW SO WORKED OVER, OVER-TIRED. I FEEL A GREAT LOSS. BUT THERE IS ALL OF THIS 'MUSIC' HERE TOO, AND WITHOUT MUZAK, ROCKS, AND MIDI'S. MUSIC WHERE OFTEN THERE ARE NO SO -CALLED SIGNS OF IT IN CULT'S SENSE; ALIVE; UNCLUTTERED. THIS HELPS ATTENUAT E THE LOSS, AND THE ALONENESS. I FIND AN ECOLOGY WHERE CARING FOR WHAT IS EN TERED INTO ANY GIVEN SPACE, CAN INCLUDE A DECISION TO NOT ENTER;---(A VERY "FAMOUS" COMPOSER SAID TO ME ONCE WHEN I WAS YOUNG ENOUGH TO BE TERRIFIED : "IF YOU DON'T SIT AT YOUR DESK AT LEAST FOUR HOURS EVERYDAY COMPOSING,   YOU ARE NOT A COMPOSER")---; SO, I AM SITTING ON MY ASS, ON ANZO'S HOT SAND, LIS TENING TO KELAH; SO I HAVE MORE THAN A (GETTING DRUNK ON SOUND) SUSPICION TH AT THESE "CRAZY" RANDOM PROCESSES I ADORE ARE REGARDED MY MANY AS HAVING NOT CARING MUSIC FOR THE SOFTENED CULTMORPHS ON WHICHEVER DESKTOP. BY THIS, I AS SUME IT IS ASSUMED TO BE A NON-CARING FOR THE "BEAUTY" OF CONVENTION;THAT IS : FOR THOSE COMPOSITIONAL-CONCEPTUAL-ORGANIZATIONAL CONCERNS SUCH AS STYLE , TECHNIQUE, AND "POSTURING" (TO QUOTE GUV'S FAVORITE DIPLOMACY); OR FOR THOSE OUTCOMES OF ORDER (+ORDERING), WHICH ONE CAN GET OFF ON, ESPECIALLY IF THEY CAN BE FOUND IN FAMILIAR-ENOUGH TERRITORY; AND MADE PREDICTABLE ENOUGH TO PR OVIDE COMFORT FOR THE WEARIED IN MOMENTS OF EXTREME COMPLEXITY. IN THIS REGA RD, THEY ARE RIGHT; ALTHOUGH I AM ALWAYS SURPRISED TO HEAR IT. AFTERALL,   I CAME FROM CULT. IT TAUGHT ME WELL. FROM IT, I ESPECIALLY LEARNED THE LESSONS OF RETROGRESSIONS, WITH REGARD TO PRECURSOR, (HISTORIC) WORSHIPS; AND THE CO MPLEX SOLUTIONS OF COMPOSING FROM "IDEA-TO-CONCRETION"; AND, TO NOT QUESTION CERTAIN IMPLICIT NOTIONS CRUCIAL TO ONE'S "DEVELOPMENT"; AND TO CONSIDER THA T EACH COMPOSITION'S END-POINT WAS A LINEAR STEPPING STONE TO THE NEXT END - POINT; A FOOT HERE, A FOOT THERE, SO-TO-SPEAK. BUT THE LESSON OF "NOT-TO-QUE STION" GOT TO ME. EARLY ON. IN TIMES OF ALONENESS, TO NOT CONCEIVE OF ANOTHE R WAY WAS A MADNESS TOO MUCH TO ASK FOR THE SAKE OF PEACEFUL CO-EXISTENCE; - --, CLICHE' GOT UNDONE QUICKLY WHEN IT CAME TO ME TO COMPOSE FROM"CONCRETION TO IDEA"; WHEN WANDERING TURNED TO WONDERING. SO SURE, THERE ARE NO ABSOLUTE S , ESPECIALLY SINCE NOW THEY ARE SO NEGATIVELY FABRICATED-CONNECTED TO THE

"POSITIVES" OF PUSHY ACOURANTS; AS IN THE WAY PASTWORKS ARE WIPED OUT BY THE
DATE THEY WERE MADE; AS IN THE WAY THE "NEW" (OF "NEW MUSIC") IS CONSTANTLYA
NNOUNCINGITSALTERNATIVE TO THE MOSTRECENT BIGBANG BY WIMPILYDRIPPINGOOZING ,
SANGUINE, ROMANCING WORDS OF THE DAY; SOUNDS OF THE DAY; NOW IN THE BEGINNIN
G; THERE IS, WAS, NO OTHER DAY. SOMETIMES NEW WAVES HAVE VERY LITTLE TO DO W
ITH ACSTOUICS, AND DISAPPEARANCE ACTS ARE HAPPENING TOOF AST TO BEGIN TO KNO
W WHAT WASN'T HEARD. BUT RADIC NOTICES THESE ARE NOT THE ONES WHO GO TO THE
CATECOMBS; WHO DENOUNCE THEIR OWN PREVIOUS WORK IN ORDER TO TAKE NEW STEPS ;
WHO ADMIT HISTORY, ---BUT BARELY; WHO ADMIRE BUT DO NOT DEPEND ON PRECEDENT.
                                                             IT RAINS.
                               BUT WHAT IS IT THAT RAINS IF NOT RAIN?
                            I REALLY MUST TELL YOU A PERSONAL STORY.
SOMETIME AGO I DID A SEMINAR AT OBERLIN IN COMPOSITIONAL LINGUISTICS.   I
PLAYED A VIDEO TAPE WORK ENTITLED "GIVE & TAKE"; ---(ONE OF A NUMBER OF GROU
P COMPOSITIONAL PTOCEDURES WORKED ON BY NMCE DURING ITS RESIDENCY AT CME-UCS
D, 1972-5. A SO-CALLED "FLASH" COMPOSITION, ---((FLASH COMPOSITION= WITHOUT-
DELIBERATION: (1) RESPOND TO A STIMULUS-GENERATED 'FLASH'; (2) FORMULATE   A
SET OF PERFORMANCE INSTRUCTIONS IMMEDIATELY; (3) PRESENT INSTRUCTIONS TO PER
FORMERS; (4) NEAR-IMMEDIATE PERFORMANCE OF INSTRUCTIONS; (5) COMPOSITIONAL R
ESULT; IN THIS CASE A VIDEOTAPE)) . THE RULES WERE VERY SIMPLE: (1) IMAGINE A
CIRCLE HAVING A DIAMETER OF, SAY, 3'; (2) EACH PERFORMER PLACES ONE OR MORE
PERSONAL OBJECTS OF HIS/HER OWN CHOSING INTO THE CIRCLE; (3) THE COMPOSITION
WILL CONSIST, QUALITATIVELY, OF THE MANNER IN WHICH THE OBJECTS ARE PLACED
IN THE CIRCLE, AND RETRIEVED FROM THE CIRCLE; (4)THE COMPOSITION WILL CONSI
ST, QUANTITATIVELY, OF PLACING THESE OBJECTS IN THE CIRCLE,AND TAKING THEM O
UT OF THE CIRCLE. GIVE-TAKE WAS PERFORMED ON A GYMNISTS MAT. SOME OF THE OB
JECTS WERE CUPS, KEYS, SOCKS, RINGS, COINS).   A LONG DISCUSSION FOLLOWED.
AT A CERTAIN POINT,A GENTLEMAN WHO HAD BEEN SILENT DURING THE PROCEEDINGS ST
OOD UP AND SAID: "THE WORK SUCKS". WE TALKED ABOUT SUCKING; (HE COULD SEE IT
WAS THE WRONG CHOICE OF WORDS). THEN HE SAID "THE WORK HAD NO FORM".I SHOWED
HIM THE FORM; (NO COMMENT). THEN HE SAID"IT WASN'T POLYPHONIC". I SHOWED HIM
THE POLYPHONIC; (O COMMENT). HE PROCEEDED THROUGH HIS LEXICAL LITANY OF ACQU
IRED TERMINOLOGIES; EACH TIME NULLED PATIENTLY; (O,O,O, COMMENTS).   FINALLY
, HE SIMPLY SAID, "WELL, IT JUST ISN,T SCHUBERT". AFTER AGREEING WITH HIM, T
SHIT HIT THE FAN FOR ME, AND I ASKED: "WHAT IN THE HELL IS SCHUBERTT DDOINGG
IN GIVE-TAKES LIVING ROOM, ANYWAY"?"I DON'T REMEMBER INVITING HIM TO THIS PA
RTY"; (O COMMENTS).THEN I SAID "IF YOU THINK SCHUBERT SHOULD HAVE BEEN IN TH
IS WORK, BY WHICH YOU JUDGED IT, THEN YOU DO NOT UNDERSTAND HIM EITHER"; (O
COMMENTS). (IT'S TOO BAD KELAH COULDN'T BE CALLED IN FROM THE EAST OR THE WE
ST FOR HELP IN THIS MATTER, BY SOOTHING HIM WITH THE LA-THROATING CALLS OF T
HE BIRD AND THE ELEPHANT; THE LA OF THE HONEY-MAKING SOUND OF BEES;   THE LA
INNERMOST WOMB-GUT SOUNDS OF THE APE; FROM THE SWIM-BLATTERING SOUNDS OF THE
FISH LA, THE LAUGHING GUT LA).THE SENSE OF AN ABSOLUTE PSYCHICAL DISTINCTION
BETWEEN THE HUMAN AND BEAST, (SO PREVALENT IN CULT, BUT I THINK ONLY FOR A
WHILE LONGER), IS HARDLY TO BE FOUND IN THE SO-CALLED "PRIMITIVE" RACES. PEO
PLE TO WHOM THE CRIES OF BEASTS AND BIRDS SEEM LIKE HUMAN LANGUAGE HAVE TAKE
N CARE, NECESSARILY, TO HEAR IT AS LANGUAGE; TO LIVE WITH IT AS LANGUAGE. TH
IS ACCORD BETWEEN THE ONE AND THE OTHER SEEMS TO BE A PERFECTLY SUFFICIENT &
BALANCED SYSTEM FOR THE SPECIES, HUMAN + OTHERWISE, IN QUESTION. SO WHAT I'V
E BEEN SAYING ABOUT SOUND, MIGHT JUST AS WELL HAVE BEEN SAID ABOUT LANGUAGE.
(IT MIGHT HAVE GIVEN THE SINGER A CLEARER PLACE TO BEGIN HIS AUDITION WITH).
SURE IT'S CLEAR BY THIS TIME. I'M NOT INTERESTED IN WRITING SAFE, HIGH- DAMP
MUSIC. BY THIS I MEAN 'ABSTRACT' STRUCTURED STUFF BEHIND WHICH ITS TRADITION
ALLOWS ONE TO HIDE; PROVIDING REASONABLE JUSTIFICATOONS,(OVERKILLING THE NOT
E,IS, AFTERALL, MERELY PART OF MUSIC HISTORY'S EVOLUTION) . THEORIES (IN ONLY,

ARE APPROPRIATE SUBSTITUTES WHEN ONE CAN FIND NO OTHER WAY OUT FOR CULT'S CUR
RENT SYSTEM OVERLOAD. AFTERALL, THE IMMENSE FAMILY OF HISTORY'S MUSICAL "HEAD
'S-OF-STATE", COULD NOT BE EXPECTED TO DO OTHERWISE THAN TO URGE THE NOW ONES
ON; (WHO SAYS SOUND IS NOT ALIVE)?, PROVIDING US ALL WITH A DETACHE' KIND OF
EXPRESSIVENESS AND CONTINUANCE, AND, CERTAINLY BY WAY OF SAFETY-IN-NUMBERS, P
ROVIDING US ALL WITH INSURANCE PACKETS FOR NOW-AUTHORS TO FANTASIZE OK-LY BY;
TO BE, (GOOD GRIEVE), "OBJECTIVE" ABOUT THE BEAUTY OF MUSIC'S QUANTA.   BUT
PRIMIT AND RADIC CAN FIND NO ESSENTIAL SUPPORT FROM THE, NEVERTHELESS, DEARLY
-LOVED GESUALDO, (THE GREAT PHANTOM), FOR THEIR CONDUCT, OTHER THAN THE WINK
OF A SLIGHTLY CONFUSED EYE. ITIS, ---SIMPLY, AND UNPRETENTIOUSLY,---(BUT WITH
CONSIDERABLE DIFFICULTY, EXCEPT WHEN IN ANZO, OR WHEN LA CAN LIKEWISE BREAK T
HROUGH CULT'S POLLUTION TO FIND US)---, WHAT ITIS; (OF COURSE, ONE CAN ALWAYS
ARGUE POLITICS)---; RAW-BONE STUFF, DRAWN FROM RAW-BONE STUFF, ---(OFTEN REFE
RRED TO AS THE "REAL WORLD"); A DIRECT SUBJECTIVE VIEW KEEPING IN MIND,A LONG
-TERM PHᴛCHOACOUSTIC JOURNEY WITH MYSELF + STUDENTS WHO HEAR, ---LEARN TO HEA
R---, WHAT'S THERE, IN EACH INSTANCE, TO HEAR, EXPRESSED IN VARIOUS COMPLEX L
ANGUAGES OF THEIR OWN. WHO'S TO SAY, OTHERWISE.   I HAVE NO IDEA:
---THIS IS WHERE HEARING-LISTENING BEGIN EACH TIME. A LA WILL COME, WHEN MIND
-BODY IS OPEN TO ONE; WHEN ONE HAS NO IDEA! THERE WAS A FAULTY ANALYSIS ONCE,
WHEN I CONFUSED LONELINESS WITH ALONENESS. WHEN I FIRST CAME TO DESERTSPACE,I
CAME LOOKING FOR AN ANSWER TO THE FORMER, BUT FOUND, INSTEAD, THE LATTER.   I
FIRST THOUGHT: "WHAT'S THE BIG DEAL"? "NOTHING IS HAPPENING HERE". BUT ALONE,
IN DESERTSPACE I CAME TO REALIZE THE POSSIBILITY OF HAVING, ---AT LEAST---, A
PSEUDO-ABSOLUTE SENSE OF TRANSCENDENCE. FOR, IF ANYTHING AT ALL, ANZO HAS A
SENSE OF THE UNCOMMITTED AND UNCONDITIONED ABOUT IT. WITH THIS REALIZATION, I
WAS LIBERATED. THE SO-CALLED BROTHER-SISTERHOOD OF COMPOSERS ARE FRIENDS FOR
SIMPLY NO OTHER REASON THAN EACH DID WHAT EACH DID, UNIQUELY. IN TERMS OF THI
S, ANY CORRESPONDENCE BETWEEN ONE OR ANOTHER IS TRIVIAL. ANY DEEP ANALYSIS, O
R SIMPLE, SENSITIVE HEARING BY DEVELOPED CONSCIOUSNESS WILL SAY THIS.   THERE
IS NO BROTHER-SISTERHOOD, IN THE SENSE OF SO-CALLED "COMMON-PRACTICE", WHICH
TODAY SOMEHOW TRANSLATES, ---BY POLITICAL LANGUAGE---, INTO MAINSTREAM. THERE
IS ONLY THE LA OF UNIQUENESS. ANZO PROVIDED THE LUSTRE FOR WHAT HAD BEEN A LO
NG-TERM METAMORPHOSIS: TO ALWAYS SEARCH FOR A NON-MIMETIC MOVE; (SO DOES JT).
I CANNOT ANSWER QUESTIONS ABOUT WHETHER "ORIGINAL" IDEAS ARE STILL POSSIBLE ;
(ALTHOUGH I DO KNOW WORKS WHICH PUT SUBSTANTIAL DENTS IN THE CYNICAL NOTION T
HAT THERE CAN'T BE. BUT, IN ANY CASE, I'M NOT TALKING ABOUT IDEAS, AS MUCH AS
I AM OF FORMULATING NEW CONCEPTS, WHICH DIRECTLY PROVIDE ALTERNATIVE COMPOSIT
IONAL PROCESSES; ---AND THEREBY, UNIQUE OUTPUTS: ESPECIALLY THOSE PRIMIT-RADI
CS INVOLVING SELF-SUBVERSION (EXCLUDING SUICIDE); ---ESPECIALLY THE LOVE OF T
HE UNKNOWN, (NOT MERELY WITH THE UN-EXPERIENCED); AND ESPECIALLY TAKING DIBS
WITH INSECURITIES, AND TROUBLE IS, "YOU DON'T TAKE CARE OF YOURSELF",   SAYS
LOQUENDI; AND ESPECIALLY, ANYWAY, WHAT KIND OF SOUND IS IT, ---THIS LA-METEMP
SYCHOSIS OF SONOROUS RAINBOWS AFTER HAVING HEARD THEIR SPECTRAL COLORS PULSIN
GAGAINST EACH OTHER, ---SLIGHTLY OUT-OF-PHASE, ONEDAY? I KNEW I HAD FOUND SOM
ETHING, (WHICH HAD NOTHING TO DO WITH "LOSING MY SENSES", IF YOU KNOW WHAT I
MEAN). IN MY EXPERIMENTAL STUDIO CAN ALSO BE FOUND MUCH THE SAME ENVIRONMENT,
AS IN ANZO; PRIMIT: ANOTHER CATECOMB WHERE INTERACTIONS AND NOT DICTA OBTAIN;
PRIMIT: WHERE STUDENTS COME FROM DANCE, AND THEATER, AND LITERATURE, AND LING
UISTICS, AND MATHEMATICS, AND ENGINEERING, AND FILMAKING, AND VIDEO, AND BROA
DCASTING, AND COMPUTER SCIENCE, AND MUSIC, ET ALIA: IN OR OUT OF CULT, TO FIN
D SOMETHING, (NOT YET LOST); PRIMIT: RUMOR HAS IT, IF ONE CAN FIND IT IN A BO
OK, OBTAIN IT IN SOME JAR OFF THE SHELF, OR PRODUCE IT FROM A PDX-647+ INSTRU
MENT, THEN ONE DOESN'T NEED THIS STUDIO; PRIMIT: THIS EXPERIMENTAL STUDIO IS
FOR ENDLESS LISTENING; IN MAKING; IN COMPOSING; IN LISTENING TO, AND CRITIQUE
ING WORK; IN DESCRIBING; IN COMING TO KNOW EACH OTHER, AND SELF; PRIMIT: ESPE

CIALLY SINCE ALL OF THE SOPHISTICATED GADGETS ,---(SYNTHESIZERS, MIXERS, TAPE
DECKS, COMPUTERS, SIGNAL PROCESSORS, VIDEO SYSTEMS, ET ALIA)---ARE LIKE LA IN
THAT NOTHING WILL HAPPEN UNTIL ONE IS READY, AND OPEN TO WHAT IS THERE, --- (
NEITHER ANZO'S LA, NOR IBM'S PC-AT WILL MAKE YOUR WORK FOR YOU; ALTHOUGH THEY
SURELY CAN MAKE THEIR'S, QUIETLY, SECRETLY RESONATING IN CIRCUIT-CHATTER LANG
UAGE)---; UNTIL ONE GETS THE WAX OUT OF EARS, HEAD OUT OF SAND, AND, AT LEAST
BEGINS TO SEE SELF, AND EACH EXPERIENCE, AS UNIQUE. IN THIS REGARD, TAPE COMP
OSITIONS ARE AS DIRECT, AND AS HELPFUL, AS ONE CAN GET. THERE'S ACTUALLY NOWH
ERE ELSE ONE CAN TURN TO WHICH WILL ENABLE THE UNDERSTANDING OF THIS KIND OF
MAKING, EXCEPT TO LITERALLY 'FACE THE MUSIC'. THERE ARE NO PROGRAM NOTES, NO
BOOKS, NO CD JOCKS, OR ELSEWHAT TO HELP. CHANGE CANNOT HAPPEN IN ANY OTHER WA
Y. IT DOESN'T HAVE TO BE INVENTED, EITHER. A GIVEN WORK DEMANDS IT; SUCH WORK
NECESSARILY FORMS PART OF ANY TRANSFORMATIONAL PROCESS. SOMETIMES, THOUGH, TH
IS PROCESS IS VERY RADIC. YET, AGAINST A STAGGERING BACKGROUND OF RECALLABLE-
HISTORIES OF SEMBLANCES; AND, BY NOW, NEAR-INSTINCTIVE COMPARATIVE PROCESSES
CONTAINED IN A BIG BAG OF LANGUAGE + MEMORY,---(WHICH RUB SALT INTO MIND-BODI
E'S NEEDED DEVELOPING SENSE OF AWARENESS, PRESENCE, AND, AT LEAST MOMENTARY F
ORGETTING)---; SUCH THAT ONE IS ENABLED TO EXPERIENCE A WORK, UNIQUELY, SOME
FUNDAMENTAL CONDITION HAS TO BE ESTABLISHED, ---(THAT IT IN ADDITION TO: I
HAVE NO IDEA). IN STUDIO, ONLY ONE "NEGATIVE" CONDITION IS MANDATORY: DISREGA
RD IN-PROCESS RESPONSES BASED ON MATTERS OF TASTE; ---(THERE IS NO ARGUING WI
TH IT, AND, SHOULD ONE ENTER THIS TRAP, THE TRIP WILL TAKE ONE ON AN EXTREMEL
Y STRETCHED TAUTOLOGICAL LOOP)---; BESIDES, A WELL-DEVELOPED SENSE OF TASTE ,
AFTER PROFOUND EXPERIENCE, IS QUITE ANOTHER MATTER. PRESUMING ONE WHO ENTERST
HISFLYTRAP CAN SOMEHOW GET UNSTUCK, THEN NEXT COMES THE PREFERRED: ASSEMBLY-
LANGUAGE STATE: A GIVEN WORK IS PLAYED AGAIN; ---(JT:"I'M A GREAT BELIEVER IN
THE USE OF THE MIND, BUT NOT WITHOUT THE EAR! SO, THE BEST WAY, I THINK, IS T
O LET THEM HEAR THE SOUND, AND THEN,---TALK ABOUT WHAT IT IS THEY ARE HEARING
. WE DO SEEM TO HAVE TO HAVE SOME KIND OF LANGUAGE TO REFER TO THESE THINGS,-
--IT'S VERY HARD TO USE THE EXPERIENCE OF HEARING,---UNLESS YOU HAVE--- SOME
WAY OF RELATING TO IT VERBALLY---")---. AT FIRST 'GLANCE', HOWEVER, NONE OF T
HE DESCRIPTIVE-LINGUISTIC BITS WHICH REFER TO THE GIVEN WORK UNDER DISCUSSION
WHICH FOLLOWS, (AND TO WHICH EACH PERSON HAS CONTRIBUTED), SEEMS CONNECTED,OR
OFTEN, EVEN ANALOGOUS; ---(NOW THE MERE APPEARANCE OF SUCH OFTEN 'CONFUSED' ,
'MANY-SEEMING VIEWS', WOULD LIKELY CAUSE A PERCEIVABLE CONSTIPATED STANCE ON
THE PART OF CERTAIN CULTERS WHO HAVE ACQUIRED A FIRM NOTION THAT ANY VERBAL D
ESCRIPTION OF A SONIC EVENT IS MORE FAITH/FULL TO THE EVENT, ---((THE CONSEQU
ENCE OF ITS "IDEA")) ---, I.E., TO ITS "LETTER", IF EXPRESSED IN SOMEWHAT MECH
ANISTIC, STATISTICAL, OBJECTIVE, ---((AND, THEREFORE, LITERAL)) ---, TERMS. TH
SUPPOSITION FOR THIS VIEW BEING THAT THERE IS SOMETHING PROFOUNDLY SINGULAR,
---((HERE I REFER ESPECIALLY TO "MASTERWORKS")) ---, ABOUT A GIVEN WORK, ---((
FOR INSTANCE ITS "UHRSATZ")) ---, THAT IS PERSONAL, PRIVATE, ONE'S OWN, ---((I
N A SUBJECTIVE SENSE)) ---, STANDING ALONE, LIKE NO OTHER, ---((ALSO IN A SUBJ
ECTIVE SENSE, BUT "LOGICALLY" ARGUED FOR AS "OBJECTIVE"))---,WHICH WOULD BE CO
MPROMISED BY UNDUELY "EXPRESSIVE", EVEN "METAPHORIC" LANGUAGE. NOW, IN THE MO
ST ADVANCED OF CULT'S BISHBONS ATTITUDE IN THIS MATTER, IS ALSO NESTED THE SE
NSE THAT THERE CAN BE NO OTHER VIEW:---((THAT ONE CULT "SUBJECT" OR ANOTHER C
AN PRESUME TO POSIT NOTIONS OF SOME "OBJECT", ---GIVEN THAT ONE CANNOT EVER F
ULLY COME TO KNOW THE NATURE OF THE SO-CALLED AND ADORED SENSE OF "OBJECT", (
((BEING MORE OF AN UNWARRENTED ASSUMPTION THAN AN ACTUALITY, IN ANY CASE))) , IS
ENOUGH TO BLUR THE BOUNDARY OF THE OBJECT AS A "THING IN ITSELF". (((WHICH DOE
SN'T PREVENT CULT-SUBJECT FROM, ---BY SOME "FURTHERMORE"-ASSUMED ARROGANCE,--
-, CLAIMING THAT IT CAN BE SO SINGULARLY POSSESSED)))---:BUT SINCE THE SO-CALL
ED OBJECT IS SO-HELD BY THE CULT-OBSERVER, THE ACTION BETWEEN THEM CANNOT BEO
THER THAN A 'NON-EXCLUSIVE' ONE)) . EDUCATED GUESSES. THAT IS, EVEN INFORMALLY

, THERE CAN, AND CANNOT, BE A SINGULAR VIEW; THERE CAN, AND CANNOT, BE A UNIQ
UE VIEW. MOREOVER, CULT'S DIFFICULTY IS THAT SUCH A DESIRED SINGULAR-LITERALV
IEW ALSO MUST ALSO "MEAN" SOMETHING; AND, THE MORE IT MEANS TO MORE PEOPLE, T
HE BETTER IT MUST BE; ---((OF COURSE THIS HAS THE APPEARANCE OF A CONTRADICTI
ON, AT LEAST TO CULT'S STAND ON SINGULARITY)) . HOWEVER, THE MEANING OF A WORK
CAN NEVER BE ESTABLISHED, SINCE THE CONCEPT OF MEANING, IN ITSELF, IS A NON-S
QUITOR)---; IN STUDIO, THE SURFACE FEATURES OF SUCH DIVERSE RESPONSES GENERAL
LY FALL OUT INTO THE FOLLOWING REACTIONS: (1) NO ONE IS TALKING ABOUT THE SAM
E WORK; (2) NO ONE SEEMS TO HAVE HEARD IT, OR ONLY HEARD IT INCOMPLETELY; (3)
SOME HAVE DESCRIBED A COMPOSITION THEY WOULD HAVE PREFERRED TO MAKE; (4) SOME
HAVE SIMPLY MAPPED ONTO THE GIVEN WORK, WORDS DRAWN FROM BAGS OF ACCUMULATED-
"MUSIC LANGUAGE", LEARNED WHO KNOWS WHERE, AND REGARDED AS A KIND OF GENERAL-
PURPOSE TOTE BAG WHOSE WORDS, (SO IT SEEMS), CAN BE PULLED OUT WITHOUT NOTICE
, AND APPLIED TO ANY GIVEN; ---(THE GIVEN, NOT BEING ABLE TO TALK BACK, SO-TO
-SPEAK, THEREFORE, DE FACTO, ALLOWS THE POLLUTION TO CONTINUE); VARIOUS OTHER
RESPONSES. NEVERTHELESS, THE PONDER-WONDER OF WHY THESE PARTICULAR LINGUISTIC
RESPONSES, AND NOT AN ABUNDANCE OF OTHERS, HAS ALWAYS FASCINATED ME. I HAVE A
N INTUITION THAT THE MUSIC, IN SOME SENSE, HAS BEEN HEARD, AND THE LANGUAGE ,
CALLED, (COUGHED?) UP, IS AN OPENING, NOT NECESSARILY CONCLUSIVE, BUT NEVER-T
HE-LESS, CONNECTED RESPONSE. IF SO, THEN SOMETHING, ---EVEN IF NAIVELY SO, --
- HAS BEEN SAID ABOUT WHAT WAS THERE TO HEAR; (CONTRARILY, "JARGON", ---WHICH
SOME OF WHAT I'M DESCRIBING MAY SEEM LIKE---, OCCURS WHEN ONE BEGINS BY AVOID
-ING WHAT IS INTRINSICALLY THERE; PREFERRING FOR ANY NUMBER OF REASONS, TO NO
T "FACE THE MUSIC", BUT, IF ASKED, WILL GLADLY PERFORM SOME FLASH DANCE OR OT
HER INSTEAD). (ALONG THE WAY, LA HELPS ME TO UNDERSTAND THAT ANY RESPONSE IS
NOT IRRELEVANT; AFTERALL, ONE MUST BEGIN FROM SOMEWHERE. SO RESPONSE LANGUAGE
IS TURNED AROUND IN STUDIO, AND IT IS ASSUMED THAT WHAT HAS BEEN HEARD HAS B
EEN IN THE NATURE OF CODES. AND CODES CAN BE DECODED). WE HAVE FOUND THAT DIV
ERSE RESPONSES WHICH DO NOT COMPRISE (EXPECTED?) SAMENESSES, (A DUBIOUS CRITE
RIA ANYWAY), NOR (EXPECTED?) AGREEMENTS, (DITTO:+, AS-IF SOME PIECE OF LEGISL
ATION WERE BEING PROPOSED), DO QUITE PHENOMENALLY REVEAL POSITIVE VALUE: HAVI
NG TO DO WITH THE LISTENER + MUSIC. ALTOGETHER GRADUALLY, MOSTLY BY AN EASY-B
UT PERSISTENT QUESTIONING, NOT ONLY OF THE COMPOSITION AT HAND, BUT ALSO OF T
HE COLLECTIVE LANGUAGE USED TO DESCRIBE IT, A KIND OF ORGANIC "CORPORATE" SEN
SIBILITY BETWEEN THE TWO BEGINS TO DEVELOP. WHATEVER THE SEEMINGLY DIALECTICA
L, PERCEPTUAL, COMPOSITIONAL, NOETICAL, ET ALIA, INTERFERENCE "NOISE" PATTERN
S ARE; NONE OF THESE LOGICS SURVIVE THE NOESIS, WHICH ITSELF BECOMES PART OF
A LIVING CORPORATE ORGANISM; (IN BIOLOGICAL TERMS, A MORPHOGENETIC "FORMATIVE
CAUSATION" IS IN PROCESS). IN ITS GENERALITY, IT IS NOT UNLIKE THE CONDITIONS
OF PARAMETRIC INTERPLAY, (INTERACTION), EXISTENTIALLY PRESENT WITHIN ANY COMP
LEX COMPOSITION, (OR SYSTEM), PER SE. LET'S SAY: IT IS NOT THAT TEN DIFFERENT
LINGUISTIC DESCRIPTIONS SUGGEST THAT EACH LISTENER HAS HEARD A DIFFERENT WORK
(WHERE, IN FACT, ONLY 'ONE' WORK, (REFERENT), WAS THE POINT OF FOCUS), ---ALT
HOUGH, IN SOME SENSE THIS TOO CAN BE IMAGINED, ---; BUT RATHER THAT A SINGLE
WORK, ---PERHAPS DUE TO ITS COMPLEXITY---, CAN EXCITE TEN DIFFERENT DESCRIPTI
ONS WITHOUT COMPROMISING EITHER THE WORK OR THE LANGUAGE DESCRIBING IT. THIS
IS SO, SINCE NEITHER THE WORK NOR THE COLLECTIVE LANGUAGE CAN BE AN ENTITY, I
N, ITSELF, ---THAT IS, EXCLUSIVELY SO---, UNDER THE CIRCUMSTANCE OF OBSERVATI
ON. IN EFFECT, A LANGUAGE WHICH INCLUDES BOTH HAS BEEN MADE. THE DIFFERENCES-
OF-VIEW OF A SAID GIVEN, ARE GENUINE DIFFERENCES; SO ARE ITS CONTRADICTIONS .
THESE CIRCUMSTANCES, HOWEVER, ARE AN ESSENTIAL FEATURE OF ANY WELL-MADE WORK,
AS WELL. (AT LAST SILHOUETTES BEGIN TO FADE). BOTH WORK AND OBSERVER LANGUAGE
, AS AN 'ORGANISM' IS NO LONGER STATIC. CONTRARILY, THE'CORPORATE ENTITY'IS N
OW ALIVE, AND VIBRATING. HOWEVER, THIS LIVING, VIBRATING ENVIRONMENT IS NOT J
UST ANY LIVING, VIBRATING ONE THOUGH, (DUE TO ITS PARTICULAR INTEGRITY AS CON

STITUTED BY ITS MEMBERS + WORK, IT NOW HAS ITS OWN KIND OF MORPHIC RESONANCE.
                                                                        I SUPPOSE
THIS KIND OF PHENOMENAL EXPERIENCE WOULD SEEM OVERWHELMINGLY UNDULGENT TO THO
SE CULT REDUCTIONISTS WHO PREFER UNIFORMLY APPLIED METHODOLOGIES IN ORDER TO
SIMPLIFY WHAT ARE, ESSENTIALLY, EXTRAORDINARILY COMPLEX SYSTEMS. WHEREAS, BY
REGARDING SOULD AS A 'LIVING' SYSTEM, THE APPREHENSION OF EACH UNIQUE WORK WO
ULD REQUIRE A DIRRERENT SET OF EARS, DESCRIPTIVE LANGUAGE, ANALYTIC APPROACH,
PERFORMANCE ATTÍTUDE, SOUND SENSE, CONSCIOUSNESS; IN EFFECT, A DIFFERENT STAT
E OF BEING.   PRIMIT
                                                                      AND
                                                                      RADIC
BEGIN WHISPERING TO ME ABOUT HOW SOUND IS "THE CRUCIAL ELEMENT WHICH HOLDS TH
ENTIRE UNIVERSE TOGETHER, CONNECTING ALL MATTER TO ALL MATTER".   THEY
ARE SAYING THIS IN THIS RESONANT FIELD WHICH I AM HEARING AND EXPERIENCING IN
MIND + BODY. AND, AS I DO SO, I NOTICE LA WHO HAS ENTERED BEGINS SPEAKING TO
LOQUENDI:

"ANIMS---
SOUL—NOTICED;
---(AND) SEES;
AND IN ITS IT
(ASLEEP)
ACCOUNT MUCH;
ACUTENESS ARE APT   KENNETH GABURO
AND SAY IT: IOWA CITY, IOWA
ALREADY---   2-10-87

THE SURVIVAL
OF AESTHETICS

This section focuses on aesthetic writings by composers Pierre Boulez, Thomas DeLio, and George Rochberg, as reviewed by composer Susan Blaustein in an article whose title is a trope on Rochberg's title, *The Aesthetics of Survival*. The value of "open form" is debated by Blaustein (con), DeLio and Sabbe (pro). Many of the issues previously aired in *Perspectives on Musical Aesthetics* are represented here, particularly the vexing question of the composer and audience, or public. Must, or should, composers fashion an "aesthetics of survival" to accommodate the music they want to write and hear to the public taste? If not, what kinds of alternative musical and social forms can be envisioned under which an unfettered art music could survive?

As *Perspectives on Musical Aesthetics* comes to a close, we might consider what music can contribute to the future of the human world. There will always be a place for folk music, for the pleasure of developing virtuosic or simply adequate performing technique, for the pleasure of playing a musical instrument, alone or in groups, and even for what Satie called "wallpaper music" for those unspecial times when even silence is unwelcome. Music to dance to will always be in demand, although the social critic might find more significance in the nature of the dances than in the sound of mass-market dance music, which almost has to be relatively simple in order to function effectively.

Where does art music fit in, music that doesn't fit, music that is unmarketable, music that is pretty essentially uncommodifiable? This is music that has been created with often exceptional passion and intelligence, music that is meant to advance the art, music that runs counter to or parallel to the slots or the grain society provides for music. Attali proposes that art music, having little or no systemic inertia and therefore capable of rapid, radical systemic change, functions partly to delineate larger shifts in culture that are only pre-nascent in other media (or in the economic substrate). Xenakis has suggested that music has tended to pioneer, inexplicitly, concepts that will appear later in mathematics and the sciences. We may remain a little wary of the familiar move that attempts to value something by endowing it with priority, or with hierarchic supremacy. Collins, via Bataille, suggests that music and art function as "heterogeneous elements" in an "intrinsically unresolvable struggle" with the homogeneous elements, Hegel without the *Aufhebung,* a sort of eternal agon—or perhaps art can at least fill the role of Prometheus's vulture. This view is appealing in its lack of partisanship, for proponents both of change and of the status quo would have to value the agon that comprises the homogeneous *and* the heterogeneous. Artists who comfort themselves that with their radical rethinking they *épater* the establishment have gnawing at their own liver the vulture of a realization that without their own-created "other" the agon would collapse, and with it the status quo. But irony is good for the blood.

The Survival of Aesthetics:
Books by
Boulez, DeLio, Rochberg

Susan Blaustein

SPEAKING IN MUSICAL TONGUES as they do, composers are among the most frequently second-guessed, misunderstood, and misrepresented of those working in the arts. We can count ourselves lucky, then, when the more literarily-inclined among them take it upon themselves to speak and to write; for whether the topic be analytic, theoretical, or more explicitly polemic in nature, in composers' words about music, cues to their modes of thinking and to their impelling ideologies abound. Also lurking in their prose are clues useful to the reconstrual of the socio-cultural context in relation to which they must work.

In two recently published volumes of collected essays, by Pierre Boulez and by George Rochberg, and in two books of essays and analyses—one written by, one edited by Tom DeLio—that deal with works by a number of living composers, we find a somewhat random but perhaps nonetheless informative and accurate sampling of the range of concerns that in the course of the last thirty years have moved composers to speak.

I shall consider each composer's writings separately before comparing approaches to issues of common interest. Finally, I will suggest one possible mode of production still viable within our contemporary musical landscape that takes off from that which these practitioners do and do not say.

*   *   *

Orientations: Collected Writings by Pierre Boulez, edited by Jean-Jacques Nattiez, translated by Martin Cooper (Cambridge: Harvard University Press, 1986)

Pierre Boulez's *Orientations* is the finally published, faithful and vivid translation of his 1981 collection of essays, *Points de repère* ([Paris]: Christian Bourgois éditeur; Éditions du Seuil, 1981; second edition 1985). These pieces range from the occasional to the analytical, and span a prodigious thirty-year period in Boulez's active life as composer, conductor, professor, administrator, polemicist, and French thinker-at-large.

Boulez's prose is a pleasure to read: literate, articulate, deeply engaged with music, and passionate about his articles of faith, he is supremely equipped to travel in most fashionable currents of twentieth-century thought and, going further, to formulate theories of cultural history and to design a future for Western music. Much to our great interest, he is by no means too shy to do just that. And because, like many self-respecting French intellectuals in the latter part of the twentieth century, he is well-read in many areas, brandishes a dazzlingly-honed dialectical rapier, and has a virtuosic flair for polemics, Boulez's words on such subjects as determinations of style, genius, succession, and taste are sharply spiced, deliciously bold, and eminently quotable. Examples follow.

On style:

> What in fact is 'style' but writing within a network of functions as limited in their intrinsic potentialities as in their historical effectiveness![1]

On the "fetish . . . of the 'creative message' ":

> Only too often we hear or read that the quality of a work depends first and foremost on 'what the composer has to say', regardless of the means he may choose. What are we to understand by this phrase? And how in fact can a composer conceive his 'message' without a morphology—a formal scheme—capable of communicating it to the listener? This whole concept of an abstract 'message' is in fact no more

than a cheap sophistry, employed only to conceal a profound misunderstanding, or indeed complete ignorance, of the circumstances of a particular historical period and, more generally, of the means of expression at the composer's disposal. This sort of myopia is a relic of romanticism in its pathetic final stages, and it reveals an inability to understand the real relationship between vocabulary and expression. I must admit that any sensibility that catches cold at the slightest draught of intellectual air seems to me to be in a pretty poor way.[2]

On his own rhetorical style:

Of course I am generalizing and oversimplifying, because to discover the truth one has to simplify and caricature.[3]

I think of myself as a gardener rather than as a woodsman: if I sometimes use an axe, it is only to cut out dead wood and give a tree a better chance of surviving.[4]

About artistic evolution and the historical inevitability of serial music (first read at Darmstadt in 1960; unpublished until now):

Now the logical evolution of any language must—and historically speaking always does—take the following form: ideas that are more 'general' and more 'abstract' at every stage replace those of the foregoing period. Thus the logical evolution of music appears as a series of 'reductions', the different basic systems forming a decreasing succession in which each one is slotted into the one that precedes it. Dialectically speaking, however, and taking into account the more 'general' and 'abstract' notions, which represent a *restriction*, or *reduction*, of previous notions, the new formal system becomes correspondingly wider than the old and in a sense subsumes it. In this way, to take an example, tonality represents a generalizing of the more particularizing modal system. Tonality generalizes the idea of modality by introducing the principle of transposition, at the same time impoverishing the older system by abolishing all the truly 'particular' characteristics of the modes. These characteristics, once integral to the modes, were in fact completely disintegrated by the new principle of general transposability.

In the same way it might be said that with such a 'generalizing' and 'abstracting' principle as permutation, for instance, the idea of the series subsumes all the other principles that have preceded it, including modality and tonality. A scale may be considered to be a series, in a restricted sense, but one with stronger, more particularized properties than the twelve-tone series; and in the same way the different modes may be said to have arisen by a simple process of circular permutation. Historically, therefore, we may lay down that no intuitive system is ever abandoned until the discovery of some method by which a study of that system can be reproduced in terms of the new 'order'. This series of logical-mathematical operations (called reductional reproductions) is *limited* in number, the order in which they occur is *necessary* and their outcome is *irreversible*, so that—for instance—there can never be a return to modal conceptions of music.[5]

On the role given the individual player in such a history:

> Every age expresses itself through the individual most able himself to assume the historical responsibilities of the society of which he forms a part. It may therefore happen that society does not immediately recognize itself in its own representative, just as a sitter may fail to recognize himself in an artist's portrait of him.…[6]

On history's treatment of these individuals in the course of its forward march:

> The history of music, as of anything else, is made *of* individuals *for* individuals: it exalts them as much as it crushes them beneath its weight as it progresses towards an absolute future, even though it means passing through our present state of uncertainty. We can at least make up our minds not to be crushed *for nothing!*[7]

On the essence and importance of criticism:

> Another essential element in criticizing a composer is a basic 'lack of respect' (a philosophical 'doubt').… 'Lack of respect' can be expressed by a maximum of radical questioning: it starts with doubt and ends in certainty, in the establishment of a hierarchy of values that will determine the new situation in which composers of the future will find themselves. But a certain Monsieur Descartes has thrown sufficient light on this point to make further insistence unnecessary.[8]

On those lacking in critical acumen:

> We still suffer from the ghastly racket of the dreadful degenerates whose total unawareness makes them innocent of the filth they produce.[9]

On the ultimate purpose for criticism:

The work of criticism will be a kind of spell to make a work germinate.[10]

This last thought is central to Boulez's credo wherein "all musical functions are inseparable and interchangeable," and, I might add, mutually nourishing: "Execution, research, experiment, propaganda and teaching should all radiate from a single central point."[11] The study of another's works, as "part of the whole mechanism of the influence of the non-self on the self,"[12] should be useful chiefly to kindle one's own creative imagination, as he makes clear in his essay on analysis and teaching:

A composition is sometimes no more than an excuse for introspection. The ultimate object of analysis is self-definition by the intermediacy of another.... This is the kind of investigation that I try to inculcate in my pupils. In a word, I want them to reach a point at which the masters of an earlier age speak to them about themselves.[13]

As Nattiez points out in his introduction, Boulez has "constructed his own plot of musical history."[14] He has hand-picked his genealogy of heroic artistic antecedents who, one can assume, "speak to *him* about *him*self." According to Nattiez, the roster includes Cézanne, Klee, Kandinsky, Mondrian in painting, Baudelaire, Mallarmé, Proust, Joyce, Kafka, Musil, Genet, Char, Michaux in literature, and Stravinsky, Schönberg, Berg, Webern, and Bartók, the five composers with whom Boulez wrestles repeatedly.

In the introduction to his book *The Anxiety of Influence: A Theory of Poetry*, Harold Bloom defines "strong" poets as "major figures with the persistence to wrestle with their strong precursors, even to the death."[15] At least in his youth, Boulez must certainly be counted among the "strong" composers, by Bloom's definition; his diatribes against Schönberg and later Stravinsky, in tandem with certain of his most suggestive works (I am thinking here of *Le Marteau,* the Third Piano Sonata, *Pli Selon Pli*), can be read as genuine efforts to match arms with these giants. Each intolerance, each noisy betrayal, each piece of music can be understood as "an act of creative correction that is actually and necessarily a misinterpretation," to use Bloom's words, an example of that "perverse, wilful revisionism without which modern poetry [for 'poetry,' read 'music'] as such could not exist."[16]

In an occasional piece from 1966 remembering one of his teachers, the conductor Roger Désormière, Boulez makes explicit his self-conscious and essentially Bloomian view of history: "Do we never want to remodel the faces of those to whom we feel in some way drawn to suit ourselves?"[17]

He elaborates on this revisionist notion when discussing the merit of unearthing sources and historical references in order to thoroughly understand the score of Berg's *Lulu*:

> It would be pointless now to try to return to Berg's sources and to concentrate our attention on the years around 1900. Berg has, as it were, destroyed those sources by his own progress as a composer and they remain his own secret, which cannot ever be discovered, though we may clear the surrounding landscape. We should be on our guard against nostalgia for the past: the work grown richer with time, as a river is enriched by alluvial tributaries. The interesting thing is to regard the composer's labour as the point of departure for another adventure, the adventure undertaken by those who make the work their own. What is valuable is not discovering the composer, but discovering ourselves through him. The difference hardly matters as long as it is fruitful.[18]

This ferocious appetite for possession is undoubtedly part of what keeps Boulez involved in as many aspects of music as he is; he needs to wholly appropriate and consume works he is interested in so as not to be consumed by them, but so he may convert them to fuel for his own creative drives.

Speaking as an opera conductor late in the same essay on *Lulu*, in "a short postscript on fidelity" in theatrical performance, Boulez writes:

> The essential thing is to re-create another secret based on the existence of the work—not to rediscover the author, but to discover oneself. *Possessing* a work and making a provisional transcription of it in our own language is something that makes one both perfectly humble and perfectly proud, free in relation to the author and the past and responsible only to one's own deeply considered options. There is no such thing as *truth*—that is something that 'masterpieces' call upon us to discover and to accept: they command our disrespect, our vandalizing even.[19]

"Perverse, wilful revisionism," proudly at work.

Boulez's insights and experiences as an opera conductor are among the most musically rewarding parts of the book. His understanding of recitative in Wagner and Debussy as the locus for motivic and harmonic development is made clear in his comments on *rubato* and "fluid tempo"[20] in *Pelléas et Mélisande* and on the necessity of "a flexible cruising speed"[21] to ensure "the dramatic effectiveness of *Parsifal*."[22] Such observations reveal him to be a feeling, skillful musician who takes great care to distinguish between modes of temporal unfolding.

Boulez's relationship to Wagner's music is surprisingly close to the core of his compositional thinking. For one thing, Wagner figures centrally in Boulez's teleology (I quote Boulez at some length here because his just-so history of the relationship between counterpoint and harmony and his aside on Beethoven are so vividly put):

> Counterpoint and harmony are distinguished academically because at one stage in the development of the tonal language the two notions did not in fact coincide except on the hypothesis of a mutual dependence. Harmonic functions became increasingly differentiated as the language evolved, and the more they did so, the more necessary it became for counterpoint and harmony to achieve a kind of symbiosis in order to exist concurrently. (The fugues in Beethoven's opus 106 and opus 133 are rare examples of counterpoint 'rebelling' against the increasing claims of harmonic functions.)
>
> With Wagner a point was reached at which the two ideas are on the brink of amalgamating and producing an overall phenomenon in which the vertical and the horizontal are projected on to each other. In this way we find tonal functions increasingly undermined by the individual power of intervals; and it was from this point that the style of first Schoenberg, and then Berg and Webern, developed. . . . Of course Wagner's obstinate insistence on uninterrupted polyphonic movement and continuity involves a number of stylistic mannerisms. . . . It is easy, in particular, to recognize in his innumerable broken cadences the seams—one might almost say scars—resulting from amputating the customary clausulae of a 'normal' discourse.[23]

Boulez-the-composer also credits Wagner with the invention of the "open structure" and the "restructuring" of time:

> There are . . . certain points in the musical discourse at which Wagner actually needs stabilizing elements to counteract the almost excessive mobility of other sections of his rhetoric, as this unfolds. He fixes on, and makes use of, at least one main stabilizing element of the musical language, whether it is tonality, figuration, a rhythmic cell or, as sometimes happens, several of these ingredients combined. The diatonic-chromatic contrast is part of a much more general technique making conscious use of the dialectic between fluid and fixed time. In the new time-structure with which Wagner endowed music he first conceived, and then realized, the absolute necessity for fundamental markers based on different, new criteria. Once these markers (which include the motives) are established, the evolution of the work's time-structure will be made clear by their distortion—a brilliant, revolutionary

conception if ever there was one!—implying that the work must be thought of as an 'open' structure never 'closed' except provisionally and unwillingly.

This explains why Wagner's conclusions are so difficult and sometimes appear hasty, arbitrary and abrupt....[24]

It is in his restructuring, researching of time that I find Wagner's real subversive achievement. It may perhaps seem something trivial compared with the grand revolutionary ambitions with which he set out, but I do not think so. The revolutions that, in the last resort, have the profoundest and most far-reaching results are revolutions in our mental categories, and Wagner initiated, once and for all, the irreversible processes of such a revolution.[25]

Unfortunately, for all his panache, powerful imagery, and strong statements, the few brief articles about Boulez's own music are less musically satisfying than those about other people's and are less interesting than the more polemical, speculative, occasional pieces gathered in this volume. His treatment of structure is abstract and formulaic. In discussions of his own works, he outlines the organizational principles at play; but only in his lecture on the "Deuxième Improvisation sur Mallarmé" does he engage with the music that results, and even there he does not address issues of pitch or succession of apparently discontinuous gestures: he speaks only about details of orchestration and their relationship to the text.

For the reader who struggled to unravel the cryptically annotated musical examples in order to grasp Boulez's harmonic "multiplication" system in *Boulez on Music Today* and wished for more pointed discussion of its use in specific works; for the reader who heard *Répons* and wants to know what's in it; for the reader who has finally got his/her hands on this expensive English version of what Boulez has presumably been thinking about compositionally during all these years of much talk, heavy research at IRCAM, and few pieces; for all these readers, these thin, superficial, recycled treatments of his own less recent pieces are a disappointment.

More than thirty years ago, Boulez laid out a clear compositional agenda to address the crisis he forecast for post-serial musical language. His stated program included the research into the potential of electro-acoustic and instrumental resources that eventually found its federally-funded home, thanks to Boulez's enormous effort and clout, at IRCAM. It included building a musical life and community that would draw in untapped and various constituencies through imaginative programming and first-rate performances. From his own example, both in his career as conductor and in all his writings about music of the past, we can read part of Boulez's *un*stated program, to include what Harold Bloom has called "the absolute absorption of the percursor":[26] that is, the self-conscious, thorough digestion of major works in the repertoire, in order to turn the lessons learned there to fodder for eventual use in his own music.

Nattiez notes in his introduction that, "generally speaking, since *Pli selon pli* Boulez does not appear to have felt the need to explain his major works in print. Instead he has used the interview...." Nattiez also reminds us that Boulez is still unsatisfied with several of his works involving electronic media, and that he considers many of his larger works to be "unfinished, or 'works in progress'."[27]

To this reader, these apologies are inadequate. Of course, the time lag before publication of such a hefty volume as *Points de repère*, not to mention its English translation, might have precluded discussion of Boulez's most recent works and thought. All the same, one would have liked some enterprising editor to have mustered at least one extensive recent interview with Boulez so that his reader might learn what he thinks now of his earlier agenda. Even if he is reluctant to discuss his recent music in any detail, we are always curious to hear Boulez's pronouncements on the state of the art: What has been accomplished? What has become irrelevant? What remains to be explored? It would be a shame if his no longer being an angry young man should deprive us of access to Boulez's undoubtedly still-provocative thoughts: How does music look, from Boulez's unique bird's eye perch as gifted and experienced conductor, administrator, composer? And how would he revise his compositional agenda today?

These are the questions on which we are "used to" hearing from him; it would be helpful to measure our *own* growth, to chart the distances traveled, if we had the opportunity to monitor our own interest in and responses to what Boulez has to say now.

* * *

Thomas Delio, *Circumscribing the Open Universe* (Lanham, MD: University Press of America, 1984)

Thomas DeLio, editor, *Contiguous Lines* (Lanham, MD: University Press of America, 1985)

In *Circumscribing the Open Universe*, Thomas DeLio looks at five pieces by five composers whom he associates by virtue of their ideological commitment to form as an open framework: "rather than representing form as an entity ontologically prior to process," the composers DeLio has selected make use of what he calls an open structure to treat "process as ontologically prior to form."[28]

Contiguous Lines contains four analytical essays by DeLio, Pozzi Escot, Robert Cogan, and Wesley York on works by Xenakis, Ligeti, Babbitt, and

Philip Glass. These four composers were chosen to reflect "the broad spectrum of compositional approaches currently in vogue throughout Europe and America" in order to convey "some sense of the breadth of current compositional practice."[29]

The analytical approaches employed in these essays, however, are by no means as varied as the pieces they treat. An *a priori* notion of hidden symmetrical structures guides Escot's investigation of Ligeti's *Harmonies* (1967), and Cogan's technique of sound spectrum analysis determines and necessarily limits his discoveries about the opening of Babbitt's *Ensembles for Synthesizer*. The pieces by DeLio (on Xenakis) and York (on Glass) do relate local detail to larger formal structures, but in general the analyses in both books tend to be "analytic" in the same sense that chemical analysis of a compound substance is analytic: constituent strains are isolated, described, labeled, listed, and the job is done; not much attempt is made to interpret, to reconstruct the whole or even part of the work.

This makes sense since, at least in the case of the "open form" works treated in *Circumscribing* . . . and for three of the four pieces discussed in *Contiguous Lines*, the exact musical result of the interaction and simultaneous overlay of various processes is not totally predictable and is unique to each realization. DeLio's essays on pieces by John Cage, Christian Wolff, and Robert Ashley are really more apologias and contextualizations than analyses per se: new symbols and procedures are explained, and statements are sometimes made about what sorts of things are likely to happen. But we find nothing empirical there—DeLio never posits a possible realization to help the prospective listener or performer imagine what textures and gestures might arise from the given materials. By his example and those of his contributors, DeLio seems to suggest that the best one can do as an analyst (and perhaps the truest one can be to the gestalt of these pieces, as well) is to elucidate these processes, turn on the machine, get out of the way and let 'er roll.

The problem for the reader is that no such elucidation matters much if he has not heard the piece, and naturally none of these isolated descriptions of individual strands is as rich or interesting as the piece itself. Some of the issues addressed in analyses of more conventional works—e.g., the influence of registral choice or of simultaneous rhythmic or pitch events on grouping structures—would apply here only to the analysis of individual realizations. Still, given the process-oriented, open-ended, interactive approach to listening and composing professed by DeLio in *Circumscribing the Open Universe*, one might have anticipated more subjective, heard responses included in preliminary or final readings of the works under scrutiny in Part I of *Contiguous Lines*.

As they stand, these essays tend to read as thin: they either sketch a rough, schematic relation between process, detail, and large-scale form, as in DeLio's analysis of Xenakis's 1965 'cello piece *Nomos Alpha* and in Wesley York's treatment of Philip Glass's *Two Pages* for electric organ and piano (1968); or else they tend to indulge in metatheoretical justifications of the compositional or analytic path undertaken, as in both the Escot and Cogan essays, which take us far beyond and beneath the work under discussion.

DeLio also engages in sweeping statements of questionable usefulness. In explaining Lucier's sound-centered compositional agenda, for example, he writes, "The result is an art which re-creates the very conditions of reality itself,"[30] and in describing the work of the sculptor Carl Andre, to which he likens that of Lucier, DeLio says,

> ... the method of this art lies more in the act of presentation than in any type of manipulation or transformation. The result is an intense focus upon presence; the presence of the object to the perceiver which is made vivid through the appropriation of unformed matter.[31]

Presentation? Presence? Presence of the object? Appropriation? Whose appropriation? The perceiver's? The artist's? The object's? Or *is* the object the "unformed matter"?

More cosmic comments on the nature of perception in Lucier's music follow:

> Perception, then, becomes the ground for cognition and the source for all consciousness of presence, both of the object and the perceiver. Thus, while experiencing the work, the listener becomes aware of himself making that transcendent leap from perception to cognition— an awareness of presence. In this sense Lucier's art may be seen as the culmination of a post-Cartesian dialectic in which perception is understood, not as the product of the thinking mind, but as the source of all thought.[32]

and finally:

> What is revealed through this music is the fact that an art's most vital function is to re-create the condition of being—not the experiences of one's life but that perpetual state of transcendence which is the very substance of life.[33]

What does it all mean? If this "condition of being" or "state of transcendence" is in fact "perpetual," then why do we need art to re-create it, and in what ways is this most vital function of art revealed in Lucier's music that distinguish it from any other music?

Indeed, it is often hard to glean from DeLio's descriptions what precisely distinguishes these composers from each other or from anyone else. In concluding his essay about Morton Feldman's *Durations* series, DeLio writes:

> As the work opens, the listener finds himself poised as if at the brink of his first contact with the world. Later, as relationships gradually coalesce, they appear to do so, not through any act of the composer, but rather through the will of the perceiving consciousness.[34]

How is this different, I wonder, from listening to any other piece of music? In beginning the essay, DeLio is more specific about the activity through which such a work emerges:

> As the foundation of his new art, Feldman proposed a language of pure process. In his art, the work and the act of creation became indistinguishable.
>
> Typically, a piece of music evolves through a series of transformations during which raw materials are carefully molded into a particular unique configuration which is then identified as the artwork. Sketches and drafts are constantly replaced or discarded as the composer slowly fashions the particular structure which he desires. Feldman, in contrast, seems to engage the entirety of this process within the very perceptible framework of his compositions. For him, the act of creating a piece becomes the very substance of that piece—its form, in a rich new sense of the word.[35]

Again, where does the contrast lie, exactly, between Feldman and any other composer? DeLio seems to imply that Feldman never revises; but aside from that, what he actually says does not distinguish either Feldman's compositional process or the aesthetic perception of his music from those involved in the work of any other composer.

This tendency toward overgeneralization leads to some highfalutin pronouncements on perceptual and phenomenological matters. DeLio regularly invokes and quotes Heidegger and Merleau-Ponty as if their work were directly responsible for the aesthetic route he is tracing; yet their actual influence on the composers whose music he treats is undocumented and is left unclear.

The broader his brush, the less meaningful some of DeLio's statements become. By the time he gets to his fourth essay in *Circumscribing*..., called "Structural Pluralism," where he discusses the work of Robert Ashley in the light of Richard Serra's sculpture, DeLio seems convinced that the commitment to open form and process by which he earlier had characterized this particular school of composers now goes for all contemporary art and thought:

> The twentieth century has witnessed the emergence of an increased awareness that structure can no longer be viewed simply as a family of relationships discerned among the elements of a single closed gestalt. Rather, a structure is a complex process evolving over a period of time, integrating an elaborate and diverse range of activities reaching out far beyond the framework of the art object itself. It is a continuum of activities beginning with a series of perceptions and proceeding through a network of interrelated transformations.[36]

Why couldn't I use the last sentence to describe my experience of Beethoven's Op. 2, No. 1? or of Schönberg's Op. 33a? or of the *Goldberg Variations*?

But DeLio is not the only one to think big. Here is Cogan, introducing his sound-spectrum analysis of the opening to Babbitt's *Ensembles for Synthesizer* :

> We ourselves are left to meet the challenge, which is to envision a framework for understanding that encompasses and embraces the superabundant sonic possibilities of the electronic medium. And then, to place all of the details and relationships of any individual piece in terms of such an all-encompassing vision. Viewed in this way, the problem turns out not so very different from the other novel theoretical challenge of our time, that posed by global music as a whole, which also requires an all-encompassing framework and the precise placement of any specific music within it.[37]

Now that is cosmic. Everything is everything, and all distinctions pale in the face of the great common drones that bind us.

There are misleading representations in DeLio's books, as well. Still speaking about Morton Feldman, DeLio writes, "Feldman's is a music in which there is no apparent structuring of sound prior to its actual unfolding in time."[38] What does he mean? That Feldman is improvising? Can DeLio be denying the meticulously weighted play of sonorities whose calculatedly precarious states of balance and imbalance create much of what is dynamic in a Feldman work?

Or, in presenting "the traditional notion of form" as distinct from the "open work":

> Within the closed work, "content" represents a type of metaphysical

reflection upon the nature of things in which the self emerges as a static entity possessing knowledge of, but always remaining separate from, all other things of the world. This separation itself stems from the illusion that thought—reflected in the notion of art as "object"— can somehow be disengaged from the process of experience, the process wherein both thought and art unfold and apart from which they no longer have meaning.[39]

What a flat and ill-informed caricature of the experience one might have where a "traditional notion of form" is in play!

In Part II of *Contiguous Lines*, DeLio and three other composers speak out on topics of more general interest: DeLio tries to show how changes in notational practices "reflect new attitudes toward the creative process itself,"[40] for which he uses Wolff, Ashley, and Cage scores as illustrations; Escot deals with the notion of what she terms "non-linearity" in twentieth-century science, arts, and letters, for which she finds antecedents in African art and music; she uses a West African tribal "Play Song" to illustrate the atomistic nature of its surface, and "analyzes" short pieces by Ligeti (*Continuum* [1962]) and Webern (Op. 14, no. 1 [1914]) as instances of "multi-linearity" and "non-linearity," respectively. At least in the case of the Webern, it seems to me that Escot all but misses the boat: by tabulating all possible events, durational "partitions," and "hidden proportions," she cannot possibly tune into the ways in which Webern builds bridges across his apparently discontinuous segments with careful, not unconventional voice-leading, rhythm, phrase structure, and meter. Alvin Lucier chronicles his own compositional evolution in tandem with developments in science and technology; and Christian Wolff writes about the conjoining of his politics with his music in his settings of political texts.

Finally, I am not sure that the essays in DeLio's books do a service for the music they set out to champion. The thinking too often ranges from murky to flaky, the writing from poor to grandiose, the actual analyses from skeletal and unsatisfying to overpadded and unsatisfying.

As for these books as finished products, *Circumscribing the Open Universe* in particular sorely wants editing. There are embarrassing redundancies (including repeated quotations in "Structural Pluralism," the essay on Robert Ashley) and many poorly organized sequences of paragraphs, particularly around quotations and illustrations from scores. Also, given the emphasis DeLio places on parallel and influential developments in painting and sculpture, photo illustrations would have been very helpful to the reader not already familiar with the works or artists under discussion.

* * *

George Rochberg, *The Aesthetics of Survival: A Composer's View of Twentieth-Century Music,* edited and with an introduction by William Bolcom (Ann Arbor: University of Michigan Press, 1984)

George Rochberg is a much venerated musician, composer, and teacher whose reflections on music, as recorded in essays written over the course of the last thirty years, have finally been published here as a collection edited by William Bolcom.

Capacious, essentialist, and passionate in approach, Rochberg's thinking appears to flow from his understanding of man's rightful place in the universe. His writings all seem prompted by his fervent belief that human thought, feelings, and sense of wonder must be the locus of commitment to an authentic, heartfelt artistic expression that ought to bear the same relation to man as man bears to nature:

> The creation of man ... is nature's way of achieving self-awareness ... of opening up through evolutionary processes increasing areas of perception of her own world. ...
>
> When we speak or sing, we are giving voice to nature's urge to communicate and express. ... The central nervous system and its incredibly subtle, interrelated perceptual capacities—all of which are windows and approaches onto the cosmos—is nature's circuitry printed on human minds which we use but do not fully comprehend as yet.[41]

One finds this imagery again and again in Rochberg's prose. Expressing himself with equal eloquence in his 1972 essay, "Reflections on the Renewal of Music," he cuts the cosmos slightly differently:

> We live within two distinct yet interrelated realities: the world of nature which includes man as a biogenetic reflection of nature's urge toward consciousness, and the world of man which includes art as a spiritual reflection of that self-awareness nature has given him. Art is neither a mirror nor a substitute for the world. It is an addition to that universal reality which contains natural man and shows the infinite varieties of ways that man can be. William Faulkner put it much more simply when he said that art was a way of declaring that "Kilroy was here." However we phrase it, art preserves the reality of man's presence on earth. ...
>
> What cannot be remembered cannot be preserved. The true intent of art is to preserve human consciousness.[42]

In Rochberg's opinion, much of contemporary music specializes in the annihilation of memory, as many aspects of contemporary life seem bent on the obliteration of human consciousness. He insists—somewhat shrilly at times, as if trying to get us to hear his warning above the clangorous and seductive clamor of what he calls the "crisis" brought about by "the triumph of abstractionism,"[43] that "rational madness"[44] that has led us astray—that we have lost our way, that we presently exist in a dangerous state of imbalance with ourselves, with our bodies, and with nature which desperately warrants our undivided attention. He sees man's age-old need for self-expression, his imagination, and his longing for "the world of the marvelous"[45] as the only hope for healing what by now is a deep and still raw wound resulting from what he reads as our possibly fatal loss of faith and self-knowledge.

The reintegration of the self with the world—that is, between man and nature—is possible "through the power of imagination," says Rochberg, expanding on Coleridge in his essay, "The Marvelous in Art": We make music, which can enter the incorporeal realm, through our imaginations—it projects itself in a sensory, corporeal form.

> To sing is to project the subtle inflections of the human psyche; to dance is to project the subtle inflections of the human body and its musculature. The renewal of music lies in the direction of reasserting both, simply and directly.[47]

In his essay, "The Marvelous in Art," Rochberg attempts to grapple with the relationship between the imagination and the ineffable. He lets *his* imagination roam from his lyrical, poetic treatment of "imagination" in Coleridge and Beethoven to musings on recent findings in modern physics, perhaps as a way of making vivid his belief that artists and scientists share the "quest to raid the infinite, to wrest from it one of its secrets, to know a little more of the unknowable," in order to "bring into living actuality in finite form something of the world of the marvelous, the world of the real."[48]

But in spite of his keen and well-fed curiosity about recent developments in science and the history of science, Rochberg is nonetheless ever alert to the artist's danger of being seduced by the lure of impressive abstract models such as those operative in the natural sciences, logic, and mathematics.[49]

In "The Fantastic and the Logical" (1973), Rochberg calls for the bringing to heel of reason's tendency toward abstraction through the grounding of imagination.[50] In his most recent essay in the volume, "The Marvelous in Art" (1982), he prescribes the invocation of an animistic sense of "wonder" to reinvest our psychically and literally endangered species with an appreciation for the value and specialness of human life.[51] But already in 1970 Rochberg was calling for the cosmological retuning of the human condition:

Physics ... is no substitute for cosmology; for it was cosmology, with its myths and magic, ritual and religion, which sustained and protected man over eons of time up to the very threshold of the age of science, largely because it allowed his image-making nature free rein to people his inner world with the fantastic, with the sense of awe in the face of forces whose power he sensed but could not know. And most of all it constrained his hubris.[52]

Always imaginative and genuine, Rochberg's thinking is largely informed by the heart—not a bad place to start from, but it is not sufficient, single-valvedly, to accomplish all tasks to which he harnesses it. For one thing, he has come around both to renouncing "Modernism" and denouncing its effect on man's ability to be expressive. In so doing, Rochberg tends to lump together and then to dismiss all twentieth-century genres, styles, and compositional methods that do not lay direct claim to earlier forms, conventions, or traditions, as "modernist."[53]

His main complaints against the turns many recent artistic movements have taken are, first, that man's expressive capacities—both as artist and as audience—have been inhibited, squelched, narrowed, and demeaned by the influence of more scientific, technologically-based modes of thinking; and second, that so many composers have seen fit to sever their connection to the great tradition and to the values it embodies.

In fact, early modernism, starting with Schönberg and continuing in the ensuing generations of composers, was largely a self-conscious translation of traditional musical values into a contemporary musical language. In the course of this process individual elements—pitch, color, rhythm, e.g.—were isolated, appropriated, and became whole areas of research in themselves, producing reams of etude-like pieces that exploit their compositional potential. But Rochberg exaggerates the flattening out that he hears as resulting inevitably from such explorations. In "Reflections on Schoenberg" he reduces Schönberg's atonal and twelve-tone works to "a one-color palette of dissonant chromaticism"[54] which,

lacking the force of tonal directedness and the availability of its great, open spaces and cadential points of rest and emphasis—necessarily leads to blurring of audible outlines, because one cannot readily grasp the sense of its tendency or of its ultimate shape.[55]

(Why not?) Rochberg goes on:

For Schoenberg the principle of the "nearest way" tended to homogenize all motions, thereby tending to equalize all harmonic values. This process of equalization, finally institutionalized in the twelve-tone method, was precisely the internal pressure which reduced identity of profile to the lowest ebb it had reached since the Baroque era and eventually opened the way to the total disintegration of identity and profile, producing a kind of music which can only be described as "forgettable."[56]

I can think of only three possibilities for such an egregiously wrong-headed statement: (1) Rochberg completely misunderstands Schönberg's dictum here, mistaking smooth voice-leading prescriptions for the desire to neuterize previously differentiated intervallic characters;[57] (2) Rochberg insists that twelve-tone music marks the final obliteration of all intervallic distinctions and neutralization "of harmonic values," and he will no longer hear of the opportunities that twelve-tone music can provide, *exactly* for the purpose of refining such distinctions through the contextual creation of clearly-defined functional hierarchies; (3) it is not precisely that Rochberg finds Schönberg's great atonal and twelve-tone works "forgettable" and wanting in "identity and profile," but rather that Rochberg blames Schönberg more as the precursor and forefather of the flood of "forgettable" music that issued in his wake and bore his methodological crest.

This misunderstanding or cluster of misunderstandings leads Rochberg to condemn almost all twentieth-century artistic movements that are not directly or obviously connected to earlier ones. In a 1979 program booklet commemorating the occasion in Philadelphia of a sixtieth-birthday festival of his music (not included in the volume reviewed here), Rochberg wrote the following explanation of his own attempt to reintegrate the past into his music as he introduces his set of String Quartets Nos. 4, 5, and 6:

I have stated many times, in various ways, my conviction that the composer of today must re-establish a deep and firm connection with music again through a rapprochement with the past and its traditions. This is the only way he can break out of the bind of a narrowly modernist aesthetic and its minimalist tendencies.

From his program notes to the Third Quartet, in the same booklet:

In my 'time of turning,' I have had to abandon the notion of 'originality,' in which the personal style of the artist and his ego are the supreme values; the pursuit of the one-idea, uni-dimensional work and gesture which seem to have dominated the esthetics of art in the 20th century; and the received idea that it is necessary to divorce oneself from the past, to eschew the taint of association with those great masters who not only precede us but created the art of music itself. In these ways I am turning away from what I consider the cultural pathology of my own time toward what can only be called a possibility: that music can be renewed by regaining contact with the tradition and means of the past, to re-emerge with spiritual force with reactivated powers of melodic thought, rhythmic pulse, and large-scale structure.

Essential to Rochberg's "aesthetics of survival," as he says in his 1972 essay, "Reflections on the Renewal of Music," is the literal recapitulation of the great tradition as the only substantive and memorable way one can write music today:

The renewal of music depends on the renewal of the art of composition itself. If we value Wagner and Brahms for the power of their harmony, why, then, have we given up harmony? If we value Mozart and Chopin for the elegance of their melodies, why, then, have we given up the melodic line? If in the combination of many voices a radiant polyphony emerges, why have we given up counterpoint? Ballet cannot exist without rhythmic pulsation and periodicities, any more than opera can exist without the accompanied aria. Both are rooted in myth, fairy tale, real or imagined history, the embodiments and extensions of man's passionate nature. Nontheatrical music is not necessarily less dramatic. It must still move and touch us. The enlargement of the timbral palette is made at the sacrifice of the melodic phrase, the rhythmic period. If there is value in this enlargement it will come only with its direct and concrete association with discernible, memorable melodies and rhythms, polyphonic combinations, and textural composites which articulate that longing for a reality which is man's best and perhaps only true claim to existence. History will not help us; but the past, which is ever-present, can.[58]

Taking cues from computer science, psychology, and Chomskyan linguistics, Rochberg rationalizes his insistence on pattern and tonality on cognitive grounds:

Was the optimum of musical communicability reached by the composers of the nineteenth century (granting some spillover into the twentieth); and are we forced to remain within the general frame of their solutions not so much for cultural as for biological-genetic reasons? In other words, does the correspondence between the natural parallel/serial functions of the human nervous system and basic parallel/serial functions of musical structure impose types of limitations which must eventually constrain today's composer to respect that correspondence or suffer the consequences?[59]

He uses the same argument to justify his disappointment in most contemporary music:

> Perhaps we have here a direct clue to one of the basic reasons for the essential failure of much new music to communicate itself directly to even the most sympathetic listeners. Its insistence on suppression of the pulse, its conscious avoidance of periodicity on all levels of structure and movement, and its consequent inability to perpetuate itself as a growing, identifiable organic structural entity apparently go against the grain of the natural functions of the central nervous system.[60]

> If my speculations have any plausibility at all, the implications for the present state of music and the direction of composition for the future are enormous. Clearly much of today's music has foredoomed itself to extinction . . . and no amount of training or conditioning in its perception, no amount of repeated hearings can eventually overcome its essential lack of correspondence with the primary functions of the human nervous system.[61]

Combining his impressive measure of newfound respect for the apparent limitations of cognitive capacities with his earlier pressing call for the return to a human-made cosmology, Rochberg rises at the end of this essay to sing his soaring compositional manifesto, his pitch for an ''aesthetics of survival'':

> A new balance needs to be discovered. It is not the world which needs remaking but ourselves. In remaking ourselves it would be well to remember that for countless milennia before the dawn of the age of science man survived without science as we know it. Instead of science he had a profound relation to the cosmos, however fantastic or superstitious that relation may appear from our vantage point. He survived not through rational knowledge or science and technology but through cosmology which peopled his imagination with myth and symbol, poetry and metaphor, image and story and song. He ritualized his existence, propitiated the gods, surrounded himself with magic. He developed the arts of language, music, dance, painting, sculpture. He learned the rhythms of his world and fitted himself into them. He survived. . . . And we? What are our chances? Can we survive our rational madness, our science and technology, our obsession for progress and change, our avant-garde, our aberrant passions for new sensations, our refusal to accept the limits of our own being? The same attitudes of mind and spirit which have brought us to this pass will not lead us out of it. We must reconnect ourselves with the alpha language of the central nervous system which is itself, I believe, a secondary derivative of the alpha language of the cosmos, and bring the

two into correspondence again, into direct connection and relationship with each other. The lesson of the avant-garde should be, if we read it correctly, to show us in concrete ways how far removed we now are from any real contact with ourselves or the cosmos, how far we have wandered from home.... [62]

Although for some reason Rochberg singles out "composers of the nineteenth century" (with "some spillover") as having attained "the optimum of musical communicability," he does not insist on that or any other period as the particular past or "home" to which composers must return. In his essay, "On the Third Quartet" (1972), Rochberg explains how he came to think of different styles as "dialects... inflecting parts of the whole spectrum of Western musical language" which

can be presented singly or in combination depending on what one wants to say and the particular size, shape, and character of the work one wants to say it in.[63]

Rochberg goes on to deliver an impassioned argument for composers' embracing a work ethic of eclecticism and pluralism:

I believe we are the filaments of a universal mind which transcends our individual egos and histories. The degree to which we partake of that universal mind is the degree to which we identify with the collective imagery, fate, wisdom, and tragedy of our still struggling species. By ourselves we are virtually nothing—but by opening ourselves to the transcendent collectivity of mankind and its experiences, we share in a totality which, however mysterious its sources, dimensions, and ultimate fate, sustains us.

Pluralism, as I understand it, does not mean a simplistic array of different things somehow stuck together in arbitrary fashion but a way of seeing new possibilities of relationships; of discovering and uncovering hidden connections and working with them structurally; of joining antipodes without boiling out their tensions; of resolving the natural tensions of contradictory terms on new symbiotic hierarchic levels....

Granting pluralism, how is a composer to deal with it? From the inside out, i.e., from the internal psychic imagery which becomes the musical gesture to its artistic manifestation. Gesture, singly or in combination, successive or simultaneous, is the determining factor—not style, language, system, or method.[64]

In his 1979 program notes for the same quartet, Rochberg shows how at least one composer has dealt with the challenge of his commitment to pluralism at the level of the musical gesture:

The inclusion of tonality in a multi-gestural music such as the Third Quartet makes possible the combination and juxtaposition of a variety of means which denies neither the past nor the present. In this quartet, I draw heavily on the melodic-harmonic language of the 19th century (even more specifically on the "styles" of Beethoven and Mahler), but in this open ambience tonal and atonal can live side by side—the decision of which to use depends entirely on the character and essence of the musical gesture.

It sounds good on paper; and perhaps as a personal solution for a man whose experience has rendered much of contemporary music inadequate for his needs, such eclecticism makes sense. But I, at least, am not convinced. What is to keep these different "rewritten" musics, however craftfully contrived, from lacking urgency and from sounding utterly glib, facile, and arbitrary in their pastiche-like juxtapositions? Does it not deprive us of *both* the past and the present to deny their separateness, their differences, to claim them as equally accessible to the various uses they could be put to by today's composer?

With music as with words, men and women have the opportunity to make, refine, and celebrate distinctions and, in this capacity, to voice their own concerns. So why would they choose instead to disregard this opportunity and level distinctions by including something of everything and insisting that all should be equal in the ears of the lord and the listener?

In short, the kind of homogenization at the level of intervallic or harmonic values that Rochberg so deplores in much contemporary music is not so different from what he advocates at a "multi-gestural" and formal level when he juxtaposes a Bartók-like opener with a slow Beethoven-like variations movement and a scherzo in the style of Mahler. It is not simply out of egotism that some composers try for coherence or singularity in their musical languages, within and across movement divisions. Without the sense that there has been some internal authorial commitment behind a work, a piece projects no apparent thrust, no integrity, no conviction. And although the notion of a compositional commitment to "pluralism" (understood here as a unity found in diversity) is a noble one, the difficulty for the composer comes in transcending the assemblage of strong, individually conjured "gestures" to forge unified, compelling, meaningful works that can communicate emotions and trigger memory, as Rochberg would also have it.

*   *   *

Having considered each of these recent volumes in turn, I should like to stand back for a moment to imagine how one might manage as a composer

inside a musical universe that permits the coexistence of such remote con-
stellations of issues. There are areas of common concern among our present
informants, to be sure; and a brief consideration of the most obvious of
these might further our eventual purpose.

First, both Boulez and DeLio & Co. have developed their interests in
the compositional exploration of sound itself—its colors, densities, textures,
constituent elements, and its potential as a structural resource.

Robert Cogan, in his well-intentioned but only moderately illuminating
attempt to analyze the "conceptual system of electronic sound or tone
color" operative in the opening of Milton Babbitt's *Ensembles for Synthesizer*
in *Contiguous Lines*,[65] speaks about the new challenge and difficulties
involved in timbral analysis:

> we are directing our attention especially toward what has previously
> been, and still remains, most elusive in musical understanding: the
> qualities and relationships of musical sound *per se*—sonic relationships,
> sometimes construed as tone color relationships. While even in the
> past these relationships have almost always eluded understanding, here
> in electronic music we are further deprived of the single, albeit
> unsatisfactory, crutch previously available in tone color discussion,
> namely musical instruments and an instrumental conception of tone
> color.[66]

Boulez-the-conductor's interest in Berlioz, his mostly orchestrational
analysis of his own *Deuxième Improvisation sur Mallarmé*,[67] and his more
recent work with computers and the 4X at IRCAM—indeed, the very existence of IRCAM—can all be understood as functions of Boulez-the-composer's fascination with sound *per se* as a compositional resource.

Rochberg understands such endeavors to be seriously misguided and
dangerous to the future of music. In his essay, "The New Image of Music"
(1963), Rochberg chronicles the reasons why "sound material of music
enjoys an autonomy never before accorded it,"[68] and considers the musical
consequences.

> This is due largely, I believe, to its liberation from what Sessions calls
> "the musical train of thought," the process of establishing logical con-
> nections between melodic phrase shapes and the harmonic progres-
> sions which support them. This liberation *permits sounds to create their
> own context*, a reversal of the traditional procedure in which the train of
> thought largely determined the individual sounds and their succession.
> The view of sounds as concrete, quantitative entities in themselves is
> revealed by such current terms as *densities, vertical pitch aggregate, sound
> structure*, and *sound object*. Since such complexes no longer derive from

harmonic functions per se, whatever structural "meaning" they have must be derived from other functions in which they now play a role.[69]

Music can no longer be said to be a purely temporal art when its very temporality . . . is at the command, so to say, of its sounding forms. The liberation of sound from tonal harmonic functions (which was the great accomplishment of atonality), the suppression of the beat and pulsation (which parallels the evolution of atonality and its subsequently systematized procedures, twelve-tone method and serialism), and the resultant emergence of unpredictability and discontinuity—these are the paths which have led inexorably to the spatialization of music and to the overthrow of a long-dominant temporal structure.[70]

The other obsession shared by Boulez and DeLio's composers, along with many others working in the late 1950s and 1960s, was the call of the open form. (As with the exploration of sound resources, Rochberg neither participated in nor condoned this new attraction.) DeLio construes openness

> as a mechanism for shifting the focus of the artwork, thereby placing the image of an emerging consciousness at the center of the aesthetic experience. . . . Form becomes a model of the self as it first encounters the world and, thus, takes on new meaning as a model for the act of becoming.[71]

> Thus, within the open work content becomes substantially the same as process as it is engulfed by that perpetual state of imminence which is the essence of each individual's experience of being in the world. . . .
> Thus, rather than representing form as an entity ontologically prior to process, the open structure treats process as ontologically prior to form.[72]

This he sets in opposition to "the traditional closed artwork," which is

> the singular product of an interaction between specific materials and one specific style. Herein lies the source of its closed nature.[73]

> Within the closed work, "content" represents a type of metaphysical reflection upon the nature of things in which the self emerges as a static entity possessing knowledge of, but always remaining separate from, all other things of the world. This separation itself stems from the illusion that thought—reflected in the notion of art as "object"—can somehow be disengaged from the process of experience, the process wherein both thought and art unfold and apart from which they no longer have meaning.[74]

The notion that form might be generated through "process" and "context" freed DeLio and the composers with whom he identifies from the inhibiting burden of their collective ancestral memory—that is, from meticulously engraved images of proper cadence formations, wellformedness criteria, and rules for motive and phrase construction. Suddenly liberated from the unwanted and constraining obligation to reproduce the music of their predecessors, these composers had finally found a way to invent their own.

At least at the time of his notorious "Schoenberg Is Dead" essay,[75] Boulez subscribed to similar promptings to dispense with the tradition. But like almost everything in Boulez, his championship of open forms and his construal of the open/closed opposition is more sophisticatedly argued, both in his prose and in his music of those years, than the passages cited above. For one thing, as we have noted, Boulez understood that even if only to subdue one's forebears, they stand and deserve to be wrestled with, and moreover that there is real pleasure to be taken in so doing.

That brings us to the third problematic culled from these composers' writings, one which all composers are forced to confront or avoid: that is, their relation to "the great tradition."

Rochberg, as if in response to the likes of DeLio and Boulez, insists that history is with us, like it or not: "The past refuses to be erased. Unlike Boulez, I will not praise amnesia."[76]

But the notion that all "modernists" believe "that the past is dead and must be buried,"[77] although characteristic of the rhetoric of certain American avant-gardists in the 1960s and some of Boulez's postures as early as the late fifties, is astoundingly naive. Even Boulez, in May 1968, in the heat of his most virulent anti-ancestry rhetoric, knew that the composer is inextricably caught in the dialectic between "the great models and an unknown future." (Indeed; otherwise, why all the fuss?) Says Boulez:

> When people tell me, 'I am taking off into the unknown and ignoring the past' it is complete nonsense. Only if one were an Eskimo and found oneself in the middle of civilization, would it be possible to ignore the past....
>
> When he shuts his eyes in order to escape, he is simply behaving like the ostrich—knocking in open doors with his head in the sand.[78]

In fact, as we have seen, Boulez's solution, appropriate to one so dialectically inclined, lies somewhere between DeLio's patricidal process-as-prior-to-form and Rochberg's filial embrace. Like Bloom's strong poet, Boulez will swallow the whole of his legacy, discard what is fruitless and integrate in his own language that which he finds useful to the fulfillment of his own musical and expressive needs.

The question of creating "one's own language" or style brings us to the final thematic that concerns all these prose-writing composers; in fact, it defines the social conditions and cultural context without which these four books could not be as ideologically diverse as they are: I refer to the concept of "pluralism," employed either as a cultural given, a compositional aesthetic, or both.

In his essay on Cage, DeLio sets forth his aesthetic in very clear terms:

It has become increasingly apparent that the evolution of the arts in the twentieth century may, at least in one sense, be understood as a manifold rejection of the notion of singularity in favor of a broader, more comprehensive world view.... Whether it be through the development of a musical language which is multi-centered or through a formal scheme which has the potential for multiple realizations, this rejection of singularity has become one of the dominant factors influencing much recent composition.[79]

This is a different kind of pluralism from that embraced and championed by Rochberg when he writes of "pluralism of gesture, language, and style":[80] as we have seen, Rochberg finds his apparently satisfying answer to the question of how to live with all of his rich and various musical influences by incorporating as many of them as he wants into any given work. However, one does not leave Rochberg's book with the impression that he is exactly open to a multiplicity of coexisting *contemporary* styles; nor do we finish DeLio's essays believing in his tolerance for what he calls "closed works."

In fact, Boulez, for all his singular and single-minded polemics, Boulez who never mentions pluralism in all 527 pages of *Orientations*, is nonetheless the most "pluralistic" among these composers in that he is the only one who finds interesting things to say about many different kinds of pieces. Now perhaps Boulez speaks as a performer at these moments; even so, one leaves his essays impressed by the evidence that digestion-and-transformation as a compositional commitment implies a sustained commitment to curiosity and appetite, as well.

And where does all this leave today's composer? We all know that there exists an overabundance of potential and contending influences, all there for the choosing; that, whatever our hand-picked lineage, our images of music-making will always bear the heavy imprint of our formidable predecessors; that the exploration of sound resources and the cultivation of musical vocabularies and grammars have become disciplines of their own that have been fertilized by the findings in other fields and have so far yielded some stimulating results, mostly in the forms of pieces; and that, indeed, pluralism flourishes, is inevitable, and will neutralize any and all theories of value that try to prioritize, thereby ultimately and permanently altering our relations to tradition, to each other, to other musics, and to the significance of our individual choices.

Given this arbitrary and democratic condition, I should like to and may as well remind us of one possible course for composers that tends to get lost in the wash of words about music, probably because most of its followers just do it and don't talk much. It is a course that borrows from the tradition without ravaging, destroying, or rewriting it; and it is a course definable only as those qualities demanded of its adherents:

—The alertness to the possibility and plasticity inherent in the musical material we are working with, and a constant attention to the changing shapes this material assumes and to the consequences these changes can have on the rest of the fabric;

—the perennial shaking awake of our imaginations so that we may invent a music that is radical *not* in the prose that accompanies it but in its composer's insistence on touching every note, on hand-sculpting each breath, on endowing every available resource with meaning;

—the recognition of the power one has to make things matter, and the commitment to taking and sharing a point of view.

These are all qualities that, to this composer, seem essential to the practice of composition today as in other days. It is tempting to speculate as to which of the three composers whose prose we have been reading would endorse which aspects of this particular compositional manifesto.

Although the first tenet listed above might well be seconded by Boulez, at least in his conductor's capacity, by Rochberg, as composer and analyst, and DeLio and the composers he treats as improvisors and process people, the second might possibly only be ratified by Rochberg. The third would probably be supported by both Boulez and Rochberg, given their personal histories of professional and ideological commitment, whereas DeLio et al. might be too committed to fluidity and the ever-openness of possibility to subscribe to such a "closed" position.

Still, when one thinks of the wide variety of musics whose composers might all subscribe to these three tenets, it becomes clear how it is possible for polemical words about music, abstract and prescriptive as these can be, to engender misalliances and suggest the strangest of musical bedfellows. This fact may get closer than we have yet to a reason for our present situation of extreme cultural pluralism, where each set of ideological assumptions is capable of generating an infinite number of musical artifacts each of which can lay claim to being a "true" representation of those assumptions.

No wonder, then, that endemic to pluralism seems to be a resistence to constructing a theory of value that would do more than acknowledge the validity of airing everything and champion a ''more-is-better'' ecumenicism.

The key question is how fundamentally this recent and increasing absence of engagement in the debate of aesthetics as we know them will alter the composition and practice of Western music as we know it. The difference remains to be heard.

NOTES

1. *Orientations: Collected Writings by Pierre Boulez*, edited by Jean-Jacques Nattiez, translated by Martin Cooper (Cambridge: Harvard University Press, 1986), 56.

2. "Aesthetics and the Fetishists" (1961), *Orientations,* 34–35.

3. "Where are we now?" (1968), *Orientations,* 452.

4. "Freeing Music" (1972), *Orientations,* 482.

5. "Time, Notation and Coding" (1960), *Orientations,* 84–85.

6. "Aesthetics and the Fetishists" (1961), *Orientations,* 38.

7. "What's New" (1976), *Orientations,* 480.

8. "The Composer as Critic" (1954), *Orientations,* 109–110.

9. Ibid., 111.

10. Ibid., 112.

11. "What's New" (1976), *Orientations,* 479.

12. "The Teacher's Task" (1961), *Orientations,* 126.

13. Ibid., 122–23.

14. Nattiez's "On Reading Boulez," *Orientations,* Introduction, 21.

15. Harold Bloom, *The Anxiety of Influence* (London: Oxford University Press, 1973), 5.

16. Ibid., 30.

17. "Roger Désormière: 'I Hate Remembering!' " (1966), *Orientations,* 507.

18. "Lulu," *Orientations,* 393–94.

19. Ibid., 403.

20. "Mahler: 'Das Klagende Lied' " (record liner notes) *Orientations,* 315.

21. "Approaches to *Parsifal*" (1970), *Orientations,* 259.

22. "Wieland Wagner: 'Here Space Becomes Time' " (1966), *Orientations,* 242.

23. "Approaches to *Parsifal*" (1970), *Orientations,* 255–56.

24. "The Ring" (1976), *Orientations,* 271.

25. Ibid., 277.

26. Bloom, *Anxiety of Influence,* 11.

27. Nattiez's "On Reading Boulez," *Orientations,* Introduction, 15.

28. Thomas DeLio, *Circumscribing the Open Universe* (Lanham, MD: University Press of America, 1984), 3.

29. Thomas DeLio, editor, *Contiguous Lines* (Lanham, MD: University Press of America, 1985), xi.

30. *Circumscribing the Open Universe,* 91.

31. Ibid., 93.

32. Ibid., 103–4.

33. Ibid., 104.

34. Ibid., 45–46.

35. Ibid., 31.

36. Ibid., 71–72.

37. *Contiguous Lines,* 58.

38. *Circumscribing the Open Universe,* 45.

39. Ibid., 2–3.

40. *Contiguous Lines,* xiv.

41. "The Fantastic and the Logical: Reflections on Science, Politics, and Art" (1973) in George Rochberg, *The Aesthetics of Survival: A Composer's View of Twentieth-Century Music*, edited and with an introduction by William Bolcom, 202 (Ann Arbor: University of Michigan Press, 1984)

42. "Reflections on the Renewal of Music" (1972), *The Aesthetics of Survival*, 235.

43. "Aural Fact or Fiction: Or, Composing at the Seashore" (1965), *The Aesthetics of Survival*, 177.

44. "The Fantastic and the Logical: Reflections on Science, Politics, and Art" (1973), *The Aesthetics of Survival*, 197.

45. "The Marvelous in Art" (1982), *The Aesthetics of Survival*, 204.

46. Ibid., 207–8.

47. "Reflections on the Renewal of Music" (1972), *The Aesthetics of Survival*, 238.

48. "The Marvelous in Art" (1982), *The Aesthetics of Survival*, 205.

49. "In Search of Music" (1964), *The Aesthetics of Survival*, 151–54, (esp. 154).

50. "The Fantastic and the Logical" (1973), *The Aesthetics of Survival*, 202.

51. "The Marvelous in Art" (1982), *The Aesthetics of Survival*, 204–6.

52. "Humanism versus Science" (1970), *The Aesthetics of Survival*, 170.

53. Rochberg's editor seems to be at least as full of spleen on the subject, and perhaps even more misguided. In his introduction, Bolcom defines what he calls "the chief tenet of modernism" as the notion "that the past is dead and must be buried." One might assume that he speaks here for Rochberg, too, with this facile and mistaken attempt at clarification of the modernist agenda, or when he audibly heaves the now-familiar sigh of relief at the passing of the "modernist" movement and all its "ephemeral submovements" "—aleatoricism, total organization, and so forth."

   "No previous style was nearly so politically adept, nor so total in its power to sway and hold the majority of artists, as modernism" (p. vii). No? What about the polemics surrounding the so-called *sprezzatura* style? Or the *conductus* style? Or the Palestrina style? What kind of statement is this? When and who exactly is Bolcom talking about, musically speaking? Schönberg's circle? Cage's? Babbitt's? Boulez's? Only one who felt excluded or utterly misunderstood could possibly take this misproportioned (and exaggerated) view of what went on among all the artists he labels "modernist" in this century.

54. "Reflections on Schoenberg" (1972), *The Aesthetics of Survival*, 50.

55. Ibid.

56. Ibid.

57. Similarly, a casual reader might mistake Schönberg's Roman-numeral chord-labelling system for a reductionist understanding of harmonic function, instead of seeing that it shifts the burden of analytic explanation to the horizontal domain: "Yes, of course it's an altered II chord, but what's *in* it, and where do those elements come from and where are they bound? And isn't it amazing that both this and that other thing over there can be called altered II chords, and yet they can be so differently configured?" In fact, our fantasized, monologuing Schönberg might conclude, "there are as many possible realizations of this simple scale-degree function as there are differing local contexts that contain it. And it is not because the differences between possible realizations don't matter that we call them all altered II."

58. "Reflections on the Renewal of Music" (1972), *The Aesthetics of Survival*, 237.

59. "The Avant-Garde and the Aesthetics of Survival" (1969), *The Aesthetics of Survival*, 222–23. Rochberg is not the only composer to advocate a form of tonal composition that will not violate the bounds of certain posited innate cognitive capacities. See Fred Lerdahl, "Cognitive Constraints on Compositional Systems," in *Generative Processes in Music*, edited by John A. Sloboda (London: Oxford University Press).

60. "The Avant-Garde and the Aesthetics of Survival" (1969), *The Aesthetics of Survival*, 228.

61. Ibid., 226–27.

62. Ibid., 230–31.

63. "On the Third String Quartet" (1972), *The Aesthetics of Survival*, 239.

64. Ibid. 240–41.

65. *Contiguous Lines*, 57ff.

66. Ibid. 58.

67. "Constructing an Improvisation" (1961), *Orientations*, 155–73.

68. "The New Image of Music" (1963), *The Aesthetics of Survival*, 19.

69. Ibid., 19.

70. Ibid., 23.

71. *Circumscribing the Open Universe*, 2.

72. Ibid., 3.

73. Ibid., 75.

74. Ibid., 2–3.

75. Pierre Boulez, "Schoenberg Is Dead," *The Score* no. 6 (May 1952): 18–22. A longer version of this article appears in French as "Schönberg est mort," in Pierre Boulez, *Relevés d'apprenti*, edited by Paule Thévenin, 265–72 (Paris: Éditions du Seuil, 1966), and in a new English translation under the original title on pages 268–76 of the English edition of the same book, *Notes of an Apprenticeship*, translated by Herbert Weinstock (New York: Alfred A. Knopf, 1968).

76. "Reflections on the Renewal of Music," 233.

77. Rochberg, *The Aesthetics of Survival*, Bolcom's Introduction, viii.

78. "Where Are We Now?" (1968), *Orientations*, 454.

79. *Circumscribing the Open Universe*, 11.

80. "On the Third String Quartet" (1972), *The Aesthetics of Survival*, 241.

Response to Blaustein

Thomas DeLio

I MUST SAY THAT I find this "review" shoddy and irresponsible. At best, it suggests that the reviewer is incapable of comprehending complex theoretical writing (or any theoretical writing for that matter); at worst, it suggests that she has not really bothered to read all the essays contained in these books.

Early in the review the author states: " . . . in general the analyses in both books tend to be 'analytic' in the same sense that chemical analysis of a compound substance is analytic: constituent strains are isolated, described, labeled, listed, and the job is done; not much attempt is made to interpret, to reconstruct the whole or even part of the work." Putting aside the obvious lack of understanding of how scientists, such as chemists, use creativity and insight to synthesize their data into coherent theories, this is a most absurd and revealing comment and suggests that the reviewer has not carefully read (or indeed read at all) either book. Almost every essay which is analytical in nature leads from detailed analysis to a consideration of larger form. In each case, the author goes to great lengths to synthesize all data gleaned from careful analytical study. Moreover, most of these essays conclude with one or more charts through which the various authors attempt to draw all analytical information together into one comprehensive view of the piece being analyzed.

Later the reviewer labels my essays on Cage, Wolff, and Ashley "apologias." I challenge the reviewer to find one sentence in either of my books that even begins to suggest that I am presenting apologias. This is absurd and easily borne out by anyone who has read these essays and observed the care and attention devoted to the explication of the work of each of the composers.

What the reviewer has labeled "chemical analyses" and "apologias" are, in the case of *Circumscribing the Open Universe*, actually a series of essays, each devoted to a detailed analysis of one work by a distinguished avant-garde composer and placed in the context of contemporary philosophy, painting, and poetry. In the case of *Contiguous Lines*, they are, in fact, a collection of essays by distinguished theorists and composers (Christian Wolff, Robert Cogan, Alvin Lucier, Pozzi Escot, and myself) on the subject of contemporary European music and American music. Clearly, the reviewer has either not understood these essays or not read them.

Referring to the Cage, Wolff, and Ashley papers presented in *Circumscribing the Open Universe* the reviewer writes: " ... DeLio never posits a possible realization to help the prospective listener or performer imagine what textures or gestures might arise from the given materials. ..." First of all, this is factually untrue (and once again, one can only conclude that the reviewer did not actually read these essays). In the Cage paper one specific, simplified realization of the score is analyzed in detail. In addition, I consider the structure of the composition as a whole. In the Ashley paper, the difference between talking about the structure of such a composition as a whole as opposed to dealing with just one realization is discussed at length. More to the point, and clearly stated throughout the book, is the fact that I consider the structure of these pieces to be more than just the analysis of one possible realization, which would constitute a simplistic approach at best.

Later in the "review" we read: "The problem for the reader is that no such elucidation matters much if he has not heard the piece. ..." Surely, as we all know, when any theorist analyzes a piece of music in a book or an essay he assumes that hearing the piece is an essential part of the reader's experience. Is the reviewer criticizing the book because it does not come with a cassette? Does she similarly invalidate all other theoretical writing which has ever been done? Ridiculous!

In the next paragraph the reviewer states: "As they stand, these essays tend to read as thin...." She then proceeds to single out the papers on Xenakis, Glass, and Babbitt. These essays, especially those on Xenakis and Glass, are among the most detailed and comprehensive analyses of contemporary works ever published. Whether or not one agrees with the analyses or likes the music, the statement that these analyses "read as thin" is patently absurd. Perhaps the reviewer was incapable of following their complexity, or more likely, merely skimmed the essays and does not really know what is in them. Otherwise she could never have suggested that they are "thin." I might add that all the essays in both books were previously published in major periodicals. The Xenakis, for example, first appeared in *The Journal of Music Theory*, whose editor and readers clearly did not find the material "thin."

Later the reviewer accuses me of making "sweeping statements of questionable usefulness." She then proceeds to reprint several statements which, in context, either introduce or conclude very complex and detailed analytical studies. Each of these studies proceeds carefully, point-by-point toward the more generalized statements reprinted in this review out of context. While this reviewer finds the ideas contained within these more generalized observations of "questionable usefulness," most scholars and students whom I have encountered over the years find such attempts at synthesis of great value. For example, the lines from my Lucier essay dealing with Carl Andre which the reviewer quotes (" ... the method of this art ...") follow a carefully developed discussion of Andre's well-known metal plate sculptures. The remarks quoted in my essay follow clearly and logically from my analysis of these works. Throughout, the reviewer seems uncomfortable dealing with complex philosophical questions, and often can't even seem to fathom their relevance to the study of contemporary music. I also find it rather curious that a reviewer who, just a few pages earlier, criticized these books for not synthesizing analytical details into larger forms now criticizes these same books for addressing general philosophical issues regarding the nature of structure and attempting to bring these issues to bear upon the analyses of specific musical works.

Later, she again misstates what is written in the text. She quotes me:

> The twentieth century has witnessed the emergence of an increased awareness that structure can no longer be viewed simply as a family of relationships discerned among the elements of a single closed gestalt. Rather, a structure is a complex process evolving over a period of time, integrating an elaborate and diverse range of activities reaching out far beyond the framework of the art object itself. It is a continuum of activities beginning with a series of perceptions and proceeding through a network of interrelated transformations.

She responds with "Why couldn't I use the last sentence to describe my experience of Beethoven's Op. 2, No. 1?" Obviously, one could, but, as I clearly state, until the twentieth century (indeed, until quite recently in the twentieth century) one did not tend to do so. Such thinking, in turn, has had a dramatic impact on the activities of composers, painters, and poets in our time. This is the essence of my discussion, as would be clear to anyone who simply takes the time to read my essay.

She then proceeds to attack Robert Cogan in a particularly ludicrous way. She quotes Cogan's essay on Babbitt:

> We ourselves are left to meet the challenge, which is to envision a framework for understanding that encompasses and embraces the superabundant sonic possibilities of the electronic medium. And then, to place all of the details and relationships of any individual piece in terms of such an all-encompassing vision. Viewed in this way, the problem turns out not so very different from the other novel theoretical challenge of our time, that posed by global music as a whole, which also requires an all-encompassing framework and the precise placement of any specific music within it.

She then mocks: "Now that is cosmic. Everything is everything, and all distinctions pale in the face of the great common drones that bind us." This appears to be a deliberate attempt to trivialize a profound statement in which Cogan calls upon theorists to work toward the development of a theoretical framework within which new techniques and media (such as electronic music) can be studied. Cogan is clearly not saying that "everything is everything." This is an idiotic reading especially in light of the complex and original analysis which follows it in his essay. He is calling for the development of a complex framework within which the richness and complexity of many different kinds of music can be revealed. As he states, this is a tremendous challenge; one for which the reviewer is clearly not prepared. She does not even recognize its existence when it confronts her in the guise of Cogan's analysis of Babbitt's electronic music. In general, the reviewer seems uncomfortable with scholars who attempt to synthesize complex ideas. Perhaps a sharper mind is needed to elucidate the work of such scholars.

All too typical is the following misleading and irresponsible statement:

> Still speaking about Morton Feldman, DeLio writes, "Feldman's is a music in which there is no apparent structuring of sound prior to its actual unfolding in time." What does he mean? That Feldman is improvising?

Again, this material is distorted out of context. This statement follows an in-depth discussion of how Feldman is able to project an *illusion* of "... no apparent structuring of sound prior to its actual unfolding in time." Later the reviewer asks: "Can DeLio be denying the meticulously weighted play of sonorities whose calculatedly precarious states of balance and imbalance create much of what is dynamic in a Feldman work?" I believe that my analysis of Feldman's *Durations* in *Circumscribing* ... is, in fact, the first to fully explore his "meticulously weighted play of sonorities," how these sonorities arise, and how they are used. To ask this and other questions leads one immediately to the conclusion that the essay was not read, for, while one may disagree with my analysis (not one word of which is discussed in this "review"), to suggest that I deny the "play of sonorities" in Feldman's music is to be completely ignorant of the content of my analysis, which is, after all, the subject of my paper. One might, in turn, wonder what the reviewer means when she refers to Feldman's "calculatedly precarious states of balance and imbalance...." This sounds like gibberish to me. Of course, I know of no examples of analysis of Feldman's music done by the reviewer. Thus, we have no way of knowing what her words mean and how she comes to make such authoritative pronouncements.

Once more the reviewer astounds us. In discussing one of Pozzi Escot's essays she states:

> At least in the case of the Webern, it seems to me that Escot almost completely misses the boat: by tabulating all possible events [this is not, in fact, what she does], durational "partitions," and "hidden proportions," she cannot possibly tune into the ways in which Webern builds bridges across his apparently discontinuous segments with careful, not unconventional voice-leading, rhythm, phrase structure, and meter.

The title of Escot's essay is "Non-Linearity as a Conceptualization in Music." Escot's subject is the study of non-linear structuring principles present in so much contemporary music (but certainly not exclusive to contemporary music). Webern's "not unconventional voice-leading" (a questionable notion to say the least) is clearly not the subject here. Thus the reviewer has actually criticized Escot for not doing precisely what she has *not* set out to do! Simply amazing! Perhaps we should also criticize Escot for not talking about Tolstoy's *War and Peace*, after all she did not set out to deal with that subject either!

Moving on, in the final section of Blaustein's article I find a particularly offensive comment: "Robert Cogan, in his well-intentioned but only moderately illuminating attempt to analyze the 'conceptual system of electronic sound or tone color' ..." Nowhere in this "review" (and by now the reader should understand that there really is no review here) does the reviewer ever tell us what Cogan's essay (or anyone else's for that matter) is all about. Cogan's work is dismissed out-of-hand with no explanation whatsoever. What are the reviewer's qualifications in the area of tone color and spectral analysis? Has she written about this topic (or any other discussed in either of these books for that matter)? Has she done research in spectral analysis? For her to so easily dismiss the work of one of the most original and exciting theorists around, without feeling any obligation to explain her remarks, reeks of smugness and self-importance and demands that we ask such pointed questions. Is her position and knowledge (?) of theory so widely and highly regarded that we must accept this and all the other blanket and totally unsubstantiated statements which fill this review? Not since I last taught freshman music classes have I encountered writing as riddled with unsubstantiated statements. As a theorist I find this entire matter particularly offensive because this reviewer, whose qualifications are totally unknown to me, has chosen to dismiss, without comment, the work of a very important, highly regarded theorist. I refer the reviewer and all readers to a fine, objective, well-written review of Cogan's own recent book *New Images of Musical Sound* which appeared in the fall 1986 issue of *The Journal of Music Theory*. (The analysis by Cogan which appears in *Contiguous Lines* also appears in this book. Thus, the reader will get a sense of how this material can be critiqued in a proper and serious review.)

As to the charge that the essays in my books "do a disservice to the music they set out to champion," I need only reprint some review comments given by one of the composers about whom I have written, Robert Ashley: "Because of Thomas DeLio's intelligent criticism of my work in other writing of his [referring here to *Circumscribing* ...] I have come to think of him as the foremost theorist of our music."

Finally, to the charge that my writing is poor and my thinking "murky and flaky"—statements which should be laughable to the readers of my two published books and over twenty published analytical papers—I need only respond by offering a few review comments from several distinguished scholars and composers regarding the two books "reviewed" here.

Circumscribing the Open Universe

This is a precious collection of essays. Five contemporary composers have been chosen for their contributions to opening the art of music. Their attitude is put in perspective with that of other artists—painters, sculptors—as well as poets and philosophers. Careful analysis of typical works helps to demonstrate the points quite clearly. The text is light, elegant, and enlightening—for musicians, artists, and philosophers.

Professor Jean-Claude Risset
Faculté de Luminy
Université d'Aix Marseille
LMA,Centre National de la
Recherche Scientifique

For obvious reasons the production of such chance composers as Cage, Feldman, Wolff, Ashley, and Lucier has long eluded scientific criticism. Here now comes an author who through a surprisingly open-minded, penetrating, multidisciplinary approach, brings to the light of rational consciousness the arcana of a fascinating universe. No one interested in the field should afford to overlook this book.

Professor Herman Sabbe
Seminar of Musicology,
Ghent State University
Senior Editor, *Interface*

Contiguous Lines

Especially for teaching purposes this book is long overdue. The essays on Glass and Lucier are to my knowledge the only ones available. Wolff's statement about his work explains, finally, ideas that have been important to composers for almost two decades . . .

Robert Ashley
composer

Contiguous Lines is an important collection of groundbreaking essays which lay the foundation for new theories of musical organization. It is one of the most important collections to be published in the last decade.

Professor Stuart Smith
University of Maryland
Catonsville

One could go on and on critiquing this "review"; citing its errors, misstatements, and pompous, unsubstantiated attacks on the work of both the composers and theorists involved. This however would be a waste of time—both mine and the reader's. Such irresponsible writing deserves no further comment.

REPLY TO DELIO'S RESPONSE

I REGRET THAT Mr. DeLio found it necessary to write such an *ad hominem* response to my essay.

I stand by my critique and encourage the eager and thoughtful to read both of Mr. DeLio's books and judge for themselves.

—Susan Blaustein

Open Structure
and the Problem of Criticism:
Reflections on DeLio's
Circumscribing
the Open Universe

Herman Sabbe

BOOKS DEVOTED TO open structure have been few and far between. Their authors have been concerned with general aesthetics (Umberto Eco, *L'Opera aperta* [Milan: Bompiani, 1962]) or music historiography and theory (Konrad Boehmer, *Zur Theorie der offenen Form in der neuen Musik* [Darmstadt: Tonos, 1967]; Gary Potter, "The Role of Chance in Contemporary Music," [Ph.D. diss., Indiana University, 1971]). None has tackled the problem of criticism as related to open structure, at least not explicitly. The first, to my knowledge, to do so is Thomas DeLio in *Circumscribing the Open Universe* (Lanham, MD: University Press of America, 1984). He does not treat the problem on a theoretical level, but each of the five essays (on Cage, Feldman, Wolff, Ashley, and Lucier respectively) which comprise the book is a practical instance of open-structure music criticism.

The problem which the (would-be) critic of open-structure music has to face is indeed a formidable one. That which he is confronted with is not the finished (readable or audible) product the conventional music critic is presented with: it is a project, a composing model, a compositional problem simulation. Also, the creative individual concerned, the composer—calling him another name, such as "project designer" does not really affect the heart of the problem—does not have here the epistemic status of a "subject": one who knows the world and "speaks" of it to us through his musical output (as was generally considered to be the case for all "great" art music throughout the romantic age and partly, still, during the modernist era).

As there is no one definite object under critical scrutiny, and as there is no subject under consideration (not even the fragmented or disrupted subject believed to be characteristic of modernist art), neither is there a predicate structure relating subject and object to turn to for interpretation.

So, criticism is deprived of both the subject of musical creation and the created object, as its points of impact. The two ways it used to approach the art work are being blocked. Criticism in the traditional sense, as centered on the interpretation of the object as an "expression" of the subject, has no leg to stand on. Even those theories of criticism based on an "objectivist" aesthetic interpreted cultural and ideological values and meanings as projected into the created object through the agency of the creative subject. Let us not forget, either, that the unequivocal subject-object relation constituted and still constitutes the very foundation of the economics of music composition: the labeling of the finished product by the name of its originator is still the prevalent functioning condition in the system of copyright, the intellectual property right as the individualized socio-economic compensation of the creative endeavor.

Even if both the status of the "subject" and the "object" have often enough been subjected to discussion—the subject being construed to mean a "plural," "collective," "aesthetic," "cultural," in one word: a "transindividual" one; and the identity of the object, in other words the musical-work identity being put to the test of methodical reasoning—ultimately the conditions of criticism always could be described as follows: to the critic, there was (is) a reality "out there," fixed and immobile under observation; therefore, criticism was (is) an act of ongoing, potentially cumulative appropriation of meanings embodied.

In open-structure music, meaning has become utterly dependent on context. In this respect, open-structure aesthetics is part of the larger cultural tendency towards epistemological indeterminacy which has been manifest in twentieth-century music ever since atonal methods have made the meanings of tone relations dependent on the specific configurations they happen to enter into within a particular composition. (In the words of Schönberg: "Twelve only mutually related tones." On the analogy of this phrasing, mobile-form compositions, evolved from the European serialist tradition, could be described as featuring "*N* only mutually related sound sequences.")

In atonality as in mobile-form compositions from the European serialist tradition (which, therefore, I term "trans-serialist"), however, contextualized meaning is, in the broader framework of the overall musical communication process, being de-context-ualized again in being textualized, i.e. in taking the form of a score as a definitive blueprint that leads to repeated and repeatable "realizations." The process that leads to real open-structure music, on the contrary, should be characterized as one of ongoing deframing, in which the act of creation gradually integrates whatever was traditionally outside it: its own performance (or rather itself as performance), its acoustic, social, and finally ecologic environment. There remain no "default options" whatsoever. Whatever meaning there is arises exclusively from the immediate, unique and unrepeatable context.

Faced with such real open-structure music, the critic finds himself in a situation altogether unprecedented. It demands of him a new type of response. In philosophical terms, this situation means at the same time the end of Idealism and of Realism. The world is not seen as fixed, or as found; whatever realities may present themselves are considered to be versions of a world of worlds in the making.

What is a critic to do? To put it in a nutshell: how should he go about appropriating a reality, the essence of which is a nonappropriative presentation of reality? How can he ever critically manage this multitude of proposed versions of a reality which is itself envisioned as merely a version of reality?

Technically speaking, of course, the open-structure project can be implemented. (Such a project bearing the closest analogy to a model stated in a "programming" language, the term "implementation" seems more appropriate here than "performance," "realization," or even "actualization.") It could even be implemented many different times, and, supposing its number were finite, the complete range of possible implementations could even be realised—though it might take the critic (even if computer-assisted!) a lifetime and more to do so.... Anyway, epistemologically speaking, the sum total of the implementations would in almost all cases remain quite beyond the grasp of any one knowing subject—unless it be some "demon" as first imagined by Laplace.

But what of a single implementation? From a didactic standpoint, it may be useful, even interesting. From a critical standpoint, on the contrary, it would not be relevant, as the significance of the project lies not in any one of its realizations, but in their very multiplicity. In terms of logics, and as far as real open structure goes, such implementation would produce an instance of a class never to be. Implementing the model surely enough restores the illusion of a predicate structure relating a subject (the composer) to an object (an implementation of the model). In so doing, the critic would surely reintroduce the very constraints of a psychological or cultural or ideological nature that the composer had set out to eliminate.

The critic should at least try and do without a predicate structure, not reinstate it; he should not reduce virtual multiplicity to explicit oneness, anarchy to order; he should make the reader aware of the necessity not to do so; he should expose the range of interpretations the model allows, not impose just one. Insofar as it is of the essence of an open-structure project that it propose procedures which eventually and diversely invite creative action by potential "performers," it is incumbent on the critic not to interrupt this "mise-en-abyme," but rather perpetuate it in stressing just that eventuality and that diversity.

I am perfectly aware that those demands upon him place the critic in a new situation altogether. His interpretation of an open-structure project cannot hope to capture the essence of the indeterminacy involved, unless it respects the very qualities of elusiveness that are "the determinants of indeterminacy." Moreoover, the conventions which underlie the intelligibility of the traditional musical work (such as causal logics, linearity, continuity, predictability) have to be discarded as criteria for critical evaluation. It would only be natural (or should I say "cultural") for a critic to be tempted to restore the familiar situation by going back to the methods of traditional criticism. It takes courage and scientific rigor to resist that temptation, and it is one of the merits of DeLio to have done so, to have devoted his critical efforts, in his own words, to "circumscribing" rather than describing or prescribing. In order to respond to a new situation, the critic has to ask new, different questions, and establish alternative criteria for excellence.

The more radical the openness of the project or model, the more fundamental the questions should be, the more radically they should be oriented toward the basic communicative intent: Does it communicate? What does it communicate? How does it communicate it?

Let us apply these questions to Cage's "Tacet piece," certainly one of the most radical open-structure projects. *That* it communicates is the message level which is most strongly, if not exclusively, emphasized here: by reducing the explicit part of the message to defining its overall time frame (4'33"), it is, rather paradoxically, its institutional layer ("this *is* an artistic message") which comes most forcibly to the fore. *What* it communicates is the situation it places its audience (which are its performers) in. And *the way* it communicates this is by each time creating an instance of such situatedness.

Questions the critic may ask in order to evaluate the degree of excellence of an open-structure project *as* open-structure project are the following: How rich is the model as a source for multiple implementation? How far does it, once implemented and in each of its implementations, guarantee qualities of openness, of immediacy, ... ? To what extent can it be regarded as a valid and valuable manifestation of a world view permeated with indeterminacy? As the representative of the audience, the critic should endeavor to make clear whether (and how) implementations of the model do (or promise to) communicate a sense of imminence, i.e. of meaning not fully embodied but rather continually deferred, of equiprobability of sound events, of a constant re-equilibration of expectations, a constant renewal of open expectation. In so doing, the critic will demonstrate how open-structure music values also relate to the ultimate values which have to do with man's presence in the world.

Should man subject his (musical) experience to rational control, or lose himself in sensuous enjoyment? Open-structure music, typically, leaves the question ... open. Whether this means that open-structure music reveals a stage of civilisation in which the ultimate value system remains largely undecided—an "open universe," beyond a world dominated by (comparable, though divergent) Calvinist/Freudian "delayed pleasure" theories of aesthetic-moral excellence—remains open to question. It will take some time yet to establish the theory and practice of open-structure music criticism. Still, it is because his five essays so compellingly invite considerations of the above type that DeLio has taken a decisive step toward doing just that.

About the Authors

MILTON BABBITT, composer and theorist, is William Shubael Conant Professor of Music Emeritus at Princeton University and serves on the composition faculty of the Juilliard School. Recent recordings of his music include *Consortini,* String Quartets Nos. 4 and 5, *Relata 1,* and *Three Cultivated Choruses.* Among his more recent compositions are *Septet But Equal, Around the Horn, Counterparts,* and String Quartet No. 6. His writings, in addition to articles on twelve pitch-class serialism, composition for electronic media, and various analytical and methodological issues, include the volume *Words About Music* (edited by Stephen Dembski and Joseph N. Straus, 1987) and a contribution to *A Life of Learning.* Andrew Mead's *An Introduction to the Music of Milton Babbitt* appeared in 1993.

ELAINE BARKIN is Professor of Composition and Theory at the University of California at Los Angeles, and since 1987 has been a performing member of its Balinese and Javanese gamelan ensemble. She is on a University of California Pacific Rim research team whose focus is new music in Bali. She has completed several texts and videos about recent gamelan music and has collaboratively improvised with and composed for the gamelan with Western instruments. Her current energies are directed toward interactive, group-centered sonic & *et alia* explorations; her recent texts concern women & music, speculations about being a composer, and the virtues of idiosyncratic ways to talk & write about and make & do music. Her *Five Tape Collages* has been recorded on the third of the OPEN SPACE compact discs. Her editorial affiliations with *Perspectives of New Music* date back to 1963.

ARTHUR BERGER, a composer, critic, and educator, is Irving G. Fine Professor Emeritus of Brandeis University, and currently serves on the faculty of the New England Conservatory of Music. He has also taught at Harvard University, Mills College, the Juilliard School, and the Tanglewood Music Center. His works have been performed by some of the major American orchestras, and among his recordings are two compact discs, issued by CRI and New World Records, devoted entirely to his music. He co-founded the journal *Perspectives of New Music* and has served as editor of *Musical Mercury* as well as music critic for the New York *Herald Tribune* and *Boston Transcript*. His 1953 monograph on Aaron Copland was the first full-length study of the composer.

SUSAN BLAUSTEIN is a composer with a degree from Harvard University who has served as a member of the composition faculty at Columbia University. She received a Guggenheim Fellowship in 1988, which enabled her to live in Southeast Asia and devote the year to composition.

BENJAMIN BORETZ has spent a lifetime creating, exploring, and thinking and writing about expressive-language behavior, particularly in the form of musical compositions, solitary and interactive soundmaking situations, verbal texts, sociomusical performance occasions, and school-based learning situations. He teaches at Bard College in New York, where he leads Music Program Zero, a continuing experiment in holistic musical development and interarts exploration. His work in soundform is recorded on INTER/PLAY cassettes and OPEN SPACE compact discs. His work in verbal/graphic textform and scoreform has been published primarily in *Perspectives of New Music*, *The Nation*, and *News of Music*. His score *(". . . my chart shines high where the blue milk's upset . . .")* for solo piano and the text/composition *Language , as a music/Six Marginal Pretexts for Composition* for speaker, piano, and tape are published by Lingua Press; his texts *Meta-Variations: Studies in the Foundations of Musical Thought, Talk,* and *If I am a musical thinker;* are published by Station Hill and OPEN SPACE. As a graduate student in the 1950s, he originated and pursued the project that became *Perspectives of New Music,* which he edited until 1983.

PIERRE BOULEZ, a composer of international renown, is a former Music Director of the BBC Symphony Orchestra and of the New York Philharmonic; he is also founder and former director of the Institut de Recherche et de Coordination Acoustique/Musique in Paris. His writings have been collected in several books, including *Notes of an Apprenticeship* (1968), *Boulez on Music Today* (1971), *Orientations* (1986), *Jalons (pour une décennie)* (1989), and *Stocktakings from an Apprenticeship* (1991). His recent works include *Répons* for large chamber ensemble and live interactive electronics and *Dérive II* for chamber ensemble, which had their U.S. premieres in 1986 and 1991, respectively.

JOHN CAGE, an American composer who died in 1992, earned a reputation as musical maverick by his ceaseless ventures into uncharted territories for composition. His aesthetic and philosophical stance has influenced several generations of composers. Among his last compositions are *Five Stone Solo* for clay pot drums and optional tape, written for the Merce Cunningham dance titled *Five Stone Wind; Fourteen,* for chamber ensemble; *101,* commissioned by the Boston Symphony Orchestra; and *Europa 5,* commissioned by Yvar Mikhashoff and Usbreker. His numerous lectures and writings have been published in several volumes, including *Silence, A Year from Monday, M, Empty Words, X, Writings through Finnegans Wake, Themes and Variations,* and most recently, *I–VI.*

DOUGLAS COLLINS is Chair of the Department of Romance Languages and Literature at the University of Washington. He is the author of *Sartre as Biographer* (1980) and *The Found Object: The Representation of Indifference in Critical Theory* (forthcoming).

THOMAS DELIO, a composer and theorist, has published articles on the music of Luigi Dallapiccola, Elliott Carter, Iannis Xenakis, and John Cage, among others. He is the author of two books on contemporary music, *Circumscribing the Open Universe* (1984) and *Contiguous Lines: Issues and Ideas in the Music of the '60's and '70's* (1985), and is co-author, with Stuart Smith, of *Twentieth Century Music Scores* (1988) and *Words and Spaces* (1989), and a forthcoming book on the music of Morton Feldman. His compositions are recorded on the Spectrum, Wergo, Neuma, and 3D labels and are published by Smith Publications/Sonic Art Editions (Baltimore) and Semar Editore (Rome). Articles about his music have appeared in *Interface, Perspectives of New Music, Percussive Notes,* and *Leonardo.*

ROBERT DUISBERG holds a D.M.A. in composition and a Ph.D. in computer science, both from the University of Washington, where he is currently on the faculty of the School of Music, teaching music technology and serving as co-director of the School of Music Computer Center. His compositions range from symphonic, choral, and chamber music to chamber opera and musical comedy. In his software research, some of which has been patented, he has explored gestural interfaces to computers. He is presently developing a connectionist system for conducting computer music performance.

DAVID DUNN is a professional composer and sound designer for radio, film, television, public installations, and other experimental per-formance venues. He was apprenticed to composer Harry Partch for four years and was active as a performer of Partch's music for over ten years. Concurrently he studied privately with Kenneth Gaburo. Since 1973 his work has explored the interrelationships between bioacoustics, music, and language. In 1990 he co-founded the Independent Media Labs in Santa Fe, New Mexico, which offers state-of-the-art computer and media services to artists and broadcast professionals. Recently he released a compact disc, *Angles and Insects,* which is available from ¿What's Next? Recordings.

ROBERT ERICKSON is a composer who taught for many years at the University of California at San Diego. In his book, *Sound Structure in Music* (1975), he pioneered thinking about the role of musical timbre. He wrote numerous compositions, often of a theatrical nature and sometimes involving timbral experimentation and innovative work with speech, as in the trombone solo piece, *General Speech* (1969).

CLAYTON ESHLEMAN is Professor of English at Eastern Michigan University, Ypsilanti and Editor of *Sulfur* magazine. Among his publications are *The Name Encanyoned River: Selected Poems 1960–1985* (1986) and *Hotel Cro-Magnon* (1989). He was the recipient of a Guggenheim Fellowship in Poetry in 1978, and, together with José Rubia Barcia, of the National Book Award in Translation in 1979 for *César Vallejo: The Complete Posthumous Poetry.*

MICHEL FOUCAULT was, until his death in 1984, Professor of Philosophy at the Collège de France, and Professor of French Literature and Philosophy at the University of California at Berkeley. His numerous works include *Histoire de le folie à l'âge classique* (translated as *The History of Madness,* 1972), *Surveiller et punir* (translated as *Discipline and Punish,* 1977), and a multivolume history of sexuality that was in progress at the time of his death. Foucault has described his work as concentrated on the history of "the objectification of the subject."

KENNETH GABURO, who died in 1993, was internationally recognized for his innovative work, including over 110 experimental compositions and numerous philosophical, aesthetic, and socio-political writings. He founded the New Music Choral Ensemble in 1960 and Lingua Press in 1974. He received a number of fellowships (Guggenheim, UNESCO Creative, Fulbright), awards (George Gershwin Memorial, Berkshire Music Center), commissions (Serge Koussevitsky Music Foundation, Fromm Foundation), and grants (Rockefeller Foundation, Thorne Foundation) for his scholarship, composing, and performance activities. He was widely regarded as a singularly profound teacher of composition and cognitive studies who persisted as one of the most creative and non-compromising artistic figures of his generation.

ERIC GANS is the author of a series of works in the domain of generative anthropology: *The Origin of Language* (1981), *The End of Culture* (1985), *Science and Faith* (1990), and *Originary Thinking* (1993), as well as other books in French and English devoted to literary and theoretical topics, notably *Musset et le drame tragique* (1974) and *Essais d'esthétique paradoxale* (1977). He is currently working on the next book in the series, tentatively titled *Deferral of Violence.* Since 1969, he has taught in the French Department at the University of California at Los Angeles, specializing in nineteenth-century French literature.

MICHAEL R. LAMPERT has resided in North Hollywood, California, where his varied musical activities include teaching improvisation and playing jazz mandolin.

FRED EVERETT MAUS has graduate degrees in music theory (Princeton University) and philosophy (Oxford University), and presently teaches in the Department of Music, University of Virginia. He has published a number of articles that concern issues involving both music theory and aesthetics; they have appeared in *College Music Symposium*, *Indiana Theory Review*, *Journal of Music Theory Pedagogy*, *Journal of Musicology*, *Music Theory Spectrum*, *Nineteenth-Century Music*, and *Perspectives of New Music*. He recently wrote a second essay on Benjamin Boretz and J. K. Randall, titled "Masculine Discourse in Music Theory" (*Perspectives of New Music*, Summer 1993).

ARTHUR NESTROVSKI is Associate Professor of Comparative Literature in the Graduate College, Pontifícia Universidade Católica (São Paulo). He is the author of *Debussy e Poe* (1986), for which he won a national book award, and has also edited the anthology *riverrun—Ensaios sobre James Joyce* (1992). In the United States, his work has been published in various journals, including *Perspectives of New Music*, *James Joyce Quarterly*, *TriQuarterly*, *The Iowa Review*, and *In Theory Only*. A member of the Instituto de Estudos Avançados at the University of São Paulo, he is also the general editor for the Pierre Menard Library of literary theory (Imago Editora) and contributes regularly to the national newspaper *Folha de S. Paulo*.

JOHN RAHN is a composer and theorist with degrees in classical languages, bassoon, and composition. His theoretical publications include the textbook *Basic Atonal Theory* (1987) and articles in various professional journals on pitch-class theory, rhythmic theory, theory of tonal music and of medieval music, theoretical methodology and formal methods, aesthetics, critical theory, and artificial intelligence and computer applications to music. Two of his compositions, *Kali* and *Miranda*, were released recently on Centaur Records CRC 2144. He is currently Professor of Music Composition and Theory and of Critical Theory at the University of Washington. Since 1983, he has served as editor of the international journal *Perspectives of New Music.*

J. K. RANDALL, a composer who has been actively involved with computer synthesis of sound and more recently with improvised, interactive performances combining musicians, painters, and dancers, taught for many years in the Princeton University Music Department. His computer-synthesized works have been recorded on the Cardinal, CRI, and Nonesuch labels; his music and writings are currently being issued by OPEN SPACE, and his interactive participations by INTER/PLAY.

RAINER ROCHLITZ, who was born in Germany in 1946 and became a French citizen in 1981, is a philosopher and theorist of aesthetics, member of the Centre National de la Recherche Scientifique and Professor of Aesthetics and Political Theory at the Université Européenne de la Recherche. He has published two books, *Le jeune Lukács* (1983) and *Le désenchantement de l'art: La philosophie de Walter Benjamin* (1992), and directs two book series, *Procope* (essays on Ricœur, aesthetic theory, and Habermas) and *Théories* (works by Rorty, Habermas, and Seel). He has translated a number of books, including those by Lukács, Benjamin, Adorno, and Habermas (into French), and by Goldmann, Ricœur, and Lévi-Strauss (into German).

HERMAN SABBE, a musicologist with degrees in law, cello, and music history, is Professor of Musicology at the State University in Ghent and at the Université libre in Brussels. He is co-founder and co-editor of *Interface—Journal of New Music Research.* His publications include books on romanticism, dadaism, serialism, and on the composers Stockhausen and Ligeti. He is currently working on a book, tentatively titled *Sociology of Music and Music Aesthetics in Western Society since 1800.*

DELMORE SCHWARTZ, an American poet (1913–66) who studied at New York University and Harvard University, was recognized within the literary world as one of the major figures of his generation. His first work, *In Dreams Begin Responsibilities* (1938), was published in the *Partisan Review,* a journal of which he later became the editor (1943–55). His early success loomed over him as a challenge throughout the rest of his life. Later works include: *Shenandoah* (1941), a verse play; *Genesis* (1943), a prose poem; *World Is a Wedding* (1948), a collection of short stories; *Vaudeville for a Princess and Other Poems* (1950); *Summer Knowledge* (1959); and *Successful Love and Other Stories* (1961).

HERBERT SCHWARTZ was an accomplished pianist who was enrolled in the graduate program at Columbia University in the 1930s. He steeped himself in Aristotelian philosophy, which he employed in his dissertation to deal with music. But since the philosophy and music departments considered themselves unqualified to evaluate results in the other's discipline, this interdepartmental project proved problematic and he was not granted his degree. Discouraged with the academic world, he disappeared from the scene, though one rumor placed him in Canada, joining a monastery. Little is known about him, though in the 1930s he did some writing for Lincoln Kirstein's prestigious *Hound and Horn*.

IANNIS XENAKIS, a composer, architect, and civil engineer, has lived in France since 1947. His architectural projects include, with Le Corbusier, the Phillips Pavilion for the Brussels World Fair (1958) and the Convent of la Tourette (1955), and on his own, the Polytope for the French Pavilion at Expo 1967, Montreal. He has put together several sonic, sculptural, and light spectacles, including those set among the ruins and the mountains at Persepolis, Iran (1971), in Paris (1972 and 1978) and in the ruins of Mycenae, Greece (1978). Many of his compositions, noted for their complex textures, introduce probability calculus and set theory into instrumental, electro-acoustic, and computerized musical means. His book, *Formalized Music* (revised edition with enlargements, 1992) describes how he has translated mathematical calculations into music notation. He is Founder and Director of the Centre de Mathématique et Automatique Musicales in Paris; he also founded the Center for Mathematical and Automated Music at Indiana University in Bloomington. He has taught at Indiana University, the University of Paris, and as Gresham Professor of Music at City University in London.